SOUTH AFRICA'S CRICKET CAPTAINS

Dear Monique
Thanks for your effort

Regards

SOUTH AFRICA'S CRICKET CAPTAINS

Trevor Chesterfield & Jackie McGlew

Trevor Chesterfield
5/2/2003

ZEBRA

Published by Zebra Press
an imprint of Struik Publishers
(a division of New Holland Publishing (South Africa) (Pty) Ltd)
PO Box 1144, Cape Town, 8000
New Holland Publishing is a member of Johnnic Publishing Ltd

First published by Southern Book Publishers in 1994
Second edition 2003

1 3 5 7 9 10 8 6 4 2

Publication © Zebra Press 2003
Text © Trevor Chesterfield and estate late Jackie McGlew 2003

Cover photographs: Alan Melville and Dudley Nourse © *The Star*;
Clive van Ryneveld © *Pretoria News*; Kepler Wessels,
Hansie Cronjé and Shaun Pollock © Anne Laing

All rights reserved. No part of this publication may be reproduced,
stored in a retrieval system or transmitted, in any form or by any means,
electronic, mechanical, photocopying, recording or otherwise,
without the prior written permission of the copyright owners.

PUBLISHING MANAGER: Marlene Fryer
MANAGING EDITOR: Robert Plummer
EDITOR: Ronel Richter-Herbert
COVER AND TEXT DESIGNER: Natascha Adendorff
TYPESETTER: Monique van den Berg

Set in 10.5 pt on 13.5 pt Minion

Reproduction by Hirt & Carter (Cape) (Pty) Ltd
Printed and bound by CTP Book Printers

ISBN 1 86872 376 3

www.zebrapress.co.za

Log on to our photographic website www.imagesofafrica.co.za for an African experience

CONTENTS

FOREWORD BY ANDRÉ ODENDAAL		vii
PREFACE		ix
1	Pathfinders, Pioneers and Rogues	1
2	Alan Melville	15
3	Dudley Nourse	27
4	Jack Cheetham	37
5	Clive van Ryneveld	51
6	Jackie McGlew	67
7	Trevor Goddard	90
8	Peter van der Merwe	103
9	Basil D'Oliveira	129
10	Ali Bacher	152
11	The Rebel Era	163
12	Clive Rice	194
13	Kepler Wessels	208
14	Hansie Cronjé	229
15	Gary Kirsten	250
16	Shaun Pollock	259
17	Mark Boucher	285
	NOTES	303
	BIBLIOGRAPHY	305
	INDEX OF NAMES	307

Photographs between pages 162 and 163

FOREWORD

Trevor Chesterfield is a veteran cricket writer exploring new ways of writing about South African cricket history.

When the first edition of this book was published in 1994, it reflected the master narrative of the past: the story of South African cricket was essentially about white men in flannels playing a British game. But democracy arrived in that year, and since then we have embarked on its cricket equivalent – 'transformation'.

One way of understanding transformation is that it involves thorough change at every level of the game, as opposed to an emphasis in the past on the 'development' of those on the margins without fundamentally addressing 'traditional' power relations, representations and cultures of cricket.

In November 1998, the United Cricket Board adopted a Transformation Charter, also described as a 'national plan for cricket's future sustainability'. The idea was to reposition South African cricket so that it could grow in an optimal way in the changing, post-democracy political, social and economic environments.

The Transformation Charter identified ten major 'thrusts' or areas for action. The key one was 'Redress and Representivity'. Another was 'Recording the full history of South African cricket'.

There was anger that existing histories negated the rich cricket traditions of those oppressed under apartheid. In line with apartheid practice, black cricketers were still mere footnotes in the story, with no real history, or so it was assumed. If this was indeed so, how then could they be taken seriously as meaningful contributors and leaders in the present?

The UCB's Transformation Charter, therefore, emphasised that it should be a priority to 'acknowledge, record and respect' the achievements of black cricketers over the past century, 'recognising our diversity as a source of strength in the process'.

Great progress has been made in this rewriting project since 1998. Besides regular newspaper articles and a number of 'recognition ceremonies' held in various provinces, several major new histories have been produced or are in preparation.

These include Junaid Ahmed's four-part film documentary, *Iqakamba*; Mogamad Allie's *More than a Game*, published by the Western Province Cricket

Association; the professionally researched *Blacks in Whites* by Ashwin Desai et al. for the KwaZulu-Natal Cricket Union; and the two-volume *Official History of South African Cricket, 1808–2003*, which is due in 2004.

A new generation of writers and historians has emerged to help undo past exclusions. A rich cricket history is being revealed. In the process, new identities and understandings, appropriate to the context of democracy, are emerging. The culture of South African cricket is slowly but surely changing.

Trevor Chesterfield has been in the field as a writer and journalist for four decades. It is to his credit that he now actively seeks to contribute to this new direction in writing. As he indicates in his preface to this second edition, he has self-consciously set out to revise old perspectives and to locate cricketing developments within the broader context of racial discrimination and apartheid. For example, a new section on black cricketers who played unofficially for their country is introduced here, and the unofficial 'rebel tours' of the 1980s are no longer given the same prominence as official Tests. Using new sources, he also goes back in time to revisit various controversial episodes in South African cricket history.

Is the author's (often controversial and distinctive) historical analysis valid? Does this second edition succeed in distancing itself from the dominant narratives of the past? That will be for the readers to decide. But, whatever their judgement, Chesters deserves our appreciation for his effort and challenging approach.

PROFESSOR ANDRÉ ODENDAAL
October 2002

André Odendaal is an historian, author and former first-class cricketer. He chaired the Transformation Monitoring Committee of the United Cricket Board between 1998 and 2002. He currently serves on the UCB's ICC World Cup 2003 Policy Committee. In March 2002 he was honoured with the Presidential Sports Award (Lifetime Achiever).

PREFACE

Much has changed in the nine years since this book first appeared in late 1994: for one thing, the shape and pace of the game. There have also been major scandals, among them the exposure of match-fixing deals, which led to the sacking of Hansie Cronjé as captain. Three new names have been added to the list of South Africa's captains: Shaun Pollock, and Gary Kirsten and Mark Boucher in a temporary capacity. Just as significant have been the important changes within the administrative guard at the United Cricket Board. Dr Ali Bacher moved out to head the 2003 Cricket World Cup organising committee, while Gerald Majola, a thoughtful administrator with forward thinking ideas, took over as executive officer.

There have been three UCB presidents, a major overhaul of the UCB and its transformation policy with the repeal of player quotas (June 2002), as well as meetings that led to the formation of an epoch-making decision body (the National Cricket Committee) and the eventual shake-up in selection and coaching structures. The last three of these events took place while the deep abrasions and scars were still visible from the 2001/02 twin Australian tours, showing impressive involvement by former players as well as administrators.

Internationally, the winds of change have swept through the game. There has been a long-delayed if considerable makeover of the International Cricket Council, the international ruling body. The old school tie, gin-and-tonic comfort zone and geriatric image that had long befuddled the game's administrative and marketing thinking and progress, has been restructured into something more in keeping with the twenty-first century.

One of the most important changes, though, has been the emergence of Asia as the new powerhouse of the sport, with the involvement of hundreds of millions of people; figures that are difficult to understand unless one has spent time in South Asia. That it took place during South Africa's years of isolation is also a matter of interest among those who have studied the game's growth along egalitarian lines.

Reasons for Asia's emergence include millions of dollars in sponsorship, television deals and media coverage, and huge spectator support. The region has produced three World Cup champions: India (1983), Pakistan (1992) and Sri Lanka (1996) as well as a losing finalist, Pakistan (1999). The power has shifted from the old Raj master, England, and its colonial buddies, Australia and New Zealand, and gives the sport a more egalitarian representation than the chauvinistic old-pals society, which had ruled for decades. Malcolm Gray, an Australian, took over the ICC presidency from Indian business mogul Jagmohan Dalmiya in 2000, and in July 2003 Pakistan's Ehsan Mani, who has already served on a number of ICC committees, including the Chairman's Advisory Committee, becomes the new president. Mani's paper on the sharing of World Cup revenues between the host and member countries had a major impact on the financial arrangements of the ICC and its members.

One area of concern has been the demise of the West Indies. After long years of domination, the pitfalls of failing to refurbish the side with young talent to learn from the old experienced players bothered Sir Conrad Hunte, Clive Lloyd and Sir Garfield Sobers. The fast bowling force that lay partly behind their lengthy success also burst a boiler as the last of a great era retired: first Curtly Ambrose and then Courtney Walsh.

Internationally, an elite panel of eight umpires was put in place, as well as five full-time match referees to meet the ever-burgeoning Test and limited-overs international schedule, with its increased demands for quality. There has also been a need to broaden the use of TV technology, with the tricky lbw decision to be included. Strangely, in March 1992, the Australian Cricket Board resisted the idea of an independent panel of umpires, which was proposed after the success of the 1992 World Cup in Australia. Fortunately, the ICC had already approved the plan in principal, and South Africa was the first country where the panel was successfully launched. Also, a new code of laws was published in 2000 and Bangladesh became the tenth Test nation.

For the first edition of this book Jackie McGlew and I relied to a large extent on our first-hand knowledge of the careers of most of the players involved post-1947. For this revised, updated edition I have also researched additional sources to ensure that all events are accurately recorded. This includes the archived files of the *Pretoria News*, the *Argus* (Cape Town), the *Rand Daily Mail*, the *Eastern Province Herald* (Port Elizabeth), *The Times* (London), the *Sydney Morning Herald*, *The Age* (Melbourne), *The Hindu*, *Times of India*, *Sportstar* (India), and the *Sunday Observer* and *Daily News* (both Colombo). Editions of *Wisden Cricketers' Almanack* from 1935 to 2001, the *SA Cricket Annual* 1955–2001, the *Wisden Anthology* 1864–1900 were also researched, as well as editions of *Wisden Cricket Monthly* and *The Cricketer International*.

With the untimely death of Jackie in June 1998, it has been my responsibility to update and revise the book with the inclusion of the three new captains

(Gary Kirsten, Shaun Pollock and Mark Boucher), and to expand the prologue and include a new chapter on South Africa's black captains. Another change has been to record the SACU rebel era and events surrounding those tours in a single chapter.

When the book was first written, the idea was to portray, through each captain, South Africa's role on the international cricket stage from the end of World War II through to the struggle and re-emergence from isolation. A pertinent criticism of South African cricket history is that it is seen largely from a white perspective, and that the narrative of books of this nature too often portrays a one-sided view. To an extent the first edition of this book *did*, if marginally, cover the race struggle issue. This revised and updated edition goes well beyond that. It examines the tricky mosaic of transformation in South Africa 200 years before it became a buzzword. (In fact, the word did not even exist 200 years ago.)

To this end the prologue has now been revamped (warts, pimples, blemishes and all) to acknowledge most of the official 16 captains as well as two unofficial captains from 1889 until 1935. In addition, there is a need to recognise and honour the seven men who led either South African Cricket Board of Control (Sacboc) or South African Cricket Board (SACB) teams between 1957 and 1990; these have been included in a separate chapter. Apart from the invaluable help of historian Krish Reddy, of Durban, and his research into the Sacboc and SACB eras, further material was forthcoming from Omar Henry, Hoosain Ayob and Basil D'Oliveira, and, before their untimely deaths, Khaya Majola and Brian Bassano. Majola and Bassano shed some private thoughts and important insights on the struggle years. There was also willing assistance from statistician Robin Isherwood, who cleared up several grey areas and made some helpful suggestions, as did Professor André Odendaal, head of the UCB's Transformation Monitoring Committee.

In recent years I have also received confidential new material through private papers from a variety of sources in the United Kingdom, India, South Africa, Zimbabwe and Australia. Some of this information sheds new light on a number of controversial issues that involved, in part, the shameful white administration (South African Cricket Association) attitudes for almost a century; included is their attitude towards Indian princes KS Ranjitsinhji and KS Duleepsinhji. It also lays bare a number of racial discriminatory issues barely touched upon in the first edition but included in this book to give the story an honest, fresh approach to this subject. It also disputes a number of preconceived notions and questions the role various administrations played down the years. Some of this is not going to sit well with many people, but disguising facts with 'faction' (fact and fiction) does even more harm to the image of the game than when the truth is revealed.

Although often in great pain, co-author Jackie McGlew, some months before his death in 1998, sent me several handwritten notes which shed fresh light on some off-the-field drama during the 1960 tour of England. Authenticated papers received from other sources show how SACA machinations in the 1890s, and up to World War I and later, had led to efforts to influence the non-selection of players of colour against South African teams in England; other reasons are also advanced to those already known for Barry Richards's controversial omission from the third, fourth and fifth Tests in the 1966/67 series against Australia. Papers made available from the UK show how, apart from the obvious John Vorster hangman act, devious political manoeuvring in South Africa and England led to the banning of Basil D'Oliveira in 1968/69, and the cancellation of the Marylebone Cricket Club tour.

One historical note that needs clarifying for the not so old is that Johannesburg has had three Test venues and Durban two. There are two Wanderers grounds, the first of which eventually disappeared under the concrete, bricks and iron tracks of the railway station in the city centre almost half a century ago, while the second is now in Corlett Drive. The third will surprise the many who visit that mausoleum-style stadium, which is better known as Ellis Park, where Tests were played against England (1948/49), Australia (1949/50) and New Zealand (1953/54). Durban's first site was a direct crib of that consecrated St John's Woods setting known as Lord's; it is not too surprising how the cheek in using this name met with a dodgy end, and the location became a more than useful building site. In 1923 Kingsmead took its place.

Lastly, my deep appreciation to Marlene Fryer, the Zebra publishing manager. Her patience and spontaneous support did much to ease the way after the first inquiry was made from far-off Weligama, Sri Lanka, in January 2002, by this eccentric New Zealand cricket nut, long transplanted in South Africa, but with new roots in Sri Lanka. She has shown a calm appreciation and has played every verbal 'googly' with a straight bat.

A complete list of sources can be found at the back. Included are several books that were either not in print or not readily available at the time of the first edition, along with various sets of unpublished papers.

TREVOR CHESTERFIELD
Centurion, South Africa
Colombo, Sri Lanka
2002

Unless otherwise marked, photographs supplied for this edition belong to the sole copyright holders, Anne Laing (Centurion) and Rian Botes (Cape Town) who have given their kind permission for their use.

For Jackie, whose idea it was in the first place, and to all future South African captains who would not mind sharing this illustrious stage with Basil D'Oliveira, Frank Roro, Ben Malamba, Eric Petersen and those others denied the opportunity to show how they could also play the game

The captain creates the moral atmosphere of his side. If he is slack and indifferent, so are the other ten; if he is keen and enthusiastic so are they. Unconsciously, the side as a whole assumes the captain's attitude towards cricket and towards a particular match.

– **Prince Kumar Shri Ranjitsinjhi,**
The Jubilee Book of Cricket, 1897

PATHFINDERS, PIONEERS AND ROGUES
Turbulent Early Years

By Trevor Chesterfield

It was once claimed that the gathering of several Englishmen on a foreign field in the nineteenth century – whether missionaries, military or diplomats – would invariably lead to a discussion on cricket, or the desire to play a game. If the gathering is now changed to a meeting of, say, several Indians, Pakistanis, Sri Lankans or West Indians, and it is moved forward from the 1800s to the 1950s, or the 1990s, or today, would not the same apply? England has long surrendered its cricket crown to the former colonies. It is hard to argue against this, especially after reading the opening words in *The Tao of Cricket* by Ashish Nandy, who proclaims with that delightfully spicy tongue-in-cheek aphorism that 'cricket is an Indian game accidentally discovered by the English'.

Now, what if a demographic blend of young South Africans – blacks, coloureds, Indians and whites – met and started talking cricket? In Soshanguve, north of Pretoria, for example, the 'most loved game' has its legion of followers who are just as passionate about it as anyone from cricket's other far-flung portals in the former British Empire.

Whether it was an accident that the British developed the game from what is a shadowy, ancient past, and later exported it to the colonies, is another matter. The fact is that they did. What they may not have expected is that the indigenous population in the lands they colonised might want to play it as well. This often gave rise to a teacher–pupil relationship, with the teacher unfortunately adopting a patronising attitude. Cricket should never be about class, race, creed or skin colour; it is about ability, skills and fair play.

If we are to believe recorded history, cricket in South Africa should celebrate its double century in 2008. Or, as has been suggested, has the sport already celebrated its bicentenary without anyone realising it? There is, of course, no evidence that members of the garrison played any form of cricket during the first British military occupation of the Cape, from 1795 to 1803 (during the Napoleonic wars). Yet the theory exists that, as several officers were known keen cricketers in England, matches were in all likelihood played. No letters to family or friends (or English newspapers or official documents) have, however, been uncovered to suggest this. The only scrap of information comes from the obituary of an officer known as Charles Anguish, who died in the Cape mid-1797. He was a member of the Marylebone Cricket Club (MCC) and was said to have played for Surrey; claims were that he was a 'crack bat'.

As organised county teams were not common in the late 1700s, and Surrey was not formed until August 1845, the 'Surrey' referred to in subsequent reports was not a recognised county team. The term 'crack' was a popular colloquialism in the 1800s meaning, among other things, 'quality'.

The first known reference to a cricket match in South Africa is a report in *The Cape Town Gazette and African Advertiser*, which said that on 5 January 1808 officers of the artillery mess would play a game for (Cape) 1 000 dollars. What is interesting here is how deep the class and social distinctions were in that era. Officers were the only ones allowed to play; the foot soldier, it is presumed, was not considered educated enough. There was a certain exclusivity about the British forces in the Cape (as elsewhere), and the officers were, at the best of times, inclined to be a snobbish bunch. It is unlikely that the garrison would have allowed or encouraged the Dutch-speaking settlers or the indigenous population to play.

Had someone as progressive and understanding as, say, the fourth Lord Harris been governor of the Cape or Natal instead of Bombay, there is every chance that politics and cricket development in South Africa could have taken a different course. Harris was a fair, benevolent ruler. With experience of India as a youth, he had a good grasp of the needs of those he was to rule. It was his encouragement that led people in the Bombay region to embrace his cricket ideals – and how they spread. Not so in South Africa; instead of encouragement, it was a matter of the 'native is to be put and kept in his place'.

Although by 1840 the game had spread to the Eastern Cape, Natal and even the Free State Republic, promotion was largely white elitist. While the coloureds and Africans were, with some enthusiasm, also playing in large numbers throughout the Western and Eastern Cape areas by the 1840s, district and club administration, such as it was then, followed a slap-in-the-face approach by pointedly failing to grant recognition. Egalitarian principles were not appreciated. It took a further 135 years before serious moves were made in South Africa to unify cricket under one banner, and even then the movement was short-lived because of a variety of political factors.

No black, coloured or Indian faces appeared in photographs of teams which played in tournaments such as the Champion Bat (in the 1880s), and MW Luckin fails to mention local players of colour in either volume of his history of South African cricket. Or was Luckin, as the South African Cricket Association (SACA) secretary, following an unwritten white establishment 'colour bar' rule laid down years before? One early example (among many) is the publication of the picture of the Boer prisoners team during their internment in Sri Lanka. On 5 and 6 July 1901 they played the Colombo Colts at the Nondescripts Club, and the photograph in Luckin's first volume shows both sides without the two coloured cooks who were used as net bowlers. The picture on the wall at the Nondescripts Club in 2000 shows the two cooks in the centre of the back row. Nor were there any Sri Lankans in the Colombo Colts side; it was hard, even on an island with such a multifarious society, to remove the barriers of prejudice mounted by the Raj to protect its society. Vigorous white chauvinism has long been blind to the needs of others.

There could be some debate about whether South Africa did in fact play their first Test at St George's Park in Port Elizabeth on 12 and 13 March 1889. As it was, the country was divided into a series of regions, with two major Boer republics, the Orange Free State and Transvaal, surrounded by the British-controlled Cape and Natal colonies. Although both Boer republics contained large pockets of English-speaking communities who played cricket, they were regarded as *uitlanders* [foreigners] and often treated with suspicion by the Dutch-speaking farmers. Therefore the term 'South African' did not really exist as a national (white) identity for another 21 years, at the inception of the Union on 31 May 1910.

Moreover, how the match ended up being granted first-class status is a conundrum. When it is considered that the 1894 side that toured England was unable to play any first-class games (and drew little public interest), and certainly no Tests, the matter of how first-class status was given to the Tests in South Africa needs to be questioned. Certainly there was no justification, although it was the first time the tourists played in a match against a full strength XI.

How teams from 1888/89 until 1904 were selected also presents a problem. Players in 1888/89 came from teams that in most instances contained as many as 22 players, and the skills quality in many cases was highly suspect. It is perhaps presumptuous of Luckin to refer to the early matches as Tests; he was not bothered by the status of the games or the strength of the selected sides.

It is also intriguing to see how the first seven captains earned their spurs. Did Owen Dunell, for example, lead the side against the England tourists at St George's Park in 1889 for no other reason than he happened to live in Port Elizabeth where the match was played? A multi-talented sportsman, Dunell was from the privileged class. Born in Port Elizabeth, he was educated in England, at Eton and Oxford University, and although failing to get his blue he was a member of the MCC, which gave him a certain stature. He also indulged in soccer against Cambridge University in 1877 and 1878. Reports of the St George's Park match do not give a checklist of his leadership skills.

The British-born Sir William Milton led the side at Newlands for the second game, and the first against Walter Read's side of 1891/92. Milton, though, did lead

3

Western Province for several seasons, and owes his captaincy of the Newlands game to his role in helping organise Major Robert Warton's 1888/89 tour: very much an old chums club situation. Educated at Marlborough College, Milton was a highly skilled all-round player, particularly as a batsman and fielder, with an accurate dart-like throw (a prototype Colin Bland/Jonty Rhodes, by all accounts). One Cape Town report claimed that 'when on the run in the field he was often a real jack in the box'. He later did much to develop the game at administration level in the Western Cape, but at the cost of black/white relations. He possessed a certain autocratic manner, which manifested itself long before he was made administrator of Southern Rhodesia. Milton College in Bulawayo was named after him. He played rugby for England.

An interesting fact about the St George's Park Test involving Major Warton's side is that the England captain, Aubrey Smith, later became more famous as Hollywood actor Sir Aubrey Smith; he also played for Transvaal and was the only player to have captained England in his only Test.

Another interesting fact is that on Read's visit in 1891/92, the last match was against a Malay XVIII, played in Cape Town, a game tagged on at the end of the tour as a benefit for the touring team's professional players. For reasons known only to Luckin, the match did not feature in the tour averages (this was mentioned in the scorecard of the match); but as Luckin was the statistician, it was glossed over by historians. Whether by design or establishment approval, it was the only time a team of colour was allowed to play a touring side.

Carrying the sobriquet 'Barberton' for no other reason than his mining connections, Ernie Halliwell was, by all accounts, a class act as a wicketkeeper and, as with most players of that era, wore a large moustache. Another South African player born in England and the son of the Middlesex wicketkeeper Bisset Halliwell, young Barberton found that standing up to fast bowlers, such as the feared JJ (Kodgee) Kotze, was preferable on matting rather than the turf surfaces in England, as it left less margin for error with catches. (Johnny Waite did the same with Dave Ironside in the early 1950s.) Halliwell took over as captain from Milton, leading the side against Lord Hawke's 1895/96 side in the first two Tests of that series. While retained as wicketkeeper for the Newlands match, he was replaced as captain by Alfred Richards who, in his only Test, seems to have assumed this role for no other reason than he was Cape Town-based and the side was chosen by those who at the time ran the Western Province Cricket Club, the owner of Newlands.

This is of course open to debate, but if some of the private papers are accurate, there was, through Sir William Milton's administrative influence, a decided bias towards Cape Town-based clubs and players. To query anything in those days was often met with swift, heavy-handed official rebuttal.

It was not the last time Halliwell led South Africa. He was recalled to the position against the first Australians in 1902 when, it appears, there was a genuine effort to select the best players after a downplayed Johannesburg-led attack on how previous teams were selected. The long North/South 'sibling' rivalry had been bubbling for some time with accusations of Cape bias.

In 1894, wicketkeeper Herbert Hayton (Fatty) Castens took the first side from the Cape to England. Another to be educated in England, Castens read law at Oxford. He holds – depending on your point of view – a unique position in sport in this country: he was captain of the country's cricket and rugby teams, a fact not well remembered by anyone other than historians. Certainly Jimmy Mayne, sports editor of the *Pretoria News* in 1968, did not think too much of this legal eagle's claim as a 'double' international because he did not play in a (cricket) Test.

The first three sides to visit England – in 1894, 1901 and 1904 – were not accorded the honour of playing any Tests, as it was felt that their standard was well below that of the English county sides. It was a fair argument as well; standards differ, and there was always the dispute, not properly settled until 1947, of what did and did not constitute a first-class match. This was established by the MCC, who after some deliberation settled the issue by claiming that in future only those games of three days or longer, and played by first-class teams recognised as such by the board of control, would be accepted as first class.

The tour of England received little publicity yet some notoriety over the omission of the Cape Malay fast bowler Krom Hendricks, simply because of his colour. Castens had seen young Hendricks in action, and when making inquiries about his non-selection was simply told, 'It would be impolitic to include a coloured [in the side].' In whose view Hendricks's selection was seen as 'impolitic' is unclear. At the time, the selectors of such teams contained strong Cape establishment influences, while the players from which the team was chosen were nominated by the regions recognised by the South Africa Cricket Association.

Milton, who took the chair of the meeting in the small town of De Aar, acted on the advice of Cecil John Rhodes, then the Cape Prime Minister, and used his executive prerogative to bar Hendricks's selection, despite the strong support the young man had. Ernie Halliwell, representing Transvaal's interests, objected to Milton's banning of the bowler. Milton may have made the 'impolitic' comment as a way of justifying a decision that would bedevil South African society for a further 100 years. It has been reported that while Read did ask about the absence of Hendricks, what may have been Castens's response was well buried by officialdom. Rhodes was prepared to put forward £500 to help finance the tour, which had been Halliwell's idea.

What upset Halliwell and the first captain, Owen Dunell, representing Eastern Province, was the way the matter was handled. They were rebuffed by Milton when the question was asked how he could use his executive powers in a matter of team selection that did not just include the Cape Colony. It can be seen from this that egalitarianism was not a noted characteristic of South African life in those years.

The following year, Rhodes turned up at Oriel College, Oxford, with Dr Leander Jameson, and in conversation with Pelham Warner, then a law undergraduate, said he did not like people of colour. In his autobiography, *Long Innings*, Warner relates Rhodes saying, 'I suppose it is the instinct of self-preservation. In South Africa we have perhaps a million or two whites and many more million of black people.'

When the name Sir Murray Bisset is mentioned, cricket is probably the last thing that comes to the mind of the average historian of colonial southern Africa. Educated at Bishops (Diocesan College) in Cape Town, where Clive van Ryneveld, Adrian Kuiper and Herschelle Gibbs learnt their skills, Sir Murray was as brilliant academically as he was as a player. He is better known by history as a politician and a judge. His playing career spanned an interesting period, in that it encompassed pre- and post-Anglo-Boer War eras. He later became the chief justice of Southern Rhodesia.

During Bisset's captaincy there was controversy over the non-selection of that brilliant Indian batsman, Prince (Kumar Shri) Ranjitsinhji, again because of Rhodes's influence, when Lord Hawke was organising the tour of 1898/99 to South Africa. Nicknamed 'Smith', Ranji was an elegant, stylish batsman who had studied at Cambridge University and had toured Australia as well as played several Tests for England in England. Bisset found himself in the middle of a selection policy row, but baulked at the thought of challenging Rhodes's authority.

Milton knew Lord Hawke, and when the side for the tour was being put together he placed pressure on the peer of the English realm to have Ranji excluded on the grounds that 'his appearance would create certain embarrassment in this country'. Lord Hawke and the MCC, then the unofficial authority administering the game in England, fell into a duplicitous role. While it was okay for Ranji to play South African sides visiting England, the now racially run SACA did not want him in teams, private or official, touring this country. It was justified, says a report, 'as there would be problems among the Indians in South Africa if they knew the visitors are to include someone such as Ranjitsinhji'.

It was naked racism, and the pity is that the South Africans were allowed to get away with it for so long. Ranji was angered by the fuss as he had toured Australia without any problems in 1897/98.

What the tough-minded Lord Hawke did do, however, over the Ranjitsinhji issue, was talk to Bisset, captain of the 1901 South African side. The outcome of those discussions is not known, but Lord Hawke was said to have been disturbed enough to accuse some South African players of having an attitude problem when they played the MCC and Ground at Lord's in early June with Ranji in the MCC side, and lost the game on a rain-affected pitch by 53 runs. Bisset's team did not play Ranjitsinhji's county side, Sussex, on that tour.

There has long been a dispute as to why there was the need for three captains for the games against Joe Darling's visiting Australians in 1902. There is no record of what policy was pursued, apart from the non-selection of coloured and African players. With no matches being organised against coloured and African sides, or mixed teams, the Australians were left ignorant of the skills and capabilities of such players. Also, unlike the Australians, who through Charles Lawrence, a Sydney publican with entrepreneurial skills, sent a side of Aborigines to the UK in 1867, no side representing South African players of colour went to England.

One of the three captains against the Australians was Henry (Tabs) Taberer, who played for Oxford University (he did not get his blue), Essex and Natal, and had a varied career. In what was his only Test, he led the side at the Wanderers, and was the first South African captain to enforce the follow on, after scoring 454; the Australians were bowled out for 296, with the Pietermaritzburg-born left-hand all-rounder, Buck (or Charlie) Llyewellyn, taking six wickets with his unorthodox/orthodox bowling style. Making his debut in this match was Arthur Nourse, father of Dudley Nourse. Taberer was dropped from the side for the second game, and James (Biddy) Anderson from Cape Town was drafted in as captain and then left out for the Newlands game when Ernie Halliwell, who had kept wicket throughout the series, was back in charge as captain and wicketkeeper.

It is perhaps ironic that it was the Trinidadian-born Plum Warner, later Sir Pelham Warner, an MCC president and once referred to as 'that grand old gentleman of cricket', who captained the first MCC side in South Africa to lose a series. Warner complained about how this particular side, in the five Tests of 1905/06, was not as strong as the team which the Honourable Stanley Jackson had led against Australia in an Ashes series in England months before. Missing were some famous names: Jackson, CB Fry, George Hirst, Wilfred Rhodes, Thomas Hayward and the indomitable Archie MacLaren. Warner had not played in the 1905 series, but had led England, for the first time under the patronage of the MCC, to Australia in 1903/04, winning the series 3–2 thanks to the help of the man who invented the googly, BJT Bosanquet. A Middlesex county colleague and personal friend of Warner's, as well as a fellow Oxford blue, Bosanquet had decimated the Australian batting on that tour. Warner regretted the bowler's absence from the 1905/06 side.

In that era, the best players were not always available, which is why most of those who had recently beaten Australia in England were not invited to undertake the tour, preferring a winter's rest. Warner does not indicate either whether he attempted to persuade Bosanquet to go to South Africa. It would have made for a more interesting series as there was the impression that England were short of a bowler, and the googly specialist might have made it more difficult for South African batsmen. It would have been very interesting to see how Bosanquet would have handled matting conditions. Warner's bowlers seemed to battle under such conditions, and it was said that, apart from the emergence of quality bowlers, South Africa's success on that tour owed much to Percy Sherwell's adroit ability as a player and leader. Yet Warner was not without complaint about the teams selected for South African tours. He once argued that until Walter Hammond's team of 1938/39, the selection of sides to South Africa did not receive the same meticulous attention as those chosen to tour Australia. The comment refers as much to the 1905/06 team, which lost the series 1–4, as to those selected for the post-World War I tours of India, the West Indies and New Zealand.

Having largely marched unchecked through South Africa during the early stages of that tour, it was not until the side arrived in Johannesburg that the first signs of resistance emerged on the home front. Sherwell led a strong Transvaal side to a shock victory over the tourists – the first success by a South African side over a visiting team. Apart from pleasing the locals at the Wanderers, it set up the start of the series when a side with strong Transvaal representation was selected. Not that this came as a surprise, for along with their poor showing, the power had moved from the autocratic, laid-back attitude of the Cape to the clout of the country's burgeoning mining centre.

Although born in Isipingo, Natal, Sherwell was taken to England in his early childhood, and learnt his cricket skills at Bedford County School and his mining experience through the Royal School of Mines. This was all before a mining career in South Africa led him to captain first Transvaal and later South Africa.

If Pelham Warner's views mean anything, Sherwell was as 'cool and as level-headed as any player I have met in the raw heat of battle'. He was also a shrewd judge of pitch conditions (in those days all games in South Africa were played on matting, which varied from ground to ground) and his bowlers. What he thought when he joined Arthur Nourse on the third and last day at the Wanderers on 4 January 1906 would be interesting. (Tests in those years were held over three days and not five.) With nine wickets down, there were still 45 runs needed for victory, with England no doubt thinking the chink of light at the end of this particular gloomy tunnel was an expected 1–0 series lead. Instead it was the light of a train gathering speed and overrunning their bowling attack.

Sherwell played two other quality innings in his Test career: the first helped South Africa beat England at Newlands in the same series. He added 94 with the No. 11 batsman, Ernie Vogler, for the last wicket to build a first-innings lead which enabled the team to go on and win by an innings, the first such success. The second was at Lord's during the 1907 series, when he pushed himself into the role of opener after becoming concerned about the indifferent form of the side. Only two of the England players in the Lord's Test had played in the Newlands game in 1906. Apart from it being their debut Test abroad, it was South Africa's first Test at Lord's. Sherwell's second-innings score of 115 and a washed-out last day forced a draw, but the series was lost 1–0, with England winning a low-scoring match by 53 runs at Headingley, Leeds, with the third Test, at The Oval, also drawn.

It has been claimed that despite the leadership qualities displayed by later captains Herbie Taylor, Nummy Deane, Jock Cameron and Herby Wade, it was Sherwell who gave the South African side the respect it needed. He was not available for the 1909/10 MCC tour led by Leveson Gower, however, and the competitive Sibley Snook was appointed in his place to continue home dominance of the MCC tourists for the second consecutive tour. Snook had already toured England in 1904 and 1907, and was surprisingly preferred to the all-rounder Gordon White, one of the famed googly quartet of the 1907 side.

Sherwell was back to lead the side in their pioneering visit to Australia in 1910/11. Although his ability behind the stumps on the that tour saw him manufacture a world record nine stumpings in a series, the Aussies were well led by the highly competitive and sharp Clem Hill, and won the series 4–1. The South African batting broke down much as it would in 2001/02, with the one success, at Adelaide Oval, a surprising turnaround for a side always under pressure. The big disappointment had been Nourse, whose top score of the series was 92, his only innings above 50. The great South African all-rounder Aubrey Faulkner was in such form on the tour that he achieved a South African record series total of 732 runs at an incredible average of 73.20. In early 1973 Tom Reddick, who had acted as Faulkner's assistant secretary and coaching assistant when he ran a coaching school in London, admitted he was shocked by the ignorance South Africans displayed over Faulkner's place among the country's great players. Here was a batsman of immense technical skill and stylish strokeplay, and whom the Australians had garlanded with impressive tributes, yet at home he is now a virtual unknown. No other South African has managed to approach such run-making levels in a Test series, yet he was forgotten. It disturbed the former Middlesex and Nottingham all-rounder to think that there was no place of honour on any mythical roll-call for Faulkner.

If cautious opinion expressed in those years really means anything, South African cricket was run by 'the gold mining bosses of the Reef'. This would explain why the MCC were often more courteous to the South African cricket hierarchy than to the more upfront Australian officials, and so eager for tours, with their extra financial rewards. The influence wielded by Sir Abe Bailey, a former Transvaal bowler and then a politician and financier, was immense. If the game was not run as his fiefdom, the power he had in England as well as in South Africa often found British administrators to do the occasional jig to his fiddle. Yet he was far from the benefactor he might seem, and unlike the humanitarian Barney Barnato,[1] he left no genuine legacy.

There was little encouragement for black cricket on the mines, though, yet it flourished among the poor and disadvantaged. The brilliance of the black Kimberley opal Frank Roro substantiates just how the culture of survival existed in such oppressed conditions, as it would generations later in places like Soshanguve. While the South African Cricket Association and its provincial affiliates may have benefited in some way, the disadvantaged were continually marginalised in all areas. It was a matter of attending the right school and club; chauvinism in its worst form tore apart the fabric and dignity of people who deserved better.

Bailey was a dictator and used to getting his way, 'as much as did Cecil John Rhodes and Sir William Milton along with Luckin, of whom it was noted was also one in the Milton mould'. Bailey could also turn on the charm when need be and 'used his persuasive and plausible argument and considerable wealth to get his way'.[2] When he proposed the formation of a world cricket body, he had in mind an international tournament. Towards those in charge of the MCC, who in a sense were the world authority in all but name, he was at his unctuous best without being too obsequious. By 1907 the major cricketing countries (including, surprisingly, the United States) had established central controlling bodies (in South Africa there was a white body, which was recognised, while those representing blacks were not).

When the Imperial Cricket Conference was formed in 1909, with Bailey as its main proponent, cricket in Philadelphia (the American headquarters) and other US regions such as New York, Chicago and California, was felt to be at its height. At the time, English judges of the game's standards considered that at least a couple of the American teams were just as strong as some of the leading English counties. Why then, at its inception, was the use of the more fussy term 'imperial' used instead of the universal 'international'? In hindsight it seems to be a matter of the short-sighted policy of 'keeping the game within the old school tie club' with its 'loyal' British Empire links.

It was said that Bailey was behind the use of the term 'imperial', and from this deliberate slight originated the exclusion of whatever influence and impact cricket may have had on that vast North American country. It might even be argued that South African mining money crippled the game's growth in the US. How often have such short-term advantages created long-term shortcomings? By the end of World War I, cricket in the US was in serious decline; no doubt those running the MCC/ICC corporate were quite smug about their actions. It took almost half a century before the ICC corrected this imbalance, but by

1965, when 'international' finally replaced 'imperial', the remedial action had come too late.

Whatever the reason for the choice of the word 'imperial' instead of 'international', cricket had reached a certain political crossroads, with South Africa and mining money behind such an introduction. It certainly added an ironic twist to the game's growing sub-plot, and cut directly across the egalitarian principles of cricket being a sport for everyone. Did this have something to do with ensuring that South Africa would control whom they would play, as opposed to whom they would not?

At the time of the 1912 triangular series between South Africa, England and Australia, South African cricket was in a state of crisis. An overweight Frank Mitchell, Bailey's private secretary, who had led the 1904 side to England, was a reluctant captain. With Bailey as your boss it was hard to refuse a request. As it was, Mitchell, a former Yorkshire and England capped player, was coerced out of retirement, with the bulk of the side made up of 11 Transvaal players (including Mitchell) and four from Western Province.

There is a theory long held in Indian circles that Bailey, who funded the 1904 South Africa side to England, ran into trouble with influential politicians at home when it was learnt that the team was to play a side from India at Lord's during the tour. There is, however, no record of this incident, yet it can be imagined. What is a pity is how the Indian visit had run into trouble of its own and was cancelled. Such a game, had it taken place, might have had long-term effects on South African sports history – something, as has been well documented, the white establishment did not want.

Louis Tancred was a specialist batsman who took over from the out-of-form Mitchell in the 1912 Triangular Tournament. It was his fourth tour of England. An opening batsman, he was solid and patient with a crouching style, but contemporary reports suggest that as a captain he showed little imagination.

Between the era of Faulkner and Dave Nourse, and the modern greats such as his son Dudley, Russell Endean, Barry Richards, Graeme Pollock, Basil D'Oliveira, Amien Variawa, Peter Kirsten and Daryll Cullinan, is Herbie Taylor, who led South Africa in 18 Tests, from 1913 to 1924. There are many who talk of Taylor the batsman, and those such as Jackie McGlew and Louis Duffus who talk of Taylor the captain. In an international career spanning 26 years, Taylor had a better batting average than most for that era at 41.86, and 30 first-class centuries. His early years, however, were more noted for his battles with the famous, often stormy Sydney Barnes, claimed to be the greatest of all bowlers, in the 1913/14 series. It is interesting how *Wisden* devotes almost two and a half pages to Barnes in their century edition and barely half a page to the spirited Taylor. It mentions nothing of the famed combat the two waged on the matting surfaces.

In four Tests on matting in South Africa in 1913/14, Barnes collected 49 Test wickets. Taylor, it is claimed, played him the best of the South African and Australian batsmen. An astute batsman on matting, he scored seven Test centuries, only one of which was in England. Yet Reddick claimed that he preferred Faulkner to Taylor if only because of Faulkner's unorthodox batting flair.

In England in an era of growing awareness of social and racial injustice, Hubert (Nummy) Deane spent more time on the 1929 tour defending the SACA against criticism of their lack of selection of non-white players than playing his defensive strokes on the field. It is also said that he was one of South Africa's finest captains of the SACA-run era. Well, as this is the sort of claim that can be made of any player who takes over the leadership of a side, it is a debating point. Deane captained the side in 12 Tests between 1927 and 1931, and began his career as the first South African captain to win the toss in all five Tests (in the 1927/28 series). It was a drawn rubber with two victories each.

The 1929 tour of England was marred by a row over the selection of Kumar Shri Duleepsinhji, nephew of Kumar Shri Ranjitsinhji. Duleep played in one Test against Deane's 1929 South Africans; he was a dismal failure, with scores of one and 12, and the elegant Indian batsman was dropped. Yet in June, July and August that year, such was his form that pointed questions were asked about his non-selection for the two remaining Tests after several England batsmen had failed in the second and third games. Sir Henry (Shrimp) Leveson Gower, then convener of the England selection panel of three, was told that South Africa were not too keen for Duleep to be included in the England side for the last two Tests.

Imagine then Leveson Gower's thoughts. He had twice been to South Africa with MCC touring teams, in 1905/06 and 1909/10, when he was captain, and here he was being challenged by South African officials about England team selection policy. He was irritated by the comments made to him by the manager, LO Frielinghaus, and Algie Frames, the SACA secretary, who had at one stage joined the tour.

When news of this broke, Deane wrote to Duleep, saying that the South Africans had no objection to playing against him, whether at county or Test level. Whatever Deane may have felt personally, and despite the disclaimers made on behalf of the side, the racist stigma stuck and raised muted questions about South Africa's position in the ICC. That these concerns were first raised by India in late 1929, when they were not a member of the ICC, was a point that was glossed over by those at Lord's and in the MCC/ICC.

Although the implication was that it was a directive sent by the South African government to the British High Commissioner and passed on to the Colonial Office, Leveson Gower fails to mention the incident anywhere in his autobiography *On and off the Field*. In fact, Duleepsinhji's name appears nowhere in his book.

There was no denial issued by either the South African government or the Colonial Office. Did this in fact mean that Pretoria was forcing its will on the touring side without consultation? Or was the 1929 episode apocryphal? Not according to a set of private papers. The thought of a century being scored against Deane's side by Duleep would not reflect well in press reports at home. Although the leading amateur batsman in England at the time, Duleep was not invited to play in the Gentlemen of England side in their annual game against the Players (professionals). It was felt that had he scored heavily for the Gentlemen; it would be hard to leave him out of the Test side. There was also a squabble of sorts within the precincts of the selectors' committee room whether Duleep qualified to play for England.

There was no doubt that he passed the qualification clauses, such as they were at that stage, just as Nasser Hussain, Mark Ramprakash, Graeme Hick and Basil D'Oliveira qualified years later on grounds of residence. In Duleepsinhji's case, the polite, scholarly prince was quite disgusted with his treatment and wanted to quit. Imagine the smirking in SACA circles had this happened. What hurt Duleep was not only the question of colour, but also that he was an Indian. Had he not been warmly welcomed when attending the coaching school run by Aubrey Faulkner, where he had been treated with the utmost courtesy? Why then this colour attitude problem with white South African politicians and their cricket administrators?

Ranjitsinhji persuaded his nephew to put the South African tour issue behind him, while behind the scenes he admonished Leveson Gower and other MCC officials for their handling of the distasteful episode. He also used his considerable princely clout to criticise those in the Colonial Office for their appalling ham-fisted behaviour, and made his views known in a pointed interview with the *Evening Standard*. Ranji found support for his views from former England captain Archie MacLaren: 'If we are going to have the best team playing for England we must include people who come over here and make this country their home.'

Leading South Africa for one Test against England in the 1930/31 series was Buster Nupen. Nupen, of Norwegian parentage and with an eye missing since he was four, led South Africa to a surprise victory at the Wanderers. The injured Deane returned to the side and led for only two games, both drawn, before it was claimed that 'business matters' before the fourth Test at the Wanderers forced him to resign. It was also rumoured that there was a disagreement with the selectors. At this point, at the age of 25, Jock Cameron was appointed, because Nupen did not want the responsibility of the job. Cameron oversaw the remaining drawn two matches for a 1–0 series victory, a surprising result, as on paper, at least, England had the stronger side.[3]

There were claims by those who played under him that Herby Wade was not a great stylist as a leader. It has also been said that he did not possess the flamboyant touches that were noted in Alan Melville's captaincy leading up to World War II, or the understated style of Jack Cheetham or Jackie McGlew. Yet, as with Kepler Wessels or Hansie Cronjé in the early post-isolation era, Wade did have some distinctive qualities. One was an autocratic manner, similar to Len Hutton's when he captained England in the early and mid-1950s. Wade and Hutton felt the need for a strict disciplinary code to get the best results out of their teams.

What Wade is remembered for, however, is leading South Africa to a 1–0 victory over England in 1935, when he exuded confidence as a thinker and leader, which contradicts the earlier view. It was South Africa's first series win over England, then led by Bob Wyatt; it was the only Test series win by South Africa for 30 years. What is interesting is that the Hilton College-educated Wade also had Jock Cameron as a contemporary.

He had the rare distinction of captaining South Africa in all the 10 Tests he played, the first five against England and second five at home against a particularly strong Australian side with the potent leg-spinners Clarrie Grimmett and Bill O'Reilly. Although not a batsman of note, Wade's leadership qualities were considered the reason South Africa beat England. Quiet, with an almost stoical approach to the job of team leadership, Wade learnt early on how to handle the South African bowling against an average England side, but the Australians, even without Don Bradman, were far too strong. Grimmett's leg-spin was too much for the South Africans, and he collected 30 wickets in the last three Tests.

ALAN MELVILLE 2
Artistic Leadership

By Jackie McGlew

The great career of Alan Melville, that graceful right-hand batsman with the classical upright stance, started long before the timeless Test in Durban in the 1938/39 season – as the grey clouds of World War II hovered menacingly on the horizon – and extended long after the 1947 tour of England. After his sudden passing on his way to the Kruger National Park in 1983, tributes poured in from all over the world. His death, at 72 years and 11 months, was mourned by a cricket-loving public worldwide. He had been a great South African cricket captain, recognised as a batting artist who holds a unique place in the country's Test records: four successive centuries against England, even if they were spread over a period of two series and eight years!

Melville was a gentleman to his fingertips: sleek, suave and sophisticated. He was a product of the exclusive Michaelhouse School at Balgowan in the Natal Midlands, and a graduate of Oxford University. His schoolmates and fellow university students knew him as the personification of grace and charm. Melville always looked as though he had stepped out of a bandbox. He was invariably turned out like a member of the landed gentry in the days when having your own personal tailor was de rigueur. And Melville's tailor would have been one of Savile Row's finest.

On the cricket field he was always immaculately dressed and the picture of elegance. His shirtsleeves were buttoned at the wrist, there were razor-sharp creases in his cream flannels and, more often than not, a sparkling white cravat knotted inside his collar.

Melville had the rare honour of representing his province, Natal, while still at Michaelhouse. This he did in the 1928/29 season, later going on to captain, in succession, Oxford University, Sussex, Transvaal and South Africa. His seasons of tenure were:

Oxford University: 1931 and 1932
Sussex: 1934 and 1935
Transvaal: 1937/38 and 1948/49
South Africa: 1938/39 and 1947 (vs England).

His remarkable career records that he captained South Africa in 10 out of the 11 Tests in which he played, scoring 894 runs at the exceptionally handsome average of 52.58, an average now recognised in an age of proliferation of Test matches as being world class in stature.

Alan Melville's name produces a nostalgic echo with both spectators and surviving players of the 1930s, because he was accepted as a graceful right-handed batsman and a commanding player in all respects. His main strength was perhaps against fast bowling. He appeared to thrive against pace with his classical drives and cool, well-timed hooks. He was of the old school in technique: upright and possessing a style and grace that had a special grandeur.

It is said that when he arrived at Oxford after leaving Michaelhouse he had not played on a turf pitch – not officially, anyway. Melville proceeded to score 132 in the Freshman's match, 78 run out against Kent and 118 against Yorkshire in his first three innings. What an unforgettable start to a first-class career in England, particularly on a ground (The Parks, Oxford) that is one of the prettiest and most charming in the country. It always remained one of Melville's favourite grounds.

Melville's development as a batsman at Oxford was as rapid as one would expect of such a talented cricketer. So it came as no great surprise when he later notched up a classic 114 for Sussex against the West Indian fast bowlers of 1933, with his driving and hooking being particularly devastating. The innings took only two and a half hours and is said to have been spectacular and solid. It must have provided enjoyment for the connoisseurs, as he received a standing ovation when it was over.

In his pre-World War II days, Melville is known to have batted with carefree flair, a light-hearted attitude that prevailed at the time throughout a peaceful world. Melville could almost have been termed swashbuckling, producing some handsome strokes that were full of joy as well as being profitable: 10 598 first-class runs at 37.80.

When he went up to Oxford, Melville played in four university matches (against Cambridge in the annual match at Lord's), captaining the side in 1931 and 1932. After leaving university he played with gay abandon, yet it was responsible and effective cricket. This culminated in his appointment as the Sussex captain for the summers of 1934 and 1935.

At this stage of his career he was a magnificently casual cricketer: popular and a crowd pleaser, the sort of glamorous amateur who delighted fans in those halcyon days. He won many fans across the length and breadth of England with his charm and debonair approach. He was also remarkably supple in movement.

After this very stylish start to his cricketing career, Alan Melville appeared to adopt a far more serious approach to the game once he returned to South Africa.

In fact, the season after assuming the Transvaal captaincy in the summer of 1937/38, he was appointed to lead South Africa in the five-match Test series against Wally Hammond's MCC tourists. The MCC team was particularly strong in batting terms, but their bowlers, apart from Ken Farnes, were not all that penetrative. This meant that the competent Springbok batsmen were able to put together some imposing totals. In addition, the pitches were apparently pretty flat and far from bowler-friendly.

Farnes, nevertheless, was capable of bowling at ferocious speeds. He was 1.92 m tall and delivered the ball from his full height. He was also able to make the ball rise very sharply because of his height, and had an accentuated flick of the wrist. In all, Farnes had the ideal build for a fast bowler.

An Essex and Cambridge University man, Farnes was almost the same age as Melville, which meant they had crossed swords on the field on numerous occasions. Sadly Farnes, a pilot officer in the Royal Air Force, lost his life in the early years of World War II. (Another member of this MCC team to die of wounds in the war was the great Yorkshire left-arm spinner, Hedley Verity.)

Farnes and Verity played against Melville in the notorious Durban timeless Test. When it is considered that the South Africans returned totals of 530 and 481, it can be seen that the English bowlers came in for something of a lambasting. However, Farnes returned figures of one for 108 off 46 overs in the first innings and four for 74 off 22.1 overs in the second innings. This was a splendid showing under the circumstances. It was in this amazing Test, played over 12 days (including three non-playing or rest days), that Melville scored 103 in the second innings, finally being bowled by Farnes.

The game was eventually abandoned to allow the England tourists to travel to Cape Town and catch the mailship home.

It is interesting to note that of the 16 players used by South Africa in the series, 10 came from the Transvaal. 'Mobil' Gordon and Chud Langton dominated the bowling, capturing 33 wickets between them. In the batting, Bruce Mitchell, Melville, Eric Rowan and Ken Viljoen all played important parts at various stages. In addition, Transvaal's Norman Gordon and Ronnie Grieveson, without serving a probationary period, proved to be outstanding players at Test level.

The timeless Test began on 3 March 1939, when Melville won the toss for the first time and South Africa scored 530, at that stage their highest ever score. Determined Pieter van der Bijl scored a solid 125, Dudley Nourse made 103 and excellent contributions were delivered by Melville (78), Grieveson (75) and Eric Dalton (57). It has been rumoured that Van der Bijl, a courageous batsman, actually wore a makeshift arrangement of towels around his thigh, hips and chest to shield his body from the fiery bowling of Farnes. Of course the protective padding devices now so common did not exist in those days. It is said that

Van der Bijl had been hit black and blue from the fast-rising deliveries the powerful Farnes was constantly hurling at him.

Van der Bijl was the father of the equally famous and competent fast bowler Vintcent van der Bijl, but sadly he died too soon to follow his son's remarkably successful career as a fast bowler for Natal and later Transvaal, and in his outstanding season with Middlesex under Mike Brearley's leadership in 1980. The elder Van der Bijl had links with Melville dating back to their 1932 Oxford days, when the future Springbok opening batsman was on a Rhodes Scholarship and awarded his blue that year.

The timeless Test was a memorable occasion because Melville scored 103 in the second innings. It is incredible that England came within 42 runs of their victory target when rain and bad light stopped play and officials were forced to abandon the game due to lack of time. England had scored an amazing 654 runs for five wickets. Bill Edrich was the top scorer with a massive innings of 219, being promoted from six to three in the order by Wally Hammond, who had great faith in the batting abilities of the Middlesex batsman.

During the MCC visit the threat of war hung heavily in the air. Steve Pitts, chairman of the Transvaal Cricket Union, voiced the thoughts of all when he expressed the hope, on behalf of all sportsmen, that war would somehow be averted.

The following comments are from a book by Hayward Kidson, and are used with his kind permission:

> The war, as we know, arrived on September 1, 1939, when Germany invaded Poland and what were to be the final round of county cricket matches were still in progress as Nazi bombs fell on Warsaw.
>
> Melville returned to Transvaal cricket in March 1946 when Transvaal matched their strength against a combined side made up of Eastern Province and Griqualand West. Alan led Transvaal to a convincing victory in the three-day match. Their opposition was outclassed when Owen Wynne and George Fullerton hit centuries, and Tony Harris, of rugby fame, notched a fine 94. Xenophon Balaskas, a former Test player who was by now a veteran leg-spinner, took eight for 65 and, just to rub it in, four for 43 in the Combined Eleven's second innings. He must have been a wizard of flight and spin. It was a nostalgic game of historic moment as it was the last first-class game to be played on the Old Wanderers ground. This was the venue which had served Transvaal cricket since 1888; no longer would summer sun fall warmly on cricket's flannelled fools at this famous old ground – a deeply sad thought.

Countless lengthy meetings took place in an attempt to save the Old Wanderers. The cricket committees formed to preserve this sacred old ground were both enthusiastic and deeply dedicated. But it was all to no avail, and as the old Arabic proverb states: 'The dogs bark but the caravan moves on.'

In the early post-war years Alan Melville was soon appointed the Transvaal captain, an indication that he would be the selectors' choice as skipper of the team to tour England in 1947, with Dudley Nourse as his deputy. As it turned out this did happen, but before the 1947 tour is discussed in full, let us broadly examine part of the pattern of Alan's cricket career.

After World War II ended, sport slowly returned to its rightful place in society, while many values and traditions were undergoing rapid change. In 1946 the South African Cricket Association was ready to reintroduce the Currie Cup competition, a necessity in the light of an invitation by the MCC for a full tour of England in 1947, and the 1946/47 season would be a period of preparation. At the time Natal were the holders of the Currie Cup, which they had won as far back as the 1937/38 season, with Transvaal finishing second. It must be remembered that in those days the Currie Cup series was placed in mothballs when official overseas teams toured the country. This archaic practice ended in the 1966/67 season when the Australians, under Bobby Simpson, were the tourists.

Nine cricket unions resumed their rivalry for the trophy, while the players eyed a coveted place in the first South African team to be selected since the end of the war. Several stars and other players from the pre-war years were still around and would be aiming for inclusion in the team, along with the many new faces. It was a fascinating situation, even more so as Transvaal cricket was as rich in talent as a Texas oil well.

Some of the really outstanding players available from the Transvaal side, probably unknown to the present generation, were Eric Rowan, Owen Wynne, George Fullerton, Alan Melville, Bruce Mitchell, Tony Harris (double Springbok in cricket and rugby), Denis Begbie, Ken Viljoen, Athol Rowan, Russell Endean (double Springbok in cricket and hockey), Norman Gordon, Xenophon Balaskas, Andrew 'Nobbie' Ralph, Ola Grinaker and Charlie Jones.

Other provinces had equally serious contenders – 'Ricey' Phillips of Border; Lindsay Tuckett of Orange Free State; Johnnie Lindsay of North-Eastern Transvaal; and others. Some of the Natal hopefuls were Dudley Nourse, Les Payne, Bob Williams, Ian Smith, Ossie Dawson, Dennis Dyer and Tufty Mann, who at the time was playing for Eastern Province. So there was an abundance of talented players jockeying for a place in the 1947 side to tour England.

Melville was the popular captain of the side; far more earnest and thoughtful than in those carefree days of Oxford and Sussex in the 1930s. War does that to people – some become more irresponsible, others the reverse. However, he was entrusted with building a young side on something of a short-term policy. What the selectors were, in effect, aiming at was an interim development of a rather long-term plan. So the elder statesman, Melville, was entrusted with some good yet raw players in international cricket. This was demanding to say the least, and there were problems to overcome. He handled these with rare dignity and aplomb. He was statesmanlike, and as the Springbok skipper showed a cool, calculated approach. He proved himself to be a shrewd and discerning student of the game and a true general on the field.

After the interruption of the devastating war years, it could be said that the tour was Melville's coming of age, because it was his first and, as it turned out, only tour as captain of South Africa.

During the timeless Test, Melville had scored 78 and 103: both superb innings, although it is the score of 103 that is all-important, because it was made in the last South African season before World War II. In 1947, during an amazing run of form, he followed the century at Kingsmead with three more Test hundreds to conclude an entertaining quartet of centuries at Test level.

At Trent Bridge, Nottingham, on 7 to 11 June, the Springbok team, with seven new caps, drew the opening match of the series. Alan Melville scored 189 as an opener in a first-innings total of 533, and Dudley Nourse scored 149; the pair took the Springbok total from 44 for two to 363 before they were parted, and shared in a record third-wicket partnership of 319. England, dismissed for 208, were forced to follow on but ended up with 551, thus leaving the tourists 227 to win in 138 minutes. This made Melville's unbeaten second-innings score of 104, also as an opener, an even more remarkable achievement. It also gave him the distinction of becoming the first South African to score two centuries in the same Test; a sumptuous contribution to his side's efforts.

The second Test was at Lord's in high summer. No other ground has more atmosphere and nostalgia than this Mecca of the game. You can feel, smell and taste the spirit of cricket in this rather special area of St John's Wood in Marylebone. It is a hallowed and sanctified territory; mystic and certainly aristocratic in atmosphere and association.

Lord's was packed with spectators for the match, which was played from 21 to 25 June. Melville rose gloriously to the occasion by scoring his fourth successive Test century. Opening the innings, he put together a stylish, calmingly influential 117 before being caught by Alec Bedser when sweeping, almost carelessly, at leg-spinner Eric Hollies – the man who a year later bowled the fateful delivery that ended Sir Donald Bradman's dreams of a Test batting average of 100.

Melville's performance at Lord's had placed him alongside Jack Fingleton, the Australian opener, as the only batsman to have scored Test centuries in four successive innings. Ironically, Fingleton's first three were against South Africa during the happy summer of 1935/36, and the fourth against England in Brisbane the following season. But along came West Indian Everton Weekes to go one better: five out of five, starting with England in Kingston, Jamaica, in 1947/48, followed by four against India, including two at Eden Gardens in Calcutta, in the 1948/49 season. And to show it wasn't a fluke, the Barbadian was run out for 90 in his next Test innings, also against India, this time in Madras. (In 2002 India's Rahul Dravid became the next batsman to score four successive Test centuries, against England and the West Indies, in what were remarkable performances of elegance and style.)

The South African captain reached the coveted fourth century early on the third morning, and was still playing skilfully when he committed his single error for Bedser to take a looping ball at short leg. His performance was lauded by all, including the critical pavilion oracles who very much admired his artistry. His skill lay in depriving the bowlers of the luxury of a maiden, which even the most patient of toilers will tell you is enough to make you think about early retirement. Melville's strokes were predominantly gentle glides rather than bludgeoning blows. He had displayed a monumental calm throughout his performance, and his timing carried the stamp of a perfectionist.

The 1947 tour could easily have turned Melville into a scapegoat, because defeat tends to do this to a captain's reputation. When a series, or Test, is lost, the name of the captain is linked to the defeats rather than the victories, or personal batting or bowling achievements. South Africa lost the series 3–0, but Melville retained the confidence and respect of his men throughout a difficult rubber. England won the second, third and fourth Tests, but South Africa could easily have won the last match at The Oval, finishing 20 runs short after scoring 423 for seven on the last day. This included a magnificently played 189 not out from Bruce Mitchell, which equalled Melville's performance of scoring two centuries in the same Test, as the Transvaal opener had scored 120 in the first innings.

In hindsight, the Springbok captain's undertaking in leading a fairly new side was a gigantic gamble, and it is apparent that the major contributions against the South Africans were from Denis Compton and Bill Edrich in what was their golden summer. Their Test records alone indicate just how they dominated the series.

	INN	NO	HS	RUNS	AVE	50	100
WJ Edrich	6	1	191	552	110.40	2	2
DCS Compton	8	0	208	753	94.12	2	4
Total	14	1	208	1 305	100.38	4	6

Awesome to say the least, particularly when it is considered that the legendary Sir Leonard Hutton averaged a modest 43.00 in 10 innings, and his famous Lancastrian opening partner Cyril Washbrook posted an average of 49.50 an innings. We also need to be reminded that in the glorious summer of 1947,

Compton, in 50 innings, scored 3 816 runs at 90.85, while Edrich, in 52 innings, scored 3 539 runs at 80.43. The Middlesex Twins cut dashing figures that summer as records tumbled. Never since has such a glut of runs been scored by two men from the same county in the same season. They remain the highest aggregates in an England first-class season.

Melville certainly had his hands full with the two great batsmen in such formidable form. It was a somewhat nightmarish experience, but he handled the problems philosophically and discreetly; he tended to emphasise the positive rather than dwell on the negative. Even the batting spectre of Compton and Edrich failed to cower him. It was not an easy tour to undertake, because in 1947 rationing was still in effect in England. Melville lost a lot of weight, something a man of his tall, almost fragile build could ill afford.

Melville was an exceptionally fine player as well as being an exceptionally pleasant person: one of the truly great cricketers of our country. In batting he never lost his elegance as a strokeplayer, his drives possessing incredible speed across the sward, and his late cut was so wristy that it had an air of virtuosity about it. His batsmanship combined power and lissome movement. In fact, he attained classic poise and the habit of long domination.

There was no mistaking that Melville was a thoroughbred. His qualities were there for all to see, and further proof could be found on the scoreboards and in the statistics. He was born to gain distinction on the cricket field; yet while he mostly gathered his runs with silky, fluent stylishness, he also scored large totals through the process of attrition.

As a fielder, too, he was brilliant. His normal position was either mid-off or silly mid-on, and Melville caught with ease: to the right, to the left, low or high. In these two strategic positions he was a source of anxiety to the batsman; ever alert and pouching many a magnificent catch.

I will always remember my first game against Transvaal during the 1948/49 season, when I was barely out of school. The venue for the match was Ellis Park, the rugby stadium, where first-class cricket found a temporary home. It was a large and foreboding edifice, dominated by the imposing old 'glass house' for administrators, VIPs and often players. Ellis Park, the headquarters of Transvaal rugby, replaced the pristine Old Wanderers, now the site of the main Johannesburg railway station. At the time the Transvaal team was one of the strongest in their proud history: Bruce Mitchell, Eric Rowan, Alan Melville (captain), Denis Begbie, Ken Viljoen, Tony Harris, Jackie Ward, Paul Loeser (wicketkeeper), Don Stewart, Geoff Chubb, Tim Heaney. It was an intimidating line-up that included Springboks of repute, as well as Chubb, who was still to be capped for South Africa. Into the bargain we were required to bat first on a wet, sticky pitch. This was a daunting prospect in those days when the ball kicked head high off a perfect length. Fortunately Dennis Dyer and I managed to see out about the first half-hour to allow the strip to start drying.

The Natal team in batting order was: Dennis Dyer, Jackie McGlew, Mervyn Lang, Dudley Nourse (captain), Billy Wade, Ossie Dawson, Deryck Dowling, Ken Orchard, Les Payne, Arthur Tayfield, Jack Plimsoll. Natal scored 427 all out with Wade contributing a classic 117, Nourse a fighting 76 and two valuable 50s apiece from Orchard and Tayfield. The best of the Transvaal bowlers were Chubb (four for 96 off 40 overs) and Mitchell with his leg-spinners, who took four for 64 off only 25 overs. Not many cricket followers know that Bruce was a wily leg-spinner and first played for Transvaal in that capacity. In fact, in March 1926, when first selected for Transvaal, Mitchell was a 17-year-old schoolboy at St John's, Johannesburg. It was in a Currie Cup match against Border in East London, and he made a remarkable debut by capturing five wickets for only 23 runs, and then six for 72. This was an auspicious beginning for a cricketer who became better known as a quality Test batsman.

In the game against Natal, Transvaal put together a colossal 560 for seven wickets, with Denis Begbie scoring a mammoth 192, Viljoen a sedate 102 and the unlucky Eric Rowan a colourful 97. The Natal bowling attack went to the shredding machine on that occasion. The teams and scores were made available by Hayward Kidson, whom cricket lovers know as one of South Africa's top umpires in his day. Before his death in 1995, he was also an author, cricket historian and statistician.

It was in that particular match that I first encountered Melville's charm and kindness to blossoming cricketers. What he did that day was really unobtrusive and not the least conceited. As I emerged from the Ellis Park tunnel and walked up the stairs that led to the field in those days, Alan (or Mr Melville as I called him at the time) was standing, surrounded by his Transvaal team, waiting to take the field. They looked most formidable. He must have noticed how pale and nervous I looked, for he quietly disengaged himself from the knot of players and strolled leisurely up to me. Putting his arm round my shoulders he gently said: 'Young man, just bat as you would in an ordinary Saturday afternoon club match.' Then, turning to Dennis Dyer, my senior opening partner, who had been on the 1947 tour of England, he smiled warmly and left with a sincere and obviously affectionate, 'Good luck, Dennis, may you play one of your classic innings that we have come to expect from you.'

That was Alan Melville, the man: his charm and dignity were present under all circumstances. Dennis Dyer was the father of David Dyer, who became the popular and highly successful captain of Transvaal in the late 1970s and early 1980s. It was during David Dyer's tenure as captain that the 'mean machine' image was born as the side recorded triumph after triumph, prospering under his level-headed and balanced leadership.

A most amusing incident occurred during the Transvaal–Natal match at Ellis Park, involving that stormy petrel of South African cricket, Eric Rowan. Poor old Eric was always crossing swords with cricket's hierarchy, thus incurring their wrath to the extent that he was frequently and unjustifiably omitted from Test teams. The selectors seemed to consider him a disruptive influence, but he also appeared to go out of his way to antagonise them.

On this occasion his wound was self-inflicted. He had opened the innings with that other famous Transvaal opener, Bruce Mitchell, against a Natal attack that included Ossie Dawson and Jack Plimsoll, two Springboks who knew how to use the new ball. The incident happened about 30 minutes before the afternoon tea break. At this stage Rowan was on about 80 and, for reasons best known to him, he allowed a cricket gremlin to take control of his batting. Unaccountably, Eric contrived to put the brakes on the fluent, free scoring he had gradually worked up to – it was almost like an artisan downing tools without explanation. Eric began to play pat ball, the crowd became incensed by his inactivity and started booing loudly and consistently slow-handclapped him. This had the effect of bringing out more devilishness in the unpredictable Rowan, who seemed to enjoy the hostility of the crowd.

He would come down the pitch to the spinners with nimble-footed flair, meeting the ball on the full toss, only instead of whipping it through the field for four, he would drop it at his feet and then grin cheekily at the baying hounds. The result of this fooling around was that his score stood on 97 when the tea break was taken. Immediately on resumption Dudley Nourse, the Natal captain, took the second new ball, and then Rowan was trapped lbw without adding to his total, depriving him of a first-class century.

The look of horror on the batsman's face was indescribably comic. Apart from Freddie Trueman, Eric had the best command of the 'second language' of anyone I know. On his way back to the dressing room he exhausted every expletive he knew. Or, more politely, and as commentators are so apt to say, 'He must kicking himself now.' Knowing that he could so easily have scored his century before tea, adding it to an already illustrious first-class list of three-figure scores, must have infuriated him beyond even the vocabulary he employed. Yet, in the final analysis, he would agree that he alone was to blame.

People have often wondered what his skipper Alan Melville thought of the episode. I am sure that, considering Alan's sense of humour, he would have chastised Eric but chuckled inwardly at the amusing events.

Melville was a man who competently coped with each occasion as it arose. One instance was when he punished the 1933 West Indian pace battery when playing for Sussex. In that innings, bumpers were being delivered after several of Melville's cover and straight drives had the bowlers resorting to more menacing tactics. But he punished them with disrespect as they whizzed around his head. He hooked elegantly yet ferociously every time they were discharged at him. As a batsman he will be remembered for his dauntless, controlled power and almost romantic, aesthetic strokes.

His captaincy was also characterised by kindness, shrewdness and bold attack, and above all artistic flair. The seasons in which he played fell in a magic era: rich and glamorous and, in their own way, a golden portion of South African cricket history. Of course World War II threw a dark, sad shadow over everything, bringing a halt to normal life. But Melville's playing ability on both sides of the war was a joy and a delight for the spectators, his teammates, the administrators and even the opposition.

He was without doubt 'Melville the Magnificent'; his name will always have a place in South African cricket's 'Hall of Fame'.

The twilight of his illustrious career came suddenly, but with an element of dignity. George Mann's MCC side visited South Africa in 1948/49; it was the first tour to this country since World War II. Melville, now an elder statesman of cricket, was preparing to wean himself gradually from active participation. At 38 he was ready to step down. The elegant warrior once again revealed flashes of his skills in the Transvaal encounter with the tourists, proving that age does not always dim the gifts of nature. He was available to lead his province in this match, held at Ellis Park in December 1948 and, in a drawn game, *Wisden* records that:

> Next to Hutton (174) the best batting of the game was that of Alan Melville who made 92 in Transvaal's huge 560 in reply to the MCC total of 513 for seven, declared. His decision during the match that he did not think his wrist sufficiently recovered from a recent fracture to enable him to be considered for the Tests was a big blow to South Africa.

This aristocrat of the flowing willow did indeed make two further appearances on the first-class field that summer: first in the third Test against England at Newlands in January 1949, when he was recalled to open the innings with Owen Wynne, and in the MCC's return match against Transvaal.

Melville was an unwitting participant in a mini-drama that was talked about for years afterwards. The ebullient Eric Rowan had failed in the first innings of the second Test of the 1948/49 series, played at Ellis Park between South Africa and England. The selectors hastily and unwisely picked the side for the third Test before the second innings of the second Test had taken place. Rowan was dropped and Melville brought in.

This obviously presented a great challenge to the fuming Rowan, who proceeded to post a defiant 156 not out (sans box and batting gloves). The occasion was made even more memorable when Rowan, during his great knock, gave the legendary Churchillian V-sign towards the pavilion where the selectors were seated. But that is another story.

Melville's unexpected return to the fold in his only Test match in which he was not captain was disappointing by his own high standards. *Wisden* says that Melville and Owen Wynne provided some excitement by attacking Alec Bedser and Cliff Gladwin in the second innings, but shortly afterwards he was stumped by Godfrey Evans off Roley Jenkins for 24. It was the end of an era for a thoroughbred who falls into an exclusive club of batting artists that includes Victor Trumper, Prince Ranjitsinhji, Alan Kippax, Denis Compton, Frank Woolley and a host of others.

DUDLEY NOURSE 3
King of Kingsmead

By Jackie McGlew

There is little doubt that Dudley Nourse is the original King of Kingsmead, the famous cricket oval in Durban that has seen many an epic Test battle. Few players before or since Nourse have fired the imagination as much as this golden batsman. Three who have come closest are Barry Richards, Roy McLean and Mike Procter, all part of a younger generation.

Roy McLean greatly admired Nourse, and he frequently paid tribute to the man he regarded as his mentor, even after he had achieved his own deserving recognition as a world-class batsman. Richards and Procter know of the name and the legend, but did not see him bat.

My first Test for South Africa was at Trent Bridge, Nottingham, during the 1951 tour. Played from 7 to 12 June, it was my privilege to witness an innings of unprecedented courage. With a pin holding the base joint of his left thumb together, Nourse produced a match-winning 208 for South Africa. It was a truly incredible performance. This is what the 1952 *Wisden* had to say about this game:

> A most remarkable match ended with South Africa gaining their first Test victory for 16 years and their second in England. Between those two successes they had failed to lower the colours of England and Australia in a total of 28 Tests.
>
> Undoubtedly the hero was Nourse, the South African captain. He carried his side with a lion-hearted not out 208. Mere figures cannot convey the magnitude of Nourse's performance. His innings occupied nine and a quarter hours, and during the whole of that time he batted under a great handicap. The left thumb, which he had broken at Bristol three weeks previously, gave him severe pain, particularly when he tried to impart any power into his strokes, and the longer he stayed the more it swelled. Nourse declined to have an injection to relieve the pain because he feared it might numb his hand and affect his grip.

How this injury to Nourse's thumb affected the tour nobody will ever know. My guess, which I admit is partial and optimistic, is that South Africa could and would have won the 1951 Test series against England if the thumb injury hadn't happened. It must be remembered that Eric Rowan was in superlative form, and with a thoroughly fit, flourishing Dudley Nourse to substantially increase the final totals, who knows what the eventual outcome might have been.

Nourse's vast experience and enormous confidence would have boosted the morale and performance of his side, especially the youngsters. The keenness of the young players in that side was admirable; they were a highly motivated group, but the captain's serious injury was a real blight on the side.

Nourse had an operation in the latter part of May to pin the bone, broken when fielding a ferocious drive from Tom Graveney in the second innings against Gloucestershire at Bristol. After his heroic innings of 208 in the Nottingham Test, a second operation was needed. From that point of the tour his form fell away alarmingly.

In the first Test at Trent Bridge, South Africa occupied the crease for almost all of the first two days of play, during much of which Nourse batted, going in at the fall of the second wicket with the score on 107 (when I was bowled by Freddie Brown, the England captain, for 40). Nourse was the ninth batsman out when Brown threw down the wicket at the bowler's end, with our captain out of his ground. It was a suicidal and sad ending to his courageous and epic innings, which had taken him 550 minutes. It was his second Test double century, and it eclipsed the record of 189 against England by a South African in England. Both Alan Melville and Bruce Mitchell had scored 189 in England during the 1947 tour: Melville's at the same Trent Bridge venue, and Mitchell at The Oval in the fifth Test; Nourse had also been a member of the 1947 Springbok team.

England seemed to have the first Test operation sewn up, as they required only 186 to win in the pleasantly comfortable time of five hours and 10 minutes; in terms of time available, it was a doddle. But the South Africans had not given up hope of victory, either. Tribute must be paid to the dynamic Eric Rowan, now acting captain for the injured Nourse, who immediately set an aggressive, attacking field when England began their quest. Eric was highly motivated, as was Cuan McCarthy, who unleashed a salvo of bumpers that must have unnerved the batsman, because Eric's brother, Athol, with well-flighted off-spin, struck a vital blow by pouching a stinging return catch from Len Hutton with the score at 23. Ten minutes after the luncheon interval Athol again held on to a return catch, this one from Reg Simpson, which made the score 41 for two.

It was at this stage, after lunch, that Athol Rowan and Tufty Mann exploited the pitch, and they were turning the ball appreciably; Mann at times was unplayable. Rowan spun the ball into the bat; Mann turned it away from the bat. It was Mann who dismissed the stubborn and technically sound Lancastrian, Jack Ikin, who had defied the South African attack for 130 minutes. Mann pierced Ikin's defence with a perfectly pitched delivery and bowled him.

Eric Rowan's dynamic leadership raised the South African fielding to great heights. Brown, the England skipper, was out to an amazing catch by McCarthy, and Godfrey Evans received his walking ticket when Clive van Ryneveld held an acrobatic catch off one of Mann's uncanny deliveries. These two catches turned the game dramatically in South Africa's favour.

McCarthy, recalled to the attack by Rowan, uprooted Alec Bedser's middle stump with a lightning delivery. Roy Tattersall then came in to join Johnny Wardle, who had been indulging in some fierce and sometimes wild big hitting. In this mood Wardle was a menace, but with his score on 30 he went for the big hit once too often, because he lofted an enormous drive to Roy McLean, South Africa's 12th man, substituting for the injured Nourse. McLean positioned himself perfectly and took the catch, which recorded an unexpected victory for South Africa with about two hours of play to spare.

When Wardle lofted that mighty skier, I was on the deep long-off boundary and McLean on the fence at deep long-on. With Athol Rowan spinning the ball away from the left-handed Wardle, I had worked out that if he went for the lofted drive the catch would surely be mine. But perversely he hit across the line of the off-spinner, directing the shot to long-on instead of long-off. I was partly disappointed and partly relieved. When you are young you long for those catches in the deep, although at times with a certain amount of trepidation. On this occasion Wardle found McLean, who always had remarkably safe hands and dropped few catches in his career.

John Waite, the South African wicketkeeper, came of age in this match when he was finally run out in the first innings after putting together a polished 76. He had shared in an opening partnership of 31 with Eric Rowan, and then he and I added 76 for the second wicket. Before his dismissal he was involved in a third-wicket partnership with our batting hero and captain, Dudley Nourse. Their association added a further valuable 82 runs to the total; for Waite it was an impressive Test debut.

When Nourse addressed the crowd from the Trent Bridge pavilion balcony he paid special tribute to the part Eric Rowan had played in the victory of 71 runs after England were bowled out for 114. The praise was fully justified, as Eric had pulled off a Houdini act, with his brother Athol taking five for 68 off 27.2 overs, and Mann with an analysis of 24-16-24-4.

It is openly accepted that Dudley Nourse was a colossus in Springbok cricket, not only in his own era, but for all time. Nourse was invariably the true drawcard of the side or, as Hollywood would have it, box-office material. Sir Donald Bradman had a similar status in Australia, although in later years this grew into reverence of the man and the legend he created. It is a great pity that Nourse and Bradman never met on the playing field, although they played their cricket in virtually the same era. Admittedly Nourse was not the utterly ruthless run machine that Sir Donald was, but they would have made admirable and exciting adversaries. I believe there would have been great mutual respect between the two batsmen.

When Nourse scored his epic 231 against Victor Richardson's 1935/36 Australians at the Old Wanderers, the touring team's attack included those twin wizards of spin, flight and mystery, Clarrie Grimmett and Bill 'Tiger' O'Reilly. Of the South African batsmen in that second Test at the Wanderers played over Christmas 1935, only Nourse seemed to realise that the only way to combat the world-class spin bowling was with the use of nimble footwork. And this is exactly how he played Grimmett and O'Reilly in that memorable match. It was memorable for being the one and only occasion on record when a fielding captain appealed against the light. Herby Wade asked the umpires, JC Collings and RGA Ashman, to rule that the light was too bad to field. This was reputedly done to protect the South African fieldsmen against the ferocious onslaught by the inimitable Australian batting genius, Stan McCabe, who hit an unforgettable 189 not out in that drawn match.

Nourse was powerful and forthright. He possessed amazingly fast footwork for a thickset, stocky man with an almost square build. Despite this, his muscles were always fine-tuned; his muscle tone and ballet-like footwork would carry him down the track to the spinners, against whom he was particularly strong. Against fast bowling, especially at the start of an innings, he could be somewhat tentative, which in no way insinuates he was weak against fast bowlers. Truth to tell, many of them suffered an awful lambasting from his merciless blade. I often saw him flay the new ball like a threshing machine in high gear.

He was one of the greatest punishing batsmen produced in South Africa because, as an attacking batsman like Graeme Pollock, he was the perfect model of the difference between a scientific striker of the ball and the risky unreliable slogger. He was always alert to the variations of pace and flight, and had a computer-like ability to place the ball into the gaps, giving vent to his insatiable appetite for runs. His hooking and driving took your breath away because of the immense power given to each shot. Despite this, it was not out-and-out bludgeoning of the bowling because there was an inbred artistry to all his strokes, as much on attack as in defence. Nourse was a spectator's delight. When he was at the wicket something enjoyable was always happening for the crowd to savour.

It is said that when Dudley asked his famous and highly successful cricketer father (Arthur William Nourse, 45 Tests for South Africa between 1902 and 1924) for a coaching lesson, 'Dave' Nourse merely said: 'Grab a fence paling and a ball and hit against the wall.' Harsh, maybe, but it did not deter the young Dudley from blossoming into maturity. There is little doubt that he possessed many of his illustrious father's characteristics, even though he received little or no coaching from Nourse senior. He made it through personal skill, sheer tenacity and an iron will: all of this helped him to force himself into the top flight of the world's great right-hand batsmen.

Today's provincial player is given more opportunities to increase his tally of runs because the seasons are crammed with extra matches. But in that era, a player could only get such opportunities when on tour.

Perhaps one of the most spectacular harvests in terms of run scoring was Natal's 664 for six when playing Western Province at Kingsmead in 1936/37, when Dudley Nourse contributed a formidable 240. In the same summer he also managed 260 not out, showing that his appetite for runs was enormous. To Nourse, batting was a delightfully perpetual battle: his follow-through was negligible and his backswing very short, so the spectators were often amazed at the speed with which the ball would rocket to the boundary. His enormous power frequently deceived the fielders in the total arc; one Durban businessman, who was also a cricket administrator, was often heard to murmur in awed tones, 'Strikes like lightning,' when watching Nourse's performances. He had an uncanny knack, too, of finding the gaps in the field.

Nourse captained Natal on no fewer than 45 occasions and conjured up some glorious gems in many fine innings. I think the highlights of his distinguished career were probably his 208 at Nottingham against England and his magnificent 231 at the Old Wanderers against Victor Richardson's touring Australians. Who knows what his statistics would have been if World War II had not broken out. Dudley was such a prolific run-getter that it is fair to assume he would have made thousands more first-class runs, and established many more records.

Nourse's technique was sound and, like Sir Donald Bradman, he always believed that psychologically he had the upper hand over the bowlers. There was an aura about him that almost defied the bowlers to take his wicket. He denied them this so often that many a toiling bowler was reduced to frustration. When taking into account that Nourse played at a time when the season included only eight or 10 first-class matches a season, it can justifiably be said that he was basically a weekend cricketer. This was a frugal diet on which to establish a remarkable career record.

It was common knowledge that much bad blood existed between Dudley and his equally famous father, and in fact they got to the stage where they no longer talked to one another. Few people knew the reason, or reasons, for this sad situation. There is a story that on one summer's day many years ago at Kingsmead, the two became reconciled. It appears to have been quite an emotional event. On 18 and 19 December 1931, Natal played Western Province at Kingsmead. Although a two-day game, it was granted first-class status (in those days any number of two-day games carried the first-class tag).

In this particular game Nourse senior was playing for Western Province, while Dudley was playing for the particularly powerful Natal side of the day. Dave Nourse scored only two and six, while his son, then only 21, scored an outstanding century. It is easy to picture the powerfully built young cricketer driving, hooking and cutting with tremendous force and, when necessary, employing his strong defence. He must have been a delight to watch, and when he got on top of an attack Dudley Nourse's dazzling supremacy could only be rivalled by South African players such as Graeme Pollock, Barry Richards, Herbie Taylor and, at his best, Johnnie Waite. Dudley was so quick on his feet, and possessed such an armoury of attacking strokes on both sides of the wicket, that when he scored a century it was always good spectator value.

Dudley described the happy ending to what had been a somewhat sad father–son relationship in his autobiography, *Cricket in the Blood*: 'It was the first time my father had ever seen me at the wicket and I wanted to show him that I had come a long way and it was not merely the name of Nourse that had secured for me a place in the team he had graced for many years.'

Dudley then records that his father walked across from slip to shake his son's hand and said: 'Congratulations, son, I hope there will be many more to follow this one.'

Dudley recalls: 'It was a proud moment but a bit too much for me, since I was out soon afterwards.'

Dudley later admitted that his captain, Herby Wade, nursed him along. On one occasion Wade shielded the young batsman from the Western Province bowlers after losing the wickets of Jack Siedle (0) and Syd Martin (4) to a ferocious early onslaught by the feared Western Province opening bowler Bob Crisp. Wade ran up a tidy 130.

It is a rarity for father and son to play in opposing teams in two first-class games. The last time this happened was in England, where New Zealanders Lance Cairns (father) and Chris (son) played in a match in the north of England in 1990.

The second encounter between the two Nourses was about a year later (almost to the day) when Natal played Western Province at Newlands on 27 and 28 December 1932. This time Dudley made scores of 27 and 54 not out, while his father Dave hit a long-remembered 219 not out. This was an incredible performance, especially when it is remembered that the age difference between the two was 32 years, which means Dave (or AW Nourse as he is now called) was 54 at the time of that innings. Dave and Dudley Nourse must have burst with pride that day. I'm sure they carried the memories of the two matches to the end of their lives. Dave (which was a nickname, as the name on his birth certificate was Arthur William Nourse) was 70 when he died in July 1948.

In January 1948 I captained Natal Schools in the Nuffield Week, held that year in Port Elizabeth. The convener of the South African Schools selection committee was none other than Dave Nourse. In the same week, Dudley Nourse captained the Natal senior side against Eastern Province at St George's Park. On the day before the provincial match, Dudley took the Natal side to watch Natal Schools play Eastern Province Schools.

It was a proud moment, I must admit, when I was selected to captain the South African Schools team, or Nuffield XI, as it was then known. Frankly, I believe that in 1948 the Natal Schools team was as strong as, if not stronger, than the South African Schools combination, because players of the calibre of Trevor Goddard, Roy McLean, Michael Melle (all later Springboks) and the brilliant Brian Pfaff, then the equal of any middle-order batsman in the Nuffield Week, were all omitted from the chosen 12.

On my return from Port Elizabeth, Dudley asked for me to be included in the Natal side to meet Orange Free State in a Currie Cup game at Kingsmead. The Free State squad included the feared Springbok opening bowler, Lindsay Tuckett. At the age of 18, I was a novice. I had replaced Des Fell, who had played in the 'Victory Tests' (England versus the Commonwealth XI) immediately after World War II. In a gesture typical of the level of sportsmanship in those days, Des sent me the first telegram of congratulations – a fine sporting gesture from a genuinely gallant sportsman. His telegram read: 'Congratulations. Wishing you a ton in your first appearance. Best wishes, Des Fell.'

Being young and inexperienced was one concern. In addition, I was the only representative from Pietermaritzburg in the team. The rest were all from Durban, and most played for fashionable Durban clubs. Although Pietermaritzburg is less than 100 kilometres from Durban, it seemed a great distance at the time.

I was extremely nervous as I boarded the Pullman at the Pietermaritzburg City Hall for the six-hour journey to Durban the day before the big event. When I finally arrived at the Pullman depot at the Durban railway station, I had to pile myself and my small canvas cricket bag into a rickshaw and set off for the old Marine Parade Hotel, which no longer exists.

There was no practice the day before the match (not for me, anyway), and no team talk. Furthermore, there was nobody there to welcome me. The only details I had were in a letter I had received a week earlier from Colonel Doug Geddie, secretary of the Natal Cricket Association, notifying me of my selection and giving me travelling, hotel and match details. That night the excitement and tension were just too much for me, and I hardly slept. I tossed and turned, wondering whether I could do justice to the occasion.

The sun had just risen when I got up, showered, had a meagre early morning breakfast and set out at 7.30 am by rickshaw for the ground. At this early hour Kingsmead was deserted, apart from the ground staff. It was quiet and eerie. Making my way to the Natal dressing room, of which I was the sole occupant until the big names started arriving, I inadvertently placed my bag on the locker in the very special corner traditionally reserved for the Natal captain. This custom was strictly adhered to and, quite naturally, respected. Imagine my stark fear and horror when the world-renowned cricketing giant Dudley Nourse arrived and demanded to know, 'Who in hell has got my corner?' Like greased lightning I shot off the bench on which I was sitting, scurried forward, mumbled incoherent apologies and swiftly removed the offending bag.

Little did I realise then that just three years later this distinguished captain's corner would be mine for almost 16 consecutive seasons. It was a privilege I look back on with humble pride and deep nostalgia.

I was not left to nurse the shame of my bag blunder for too long, as Dudley Nourse won the toss from the Orange Free State skipper, 'Kappie' Kaplan, and elected to bat on a hard, fast pitch. He told me to pad up as I was to open with that fine left-hander, Mervyn Lang. When we went out to bat I nervously asked Mervyn if I could take strike, which was my preference. He suggested that I go to the non-striker's end in order to get acclimatised to the light, the pace of the pitch and so on.

If I remember correctly, the famous Lindsay Tuckett took the first stride from the Umgeni end at exactly 10.30 that morning. Tuckett was definitely more than medium-fast. His first delivery was one of the most devastating I have witnessed. Superlatives are inadequate to describe this flawless gem. The ball pitched middle and leg, right on a perfect length, and cut off just about at right angles. Lang was a left-hander, so pitching middle and leg it opened him up square, then lifted straight across to beat the bat and clip the off-stump. Believe it or not, at that very moment Mervyn Lang's wife gave birth to a daughter! Or so it was reported.

The bail, after Lang had been bowled, carried over the heads of the slip fieldsmen. A forlorn Lang just stood and stared open-mouthed at the undemonstrative Tuckett. My heart missed a beat and I felt overawed by it all. The speed with which the ball hurried off the pitch was unnerving. The next ball, to our number three Derek King, was edged hip high and also at catchable height between first and second slips for four runs. My heart now started to develop what I think Victorians referred to as the flutters. When my turn eventually arrived to face the awesome Tuckett, my bat must have been shaking so much that I could hardly hold it still, as I asked the umpire for two leg.

I often wonder if my career would have ended on the scrap heap if I had been bowled without scoring. For that is almost what happened to me. In my nervousness I was still lifting my bat when the ball cut back at me like lightning and caught the inside edge of my bat. The ball then flew down to fine leg for four. Fortunately for me, after that Chinese glide to leg I settled in and batted with a lot more assurance, before being run out while putting together a moderate stand with my skipper, Dudley Nourse.

Critics have claimed that the influence of Dudley on Natal cricket in this period cannot be remotely overestimated. This I can believe, because watching the cavalier way he dealt with the Orange Free State bowlers that day was a revelation. This includes Tuckett, who came off a run of only about 11 metres. He covered the ground from bowling mark to delivery stride in loping, almost lazy strides, swinging the ball in sharply and late to the right-hander. His pace off the pitch was often devastating, and he was known for his long bowling stints, even on the hottest of days. He captured 65 wickets on the 1947 tour of England, playing in all five Tests, and making his debut in the first. On this particular day, Nourse played Tuckett like the batting maestro he was: swift footwork and always on to the line of delivery.

Nourse was a born ball player: outstanding at both baseball and soccer. He represented his province in both sports. Like so many top international cricketers in his day, he was a multi-talented sportsman. But cricket was his first love and it was the game that turned him into a celebrity; with his broad shoulders and blacksmith forearms he could strike the ball with explosive power. Against spin bowlers he would often move yards down the pitch to drive them. However, it was off the back foot that you could gauge the fierceness of his strokes, particularly when hooking and square cutting. He was a naturally bold and aggressive batsman.

Once his apprenticeship was over, he became a permanent fixture in the Natal side until he retired in 1951; yet a serious bout of pneumonia in World War II, while serving in the Western Desert, nearly caused his death. This would have cost both South Africa and Natal dearly, because he scored an enormous number of runs after the war.

For instance, he was Alan Melville's vice-captain on the 1947 tour of England, where his highest score was 205 not out against Warwickshire at Edgbaston. On that 1947 tour he scored 1 453 runs at 42.73. Only Denis Compton scored more runs in the Test series than Nourse, when the Natal master batsman scored 621 at 69 in the five matches. Later he succeeded Melville as captain of South Africa. At home against George Mann's 1948/49 England side, Nourse collected 536 runs in 10 innings at 76.57. The following summer, also at home, he was less successful against Lindsay Hassett's Australians in the 1949/50 series, scoring 405 runs at 45.00. However, it was the fifth successive series in which he headed the South African batting averages. His last Test century in South Africa was at Newlands, Cape Town, where he scored 114 in a game that the powerful Australian side eventually won by eight wickets. Despite this, the best of the famous Nourse technique and style was on display. His first innings of 65 was a study in stubborn artistry against a strong bowling attack: Ray Lindwall, Keith Miller, Bill Johnston and the leg-spinner Colin McCool formed the basis of the attack.

For Nourse to top the Springbok Test batting averages five series in a row, including the three after World War II, was a Herculean task. I have not seen, in all my research, any reference to such an unusual achievement, yet it is one worthy of the highest respect from cricketers in all quarters.

Dudley Nourse was only one of two batsmen who was able to successfully savage the bowling of Martin Hanley, that fine Western Province off-spinner, at Newlands. Hanley was known to wear the skin off his fingers when imparting his huge spin. He possessed the deadly combination of bite, flight and turn and, when bowling into a southeaster, was almost unplayable. Only the great Athol Rowan prevented Hanley from playing regularly for South Africa. Then, of course, came the incomparable Hugh Tayfield. In the 1952/53 season, Natal did not make an impressive start. The South African side were on tour in Australia, which meant John Watkins, Roy McLean, Hugh Tayfield, Headley Keith and I were away with Jack Cheetham's side.

Because of the team's poor start, it was decided to recall Nourse to arms. He emerged from retirement to rescue Natal from relegation. He finished third in the Natal batting average with an aggregate of 380 runs from only six matches, averaging 43.22, and scoring an invaluable 106 against Orange Free State in Pietermaritzburg during February 1953 before being caught off the bowling of left-arm spinner Jimmy Liddle.

It was Dudley's last season (half a season, more accurately) for Natal. Today he would easily have earned a benefit of more than R200 000, and I have no doubt that over his entire career he would have earned over five times this amount through sponsorship and other endorsements. Appearance money would have been 10 times as much. His contribution to Natal cricket was incalculable.

Note: The term 'first class', as applied to cricket, dates only from July 1947, when the Imperial Cricket Conference, at its annual meeting, sanctioned what were previously known as representative games, i.e. those played between teams recognised as representative by the governing body of ICC member countries. Matches of two-day duration, such as those in South Africa before July 1947, along with similar matches in other ICC countries, were, for the sake of continuity as well as statistical data, granted first-class status. The definition of what constitutes first-class status was redefined in 1965, when the ICC became the International Cricket Conference. Definitions and playing conditions were further widened in 1992 to cover all full members of the ICC, now reconstituted as the International Cricket Council, and can be found on pages 1283 and 1284 of the 1994 edition of *Wisden Cricketers' Almanack*. At no stage was the MCC, until 1947, involved in the granting of first-class status on games, and then only with teams within the United Kingdom.

JACK CHEETHAM 4
Captain Capable

By Jackie McGlew

Known to all as Jack, John Erskine Cheetham was dedicated to the point of fanaticism. It is easy to imagine him as a little boy saying, 'Mum, when I grow up I want to be the captain of South Africa at cricket.' He was so keen on the game that he would drive, ride or walk any distance just to play in a game, be it a Test or even at some village green, and as a youngster he was forever watching or playing in a match.

Jack's greatness as a captain was firmly established during the Springbok tour of 1952/53. This was when every pressman, without exception, gave South Africa no chance against the mighty Australians. The touring party was referred to as a bunch of total no-hopers, an opinion universally held in the cricket world.

Recommendations were made that the South African Cricket Association's board consider cancelling the tour, as it was strongly felt in most quarters that the Springbok team would be sorely embarrassed from every angle. It was believed that gate receipts would be so poor that they would not nearly cover the costs of the boat trip from Cape Town to Fremantle, the hotel bills, and other travelling and incidental costs. Every minute detail was discussed as the side was harshly belittled.

All these misgivings and a host more were voiced by the press. Even the doyen of South African journalists of the day, Louis Duffus, appealed to have the tour cancelled. This was probably because a devastating drubbing at the hands of the seemingly invincible Australians would damage Springbok morale beyond repair. Little credit was given to the resilience and burning ambition of youth.

Fortunately for the long-term good of South African cricket, the tour was allowed to go ahead, and it now forms a proud part in the annals of the game. When the *Dominion Monarch* sailed from Cape Town in late September 1952, Jack had under his command a team of which legendary Australian cricket writer and commentator, AG ('Johnny') Moyes later gave the following potted pen pictures in his book *The South Africans in Australia: 1952/53*:

> John E Cheetham (Western Province) 6ft 1in, captain; a cheerful sportsman who had the confidence of his team. Born May 26, 1920.
> Derek John McGlew (Natal) 5ft 6ins, vice-captain; sound opening batsman, superb fielder. Born March 11, 1929.

Kenneth J Funston (Orange Free State) 5ft 9ins. Splendid batsman and grand fielder. Born December 3, 1925.

Anton RA Murray (Eastern Province) 6ft 3ins. Splendid medium-paced bowler, good bat, grand fielder. Born April 30, 1922.

W Russell Endean (Transvaal) 5ft 9.5ins. First-rate batsman, splendid fielder, who took some dazzling catches, and useful reserve wicketkeeper. Born May 31, 1924.

Eric B Norton (Eastern Province) 6ft. Solid bat and fielder, born December 5, 1919.

Gerald B Innes (Western Province) 6ft. Technically possibly the best equipped batsman in the team, but lacked confidence. Born November 16, 1931.

Roy A McLean (Natal) 5ft 10.5ins. Lovely aggressive bat, able to turn fortunes of the games but sometimes a little too adventuresome. Grand fielder, born July 9, 1930.

John HB Waite (Eastern Province) 6ft. Accomplished opening batsman and first-class wicketkeeper. Born January 1, 1930.

Percy NF Mansell (Rhodesia) 5ft 10ins. Useful slow spinner and batsman and good fielder. Born in England, March 16, 1920.

Edward ('Eddie') Fuller (Western Province) 5ft 8.5ins. Fastish right-hand bowler and extremely good fielder. Born August 2, 1931.

John C Watkins (Natal) 5ft 11ins. Medium paced right-hand bowler, who developed splendidly as a batsman and who was in general a fielder who rarely missed a catch. Born April 10, 1923.

Headley Keith (Natal) 5ft 10ins. Left-arm spin bowler and batsman, born October 25, 1927.

Michael G Melle (Transvaal) 5ft 11ins. Fast bowler and fine fielder with a superb throw. Born June 3, 1930.

Hugh J Tayfield (Natal) 5ft 11ins. First-class right-hand off-spinner and useful bat. Born January 30, 1928.

Ken J Viljoen. The manager and a remarkably efficient one.

That is what Moyes, a noted critic, thought of the side. Unfortunately other statements and views were almost diabolically hostile, particularly before the team's departure. Their detractors were proved wrong. I dwell on this phase of Cheetham's captaincy because it is of paramount importance in his entire career. It was this period that established him as one of the all-time great captains, and attributed to him the virtual reincarnation of South African cricket.

In my book titled *Cricket for South Africa*, after the England tour of 1960, the following paragraph appears:

This I will say of our side in Australia that summer, that I doubt whether any captain had a team more loyal, more firmly decided to give him of their very best than Jack Cheetham had on this tour. There was a purposeful air about the whole party: it would prove itself, despite the carping criticism of the many who had tagged it as 'no hopers'.

It is my firm belief that no team in the history of South African cricket worked more tirelessly for their captain than the 1952/53 side in Australia. Perhaps other tourists have given equal allegiance, but certainly not more, because there was no more to give. This team of hard-working tourists stood four-square behind Cheetham.

This is also an opportunity to discuss Cheetham the man and Cheetham the captain. Jack would not have won any beauty prizes for his batting; he was certainly no stylist, but no one would disagree with the description of 'doggedly determined'. He possessed deep resolution and tenacity, which was both admirable and inspirational; otherwise how could he have completed a first-class career, ranging from 1939 to 1955, with an average of 42.20 from an aggregate of 5 697 runs, which include eight centuries? He was certainly a doughty opponent, although not a prolific run-getter in Test matches. He was a firm force in the field, where he patrolled his mid-off area with dogged determination. Little escaped him there, and he earned a worthy reputation as a safe catch. He practised endlessly, and of necessity he had to rely overmuch on defence, but he always showed a dour fighting spirit that was invaluable whenever his side was in trouble. He fought many a rearguard action.

As a man, Jack was a cheerful sportsman, whether in triumph or adversity. He was a charming person who enjoyed the confidence and affection of those who played under him.

He was injured in the second first-class game at Adelaide against South Australia, and I then had the awesome task of taking over right up to the first Test in Brisbane some four weeks later. Nevertheless, Jack was ever-present with warm encouragement. I think Jack's injury would have broken the spirit of most people, but he was an eternal optimist. 'Smiling Jack' was an apt name for him, because when he did smile, which was frequently, his face lit up like a beacon. Coupled with this, he had a hearty laugh and an infectious chuckle. He was always cheerful company.

Jack, of course, will always be remembered as a captain. He is especially remembered as the skipper who would never have allowed his players to lose faith in themselves. There was no doubt that at the time he was taking a team of Cinderellas to Australia. The chosen 15 left home amid groans of despair from the South African cricket public. When the tour was over, however, the side returned home to paeans of praise.

Such was the delight at the South African performances in Australia and New Zealand that summer, that a classy mayoral reception was arranged for us in the Cape Town City Hall after we had disembarked from the *Dominion Monarch*.

Jack Cheetham died on 21 August 1980, at the relatively early age of 60, and did not live to see his dream of total cricket unity and reacceptance as a full member of the International Cricket Council on 10 July 1991 fulfilled. Norma, his wife, was heartbroken, and his three loveable sons, John, Robert and Peter, were devastated. Norma never got over Jack's passing, and this led to her death, also at an early age.

Cheetham was a successful pupil of the South African College School (SACS) in Cape Town, which also produced modern batting luminary Peter Kirsten. I remember the school well, because that is where the Natal side was billeted in 1946 in the annual Nuffield Week. Jack went to the University of Cape Town where he obtained a BSc Engineering degree, which stood him in good stead. After several years with the South African Railways, it was cricket devotee and benefactor Wilfred Isaacs who apparently arranged a job interview with the construction firm of Murray & Roberts, who employed him. In his own dedicated way, Cheetham helped build them into the giant they are today. His employers held him in such high esteem that they have named a boardroom after him, and it contains a lovely picture of 'Happy Jack', as he was affectionately known to all his friends, smiling that broad, familiar, unforgettable smile.

On his first tour of England as a member of Dudley Nourse's 1951 side, Jack ended the eventful trip second to the prolific Eric Rowan in the team's batting averages. In 33 innings, Jack had an aggregate of 1 196 runs with a highest score of 133 not out, and a handsome average of 42.71. He scored three valuable centuries on that tour: the 133 not out against Combined Services at Portsmouth; 127 versus Lancashire at Old Trafford; and 116 not out when we met Warwickshire at Birmingham. He also just missed a century against Oxford at The Parks when he was stumped by Peter Whitcombe off one of Donald Carr's left-arm spinners, which he bowled out of the back of his hand. At that stage South Africa were really chasing the runs, as Rowan was looking to make a declaration.

When Cheetham scored his century against Combined Services, he and George Fullerton were involved in a partnership of 113 made in only an hour. The Combined Services bowling line-up that season consisted of Alan Moss (Middlesex and England), Brian Close (Yorkshire and England), Arthur Underwood (Notts), Jim Parks (later an England wicketkeeper), RG Wilson, Fred Titmus (England) and Louis Devereaux. This match immediately followed the second Test at Lord's in late June, where Jack scored a dogged 54 on a rain-affected pitch before being bowled by Statham.

The game before the second Test was against Lancashire at Old Trafford from 16 to 19 June, where Cheetham scored a fine 127 before being bowled by Roy

Tattersall, then also representing England as an off-spinner. Jack's innings in this match was put together with a heavy reliance on the straight drive, which he played so very well, hitting a six and 10 fours in what was his first century of the tour. The Lancashire bowling attack was littered with names of players who had either played for England or were close to Test call-up: Malcolm Hilton, CS Smith, Alan Wharton, Tattersall, Jack Ikin and Ken Grieves.

Then, on 8–10 August, South Africa squared up to Warwickshire at Birmingham, and it was here at Edgbaston that Cheetham hit his third century of the tour. The Springboks had been skittled for 77 in their first innings and were in trouble in the second, before a sound partnership between Roy McLean (80) and Cheetham pulled them out of trouble. Cheetham hit 116 not out and proved to be the saviour of the side. The Warwickshire bowlers who were used in the second innings to dislodge us were Charlie Grove, Ken Dollery, Ray Weeks, Alan Townsend, the New Zealand trio of Ray Hitchcock, Tom Pritchard and Don Taylor, and Bert Walton. But with Cheetham standing fast and Athol Rowan hitting a useful 48 at number seven, the Springboks held on to a draw with 290 for six wickets.

Cheetham added a fourth century to his impressive tally when he scored 114 against Minor Counties at Norwich, but since it was in a two-day game, played on 5 and 6 September, it does not qualify as a first-class game or ton. Yet in all he enjoyed a most successful first tour, and apart from his batting he was also a versatile fielder with a safe pair of catching hands.

Cheetham's next tour was to Australia and New Zealand as captain, and what a fine job he did. After the tour he produced a book titled *Caught by the Springboks*, which is now unfortunately out of print. This is a great pity because it makes for good reading, as does his later book, *I Declare*. This was published at the end of his reign, when he had decided to retire. In the first book he covers the South African tour of Australia and New Zealand in the minutest detail, even giving comprehensive tour statistics of both first- and second-class matches.

It was on this tour that Jack Cheetham came up with his 'Poor Kangaroo' joke, which is still remembered by many South Africans and Australians. Jack tells it in his own words in his book, published in the 1950s:

> After introducing the players, one by one, and giving a short description of their capabilities, I struck on a happy thought. The Honourable Mr Simpson had mentioned the wild flowers for which Western Australia is justly famous, and in particular the 'Kangaroo Paw'. I led up to this and before thanking the Lord Mayor for the hospitality shown to the team, said, 'The first wild flower I was shown in Western Australia was the Kangaroo Paw; by the time we get back here in March, I hoped it will be a case of not the Kangaroo Paw but the Poor Kangaroo!'

Although I did not know it then, the words were prophetic, because none of the sporting critics of both South Africa and Australia held any hope for us whatsoever.

Little did the critics to whom Jack refers know that South Africa would win both their Test matches at Melbourne: the second and fifth matches of the series. In the second, the South Africans were the victors by 82 runs, after having gone down to Australia by 96 runs in the first Test at the Woolloongabba, Brisbane, played in a heatwave from 5 to 10 December. It was a Test where the nerves of both teams were tested to the full. There were three reasons: the first being that the Queenslanders threatened to boycott the game because their own Test hero, wicketkeeper Don Tallon, who had been in superb form, was omitted in favour of Gil Langley. Langley had kept wicket in the previous home series, against the West Indies, and was the incumbent. Secondly, on the matter of team selection, the Australian public resented that preference had been given to the states of Victoria and New South Wales. The reason for the criticism was that the selectors had seen fit to select six players from Victoria and four from New South Wales, who had just beaten the South Africans soundly in Sydney. That particular New South Wales side contained such illustrious names as Arthur Morris, Jimmy Burke, Richie Benaud, Sid Barnes, Keith Miller, Jimmy de Courcy, Ian Craig, Alan Davidson and Ray Lindwall. Only Morris, Miller and Lindwall were selected, with Benaud the 12th man, for the Test. This was a major bone of contention with the cricket public, who were clamouring for the infusion of new blood.

Although beaten by Australia, South Africa was in no way humiliated, scoring 221 and 240 in reply to Australia's 280 and 277. We were in with a chance, but in a way I 'flogged' it when I got out for 69, lbw to Lindwall on the fifth and final day. Ken Funston and I shared a threatening stand of 96 before my wicket was the third to fall, and Funston followed shortly afterward for a fine innings of 65, with the wickets falling at 153 and 170 respectively. It was an absorbing match.

But back to the reasons for the threatened boycott. Two have been given: the omission of Tallon and the general make-up of the team. The third reason was the exclusion of Sid Barnes, the stormy petrel of Australian cricket at the time, who was in prolific form with the bat. The overlooking of Mr 'Chappie' Dwyer, as selector, also raised a great deal of anger.

A certain section of the crowd at the Gabba misbehaved and constantly made insulting remarks to Gil Langley, chosen instead of their own Don Tallon. They regularly jeered the efforts of the Victorians in the field. It did the Queensland cause no good at all. At the time they were fighting hard to retain Brisbane as a Test venue, as there were those who wanted Perth as a Test venue instead.

The denouement of the series was most interesting. The second Test was won by the Springboks by a margin of 82 runs at Melbourne over Christmas 1952. However, Australia trounced the South Africans at Sydney by an innings and 38 runs in the vital third Test, played from 9 to 13 January 1953. In the fourth Test the Springboks were very lucky to hold on to a draw. The fifth Test brought honour and glory to South Africa when Jack Cheetham's 'no-hopers' hit back to win by six wickets. Golden glory from the greenhorns.

In the second Test, where South Africa were victorious, the success was – as always Down Under – a team effort, but it would not be wrong to single out Russell Endean. The catch he took on the boundary edge off Tayfield's bowling to dismiss Keith Miller – then in full cry – for 52, is almost folklore in South African cricketing circles. Endean received a standing ovation for what seemed like five minutes for his miraculous catch. Russell balanced on the edge of the boundary, poised on his toes, and then leapt into the air to pluck the ball 'out of the sky'. His efforts stunned Miller, who at this stage was replying to a sincere compliment of 'well hit' from Johnnie Waite. Miller's response when he realised Russell had taken an impossible catch is unprintable.

Johnny Moyes, in his very readable book *The South Africans in Australia*, saw the catch slightly differently to me, but I was fielding near Russell on the mid-wicket-cum-very-wide-long-on boundary. It was a position that I believe present-day players call 'cow's corner'. This is Moyes's account of the incident:

> Miller was now Australia's hope, and he began playing strokes of power and royal lineage which are part of his heritage. He ran to 52 while others found the going against Tayfield extraordinarily difficult. Then came a mighty hit. The ball could be seen soaring towards the long-on fence. Endean moved back with it, hands held high above his head, but it seemed that this was but a gesture. The ball was certain to clear the fence and disturb the spectators sitting close behind it. Suddenly they rose, and everyone sensed a hit for six, but their rising was merely a prelude to loud and vociferous cheering, for Endean had plucked the ball out of the air with his right hand as he leaned back over the railings. An incredible catch! It took away one's breath ... or nearly so, for a commentator can always find a reserve somewhere to permit him to continue his description or comments. As for me, I was staggered by the amazing splendour of it all, and I believe, from what I have been told that it seemed that I might in my excitement at this cricket miracle, have appeared right through the microphone.

Whatever embellishments have been made, it was nonetheless a miraculous and unforgettable catch.

In addition to this legendary catch, Russell Endean contributed a truly magnificent 162 not out for South Africa to total 388 in their second innings.

If they had such a thing as a man of the match award in those days, then Russell would have received that accolade. His all-round performance was superb.

The same could be said of Roy McLean in the fifth Test, when South Africa were again victorious in Melbourne. This was a nerve-wracking contest for the Springboks, who batted last on a slightly dusty pitch, which contained cracks. South Africa now required 294 runs to win in the final innings. Chasing a total of 300 seemed, at the time, an almost impossible task. But it must be remembered that Australia were without the services of the most feared opening bowling pair of that era, the inimitable Ray Lindwall and Keith Miller, both omitted from the Australian team because of injury.

Again it would be appropriate to quote, this time from SA captain Jack Cheetham. In his book *Caught by the Springboks*, Jack had, among many other things, this to say about an agonising stage of the game:

> In the pavilion, Fuller was sitting at the end of the bench counting the score, but, although the scoreboard was in full view, he kept us informed that we needed 108 runs, 107 runs, 105 runs, 104 runs – and with that number still to go Benaud bowled a top-spinner which Funston played no stroke at, for the ball to hit the off-stump. Funston stared down at the wicket, and couldn't believe his eyes – thinking that the ball had rebounded from the 'keeper's pads. There was no doubt though and there was an uneasy hush in the dressing room as McLean picked up his gloves and bat, and started for the door.
>
> All my gear was next to McLean's and I moved over to wish him luck, murmuring it was up to him to play his own game and not throw his wicket away. Roy tugged his cap on and said 'Don't worry, Pop, I'll get them for you' and he certainly did in a manner which I for one and all who saw the day's play, will never forget.

Then Cheetham portrayed the grand finale in this vivid manner:

> Sir Donald Bradman moved into our dressing room, to be the first to congratulate me, but, with 10 runs to go, I preferred to wait for the kill, and with the police moving onto the field, Hassett took the ball for what was to be the final over, the rubber saved, and Sir Donald wringing my hand. Slowly the tension drained away, leaving me almost light-headed, and my eyes filled with tears.

Yes, it was a most memorable and emotional occasion. There was no doubt that Roy's 76 not out made him the hero of the match in our books. All the Springboks had, of course, contributed in their own way to the win, and none more so than the courageous Headley Keith with a plucky, well-played 40 not out. He was at the non-striker's end when McLean levelled the series with a crashing four off Lindsay Hassett's sporting over, from which 12 runs were scored off only five balls.

Then it was on to New Zealand, where South Africa won the two-match series 1–0. The Springboks won the first Test by an innings and 180 runs, but the New Zealanders held us to a draw in the second in Auckland. In October 1953, the New Zealanders arrived in South Africa under the leadership of Geoff Rabone and the guidance of the well-liked manager, Jack Kerr. This must rank as one of the most popular sides to come to the country, and not because the Springboks won the series 4–0. In fact, the *South African Cricket Annual* of 1954 records: 'The first-ever New Zealand team to visit South Africa lost four of the five Tests matches played BUT on at least two occasions, in the memorable second Test at Ellis Park, and again a few days later at Newlands, there were moments when an initial New Zealand Test victory appeared inevitable.'

It was indeed a memorable second Test at Ellis Park, one that is still spoken of to this day. Neil Adcock, in only his second Test, was bowling at a great pace on a pitch rarely seen in cricket today – a green top. In fact, at least 50 percent of the games played in those days commenced with a green pitch; however, Ellis Park had become known as 'Adcock's Alley'. This was because it was invariably a green track and Neil Adcock, more than any bowler around, could extract lift and life from that pitch: he was a batsman's nightmare.

On the second day of this Test, a pall of gloom descended on the New Zealand dressing room. This was because Bob Blair was informed of his fiancée's death in a train accident in Tangiwai, New Zealand, on Christmas Eve. When we arrived at the ground the flags were flying at half-mast. Although not as horrific as that sad news, high drama awaited the Kiwis on the Ellis Park pitch, and Adcock was almost unplayable for a period. He was bowling at a fearsome pace and causing the ball to lift head high from just short of a good length. Geoff Rabone was brilliantly caught by Endean in the slips off an inside edge, but it was Adcock who was causing devastation in terms of physical danger and the taking of wickets. He bowled Murray Chapple for eight, knocked back Matt Poore's stumps for 15, and then had John Reid caught at slip by Endean for three after pinning the all-rounder on the left chest with a lifter. The sheer savagery of his bowling can be imagined when it is recorded that both Bert Sutcliffe, a really great left-hander, and Lawrie Miller, batting at number six, had to be taken to hospital after being struck by Adcock's thunderbolts. Neither batsman had scored at the time, and Adcock felled Sutcliffe with a frightening blow on the head when the batsman mistimed his hook shot; then he struck the lean, balding Miller a sickening thud under his heart, which caused him to start coughing blood on the pitch. With these two receiving attention in hospital, New Zealand were in the precarious position of 23 for three, with two others in the casualty ward of the hospital. It was a precarious situation for the tourists. They were being put to the sword.

Sutcliffe eventually returned to the battleground, his head swathed in bandages. There was an air of fierce determination about Bert, and he proceeded to play an electrifying innings, bludgeoning the second ball he received from Dave Ironside for a mighty six. Sutcliffe's subsequent exhibition of attacking batsmanship was one of the finest one could wish to see. The spectators' thunderous applause was testimony to this as they greeted each boundary with deafening appreciation. In this beautifully timed display of big hitting, he saved the follow on with a colossal six. His explosive strokeplay saw him race to 80 not out – all this, according to the statisticians, off only 27 scoring strokes. It was an incredible innings to watch. Although we were on the receiving end, it was a privilege to have witnessed one of the finest displays of big hitting in the history of Test cricket: an innings that also saw Sutcliffe become the first New Zealander to score 1 000 Test runs. He had support from a stubborn Frank Mooney, New Zealand's wicketkeeper, who contributed a plucky 35. Sutcliffe and Mooney's defiant partnership realised 56 runs in even time, made at a crucial stage. At one stage Mooney was also felled by a terrifying lifter from Adcock, and in our excitement I thought the ball had hit his bat as there was a sharp crack. 'Catch it!' I shouted, only for the gutsy New Zealand wicketkeeper to stagger to his feet, holding his head. 'Come off it, mate!' he said, aggrieved. 'It hit me on the head!'

When the grief-stricken Blair emerged from the tunnel to join Sutcliffe, he was greeted with a standing ovation of sympathy from the 22 000-strong crowd. Blair and Sutcliffe added 33 invaluable runs in only 10 minutes before Blair was out to a lightning stumping by Waite off Hugh Tayfield; Blair's contribution was six, which came off a single blow from Tayfield's bowling.

This Test was a close call for South Africa, as at one stage the Boks were 44 runs for five wickets in their second innings, and were eventually all out for 148 runs. In turn, New Zealand could muster only a paltry 100 runs and lost the match by 132 runs.

The series was played in the finest spirit I have ever known, and I think that the two captains were largely responsible for this happy atmosphere. Jack Cheetham was fifth in the Test averages for this series at 37.83.

Rabone's touring team contained a bunch of sporting cricketers who were a great deal better than their 4–0 drubbing will ever suggest. As for Cheetham, he must have been highly delighted with his team's performance, although they gave him cause for alarm at times, and were responsible for him smoking a lot more cigarettes than usual.

Jack Cheetham was rightly rewarded for his gallant services to South African cricket when he was appointed captain of the Springbok team to tour England in

1955. This was probably the best South African side in which I had the privilege of playing. The touring party was:

Jack Cheetham (34), captain, Western Province
Jackie McGlew (26), vice-captain, Natal
Russell Endean (30), Transvaal
Neil Adcock (24), Transvaal
Chris Duckworth (22), Rhodesia
Eddie Fuller (23), Western Province
Trevor Goddard (23), Natal
Peter Heine (26), Orange Free State
Headly Keith (27), Natal
Percy Mansell (35), Rhodesia
Roy McLean (24), Natal
Anton Murray (33), Eastern Province
Ian Smith (30), Natal
Hugh Tayfield (26), Natal
Johnnie Waite (25), Transvaal
Paul Winslow (25), Transvaal
Manager: Ken Viljoen, Transvaal.

Although they lost their first match, this team produced some outstanding cricket in every department of the game, including Johnnie Waite's brilliant wicketkeeping. They departed from Jan Smuts Airport, the first South African cricket team to travel to England by aeroplane. In the past they had always gone by sea.

This was a great series, with England fielding a powerful combination in every Test. There were such great names as Peter May, Trevor Bailey, Denis Compton, Brian Statham, Johnny Wardle, Tom Graveney, Frank Tyson, Godfrey Evans, Ken Barrington, Bob Appleyard, Colin Cowdrey, Fred Trueman and several others, all of whom would be remembered by cricket lovers. It also marked the end of Sir Leonard Hutton's career, the highly successful England captain and opening batsman being forced to retire after being named captain for all five Tests of the series. Those making debuts in the first Test were Trevor Goddard for South Africa and Ken Barrington for England.

South Africa were pulverised in the first two Tests, then came back to gain victories in the third and fourth matches of the series. The fifth match was unfortunately tainted by a number of highly controversial decisions, which time and again went against South Africa. England ran out the winners in the fifth Test by 92 runs, and of course they may have done so despite the controversial decisions. However, it did leave something of a nasty taste, especially as it was the deciding match of a highly exciting, ding-dong series that had produced fine cricket on both sides. Nevertheless we felt that it was true to say that our team suffered far more from the vagaries of decisions than did our English counterparts. Jack was, sadly, highly criticised for returning to the team after an absence of two Tests, both of which South Africa won. As it was, he offered to stand down, but the touring selection panel and I, in particular, were adamant he take his rightful place at the head of his team. Jack was fit, and including him was the correct thing to do. The fact that South Africa lost the final Test had nothing at all to do with the decision to allow a fit Jack Cheetham back to skipper his own side. In his last two county innings he had scored 36 not out against Gloucestershire and 18 not out against Leicestershire. He had also been sprightly in the field and taken three good catches.

What caused Cheetham to miss the third and fourth Tests was an unfortunate injury in the second Test at Lord's. He was the unlucky victim of an incident during the last ball of the third day's play. It was a fiery delivery from Freddie Trueman that lifted sharply and struck our captain a painful blow on the elbow, crippling his arm. Cheetham was taken to Middlesex Hospital, where an X-ray revealed a chipped fracture of the radius bone; the elbow was grotesquely swollen. The worst part of the whole affair was that the light was so bad the players should not have been on the field, let alone having to face Trueman and Statham in the gloaming. These days the players would have been off long before that fateful over had started.

In his book *I Declare*, Jack describes quite graphically the events leading up to the ill-fated final ball of the day:

> Quarter past six, and a dull gloom settled over the ground. Twenty past six, and Trueman bounced a ball past Goddard's head, and then at twenty-six minutes past six Statham once again struck a faster ball catching the shoulder of Goddard's bat, for Evans to yell joyously as he held the catch. Tayfield – that man of many parts, and the best night watchman I have ever had in a cricket side – strode out briskly. I met him half way and told him he would not have to face a ball, as there was but one over to go, and I would take all the deliveries from Trueman.
>
> It is ironic to look back and realise that we could have taken a single off the fourth ball when I played it down toward third man – instead I faced up to the last ball of the day, as Peter May brought the fielders around me in a menacing ring, determined to keep my wicket intact. The ball, short pitched, lifted off the wicket, and I pulled my bat away only to feel a crack on the elbow where the ball struck me. I was conscious only of the sharp stabbing pain and Denis Compton rushed forward from the gully, I dropped my bat and holding my elbow walked dejectedly into the pavilion.

That was how we lost our courageous captain for the third and fourth Tests. And the worst part of it all is that it could have been avoided so easily. As depressed as he was about his injury over the next few weeks, Cheetham was remarkable in his ability to laugh, joke and generally remain in high spirits.

The results of this stimulating and hard-fought series were as follows:

FIRST TEST: Cheetham lost the toss in the match played at Trent Bridge, Nottingham, on 9, 10, 11, 13 and 14 June 1955.
England won by an innings and five runs.

SECOND TEST: Cheetham lost the toss in the match played at Lord's, London, on 23, 24, 25, 27 and 28 June 1955.
England won by 71 runs.

THIRD TEST: McGlew lost the toss in the match played at Old Trafford, Manchester, on 7, 8, 9, 11 and 12 July 1955.
South Africa won by three wickets three minutes from time.

FOURTH TEST: McGlew won the toss in the match played at Headingley, Leeds, on 21, 22, 23, 25 and 26 July 1955.
South Africa won by 224 runs.

FIFTH TEST: Cheetham lost the toss in the match played at The Oval, London, on 13, 15, 16, 17 and 18 August 1955.
England won by 92 runs.

Although we barely lost the Test series, Cheetham told me he considered the tour, as a whole, a stimulating experience and a huge success. He finished third in the first-class averages on that tour, with his average standing at 34.77. He scored one century, against Kent at Canterbury.

It was immediately after the tour that Cheetham announced his retirement, and while he was a distinct loss as a captain and player, he was fortunately not lost to South African cricket.

He soon established himself as an able administrator and a competent selector. His toughest battle was fought off the field over what has become known as the 'D'Oliveira affair', when he went to England with Arthur Coy with a grim message for the MCC that, for reasons beyond the control of the SACA, the 1968/69 MCC team, which included Basil D'Oliveira, the Cape Town-born all-rounder who played for Worcestershire and England, was not acceptable in South Africa.

In the early 1970s Cheetham, as chairman of Transvaal, and acknowledging the wrongs of the past, helped pioneer the organising of invitation teams to give cricket an avenue to help survive those early years of isolation. Transvaal organised the first of four tours of the country by the Derrick Robins teams during those first years. But during his years as the SACA president from 1969 to 1972, Cheetham worked especially tirelessly to have South Africa readmitted as a member of the International Cricket Conference. It was, as he admitted in 1973, becoming a futile exercise, but a worthwhile experience.

Had he lived to see them, the events of the past ten years, such as the formation of the United Cricket Board of South Africa, the historic tour of India, the World Cup series and West Indies adventure, as well as the first momentous home season free of the restrictions of isolation, would have given Jack Cheetham great satisfaction. There is little doubt that he would have been among the first at Jan Smuts Airport to greet Mohammad Azharuddin on that momentous day when the Indians arrived from Harare; and he would have agreed that the Total International triangular series with the West Indies and Pakistan meant that South African cricket had at last found a rightful place in terms of global cricket. It was, after all, Cheetham's greatest hope that South Africa would one day play all Test countries.

CLIVE VAN RYNEVELD 5
The Gentleman Captain

By Jackie McGlew

In certain circles Clive van Ryneveld was considered, in the kindest possible way, an eccentric. This probably had something to do with him being a deep thinker as well as a forward-looking person. Both an academic and a sportsman, he was in many ways a perfect product of Bishops (Diocesan College) in Cape Town: a kind, considerate sort, who even in the often bubbling cauldron of a Test match would introduce his own high standards of what he considered to be fair play to overrule anything that he felt was underhand. He was a throwback to the more relaxed pre-World War I Edwardian era.

It was once said of CB Fry, the great all-round English sportsman who epitomised the 'Boys Own'-style hero of the late Victorian and Edwardian years, that 'he was too various for the single aim; he lacked the ruthlessness that is present, however deftly disguised, in the careerist'. Such remarks also apply to Clive van Ryneveld in his early years.

However, it is almost paradoxical to add that in his own way Van Ryneveld made a career of all he did, or undertook to do. That is probably where the eccentric label originated, because it was a case of 'I'll do it my way', as Frank Sinatra might have put it.

Two prime examples of this occurred during the 1957/58 South Africa–Australia series: the first in the third Test at Kingsmead, Durban, and the second on the fourth and last afternoon of the fifth Test at St George's Park, Port Elizabeth.

Neil Harvey, Australia's great left-hand batsman of the early post-World War II years, was involved in the first incident at Kingsmead. At the time he had about 53 runs, and was batting with the often doughty customer, Slasher Mackay, when Mackay squeezed the ball past fine leg, where Russell Endean had been positioned. Instead of Endean going after the ball, Hugh Tayfield, in the slips, gave chase at full pace, putting out his foot at the boundary edge to stop a certain four. Both batsmen by now had slowed to a walk, thinking the ball had crossed the boundary. At this point Tayfield hurled the ball back in such a manner to the Springbok wicketkeeper Johnnie Waite, that it indicated the ball had not crossed the boundary. Mackay was now making his way toward Waite, but Ken Funston, quick as a flash, called for the ball at the other end. Waite could quite easily have run out the Queenslander, Mackay; instead he looped the ball to the other end where Van Ryneveld was now standing.

With almost playful ease the Springbok captain, urged on by Ken Funston, removed the bails – at which point Harvey looked on, at first almost hypnotised by the action.

'Hey, you can't do that,' he said, not quite believing what was happening. 'It was a boundary.'

The umpire, Bill Marais, himself uncertain, checked with Tayfield, who was now at point. But the off-spinner quite vigorously shook his head and told the umpire that it was not a four. While an appeal at that point would have left the umpire with no alternative but to give Harvey out, Clive ended it there when he shook his head and indicated that there would be no appeal, suggesting that the game continue. Trevor Goddard bowled the next ball, much to the relief of all.

Harvey continued his innings and went on to score 68, which not only held the side up, but may have been the reason why South Africa was held to a draw. But I am convinced that the Aussies wouldn't have reciprocated the favour if one of us had been the batsman.

The St George's Park incident is full of irony: the Aussies wanted about 68 runs in the second innings to win the series 3–0, and with a day to spare they faced an easy task. Wally Grout opened with Colin McDonald, as Jimmy Burke was injured. Peter Heine's opening over of that particular innings indicated that he wasn't in the mood to give anything away, and McDonald picked up a single. But Neil Adcock's first ball of the over to McDonald was as perfect a bouncer as you would find and caught the Australian by surprise, forcing him to duck out of the way, but only just. The next ball zoomed in on the batsman with the speed of a thunderbolt, and the Aussie was forced into a hurried stroke. It was at this stage that Adcock realised that the 'game was really on', and bowled about the fastest he could remember at any stage of the series. He did have the advantage of a following wind, and his deliveries hurried at the batsman like bolts of forked lightning.

It should be remembered that in those days they bowled eight-ball overs, and the Victorian found himself taking an edgy single to get away from his tormentor – only to face the ever-robust, fiery Heine at the other end. South Africa has had fast bowling combinations before and since, but for a time the Adcock–Heine combination was acknowledged to be the meanest around. So, when Heine let loose with a fierce opening over, McDonald knew what to expect. McDonald went for four, picked up by Tayfield, with the wicket falling at four. Grout somehow managed to survive the torrid attack, and his new partner, Harvey, found himself battling to keep his wicket intact. This was far from easy under the circumstances, but crucial to the Australian cause, as the pacemen attempted to save some face for South Africa at the end of a series that had not fulfilled its promise of being a close contest.

Adcock and Heine bowled only seven overs between them for 30 runs, and while the pace was fast and furious, it was a bouncer Adcock aimed at Grout that forced Van Ryneveld to intervene and take both bowlers out of the attack, although umpire Marais had already talked to Adcock about the number of bumpers he had bowled to the Australian opener.

'I was not at all impressed by the reasoning Clive gave me. Here was a chance to knock over a few wickets, and we were told, "This is not the way we play cricket",' the admonished Adcock later recalled. 'I can tell you now the Australians would not have bothered one hoot about such niceties had they been in our situation. They would have gone flat out to knock off our blocks. What would a few bruised knuckles or ribs be to Ian Craig [the Australian captain in that series], and particularly the rest of the Aussies?'

Grout scored 35 not out and Harvey 22 before he was caught and bowled by Tayfield, who had a hand in both dismissals that innings, and Richie Benaud was not out with six, as a third-wicket partnership of 15 negotiated the pathway to victory.

Van Ryneveld had much in common with that other 'gentleman captain', Alan Melville. Both were products of the South African private school system: Clive van Ryneveld from Bishops and Alan Melville from Michaelhouse; both had the privilege of attending Oxford University. They were thorough gentlemen who conducted themselves with dignity but never lost their impish sense of humour, which often delighted their colleagues. Clive and Alan were tall, slim and impeccably neat and well spoken. It must be added that while Van Ryneveld possessed all the trappings of an upper-class background, he never lost the boyish enthusiasm that endeared him to his associates. He was interested in whatever subject was being discussed, and was a clear-thinking, articulate debater. All these academic qualities and his legal qualifications were adjuncts to his phenomenal versatility as an international sportsman, for in truth he was a natural ball player.

Van Ryneveld is generally regarded as being South Africa's greatest natural athlete since the halcyon days of the great multi-talented Tuppy Owen-Smith – also an Oxford University graduate. Perhaps it was his overwhelming versatility, along with his excellence of mind and body, which made him a sure-fire success in all he tackled. In a wide-ranging sporting career he earned coveted cricket and rugby blues while at Oxford, and was then selected to play rugby for England and cricket for South Africa. Indeed, by the time he was 23, he had been capped five times for South Africa at cricket and four for England in the winter code, where he excelled as a centre three-quarter. But it was his cricket exploits that earned the more deserving recognition and the headlines.

When the South African team toured England in 1951, several top rugby critics told us that in his days as a rugby player at Oxford, Van Ryneveld was rated as the best centre in Europe. His brilliance apparently lay in his speed, change of pace, body swerve and incredibly safe hands in a sport where safe hands are a necessary by-product of class and quality in a player.

It is sometimes forgotten that while Van Ryneveld was the Oxford cricket captain in 1949, he led the university to a singular victory over Walter Hadlee's Kiwi tourists, who otherwise went through the tour unbeaten, drawing the four three-day Tests. It may be true that winning the toss could have had something to do with the victory, because rain affected the pitch later in the match, but the way he handled his bowlers earned him much credit – and not only from the New Zealanders. As it transpired, there were three budding Test players and captains in that 1949 Oxford team: Clive, Donald Carr (England) and AH Kardar, perhaps better known as Abdul Hafeez Kardar (India and Pakistan), who led Pakistan in their first 23 official Tests. Top scorer for both sides in that match was another South African and double blue, Pretoria-educated Murray Hofmeyr.

It has been argued that Van Ryneveld modelled his batting technique on that of Herbie Taylor, but those of us who played with and against him have their doubts about such claims. He was far too adventurous, even daring, in his batting to allow a comparison with the immaculately sound and clinical batsmanship of Taylor who, by all accounts, easily ranks with Graeme Pollock and Barry Richards as South Africa's finest.

Hallmarks of Van Ryneveld's enterprising batsmanship were his deceptively long reach and glorious cover driving. He was one of the few batsmen I have seen who, on an easy paced pitch, could and would consistently drive the ball on the up, to the consternation of the bowler. This was done mainly between the arc of the non-striker's stumps and somewhere between cover and point: the shot was always played effortlessly and with an almost enchanting elegance. At his best he was always comfortable against any type of bowling, but his great strength was his manner of dealing with spin bowlers. Using his height and swiftness of foot, he could go down the pitch, or get well back (and across if necessary) on his stumps. He was capable of savaging the spinner, or playing so delicately that one did not notice he was scoring at a steady, consistent rate, over after over.

Van Ryneveld's first-class career extended from 1946 to 1958, and in those 12 summers at home and abroad he scored 4 783 runs, including four centuries, for a batting average of 30.27. He was not a chaser of records, nor did he harbour a Geoff Boycott-like desire to amass more runs than anyone on this planet or anywhere else cricket might be played. He played for the sheer fun of it. The grim, joyless concentration applied by some cricketers wasn't his style, although he was capable of fruitful concentration when it was demanded. He believed that cricket was a game to be enjoyed, and the long, golden summer hours should provide pleasure, sporting deeds and cheerful exploits that would long be remembered. He cherished all that was good about the game, unfortunately allowing sportsmanship to backfire on the rare occasion: as with the Harvey run-out incident at Kingsmead, and the fast-bowling episode in the same series at St George's Park.

Van Ryneveld's cricket career for South Africa covered the 1951 tour of England, and at home he represented his country against Geoff Rabone's New Zealanders on their 1953/54 tour, Peter May's 1956/57 England touring party (four Tests as captain) and Ian Craig's Australians of 1957/58 (again four Tests as captain).

On the 1951 tour of England, Van Ryneveld played in 22 first-class matches, scoring 983 runs, hitting a century and six 50s, and ending with an average of 29.79, placing him seventh in the South African averages. He was a cheerful, motivated member of the touring party, and it was always a pleasure to be in his company. His highest Test score was 83 against England in the drawn fourth Test at Leeds, where he and Eric Rowan added a record 198 runs for the second wicket, beating by 43 runs the previous record of 155 established by Bob Catterall and Herbie Taylor at Newlands in the 1922/23 season.

Once Van Ryneveld and Eric Rowan had raised the record to 198, Clive was out to an easy caught and bowled dismissal by Lancashire left-arm spinner Malcolm Hilton. In that same match he captured the valuable wicket of Len Hutton (later to be knighted), bowling him with one of his tweakers for exactly 100. Given only eight overs by the captain, Dudley Nourse, he ended with one wicket for 26.

This Test is memorable for three other feats: Eric Rowan created a South African batting record by scoring 236 before being caught by Alec Bedser off Freddie Brown's bowling (the innings made him the oldest South African to score a double century in a Test). Eric batted for 575 minutes while establishing this record, not giving a bowler a chance until passing the 200 mark; the achievement was accomplished on the second day, as was another record. The South African total of 538 was recorded by the immortal *Wisden* as being five runs more than the 533 scored against England by Alan Melville's 1947 team at Trent Bridge, Nottingham, in the first Test against England in that particular series, and the first encounter between South Africa and England after World War II.

Peter May, often referred to as 'PBH' [Peter Barker Howard], made an auspicious Test debut at Leeds. When finally bowled by Athol Rowan's off-spin, May had scored a century. He was only 21 and a student at Cambridge University, and the 138 was an auspicious start to what became an illustrious career. It was an innings that proved that schoolboy prodigies sometimes justify predictions. PBH went to Charterhouse, one of those fine British public schools that produced an army of fine county and Test players until the demise of the amateur in 1963, when the status was removed from the game in England. The knowledgeable George Geary, the former Leicestershire and England all-rounder, gave May a sound appreciation of the fundamentals, which did a great deal for his game.

In a way, May was not unlike Clive van Ryneveld. The 1952 *Wisden* has this to say about PBH May:

> The story of May's cricket ascent is that of a boy reared, as it were, with a ball in his hand or at his feet. The urge to kick or hit the ball came to him strongly at an early age and, with youthful zest, he spent hours doing so in the garden and on the hard tennis court of his parents Reading house. He made no attempt at specialisation. All games provide enjoyment. Thus he acquired a ball sense which became the foundation of all-round sporting ability.

I quote the *Wisden* assessment to show that May and Van Ryneveld had an enormous amount in common. May, too, was an outstanding all-rounder, captaining Cambridge for the 1951/52 season in both soccer and fives – a stunning university achievement.

It was on the 1951 tour of England that Clive hit a career-best first-class innings of 150 against Yorkshire at Bramall Lane in June. It was a flawless innings in a high-scoring match that appeared doomed to an inevitable draw from the first day; the pitch was docile to the extent of being overly batsman-friendly. Batting first, the South Africans posted 454 runs for eight wickets and then declared. Yorkshire replied with a mammoth 579: Len Hutton and Frank Lowson shared an opening partnership of 286, the highest for Yorkshire since the end of World War II. The partnership was responsible for laying the foundation for the highest total recorded against the South Africans that summer, an amazing answer to the huge score amassed by the tourists.

At one point the South African innings stood at 148 for four. Enter first George Fullerton, then the young Roy McLean. The score when the next wicket fell was 304. Fullerton had scored a scintillating 63 before falling lbw to the Yorkshire captain, Norman Yardley. Clive and Fullerton had added 156 in only 105 minutes for the fifth wicket, a devastating onslaught that included some glorious shots from both batsmen. Immediately after the compulsory Sunday break, Van Ryneveld was bowled by Whitehead, failing to add to his magnificently played 150. The wicket fell when the South African total was 365. This allowed McLean to provide a brilliant pyrotechnic display of powerful hitting all around the wicket. Roy was eventually caught by Leadbeater, bowled by Whitehead, ending an innings that yielded 88 runs and provided a splendid exhibition of controlled, hard-hitting strokeplay.

Clive van Ryneveld emerged as a batsman of some quality and skill at Test level in the five-match series against New Zealand in South Africa in 1953/54. It was a unique series, as it was the first time the Kiwis had played in a rubber of five Tests, and the former Oxford captain headed the Springbok batting averages. His statistics were: played five matches, batted seven times with two not outs and a highest score of 68 (not out), for an aggregate of 234 and an average of 46.80.

This graceful all-rounder was consistent, if not prolific, in his batting against the Kiwis, with the following scores:

First Test: 68 not out
Second Test: 65 and 17
Third Test: 23
Fourth Test: 11
Fifth Test: 40 and 10 not out.

In addition, he scored a further 57 when captaining Western Province against Geoff Rabone's team at Newlands in the opening match of the tour. He was named one of the five cricketers of the year by the *South African Cricket Annual*, with the annual mentioning that Herbie Taylor was his mentor as well as his coach 'who trimmed the rough edges and on whom Clive modelled his style of batting'. However, being coached by someone and modelling yourself on his style are so often two very different things. Van Ryneveld could hardly have modelled his batting on Taylor's as he never saw the great man in action at the height of his career, and furthermore Taylor was recognised as the undisputed master of batting on matting pitches. Clive van Ryneveld was just too adventurous to be seriously compared with the scientific Taylor.

Of course both were majestic and graceful to watch and some of Taylor must have rubbed off on his pupil; but in the final analysis Taylor is Taylor and Van Ryneveld is Van Ryneveld. Both will be remembered for their own style of cricket.

Having said this, I have no doubt that Taylor had a great influence on Clive's success and his approach to the game.

When May's MCC side was to tour South Africa, the name of DJ McGlew was announced as captain of the South African team. This was not to be. It was, in fact, an ill-fated tour for me. During the season I was forced to have a cartilage removed from the inner meniscus of my right knee and, to make matters worse, I had a displaced collarbone for the best part of the season. I tried to play anyway in the second Test in Cape Town, but with disastrous results. My injuries were really too severe even to attempt the game, and by playing I not only let myself down, but also my teammates and the selectors; I did so purely out of a deep-rooted desire to captain my country at home.

However, as they say in darts circles, there is no such thing as a bad dart, because whether the dart is a bullseye or doesn't even hit the board, one of the sides will benefit. In this case the beneficiary was Western Province's captain Clive van Ryneveld, and he made such a fine job of it that his services as captain were retained the following season when Ian Craig's Australians were the tourists.

The only joy for me during the 1956/57 season was when I captained a South African XI that defeated the MCC XI at Loftus Versfeld in Pretoria. This was an ironic venue for what turned out to be an historic result, as the ground was part of a famous rugby complex. Although local club cricket was regularly played on the B-field until the mid-1960s (and it was also a major tennis venue until 1991), this was the first game of cricket on a patch of turf better known for its rugby international duels. That South African XI was the first South African side to beat an MCC team outside a Test for 43 years. It was an exciting match, and a very gratifying one for those of us who had the opportunity to play in it.

As I was injured, I made way for Van Ryneveld in the first Test, played at the (new) Wanderers over Christmas 1956, when a South African record 100 000 spectators crammed into the new stadium over the five days. Clive lost the toss and South Africa ultimately lost the opening match of the series by 131 runs. A similar fate awaited me in Cape Town when I lost the toss and South Africa – batting last on a dusty, turning Newlands pitch made for the spin wiles of left-arm Johnny Wardle (seven for 36 in 19 eight-ball overs) and off-spinner Jim Laker (two for seven in 14.1 overs) – tumbled to a 312-run defeat when we were bowled out for 72.

For me it was back to Pietermaritzburg and hospital, but for Van Ryneveld it was on to Kingsmead and eventual glory. From this point on, the Springboks fought back courageously from a 2–0 deficit to square the series. The Kingsmead Test ran to a draw, but was nevertheless a most absorbing game, probably the most entertaining from the spectators' point of view. It was played over five days in late January 1957. On the first day Hugh Tayfield created a record by bowling 14 consecutive maidens, an incredible testimony to the most accurate off-spinner produced by South Africa. Tayfield achieved this remarkable record between 2.30 pm and 4.55 pm. He showed pinpoint precision, and his full analysis for that first England innings read 24-17-21-1 – and it must be remembered they were eight-ball overs. The scores were England 218 and 254, while South Africa responded with 283 and then pluckily held on to record 142 for six wickets.

Although only a draw, it was a platform from which South Africa could fight back, and fight they did, bouncing back to win the fourth and fifth Tests. The fourth Test was played at the Wanderers from 15 to 20 February 1957. It was in this game that Van Ryneveld scored his highest individual innings of the series, posting 36, and batting at eight in the first innings. Although he averaged only 20.75, Clive's inspirational leadership encouraged the Springboks to summon up that something extra to pull off a fine victory in the fourth Test against May's powerful England team.

In the first innings Trevor Goddard and Johnnie Waite, now promoted to three, added 112 for the second wicket, becoming the first century partnership against England in the series. In South Africa's first-innings total of 340, Roy McLean was only seven runs short of his second successive century when he was run out. What disappointment he must have felt, especially after batting so brilliantly, hitting a six and 14 fours in a spectacular innings.

When the last day of this match dawned, the task facing England – given their formidable batting strength – was relatively easy: their objective was 213 runs with nine wickets standing. They had started shakily, losing Trevor Bailey to Tayfield's off-spin for one, just before the close the night before. Richardson was not out on the penultimate evening, only to become Tayfield's second victim, for 39, with the score on 65. What really drove the nails of defeat into England's coffin on this exciting final day was the loss of May and Denis Compton for only one run between them. May was caught by Russell Endean for a duck off a Tayfield delivery, and Compton succumbed to the same bowler when neatly caught by Goddard for only a single.

Doug Insole played his second fine innings of the match when he scored a fighting 68, and with Richardson shared in a 55-run partnership in 72 minutes for the second wicket, indicating that England had decided to adopt bold batting tactics, which nearly paid a handsome dividend. Colin Cowdrey also made a brave effort with an innings of 55, and daring hitting by Wardle kept them in with a chance.

But throughout the innings the incomparable Tayfield was just too much for England. His subtle flight, sufficient spin and wily variation overcame the class opposition. His astonishing spell brought him a return of nine wickets for 113 runs off 37 overs, as Van Ryneveld backed his spinner against the batting might of England on the most important day of the series for both teams. It was vintage Tayfield: his length and line did not falter as he dropped the ball on the proverbial 'tickey'. It was a fairytale ending for the off-spinner to capture nine wickets in one innings, and ensure an important victory for his country. In fact, he had a hand in all 10 dismissals in the England second innings, catching Insole off Goddard's left-arm bowling, which opened up the middle order.

Wisden describes the ending of this vibrant game thus:

> At tea the game was still open, England wanting 46 with four wickets left, but the end came 50 minutes later with Arthur Tayfield, fielding as a substitute for Funston, who hurt a leg, catching Loader on the long-on boundary off his brother's bowling. Hugh Tayfield was deservedly chaired off the field, having bowled throughout the four hours and 50 minutes on the final day, sending down 35 overs, and although heavily punished by the early batsmen, always

looked menacing. Cowdrey, finding himself running out of partners, tried attacking him, but when he gave a return catch, after staying three hours 20 minutes, the end was in sight. After a closely fought and keen struggle South Africa went into the last Test with a chance to share the rubber – an excellent effort considering they were two down after two matches.

Van Ryneveld was over the moon with this victory by 17 runs. Inspired and emboldened by the Wanderers result, he was able to lead South Africa to a 58-run victory two weeks later at St George's Park in Port Elizabeth in a low-scoring game. Clive himself managed only 24 and 13, but both contributions were valuable in small totals of 164 in the first innings and 134 in the second. But more important was the captain's enthusiasm and optimism that victory was a strong possibility.

The condition of the pitch for this match was roundly criticised by the media, both in South Africa and England. Even *Wisden* conveyed a note of censure when it said:

> Considerable controversy arose over the condition of the pitch. In order to improve it the authorities imported special soil from the Durban area. They might have learned their lesson from Pretoria where similar efforts were made to relay a pitch in two months. This time three months were allowed, but it would have been a remarkable achievement to get a Test strip ready so quickly. The result was a dead, slow pitch from which the ball kept exceptionally low from the end of the first day onwards and the number of shooters is more than one sees in a full season.

Perhaps this critical observation is justified up to a point but, to be fair, the circumstances in the fifth Test were really the same for both sides, although it is claimed that the winning of the toss was of vital importance because it gave South Africa the opportunity to bat before the pitch became thoroughly awkward. The devil in the pitch caused the ball to keep predominantly low, with the odd delivery shooting off like a rocket.

Neil Adcock, with some humour and perhaps a little relish, recalls that Trevor Bailey kept stretching forward to play the ball. This is always a good tactical counter if the ball is keeping consistently low, but on this occasion Adcock got one to fly from just short of a good length, and on its way up the ball hit Bailey's cap. Still on the front foot, and in the posture of the forward defensive, the England all-rounder looked up at Adcock, fluttered his eyelids, and with his well-known smile said, in a plummy English accent, 'Oh, I say, well bowled, old chap!'

Bailey showed his sterling qualities as a man and his unqualified fighting ability as a batsman when he top-scored in England's first innings with 41. In the second innings he contributed a hard-earned 18 out of England's meagre total of 130. Bailey was successful because he was essentially a front-foot player, whereas backfoot batsmen were at a severe disadvantage in such conditions. Apparently the faster bowlers were particularly devastating from one end. They were able to produce some almost unplayable deliveries, which meant England sorely missed one of the world's greatest opening bowlers of all time in Brian Statham, who did not play in this Test because of a foot injury. He might have dramatically changed England's fortunes. I know Clive van Ryneveld would have wished Statham no ill, but I am positive he must have been relieved that such a devastating match winner would not be hurling his thunderbolts at the Springbok batting line-up.

Adding to England's woes, Peter Loader was hit on his instep off the first ball he faced, and the bruising was so severe that he could only bowl four balls on the Monday of that game. A hamstrung Peter May could do little but wonder at the blow fate had dealt him, being robbed of Statham before the match and Loader during it.

Endean, in making 70 out of the South African total of 164, could not have chosen a better time to play his only quality innings of the series. It was a solace to this outstanding batsman to end the series with, in its own way, a match-winning innings.

Although set only 189 runs for victory, England never looked to be in the race and were dismissed for 130, allowing South Africa to tie what had been a tremendously exciting series. Tayfield, the bogeyman of the England batting throughout the series, captured a further six wickets, mainly because the batsmen went out of their way to get after him as they could not score off the fast or medium-paced bowlers with any confidence. The six for 78 off 24.3 overs pushed his wicket haul to 37 for the five Tests, a record total for a South African bowler in any series.

Van Ryneveld's success was hard earned, and the triumph of conquering the strong England team in the final two Tests was, under the circumstances, a memorable effort. Sadly the next season was to be his last, and he did not enjoy the same success. He was the automatic choice as the South African captain, but had the misfortune of seeing his side go down 3–0 to Ian Craig's Australians.

In many ways it was a fascinating series. We South Africans firmly believed we had the beating of the young tourists, but the results just as firmly burst our bubble of optimistic hope. To this day, many of the Springboks who played in that series harbour the theory that things could so easily have been different.

For the first Test at the Wanderers, Van Ryneveld was unlucky to arrive in Johannesburg with the webbing between his thumb and index finger badly split, and the selectors asked me to take over the captaincy. It was somewhat ironic.

Winning the toss I decided to bat first, and we put together a pretty solid 470 for nine wickets, declared. Goddard was most unlucky to miss what would have been his first Test century, as he batted well for his 90 before Ian Meckiff shattered his dreams of achieving three figures at last. His teammates shared in his disappointment. Johnnie Waite batted beautifully and supplied us with a bountiful 115 runs, all scored with grace and elegance, while McLean and Endean helped swell our store of runs with half-centuries.

When Australia batted they had an uphill struggle until Richie Benaud arrived at the crease: they had slumped to 62 for four and were then 177 for six before Benaud's transformation with the assistance of Bobby Simpson, playing in his first Test. But for Benaud, Australia would most assuredly have lost the match. He produced a superb innings of 122 before being caught by Peter Heine off Adcock's bowling, while Bobby Simpson fell lbw to Tayfield for a well-played 60 – an excellent Test debut.

I am convinced that if Tayfield had been in only half the form he was in the previous summer, we would have won the Wanderers Test easily, as the pitch was taking the type of spin he revelled in. But Tayfield was unable to exploit the conditions. His figures in the match proved that he was a shadow of the spin wizard of 1956/57, when his 37 wickets against England were at a cost of only 17.18 runs a wicket. Against the Australians, his 17 wickets were earned at the high cost of 37.50. He bowled accurately but his strike power had deserted him. When a man's form falls away so quickly in the Test arena, there are almost always outside reasons, and I certainly know it to be true in my case.

In Tayfield's case, he wasn't fit: he looked pallid, and it was common knowledge that he was experiencing a number of personal problems. Had he been at his peak, as he was the previous season, the outcome of the series against Australia might have been drastically different. He should have been our ace, but it did not turn out that way and his decline was a worrying factor.

Australia held out to a draw and, although honours were basically even, the Aussies were fighting an uphill battle for much of that Test. The number of rearguard actions they had in that particular game speaks volumes.

Van Ryneveld returned to captain the side in the second Test in Cape Town over the New Year of 1957/58. The match started on 31 December and ended on 3 January – disastrously for the South Africans, who lost by an innings and 141 runs. The destroyers were Benaud and Lindsay Kline, who between them had the Springboks up a gumpole with their well-controlled spin.

Batting first on the typically flat Newlands pitch of those days, the Australians amassed 449. As it turned out, winning the toss was the decisive factor: it was always the golden bonus at Newlands. Jimmy Burke and Colin McDonald gave the tourists a prolific start with a slow but most effective stand of 190, in which they wore down the Springbok bowlers over a period of four and a half hours. Burke went on to score a mammoth 189, while the luckless McDonald missed his century by only a single, caught behind the wicket by Waite off the bowling of the Western Province bowler Eddie Fuller.

Although South Africa had a sound start of 61 before the first wicket fell, only Roy McLean (38) and the skipper, Van Ryneveld (38), at number eight, managed any sizeable contributions to the first-innings total of 209. Following on, South Africa's batting was humiliated, being bundled out for a paltry 99. Benaud took five for 49 off 21 overs, and adding insult to injury Kline performed the magic by conjuring up a hat-trick with his deceptive left-arm spin out of the back of the hand – dismissing Fuller, Tayfield and Adcock with successive deliveries.

The Springboks were bitterly disappointed at the end of the Test, and captain Clive van Ryneveld was no exception. Before leaving the Newlands Test behind as a bad memory, I must comment on how the Australians had grown in confidence, with Benaud and Neil Harvey acting as the chief and constant advisors to the young skipper, Ian Craig. At one stage, when Burke was batting particularly slowly and a wicket had fallen, in strode Benaud. He called Burke over and in no uncertain terms told him that if Australia were to win this Test, Burke had better get himself into top gear. Benaud then set to work on the South African bowling with a mission in sight, and scored a swift 33.

The third Test at Kingsmead, Durban, was the one in which I scored the then slowest Test hundred in history. Although this unenviable record was later broken by a Pakistani, Mudassar Nazar, it earned me unjustified criticism from the press, who had no idea of the circumstances in which it occurred. However, I do not intend to discuss this now. Poor Johnnie Waite came in for the same cruel criticism. We joined each other with the score on 28 for two, Dick Westcott and Endean being the batsmen dismissed and a breakthrough imminent for the Australians. Waite and I went in after lunch and were still there at the close on the Saturday evening.

The next day we were hailed as the heroes of South Africa in the Sunday newspapers and by the public. But on Monday when we resumed, we went on batting painfully slowly, so by the end of play we had become the villains of the piece once again. It is an innings I would like to forget, but human nature being what it is there are many people who choose to remember only that particular innings of my career. While I am not proud of that innings, I am sometimes tempted to come up with Adcock's style of comment, a sarcastic 'Have you ever scored a Test century?' I find, however, that it is better to ignore those who are ignorant of the context.

Two incidents stand out in this partnership: the first occurred when there was a sudden round of applause and Australian wicketkeeper Wally Grout asked Waite what it was all about. Waite replied that 'it must be some kind of record'. Grout's reply came back as quick as a stumping attempt: 'It must be a long player!'

Grout was also involved in the next bit of fun when I finally reached my hundred. He walked past me at the end of the over and said, out of the corner of his mouth, 'Congratulations.'

'Thank you very much, Wally,' I replied.

'Yeah,' he followed. 'It was the worst b... hundred I have ever seen.'

My reply was equally belligerent. I inquired whether he had ever scored a Test hundred, and when he told me he had not, I told him to keep his remarks to himself until he had – and my phraseology wasn't exactly Etonian either.

Waite went on to score 134, and, although slow, it was full of classic technique, while Goddard, batting in the unaccustomed position of five, posted a well-hit 45, and the captain, Van Ryneveld, was not out on 32.

I have always felt that the selectors erred in breaking up my partnership with Goddard by bringing in Westcott. In the game before the Test, when Natal played the Australians in Pietermaritzburg, we scored 121 for the first wicket. Surely that should have convinced them we should have remained together as South Africa's Test openers? Players today complain about the attitude of selectors. They should have been around in those days when the captain had no say at all in crucial team matters such as selection and batting order. I have played in many games where the selectors contributed greatly to our defeat. Clive van Ryneveld also had this problem sometimes, but he kept his own counsel, although there must have been times when he was unhappy with teams under his command. He was selected to lead, and in those days to query selection was inviting the termination of a Test career, no matter what the quality of the talent being placed in permanent mothballs.

The Test was drawn, but will be best remembered for some fiery bowling on the first morning by Adcock and Heine. It is always something of a spectacle to see two fast bowlers operating in tandem on a lively pitch. The Australians were most uncomfortable against the pace merchants, who were getting the ball to lift alarmingly. They were bowled out for 163, with Heine taking two for 30 and Adcock six for 43, but it should be remembered that Craig had won the toss and elected to bat first. Adcock and Heine were at their fearsome best.

Wisden said of the match that we had our first chance of beating Australia in South Africa and that we were the better of the two sides in the contest, blaming our slow batting for our failure to win. But there is a lot more to it than that.

We had a first-innings lead of 221, and when they reached that target for four wickets, the match was over. Tayfield gave about his best display in the series with three for 94 in another marathon bowling spell of 59 overs; only the penetration Clive wanted from his bowlers on this occasion was missing, although he took two for 37 in 17 overs of leg-spin. The man who really frustrated us was Queensland all-rounder Ken Mackay, known throughout the cricket world as

'Slasher'. He was just as uncompromising as England's Trevor Bailey when it came to match-saving performances. It would have been nice to go to the fourth Test at the Wanderers with the series squared at 1–1, but it was not to be. That barnacle, 'Slasher' Mackay, had thwarted our optimistic hopes.

The fourth Test saw the Australians win by the uncomfortable margin of 10 wickets. Clive's bad luck with the toss continued as Craig called correctly for the third successive time, and then rubbed it in by making the most of perfect batting conditions by amassing 401. Benaud, batting at four, set it up with another cracking innings, scoring exactly 100 before becoming one of Heine's six victims. Opener Burke (81), Mackay, with a gritty 83 not out, and Alan Davidson, that great left-hand all-rounder, with 62, continued our humiliation. Heine was forced to carry the pace attack on his own for much of the innings – later being restricted by a damaged ankle – while his partner, Adcock, was confined to bed with flu. Firing together they were always good value in the cause of South Africa, and how we missed their venom in this match.

About the only worthwhile batting in our two innings at the Wanderers this time came from Ken Funston, with innings of 70 and 64, and we were bowled out for 198 in the second innings. The Aussies needed only one run, with Roy McLean bowling the only four balls of his Test career.

I have already discussed the outcome of the fifth Test, won by Australia by eight wickets, giving them the series 3–0 and sadly bringing the curtain down on Clive van Ryneveld's Test career. He scored 26 and five at St George's Park, ending sixth in the South African batting averages with 21.4 from seven innings. And despite the drubbing we were given, he remained cheerful and enthusiastic, doing his best to keep morale at a high level. He was to be admired.

The major factor in Australia's success was Benaud, who had made gigantic steps both as a batsman and bowler. During the tour he captured 90 wickets, 30 of them in the Tests, taking five wickets in four innings, as well as scoring two centuries. Throughout the series he was a prickly thorn in the side of Clive van Ryneveld and his Springboks, while 'Slasher' Mackay presented the other headache for the South African captain. Mackay had the astonishing average of 125.00 from seven innings, with a top score of 83, all boosted by four not outs. Ian Craig captained well and his side just clicked, slotting together like a jigsaw. To us it was 'a turn-up for the books'.

I often doubt whether we realise the greatness of our sportspeople, because many would rather remember the defeats and negatives than concentrate on the positives. As an example I take the captain in question: Van Ryneveld, one of the most brilliant fielders South Africa possessed. He bounced around the field like a rubber ball. I saw him dive and catch a ball with his left hand that was speeding past him in the short gully position; and woe betide anyone who hit the ball near him in the covers, mid-wicket or in any other area where he lurked. Risking a single to him was a perilous decision.

In this day of television cameras and vast media coverage, Van Ryneveld would be considered a sensational fielder. He would have packed them into the grounds for Test matches; and while not linked with other great fielding names, he was right up there with them in skill.

His leg-spinners, while not always accurate, were nevertheless the genuine article. He was not your average common or garden roller variety, but he gave the ball an authentic 'tweak', and on a responsive, turning pitch, was capable of delivering that mystical, unplayable ball. He gained a place in the touring side to England in 1951, when he took nine wickets in one innings during the trial match held at Kingsmead. I believe he would have secured a place even without this performance, such was his natural versatility and all-round ability. Posterity should remember him in his proper place and not categorise him as just another talented all-rounder.

When Clive retired from the provincial and Test scenes, he entered the world of politics for a while and was later elected to the House of Assembly. He also gained admission as an advocate to the Cape Bar. Interestingly, he wrote occasional letters to newspapers on the subject of South Africa and international cricket links. One was to the *Daily Telegraph* in 1961. By now South Africa held only observer status at the ICC because of our departure from the British Commonwealth. In brief, the letter appealed for South Africa's readmission as a member of the Imperial Cricket Conference (changed in 1965 to International Cricket Conference, and in July 1989 to International Cricket Council). There was careful reasoning behind Van Ryneveld's letter. The eminent cricket writer EW Swanton had suggested in an article that the South African Cricket Association declare itself 'in favour of including non-white cricketers in national teams on merit and of matches against non-white countries'.

Van Ryneveld said he would welcome such a statement from the SACA, because it would assist the ICC over the troubled question of South Africa's membership readmission, and would have the support of the majority of cricketers in the country. Nevertheless he felt there was an inherent danger in making such a declaration. He warned that it would invite government action to stop the interracial sporting activities that were quietly developing.

It took another 30 years before the game was totally normalised under the banner of the United Cricket Board of South Africa and membership of the ICC restored.

JACKIE MCGLEW 6
The Little General

By Trevor Chesterfield

Memories of burnt-out summer days long past leave a few faded impressions of fine innings set against the varied backdrop of Test arenas. Two of those blazing hot days that are entrenched in the mind recall the powder-blue canopy of an early autumn day at Wellington's Basin Reserve, where a buzzing crowd watched Jackie McGlew score an undefeated 255. It was an innings that stencilled his name in the annals of all-time South African Test records. It was also one of the great comeback innings.

After a month's inactivity caused by a broken finger, McGlew, the team's vice-captain, was back in the side for the first Test against New Zealand. It had been a frustrating month, too: he had sat, perturbed at his inactivity, in the pavilion at the Melbourne Cricket Ground, while South Africa recorded that famous fifth Test triumph. Then, uncertain of his form, he was pushed into the side for the game against New Zealand in Wellington.

Yet for the tourists, the visit to New Zealand, even after the successful 1952/53 tour of Australia, was not always the comfortable cruise it seemed to be. McGlew had already sat out the four games played between the Melbourne triumph and near-disaster in Christchurch against Canterbury, before his re-emergence in the first Test in Wellington. At Lancaster Park in Christchurch, in the second game of the New Zealand leg, Jack Cheetham and Anton Murray rescued the South Africans in a partnership against lively Canterbury bowling, which underwrote the touring party's success. In the pavilion Jackie watched, an anxious bystander, as the top order collapsed. At a decidedly uncertain 155 for eight, the fickle finger of fate hovered over the New Zealand tour. But, along with Michael Melle, the tail-enders added 201 runs in a timely rescue act. Murray had joined Cheetham and the tall schoolmaster – later to become the first headmaster of St Alban's College in Pretoria – put together his first century of the tour. The match saved, the team moved to windy Wellington for McGlew's date with destiny.

From the first game he ever played, Jackie McGlew applied himself in the same dedicated, astute manner and with the bulldog discipline that underpinned his playing career. But this is true of anyone who became addicted to the game as a mere four-year-old. For years his mother had a picture of him holding a bat about three or four sizes too big for the future South African captain, the chunky face staring at the camera and the bowler with an expression of great determination.

Those early years were not easy for the McGlew family. Jackie and his brother Robin, also a victim of cancer some years before Jackie, virtually grew up fatherless, and only when he started going to Maritzburg College was there a stepfather to encourage them. Gerald Fender, born in the Pudsey area of Yorkshire, home of those great opening batsmen Sir Leonard Hutton and Herbert Sutcliffe, fanned the bright flames of interest in the game. 'Test' matches were played with Robin and a few friends in the street outside his mother's Pietermaritzburg home. The World War II years also meant shortages, but his early days at Merchiston Preparatory were important in his development as a batsman. He made the first side by the time he was in Standard 3, and captain the last two years. He spread his sports interests as the school's first rugby team's vice-captain, and was an above-average middle-distance runner, twice coming second in the marathon event. He achieved this despite suffering two serious illnesses and enduring 12 months of inactivity. He overcame diphtheria and a bout of rheumatic fever that left him with a mild systolic murmur of the heart. Yet so eager was he to win the marathon that he trained for it secretly in the back garden. His dog helped him in his clandestine training sessions. They ran around the fruit trees, out of sight of Jackie's mother. The boy had worked out that he could spend enough time at this exercise in the afternoons after school to cover the same distance as the marathon. He continued this exercise for several weeks, gradually improving his stamina and confidence. He came second in the open marathon. In his last winter at Merchiston he was vice-captain of the rugby side, a sport he flirted with enough at senior club level after leaving school to be included in two Natal rugby trials.

It was as captain of the 1947 Natal Schools side at the annual Nuffield Week that McGlew won his first honour. Leading a side was the envy of any school captain. Including McGlew, there were five future Test caps: Trevor Goddard from Durban Boys' High School, and the Hilton College quartet of Roy McLean, Mike Melle, Johnnie Waite and Brian Pfaff. Pfaff went on to play cricket and rugby for Western Province, as well as earning himself an international rugby cap. Jackie felt firmly, however, that Pfaff should have been a double international, such were his batting credentials in those years.

Jackie's 1948 Natal Schools side again contained Waite, also capped by South African Schools in Port Elizabeth that January, and later an important member of the 1952/53 side Down Under, who played in the epic Basin Reserve match.

As it was, the South African side for the first Test against Merve Wallace's Kiwis was not easily settled. There was still a view in the South African camp that McGlew should sit out the game at the Basin Reserve and wait another few days until the second Test in Auckland. The debate over who would open the innings with Waite topped the list, with Cheetham and manager Ken Viljoen feeling that McGlew's fielding would be a bonus.

'We did have a lot to consider as most of the players were tired after the long tour of Australia,' was Jackie's comment on that selection meeting. 'We had actually drawn a series against the uncrowned world champions of the day. A lot of people are inclined to forget that now, just as they forget that the Australians had thrashed the West Indians the season before and England before that.'

Even today, the achievements of the fine sides of the 1960s and those since the end of isolation are inclined to overshadow the success of the 1952/53 team, which drew a series against a side that had not lost a series since the infamous bodyline tour, designed to curb the batting brilliance of Sir Donald Bradman, 20 years before. Ray Lindwall and Keith Miller were bogeymen to haunt any touring side. Indeed, it had been suggested that the tour should not take place at all, with critics in South Africa and Australia saying that financial fiasco loomed. It was a side selected under controversial circumstances (as were all sides in those days), lacking a strike bowler with Cuan McCarthy being overlooked. In a show of faith the South African Cricket Association stuck to its decision to send the side on a 'learning experience'. Yet it must also be said that there was a vast difference in strength between the Australian team of 1952/53 and the sides Bobby Simpson led to South Africa in 1966/67 and Bill Lawry brought over in 1969/70. The bowling attacks under Simpson and Lawry were inferior by international standards, resulting in South Africa winning seven of the last nine official Tests they played before international isolation shut the South Africans out for more than 20 years. Since their return, South Africa's record against all teams but Australia and England has been one of remarkable improvement.

There is much about the Basin Reserve match to remember. But it takes some of the players involved, like Bob Blair, the New Zealand fast bowler who at the age of 20 made his Test debut, and Jackie, to rekindle the memories and other facts of that particular game. Jackie's polished efforts were watched by a rookie leg-spinner from the spartan comfort of a wooden bench, and it was carefully noted how he handled left-arm spinners Tom Burtt and Alex Moir, and how he moved out to meet them. Leg-spinners and left-arm spinners have one thing in common in that they move the ball away from the bat. On that day Jackie's textbook artistry, perhaps more artisan than stylish, came into play, and his ability to handle the spinners was a clear example of this skill.

To some Jackie McGlew was a dour batsman, or what they call a 'safe anchor', while Ken Funston and Roy McLean were the strokeplayers, or the fashion artists of the trade. Only on that first day both were out early in their innings: Funston went for two, bowled by Eric Fisher, and McLean bowled by Blair through the gap between bat and pad.

'I was young and eager in those days, and hadn't quite learnt the art of conserving my speed or energy,' said Blair, whose initial burst on his Test debut was three for eight off 10 overs. 'All I saw was a new batsman and I wanted his wicket; that was the big prize.'

From the start of his innings McGlew had to bat carefully, yet remain ever purposeful and vigilant as he gathered his runs. He was like a clucking hen accumulating a batch of eggs, ever mindful of danger, with his injured finger. Occasionally he took the bottom hand away from the bat at point of contact, the top hand sliding down the handle to guide the stroke if the ball hit the bat with force. With the ball coming onto the bat slowly because of the spongy surface, he was able to do this without worrying about excessive jarring of the injured finger, especially when facing Blair, bowling mostly downwind from the Newtown (south) end of the cramped ground. There were also pushes into the on-side gap, or drives, usually along the ground with the ball finding gaps in the field.

There was a correctness about his batting many a young hopeful would have done well to copy, but never imitate; for, as Sir Donald Bradman often said, imitation leads to technical errors, and such usurpers of method and style are quickly sorted out as flaws creep into their technique.

McGlew, the 'Little General', body always in position and bat behind the line, always seemed to know where his legs were in relation to the stumps. This is a fundamental basic so often forgotten by today's willow wielders, brought up on a diet of one-day games where the line of attack is all too often directed at the leg-stump to curb strokeplay. Jackie's general balance showed that he was always ready to defend when he had to, but generally it was an innings where he attacked as much as he possibly could. There were few false strokes, but on the second day, after weeks of inactivity, a tiring body forced him to commit an error at 179, and a catch was grassed. Twenty runs later he edged a well-angled Blair delivery into the hands of all-rounder Eric Fisher at wide leg-gully, only for the fieldsman to carpet this chance as well.

At that point Anton Murray, his partner, tapped the toe of his bat in annoyance at the rashness of the stroke, and advanced down the pitch to talk to his shorter partner, telling him to look at the scoreboard and remember that a score of 200 reads far better than 199. His sober comment prevented any over-adventurous carelessness that could have led to the downfall of a monumental achievement in terms of South African Test history. Years later, Jackie admitted that the Eastern Province all-rounder's remarks were opportune: 'He brought home to me the importance of being more responsible and putting the needs of the side above my own. You are inclined to think differently when you haven't had a bat in your hand for so long. It gets like that; you want to score as many runs as possible to make up for those chances you have missed, and build your confidence after so long away from the crease.'

McGlew also remembers the trouble the Springboks were in when Murray joined him at 238 for six; a small recovery after the team had again stuttered along to 189 for five. It is always easy to hide the cracks in an innings of 524 for eight, declared, and to forget the often untidy middle passages that led to such a commanding score.

'The Kiwis,' McGlew regularly argued, 'always had fine bowlers before Sir Richard Hadlee came along.'

Blair, in his Test debut, had four for 98 off 36 overs, showing as always that he was a quality bowler. There was some untidy fielding on the first day of the Basin Reserve Test, which let the New Zealanders down. And there were errors in selection, too. Fisher, an all-rounder, who had had a fine season for Wellington in the short Plunket Shield series, was preferred to either Matt Poore or Tony MacGibbon for the Test, because of his ability to cleverly use the wind with left-arm swing bowling at the Basin Reserve. While Fisher was at the peak of his career, the selectors admitted their mistake and, looking ahead to the tour of South Africa the following summer, brought back Poore and MacGibbon for the second Test at Eden Park.

While not all Jackie's innings during his career were played with the same authority as the one in Wellington during those balmy March days of 1953, few were as rewarding. Psychologically the Basin Reserve innings was of profound importance: it was a signpost for the future. Failure at Wellington would have been easy to take, but success and the desire to see the side well on the way to victory was of paramount importance. Yet the undefeated 255 in Wellington – the record Test score by a South African until Graeme Pollock's 274 at Kingsmead, Durban in 1969/70 – was a cameo of his own life, which was moulded to be one of his country's finest sportsmen. Pollock's score has been surpassed by Daryll Cullinan (against New Zealand in 1999) and Gary Kirsten (against England in 2000), with innings of 275. Cullinan was not out when Hansie Cronjé applied the declaration.

As Cheetham's tour deputy in 1952/53, McGlew had been eager to show his ruthless streak against the Australians, whom he admired greatly, since they played the game with the same toughness. Yet his capabilities as a Test captain were recognised early on in his career: former South African captains Alan Melville and Dudley Nourse commented on his astuteness and his handling of the Natal and South African Schools teams in 1948. They recognised him as a high-quality player, a thinker whose strategies often ran counter to Cheetham's own train of thought, and a fitness freak who slaved away religiously at tough preseason training schedules.

Make no mistake, McGlew deserved the grudging praise, and later the recognition as South Africa's best Test captain in the pre-isolation era, as well as being placed above his mentors Melville and Nourse in the all-time, pre-unity Natal side. Such tributes do not come easy, especially in the more hard-boiled, cynical era in which we now live. Yet McGlew's record speaks for itself. His long run of success as Natal's greatest captain, with 75 matches to his credit between 1951 and 1966, is an example of his consistency in maintaining the high level of playing skills that enabled Natal to win the Castle Currie Cup season after season. And few will remember that there was a chance that McGlew, and not Cheetham, could have led that highly successful South African side in Australia.

As part of the 1951 England tour plans, a game was organised for Kingsmead in March 1951 to select the side, with the respective teams led by Nourse and Eric Rowan. At the time, McGlew was the least fancied of the six opening batsmen used in the trial; what turned that around was his innings of 138. For one thing, it convinced the national selectors that he was fulfilling the promise first noticed when leading South African Schools in 1948. (Nourse later denied that he had anything to do with his selection, but he did show his pleasure when Jackie's name was announced in the touring party.) It was not that he was a fresh face just out of school. Already there had been three summers as a provincial opening batsman, being drafted into the Natal side a few days after leading SA Schools against Eastern Province; but after a steady, if moderate, performance against Free State at Kingsmead, he was brought back to terra firma with a duck in his first club outing. It was not his first failure, and it certainly was not going to be his last minor setback. Take that first tour of England: his first three innings were ducks, one a first-baller in a warm-up game at Maidstone when he was the victim of England Test all-rounder Bill Edrich.

His fourth innings of the tour was against Glamorgan, batting at number three, and the three failures ran through his mind as he went out to bat. He was determined to get off the mark, having been delayed for three hours by a profitable partnership between Rowan and Waite. Psychologically he was torn between the desire to get among the runs and not to lose his wicket early on. At the age of 22 he was a mere yearling in the cauldron of the first-class game, yet mature enough to bat with an outer calm that surprised his teammates. However, his inner turmoil wound him up tightly at times. The result was a satisfying innings of 110. The 'Little General' was back in action, a little happier with himself, but mindful of the pitfalls that are so much a part of batting. Cricket is, after all, a team game, played by individuals in which one performance can turn the batsman, bowler, fielder or wicketkeeper from hero into villain several times over during the progress of a game.

The next tour match, against Gloucestershire, taught Jackie the ever-important lesson of accepting the umpire's decision, even in highly unusual circumstances. Still hungry for runs after the century against Glamorgan, he took out the strokes still in their textbook wrapping and reeled off a highly polished 90. Then he was trapped lbw by the tall off-spinner John Mortimer, who later played for England, with the ball hitting him on the buttocks. This brought an appeal from the bowler and wicketkeeper, and when he looked up, Jackie saw the umpire's raised finger. He looked at his feet and at the wickets, then back up the pitch to see the umpire unmoved by this silent remonstration. So he walked back to the pavilion shaking his head, and shaking it again as he passed the umpire.

He sat down in the dressing room, totally satisfied with his innings and the way it had been put together. As he looked up, the huge frame of Dudley Nourse burst through the door. Instead of a 'well done' or 'hard luck' comment, he received a severe rebuke from his captain for his display of churlish behaviour. The next time Jackie showed dissent at an umpire's decision, Nourse informed him, 'you will be on a ship back to South Africa via China, and I'll make sure that you get back after we do'. (That would also have meant the end of his Test career.)

Yet Nourse was also quick in his praise of his young understudy. As soon as he returned from the battles of the 1951 tour, Nourse retired. The thumb damaged in the Trent Bridge Test had forced this great South African batsman to pack away his kit. When asked who he felt should take over, he unhesitatingly recommended Jackie, which surprised most critics as it had long been thought John Watkins would get the job. He was six years older than Jackie, but his decision to miss the 1951 tour of England was probably a contributing factor. During this tour, McGlew's growing knowledge of the game often showed. Nourse had been so impressed by him that he could give unqualified backing to the young student of the game. 'You don't have to look further than Jackie McGlew,' he told the Natal selection committee before the start of that summer's campaign. 'He should be your next Test captain as well.'

And what a start to the 1951/52 season: 186 off the Western Province bowlers at Alexandra Oval, with Cheetham getting a good eyeful of solid batting technique from either the slips or mid-off. It was a record score for a Natal captain on a debut. But as Jackie (and Bert Sutcliffe) once said, they did not think in terms of records in those days. It is also true of most of today's players; record partnerships, individual scores and bowler performances are merely extra material with which writers embellish their stories, and to give readers examples of how to judge an exceptional performance. It was only later in the season that it was suggested Jackie might indeed captain the side to Australia and New Zealand.

At the time he was only 22, yet light years ahead of others his age as a thinker of the game, and had shown remarkable qualities in leading Natal to the Currie

Cup title that season. It was said that Jackie's field settings for Hugh Tayfield had much to do with the then 24-year-old off-spinner heading the 1951/52 Currie Cup bowling averages: 39 wickets at 19.38. Some years later Tayfield said that the 1951/52 season had given him a 'whole new direction'. It has always been a contentious point, but there is little doubt that without the McGlew influence, Tayfield might not have been such a success in Australia on the 1952/53 tour.

Perhaps because the tour turned out to be such a success, it is often forgotten that some believed Eric Rowan should have captained the side. Jackie even felt that 'in those conditions, he would have made a packet of runs'. But the older Rowan was out of favour and overlooked 'for reasons other than cricket'. The 1951 side in England was divided into Nourse and Rowan camps, and the situation was exacerbated by the notorious sit-down strike at Old Trafford. It added to the friction within the camp, and later the SACA became involved in a court case with Rowan. The po-faced establishment could not afford to have 'that particular man on tour at any price'. This was confirmed by reports of the case between Rowan and the SACA. Another factor forgotten in the mists of time is that the SACA were footing the bill for the Australian tour (funds were supplied by several benefactors), and it was only on the Saturday of the fifth Test in Melbourne that Ken Viljoen, the manager, could afford to smile. Not only was the tour paid for, there was a handsome profit at the end of the New Zealand leg as well.

The following summer Jackie led Natal in a couple of friendlies when New Zealand, under the captaincy of Geoff Rabone, made their first tour of South Africa. Depth being what it was, the Kiwis were not considered too strong: certainly no match for the South Africans, but capable of an upset and even causing a scare or two if they had held their catches. For Cheetham it was a 4–0 success, the first home triumph in a series, and for the Kiwis it was a learning experience.

If anything, the tour is remembered for Bert Sutcliffe's marvellous batting at Ellis Park on a fiery pitch on Boxing Day 1953, when Neil Adcock, in only his second Test, sent two batsmen to hospital. The Ellis Park game, eventually won by South Africa by 132 runs, saw the left-handed Sutcliffe flay Hugh Tayfield. Felled by an Adcock delivery before he had scored, the left-hander, head swathed in a bandage, returned from the hospital to put together one of Test cricket's most remarkable performances. In an innings of 80 he hit seven sixes, the runs coming off 106 balls. Several glasses of whisky were lined up for him to knock back as a way to dull the throbbing pain. It was also an innings that saw Sutcliffe become the first New Zealander to score 1 000 Test runs. With a grieving Bob Blair, who had lost his fiancée, Nyree Dawn Porter, in New Zealand in the Tangiwai rail disaster, Sutcliffe added a remarkable 33 for the last wicket.

The other feature of the tour was the draw at Newlands, with John Reid scoring 135 and John Beck, run out on 99 in his Test debut, helping the tourists to a then

New Zealand record aggregate of 505. Rabone's spin and seam mix then earned him six for 68 in 37.7 overs (they were eight-ball overs in those days), and the New Zealanders forced a team to follow on for the first time in their Test history.

It was obvious that the South Africans were too strong for Rabone's men. Adcock, then only 22, made his debut in the first match of the series at Kingsmead, with a string of hostile contributions. The New Zealanders had fine bowlers but, Sutcliffe and Reid apart, lacked batsmen with skills and technique. Yet the bond between the two sides was so close that they went everywhere together and exchanged gifts at Christmas; in most cases the friendships lasted a lifetime for players in both camps.

However, South Africa's fine fielding standards remained, although Adcock at times found it hard to match up to the unerring demands. One indication of just how good the levels were is Jackie's own comment that while technical excellence and skills have improved the modern game, the fielding of the South Africans from 1952/53, right through to 1955, was on a par with today's sides at limited-overs level.

During the 1955 tour, Jackie began to assert more authority as captain than he had done in the previous two series. Against New Zealand he had been an unofficial vice-captain (none was appointed for the series), while Down Under he led the Springboks around Australia for a month after Cheetham was injured in a match in Adelaide. It was initially claimed that the famous fielding techniques of the 1952/53 side were moulded around a plan devised by Cheetham and manager Viljoen as one area where they were ahead of the Australians. While Jackie, because of his role as the team's vice-captain, does lay some claim to the fielding thesis formula, it emerged in 1988 while in conversation with Waite and Roy McLean – and was confirmed by Jackie – that it was the players themselves who put the plan into action through their hard work during those first days in Perth. It can also be said that the plan was based on a fielding thesis devised by Jackie during the winter of 1952. He had written to Dr Danie Craven at Stellenbosch seeking advice about keep-fit exercises, and by return post received six foolscap pages of callisthenics and a lot of good wishes. They helped Jackie all right, as did the surya namaskars, or hatha yoga [physical yoga] or, in simple terms, exercises. This required about 50 pendulum-type exercises every day, which the future Test captain admitted were 'very hard at first'.

Leading South Africa to successive victories in the third and fourth Tests over England in the 1955 series did much to enhance Jackie's credentials as South Africa's captain for the matches against England in 1956/57. He was forced to take over from Cheetham, whose chipped elbow in the second Test at Lord's left Jackie with a similar role to the one he had played in Australia. But in 1955 the 'Little General' not only led the tour averages, he was also the leading run-scorer with 1 871 at 58.46 (20.36 better than McLean, the next best in both aggregate and averages), and topped the South African Test averages (476 at 52.88 from 10 innings, which was almost double the next best South African, Waite's 265 runs at 29.44). He scaled run-making levels during the tour that placed him above anyone else in the side, with five centuries: 161 twice, the first against Leicestershire and the second against Kent, along with Test scores of 104 not out in the third match of the series at Old Trafford, Manchester, and 133 in the fourth at Headingley, Leeds, when he was captain in Cheetham's absence. South Africa won both Tests. At the other end of the batting scale, he faced only three balls at Lord's, where he bagged a pair: twice the victim of Brian Statham, a rare error in an amazing run-making credit balance.

In 1955 his batting and his captaincy earned him a place on a rather special roll of honour, as one of the five cricketers of the year in the 1956 edition of *Wisden*. 'To England's bowlers he became a solid, unflinching and likeable opponent,' and was likened to Bruce Mitchell and Eric Rowan, as much for his ability as his approach. And while he rarely approached such batting mastery during the remainder of his career, he was, as yet, untested as a Test captain. Among the gallery of stars who were conferred with the player of the year (1955) 'knighthood' were legendary fast bowler Frank Tyson, the classy off-spinner Hugh Tayfield, and the former chairman of the International Cricket Council, Sir Colin Cowdrey. (Later to become Lord Cowdrey of Tonbridge.)

If England 1955 was Jackie's summer of glory, those of 1956/57 and 1957/58 in South Africa were seasons of tribulation, some of it self-induced because of an eagerness to lead his country. Always aware of the problems players faced with regard to physical fitness, and always alert to the needs of the 'team above all', he faced a terrible moment of truth on the eve of the first match of the series against Peter May's side, when he was finally forced to withdraw from the match at the Wanderers. Before that game, however, he had struck a moral blow by leading the South African XI to victory over the MCC side at the most unlikely venue for such a major game, Pretoria's ugly edifice to sports fame, Loftus Versfeld. The pitch had been laid at the end of the rugby season, only three months before, and by all accounts was unfit for a club game, let alone a match of this nature. It had, in technical terms, a loose surface, and was bare, dusty and slow, giving the spinners much sideways movement throughout. This made scoring difficult, but ensured a triumph for Tayfield's off-spin: 12 wickets for 83 with a remarkable second-innings return of 36.5-18-47-6. This was the first defeat on turf in South Africa by an MCC team, the first since 1930/31 and the first outside a Test since 1913/14.

May did not play in this historic match, for which the MCC fielded a particularly strong side. His place was filled by the vice-captain Doug Insole, who won the toss and invited Jackie to bat. Jackie's performance was typically gritty and dogged, with 41, second top score in a restless, low-scoring game, often plagued by outright acrimony. Some of it had to do with the sub-quality pitch, although the two umpires, George Fitzpatrick and George Hawkins, were later unfairly criticised by Insole for their role in the 'walk-off incident' over the interpretation of the playing conditions agreed on before the match. As it transpired, it was Insole who was wrong.

During a function for the team hosted by the British Embassy, the MCC team manager, Freddie Brown, confided in a local official, Arthur Grace, that it was his and Insole's view that the pitch had been deliberately prepared to help the spinners. This in turn gave rise to a vague suspicion that the South Africans were cheating. There is no doubt that Insole was also decidedly miffed at leading the first MCC team to be beaten in South Africa for more than 40 years.

With the first Test only 13 days away, the MCC's defeat was psychologically disastrous for their build-up to the opening game of the series at the new Wanderers. Also, it was soon realised by the tourists that Tayfield would, despite Adcock and Peter Heine, be the key bowler in the South African attack. And so he proved to be, with 37 wickets, playing a major role in sharing the series 2–2. Suddenly the tourists, who had swept through the country on their march to Pretoria unchecked, looked vulnerable and edgy as Jackie exploited the pitch conditions with cunning field placings to Tayfield's bowling. The MCC were a shaky 90 for eight, seeking a total of 147 to win at the close of the third day, when Jackie ran off the field to consult Insole, seeking the agreed extra 30 minutes in a bid to finish the match. The not out batsmen Trevor Bailey and Tony Lock followed him. There was some confusion as to whether eight or nine wickets had to be down in the fourth innings for the extra half-hour to be claimed.

It was at about this point that May arrived, and with manager Freddie Brown agreed that McGlew's interpretation of the playing conditions was correct, and that the match should continue for an extra 30 minutes that third day. A disgruntled Lock and Bailey resumed, with Lock complaining of Jackie's shadow on the pitch as the acrimony spilled over. He moved from silly mid-on to a wide silly mid-on, and still Lock grumbled about the shadow. In the end he took up position at a very wide silly mid-on to Lock who then, to his chagrin, drove a catch straight to Jackie. Had he said nothing Lock may have survived, but he failed to score and stormed off.

May's comment, made years later, was that there had been ambiguity in the playing conditions, but that the MCC side had not been blameless and 'we [the side] did not perform to the greatest credit'. The gentlemanly Cambridge University graduate must have been more than vexed at what he felt was a transgression, by his own high standards, of cricket's civilised code of conduct. It seems he read his own private riot act to all members of the side, making it pretty clear that he would not tolerate a repeat of the Loftus Versfeld incident.

Bowled out for 107 and 109, the MCC were a sorry bunch as they left a dusty Jacaranda City for Durban. Yet Ken Funston's technical brilliance, which saw him score 55 for the top score of the match, lingered for some, the selectors included.

Jackie was named captain for the series, a particularly singular honour after being vice-captain in three series to Jack Cheetham. He would be the first to admit that he erred by not telling the selectors of his injury problems, a displaced clavicular bone and a torn cartilage, before the series started. It was to cost him dearly. There was a lot of unease about the effect his withdrawal from the team at the Wanderers would have on the side's preparation for such an important game as the first in a Test series.

Clive van Ryneveld took over at the Wanderers, which drew a South African record 100 000 spectators over the five days. The match was won by England by 131 runs. But Jackie was back for the second Test, at Newlands over the New Year, to captain his country for the first time at home. However, the game was hardly an hour old when he realised he had made a serious mistake in playing, and he contributed only 14 and seven in his two innings. South Africa's batting failed abysmally a second time in the second innings – 72 all out with the first 'handled ball' dismissal recorded in a Test. Russell Endean was the culprit.

So what should have been a summer to remember ended in frustration and disappointment, with Van Ryneveld rightly retaining the captaincy for the following season's series against Australia. However, the all-rounder, carrying an injury, missed the first match at the Wanderers, with Jackie in the caretaker role. It was in this drawn match that Jackie and Trevor Goddard scored a record 176 first-wicket partnership against Australia.

Throughout this Test series, and the first two Tests against England in 1960, South Africa's batting weakness was their second-innings performances. Anything above 150 was regarded as a miracle, anything less than 100 a regular event. At Newlands circumstances were slightly different in the second Test, with left-arm spinner Lindsay Kline, who employed the clever use of the off-break as well as the googly (or the chinaman), taking a hat-trick to wrap up the South African innings for 99, snapping up three for 18 in 10.4 overs. It was with this in mind, and the appeal from the manager for occupation of the crease, that Jackie and his new partner Dick Westcott opened the innings at Kingsmead. Recalling the game, Jackie had firm views on what had happened:

> When we went into bat, about half an hour before lunch on the second day, we had bowled out the Aussies for a low score. We then lost two quick wickets: Dick Westcott, bowled off the inside edge by Gaunt without scoring, and

Russell Endean, snapped up by Simpson off Benaud just before lunch. We were then two for 28, not at all a good position.

I remember as Johnnie Waite and I went out to resume, Ken Viljoen, our manager, said to us that occupation of the crease was all-important. We did just that for the rest of the day. The next day we were the heroes of South Africa in the Sunday papers. But by Monday afternoon, we were the villains of the piece. I must admit it's an innings of which I'm not too proud – then the slowest test century in history. It seems to be all that some people want to remember of my career.

As it turned out we were eventually blamed for costing South Africa the Test. Yet, if the truth was known the pitch was starting to wear, and I pleaded with Clive [van Ryneveld] to bowl himself and Hugh Tayfield. He did, but it was then too late. I am convinced that had he brought himself and Hugh on a lot earlier we would have had the Australians in a lot of trouble.

Although South Africa was favoured to win the series, the Australians, under Ian Craig, developed so much on the tour that they ended up 3–0 victors. The tour result was more a reflection of how South Africa played than of the performance of the visitors, who became a far better all-round side. Also, Richie Benaud emerged as a force behind the Craig throne in the Australian dressing room. As Trevor Goddard explained, the Benaud factor was particularly strong: he was an aggressive, positive leader. He had been disappointed at being passed over for Craig, but accepted it. Conrad Hunte, that delightful West Indian batsman with his warm, engaging smile, was bitterly disappointed when Gary Sobers was preferred; at the time he refused to accept the lesser role. Yet he grew to accept the secondary position, as did Jackie with Van Ryneveld.

'It is often so hard to know that there are those who feel you do not quite match up to what they are looking for in a captain,' Hunte said of the West Indies selectors at the time. 'Gary was all charisma as well as talent: there was greatness whether he batted or bowled or fielded. I was none of those. I knew too he needed my support.'

Jackie, in a sense, felt the same about his place in the South African team when Van Ryneveld was captain. It did not matter what his personal feelings were; he had made a mess of it and would have to wait his turn.

* * *

In the chill of a late spring morning, Worcester's famous church spire seemed to take on a pious look as the 1960 South Africans opened the fateful and troubled tour of England. It was as though the spire was sitting in judgement on a group of sportsmen beset by problems not of their own making, but of their white establishment and the hard-line Verwoerd regime. Yet, as Jackie discovered, he had added worries thrust on him on that tour.

It began long before the side flew out of Jan Smuts Airport for Heathrow. First came the selection of Geoff Griffin, which had bothered Jackie from the time he knew of the selectors' thinking. The selection of the side had sparked a serious disagreement between Jackie and Alan Melville, and added to this was Jackie's concern over the witch-hunt taking place in England against 'chuckers', no matter whether they were English, Australian, West Indian or South African. Then there was still the stench of death from the Sharpeville massacre, as a bitter political backlash to the tour gathered momentum. There were placard-waving demonstrators (the first to follow South African sports teams), and the harassment of letter writers and occasional phone calls. It was the start of a new phenomenon, the first signs of what was to face white South African establishment sports teams as the 1960s gathered pace – the first rays of an icy cold dawn leading to total isolation.

As Jackie admitted during deeply personal conversations in 1995, which revealed much, democracy in South Africa in 1960 was democracy for the whites; the blacks had no franchise. It was something that was thought about but not discussed. He agreed that his own political philosophy had also been tainted with acceptance of the government's laws. The side was an easy target for political activists because of the events in Sharpeville, which he agreed had been a reprehensible act against unarmed people.

Minutes before the squad left the international departure lounge, Jackie was quietly drawn aside and handed an envelope by the SACA secretary, Algie Frames. It contained two neatly typed sheets, which were not official SACA paper, and contained a list of what to say and what not to say at the press conference at Heathrow. Although already warned by officials from the departments of foreign affairs and the interior of 'possible negative reaction', he did not realise that the players' responses would be monitored and reported back. Equally uncertain was just who would get the reports. Jackie was shocked by the turn of events. It was supposed to be a cricket tour, not a political exercise. For the first half-hour, the first press conference centred mainly on matters other than the tour or the team. Not surprisingly there were as many political journalists as there were sports reporters and cricket writers. There was the need, though, for a diplomat to answer the political questions; at the time, however, the team were left to their own devices.

Yet Jackie and the team's manager, Dudley Nourse, had more immediate problems to deal with in the shape and form of the players selected. They were far from ideal for English conditions, and surprisingly the captain had no say at all in the side's selection, which placed him under a pressing handicap. In those years the national selectors not only picked sides without consulting the captains, but in South Africa they also made suggestions on what the batting line-up might look like.

Early in the 1959/60 season, when the selectors were looking for what he assumed would be a stable bowling attack for the England tour, Jackie wanted to hear the selectors' thoughts. His first opportunity was at the Wanderers, where the Commonwealth XI were playing a South African Invitation XI. There he sought the views of Alan Melville, the convener, Johnny Lindsay and Lindsay Tuckett. It was a friendly enough discussion, until the subject of the composition of the bowling attack came up. It was known then that Peter Heine was considering retirement, but Melville declined to ask the fast bowler that, if he were thinking of retirement, would he not reconsider because of the England tour? Melville may have been an astute captain and know a thing or two about a player's ability, but there were times when foresight was decidedly missing. It also emerged later that some of the selectors did not like Heine's frank views or bluntness.

'We'll do all the worrying about the team's selection, Jackie,' had been Melville's comment. 'All you need to do is lead the side.'

It was not what McGlew wanted to hear. England were strong in batting, and a side without penetrative bowling would suffer. Although at the time, and even years later, critics felt the bowling was fairly balanced, McGlew did not agree. There was a blend of youth and experience, but there was also some serious inexperience. Losing all five tosses in the series did little to help the team's cause; it meant they were always under pressure.

Jackie had wanted the aggressive Heine, Jackie Botten and Joe Partridge to be considered; if Heine was not available, at least consider the other two. Instead he was given Geoff Griffin and Jim Pothecary; the first had a dodgy action, and the second was inadequate to the demands made on a Test bowler.

In 1960 Jackie was held responsible for a number of players failing to be included, and faced heated criticism that should have been aimed at the selectors. While he diplomatically steered clear of voicing his opinions on who should have gone and who should not, a couple of former officials, Jack Cheetham being one, admitted that several blunders were made in the selection of the team. Apart from Heine's omission, Russell Endean was left behind because he refused to sign an undertaking that his wife would not be in the British Isles at any time during the tour, and Ken Funston was also left behind. It partly explains why the side was an ordinary one.

It is still a puzzle why Griffin went and Botten and Heine stayed at home, as Griffin had twice been called in matches before the side was announced. The first was by Des Fell, a Test umpire and former Natal batsman, at Kingsmead in a Currie Cup game against Transvaal from 20 to 23 February. The second was in an end-of-season trial match in East London 11 days later, when Arthur Kidson, a

Border umpire and cousin of the Test umpire Hayward Kidson, called him. From 7 March 1959 to 7 June 1960, umpires in Australia and England found that six bowlers infringed the wording of the law as it was at the time, in nine matches: one of them, DB Pearson of Worcestershire, was called in three games, as the word went out to rid the game of chuckers.

There is no doubt that the South African selectors erred, although it seems that they did consult the umpires on the legality of the action and were assured Griffin would pass muster; an incongruous, if not presumptuous line of thought, considering what happened later. Who were the South African umpires to say what the umpires in England would think? It was not only unfair on the team, already under pressure from a political quarter, but also on Jackie to have to confront a controversial situation alone. Griffin had passed what Melville and Nourse felt was the crucial trial when Fell had passed him in a match without comment. Jackie could not believe what he was being told an hour before the team's names were officially released.

There were problems with Nourse as well. The manager declined to go to London in the middle of the match against Leicestershire to face a committee of inquiry into the suspect action law. There were other times during the tour when Jackie had to tackle managerial duties. One was in the middle of the match against Somerset, when he had to leave the field for television and radio interviews because Nourse would not handle the growing demands made by the media. As a batsman and captain Nourse may have been one of South Africa's great players; as a manager he was a public relations disaster. There were also times when he was unapproachable, and there were mixed feelings over the growing Griffin debacle.

The 'did he or didn't he' throwing controversy simmered at the start of what turned out to be a typically damp English summer. By the time the side arrived at Lord's for the match against the MCC, Griffin had been seen and commented upon, but not called. The South Africans felt uneasy before the start of the Lord's match, although they couldn't put a finger on the reason. The Natal fast bowler was the main support backup for Neil Adcock, and the game against the MCC was seen as a trial run for the Tests, as well as an opportunity to check on Griffin's action. It was John Langridge who finally burst the bubble, and when the call came Jackie and Johnnie Waite, the wicketkeeper, were stunned by its suddenness. Langridge called him twice and Frank Lee once in the match, played from 21 to 24 May.

Langridge later claimed he would have called Griffin in an earlier game, when the South Africans played Essex at Ilford, but declined because 'of not wanting to be seen taking heed of the opinions of the spectators'. The calling at Lord's found the team's executive taking a stand in fighting the issue head-on so as not to upset the team's jolted morale. But Griffin was found to be throwing in the match against Nottinghamshire at Trent Bridge. The press contingent, because of the growing controversy, had swelled considerably for that game, so there were large numbers of 'experts' ready to add opinion to the major topic of the week. Fleet Street tabloids salivated over such a juicy issue, and even news agencies got in on the act. Everyone was more intent on what the square-leg umpire was going to do than how Griffin was going to bowl; it was all very uncomfortable and explosive on the field and in the press box.

Griffin went to Alf Gover's cricket school to have the bend and jerk in the action smoothed out, while the team's executive asked the SACA to consider sending out Heine, who had retired at the end of the 1959/60 season, but then made himself available for the tour. The SACA rejected the request for Heine, and those responsible for team selection on tour were left with no option but to carry on and hope Gover would find a magic formula to save their fast bowler. The team went off to matches in Stoke-on-Trent and Cardiff, where the Natalian rejoined them, playing against Glamorgan and negotiating the three days without undue concern from umpires Harry Baldwin and Emrys Davies. This encouraged the selectors to pick him for the first Test at Edgbaston, where Griffin bowled 42 overs without the umpires, Langridge and Eddie Phillipson, calling him. England won by 100 runs as South Africa's batting twice failed, and the limitations that were to worry Jackie throughout the tour became all too obvious.

Fleet Street howled with indignation over Griffin's selection for the first Test, but Jackie and other selectors had faith in their man and the English umpires, and felt the exercise at Edgbaston justified their gut feel about the blond bowler. Because of that success, Griffin found himself an automatic choice for the second Test at Lord's, where the umpires were Lee and Syd Buller, a couple of tough nuts in pressure situations. The queasiness some team members had felt before the MCC game returned. Lee went to square-leg and Jackie to point, and the first two overs by Griffin passed without the twitching of an eyebrow. Then at the last ball of the third over it came ... a chilling cry of '*no ball*' ricochetted around world cricket's headquarters as Lee's right arm was pushed horizontally, starkly signalling the death knell of the career of a fast bowler, while the buzz in the crowd grew and the press benches hummed. The next ball received the same treatment, and a disappointed Jackie moved to Griffin and told him to 'carry on' as he tried to cushion the blow for his teammate.

It was a tough moment for the Springbok team, but for Jackie, who had to think decisively and clearly and without displaying too much emotion, the team was his first priority. Griffin tried to smile at his captain through the numbing realisation of it all, but no one really felt like smiling. The first thing to do was for him to finish the over. When that was finished the game could continue, but in the back of Jackie's mind lurked the disturbing fear of a repeat of the incident. Griffin was later given another chance to re-establish his confidence and credibility, and the bowler did motor in speedily, getting lift and life out of the pitch.

The first day, curtailed by rain and later bad light, passed with only two more calls, but the second morning came and Lee's calling and horizontal arm signals on several occasions stung both Jackie and Griffin. In the middle of this emotional drama came the hat-trick: the first and only one at Lord's. Mike Smith was the first victim with the last ball of an over, caught by Waite behind the wicket on the tantalising figure of 99. Peter Walker was the second victim off the first ball of the next over when bowled by Griffin for 52. Griffin then castled Freddie Trueman for a duck, at which point he became airborne before collapsing into the arms of Adcock, as teammates zoomed in while the crowd roared approval for his courage and determination. He was not to bowl again in the match; in fact, it was his last official over of the tour. The short, traumatic Test career of Geoff Griffin was at an end, although the agony wasn't quite over. South Africa's batting wilted before Brian Statham's pace, lift and swing in their two innings; the accurate Lancastrian earned an impressive 11 for 97 off 41 overs, with first-innings figures of six for 63, as the heavy atmosphere suited his style of rhythm and swing.

Bowled out for 152 and 137 to lose the Test by an innings and 73 runs, Jackie agreed to an exhibition game (he referred to it as a 'buns and fizzies') to give the spectators who stayed something to remember while the South Africans waited for the Queen to pay her annual visit to Lord's. The Test was over some time before the Queen's arrival after lunch, and Jackie wanted her to meet the South Africans in front of the stately pavilion.

Sitting in the Mound Stand with the idea of getting a back view of Griffin's action through binoculars was an interesting exercise. Out came the umpires, Buller moving to square leg, like an axeman from the Tower eyeing his victim, as Griffin moved in to bowl. When the first call came most of the players knew that it was the end of the blond bowler's career. Jackie was stunned as call after call rang out. Up in the Mound Stand they began muttering, calling for the disgraceful scene to be brought to a timely end. Little did most know at the time that Griffin was the victim of circumstances, as a decision had been made to purge the game of such bowlers, and Buller and Lee were the hit men tasked with carrying out the instructions. Gubby Allen, later Sir George Allen, chairman of the England selectors in 1960, did convey in a clear message to Nourse that he thought the South Africans were 'utterly foolish' and 'doing the wrong thing in playing Griffin', adding 'I don't think you will get away with it. I know you won't.'

They did not.

On 3 November 1960, England and Australian officials announced details of an agreement on throwing as related to the 1961 Australian tour of England, giving bowlers with suspect actions a five-week amnesty. This was later rejected by the counties, who were quite happy with the tough action taken by umpires with the backing of the MCC – the custodians of the laws – to root out chuckers.

To end the mockery being made of the exhibition game, Jackie went to Buller and asked how Griffin should end the over. The umpire indicated that the bowler should do it underarm, which he did, only to earn a swift rebuke in the form of another no-ball call, this time from Lee at the bowler's end, for failing to inform the umpire (who would then inform the batsman) of his intentions.

And so ended a sad affair. For Jackie it was the final straw in a series of unhappy episodes, and he admitted some years later how the whole sorry chapter had indeed affected the team's Test performances, with South Africa failing 3–0 and the bowling attack lacking extra penetration. Jim Pothecary, always willing but rarely performing as a Test bowler, should never have won a Test cap. His bowling was an embarrassment at times.

As for Jackie's batting contributions, the series was a dismal failure with a top score of 45. But what could be expected of the man who had been given an almost impossible job as captain? His batting suffered in the Tests mainly as a result of outside pressures, for his county form was generally good. It was not the easiest of tours, yet he was recognised as being an astute and cunning captain, finding answers to near-impossible problems in the field with limited resources; often relying on his own counsel in solving tricky situations on and off the field. Little wonder he earned the reputation, starting with the two 1955 Tests at Old Trafford (Manchester) and Headingley (Leeds), of being South Africa's best Test captain. In fact, he was honoured in this respect several years ago when, during Natal's centenary year, he was voted the province's top all-time captain, ahead of Dudley Nourse, and was slotted in as opener with the great Barry Richards at three.

Jackie, as a captain, always placed a heavy emphasis on being able to lead from the front, as well as on having the respect of his players. In 1960 he had the respect of his players for the way he handled the tour issues; always looking for the positive. But it is hard to continuously lead from the front when under such intense pressure. He scored two centuries, managed only 189 runs at 21.00 in the five Tests (batting standards on both sides were generally disappointing), but he did head the tour averages with an aggregate of 1 327 at 42.80, which was something.

His last series was against John Reid's New Zealanders in 1961/62, when South Africa's selectors, at his urging, finally introduced the nucleus of the great teams to follow. There were seven new caps in the first Test of the series, shared 2–2, at Kingsmead, Durban from 8 to 12 December 1961: Eddie Barlow, Colin Bland, Harry Bromfield, Kim Elgie, Goofy Lawrence, Peter Pollock and Ken Walter. Four of them, Barlow, Bland, Elgie and Pollock, were members of the

Fezelas side, which had a highly successful tour of England in 1961. It was a trip that was designed to be an open-air classroom, only this group of talented players ended up being the teachers. Perhaps some were arrogant in the way they played, but as most of them later became world-class players, they had some right to feel that they were better than most.

In the Kingsmead Test, Jackie became only the fourth South African to carry his bat through an innings, scoring another technical masterpiece as he put together 127 not out – helping South Africa to a first-innings score of 292 and eventual victory by 30 runs for the Boks, to go 1–0 up. Bernard Tancred (1888/89), Billy Zulch (1909/10) and Trevor Goddard (1957/58) were the other three, with Goddard scoring 56 not out when Lindsay Kline took the hat-trick at Newlands and South Africa were bowled out for 99. The first three performances were at Newlands.

It was in the series against New Zealand that Peter Pollock discovered what a brilliant technical cricketing brain his captain had. In his early days Pollock was inclined to be brash, but he had every right as he was a fine specimen of a fast bowler; far better than a number of the modern breed passed off as match winners. A down-to-earth sort, warm and understanding, his knowledge of the game, like the man, has grown over the years. Although this opinion of Jackie was expressed more than a decade ago, Pollock was quoting from his book, *The Thirty Tests*.

> Maybe some of the others won't agree but I do single Jackie McGlew out as an outstanding tutor in those more formative days. Maybe he had a chip on his shoulder over certain aspects of that New Zealand tour (all of it to do with selection policies), but if you were prepared to listen and learn, there was much to be gleaned from Jackie. He was the dedicated never-say-die, lead-by-example skipper and I say it again, he taught us plenty during that series.

There was a certain amount of what is these days referred to as 'street fighting', or sledging, in the middle; an earlier era called it 'verbal fun and games', as some of the more aggressive players tried to psyche out their opponents with a variety of comments.

Also, the ghost of the Griffin episodes in England was resuscitated as Gary Bartlett, a chucker right enough and the Kiwis' main weapon, let rip at Newlands. The indignant McGlew threatened retribution for the fourth Test at the Wanderers where South Africa, with Tiger Lance making his debut, went on to win by an innings and 51 runs with about 85 minutes of the third day remaining. Neil Adcock and Peter Heine were recalled as part of the plan to subjugate the Kiwis after Newlands, and although no one knew it then, it was the last time the two pace warhorses were in action together.

It was also a Test in which Jackie made a skilful 120, top score in an innings of 464, and his last Test century, for at St George's Park, Port Elizabeth, he batted at three in the second innings and was run out for 26. His shoulder had been badly injured from a dive in the covers on the first day and had turned him into a passenger for most of the match. To Jackie's chagrin, Heine was left out of the South African side on the morning of the match for 'disciplinary' reasons. The move angered Jackie as he felt such steps were uncalled for, but the national selectors went ahead. Peter Pollock was brought back to share the new ball with Adcock, the bowler on whom he had modelled himself when a schoolboy, as a proud fast-bowling era slowly drew to a close.

Although asked if he would captain South Africa on their next pathfinding mission, to Australia and New Zealand in 1963/64, growing business commitments and personal matters forced him to reluctantly decline what would have been an emotional farewell tour. Had he gone, who knows, South Africa may have won the series in Oz, and also possibly in New Zealand. Both series were drawn.

Sport rarely produces men like Jackie McGlew. He was always there when needed, not the spectacular type perhaps, but very effective; an aggressive and intelligent captain, and for several of the teams of the 1960s, certainly the best they played under. It was his captaincy that enabled Natal to win the Currie Cup in his last season in 1966/67, a time the side was going through an important transitional process. If further proof was needed of his greatness in cricket leadership, it came the following summer when Berry Versfeld and the rest of the Natal team wanted their guide and mentor, now retired, to share the glory of winning the 1967/68 Currie Cup by inviting him to their celebratory dinner as guest speaker.

In later years when his opinion was sought by batsmen troubled about their form, or worried captains whose tactical oscillations showed a lack of planning, it was readily given but not always appreciated.

As convener of the South African Nuffield school teams at the annual Coca-Cola Nuffield Week from 1979, he saw the rise of the top cricket youth and predicted that the teams with which Hansie Cronjé and Jonty Rhodes were associated would, in time, see an upliftment in standards. What he would have made of Cronjégate and Cronjé's tragic death is another matter, as he felt that the game's creed dictates 'play it hard but play it fair'; honesty is always the best policy.

In 1992 Jackie achieved another lifetime ambition when appointed manager of the South African Youth Team to the West Indies on an historic journey: leading a fully unified South African side on a pathfinding mission. For him the Windies visit was special, as from his early provincial days he admired the great West Indies captain and batsman, Sir Frank Worrell, and in some ways the visit would be a pilgrimage to honour the great man in what was for Jackie the autumn of a rich and often rewarding cricketing life.

He gave up his Schools selection convener post after trials at Centurion Park selected a side to tour England in 1995, and he supported Khaya Majola and Anton Ferreira, then the under19 coach, for the inclusion of Paul Adams in the team. The sceptical schoolmasters were unhappy. How the trio smiled when Goggamania gripped the nation in the summer of 1995/96, nine months later, when Adams, at 18, became the youngest South African Test debutant, playing England at St George's Park in Port Elizabeth. Not one to point an accusing finger at a fellow selector, McGlew often wondered how schoolmasters viewed selection, and whether it was a matter of getting as many of their players in the side at the expense of others who later came through, while those selected failed.

'Selecting can be such a tricky business,' he said in April 1995, during the trials in which Paul Adams bowled at Centurion Park. 'You make what you think are the right choices, yet when you look at a national Test side or the South African A side, the question often arises of, "How did we miss this one?" or even "Why did we not spot this one?"' He is not one for examples, except in the case of two country players, Fanie de Villiers and the late Tertius Bosch. They had shown exceptional talent at primary school level and even at under15, but they became lost in the system, only to emerge at tertiary level. He blamed the haphazard way selection in country areas and at schools was handled in the 1970s and 1980s.

From his early association with Khaya Majola in 1992, Jackie began to understand the suffering of the less privileged players who, like the Afrikaans countrybred lads, battled to attract attention. How many Fanie de Villierses were lost, how many Makhaya Ntinis? Paul Adams was given the opportunity, but he had to go through another route to earn notice; and the schoolteachers were claiming they had wanted him in the side. Frankly, McGlew's ethic, as well as Majola's and Ferreira's, was far more transparent than that of the schoolteachers with their agendas to get in their quota of players from certain schools, whether or not they deserve selection.

What did please Jackie was an incident that occurred during South Africa's Test at Lord's in 1994. He was on his way to his seat with Denis Compton when they were waylaid by a youngster, asking them to autograph a book. It did not take long before there was a queue, and both Jackie and Compton missed the first over of the second day's play while they signed autographs. As one youngster explained, 'There were some shots of you batting on TV the other night, and it was impressive.'

From late 1996, however, there was a noticeable deterioration in Jackie's physical condition. He was a regular at matches involving Northerns at Centurion Park, and he and the author spent much time talking about the game and the way forward. Yet the pain he went through was traumatic for his wife Patricia and daughter Jacqualine. He slipped away peacefully on 9 June 1998, shortly before the Lord's Test. The South African team wore black armbands when they took the field, and Barry Richards paid a special tribute.

One lasting memory is of a flashing cut off Eric Fisher's bowling at the Basin Reserve, which brought him his double century in that first Test; it was poise and elegance and fashioned the way he liked. You can't do much better than that.

7   TREVOR GODDARD
Passion from the Pulpit

By Trevor Chesterfield

If you had asked Jackie McGlew whom he would take with him into the trenches in a Test, he would unhesitatingly have nominated Trevor Goddard. For him, the tall, spare all-rounder, now living in Cape Town, would go through a wall of fire for his side. These days Trevor spends some of his Sundays profitably healing souls and spreading compassion among his congregation, telling them about God and the importance He has in their lives. Both vocations present a compelling challenge for this disarming man, whose ability at Test level once caused widespread apprehension within the ranks of the opposition, and who in 1963/64 captured the imagination of the country as he led South Africa in a brave attempt to beat Australia Down Under for the first time.

The great all-rounder was also one of finest left-arm seam bowlers in the game when South Africa toured England under Jack Cheetham and Jackie McGlew, his Natal captain, in 1955. It has been acknowledged that it was McGlew's astuteness that won the third and fourth Tests when Cheetham was out of action as a result of a devastating elbow injury, caused by Freddie Trueman in the second Test at Lord's in light so bad, today's batsmen would have bellowed with indignation at the gloom enveloping that historic venue.

Trevor Leslie Goddard became South African captain because there was no one more qualified. After McGlew's retirement due to pressing business reasons, Goddard led a fine young side to the Antipodes in 1963/64. Packaged and labelled as Goddard's Cinderellas, the team embarked on the tour that brought fame to Eddie Barlow, Graeme and Peter Pollock, Peter van der Merwe and Colin Bland, and established Goddard as a thoughtful captain who gave the side a sense of self-belief. At first he was a buffer between players and manager Ken Viljoen, whose overt style of discipline caused early tour friction, especially among some younger members of the side who were adults and wanted to be treated as such by management. Although they respected Viljoen's cricket knowledge and his familiarity with Australian conditions, which he came to know while manager of Jack Cheetham's heroes 11 summers before, the young men of 1963/64 found his strict regimen highly irksome.

While those critical of Trevor's captaincy claim that perhaps it wasn't as skilful as, say, McGlew's, Cheetham's, or Van der Merwe's, he was given the important role of leading a side on which the foundation of the great Springbok era of the 1960s was based. This was in a sense a Natal effort in that McGlew started it in the 1961/62 series against John Reid's Kiwis, and Trevor continued the process Down Under three seasons later, as the talent nurtured under McGlew expanded their impressive playing record by drawing the series.

The youngsters under Trevor's care could not have had a better teacher, as there were few technically better equipped cricketers from whom to learn. As it is, there was no finer defensive bowler in the 1950s and 1960s, and such was his accuracy that he would have been ideal to combat batting techniques in the limited-overs games of today. Yet he was more than a defensive bowler: his technical brain rapidly analysed a batsman and told him where the errors lay. He would then, with the uncanny knack of a skilled performer, put into practice the art of taking wickets almost at will. He did that on one hot Sunday in Witbank, a Transvaal coal-mining town of rather unpleasant odours, when playing for Harlequins in a rare club match in the second half of the 1966/67 season. He took an incredible nine wickets in the first innings and six in the second, and top-scored with a clinical 78.

He was a true sportsman in that whether it was club, provincial or Test cricket, he gave 100 per cent. There was no playing only when he felt like it – if your team needed you it was a good enough argument, although at times the workload was heavy enough to make even the brave want to take it easy.

The artistry of a magnificent bowler was always in evidence that day in Witbank. Rupert Hector was, according to the all-rounder Goddard, uncertain of where his off-stump was and was comprehensively bowled, with the left-hander swinging the ball back sharply and cutting it off the seam. With three nondescript batsmen falling in rapid succession – two caught in the slips while a third was yorked – Trevor had picked up five of the nine wickets for only 15 runs off nine or 10 overs; and eight of those runs were from thick outside edges, which had eluded the sleepy gully. This particular spell of bowling from the all-rounder was an example of how an ordinary club side relies all too often on their star to win matches: he scored the bulk of the runs and took most of the wickets, and played a pivotal role in North-Easterns winning the Currie Cup B Section that season.

It has been a source of amazement that, like McGlew, Trevor has rarely been accorded the international recognition he so justly deserves. In some of the more recent books on the best bowlers, or in McGlew's case, the best batsmen, they are conveniently ignored; perhaps forgotten, as the shadows of isolation lay heavy over South African cricket for more than 20 years. This is a sad indictment, because some of their cricket is becoming a fading memory. Goddard, one of the great all-rounders of his age, is now almost overlooked for the role he played in

South African cricket during times of fecund success, particularly in the two series against Bobby Simpson's Australians of 1966/67 and Bill Lawry's 1969/70 side. While he did perform as a batsman and bowler in the rather boring 1964/65 series against Mike Smith's team, the last MCC side to visit South Africa, there was a time when the selectors, led by Arthur Coy, considered removing him as captain because they felt he lacked the flair needed to win a Test to square the series. But the overlaying criticism of those Tests was that the pitches prepared suited Smith's side rather than the Springboks. It is an old complaint, and one offered in the 1992 World Cup tournament in Australia and New Zealand for the demise of Allan Border's side. But it is not a convincing argument, as Australia were tired from having played in a madcap series of one-day games before the big event.

In the 1964/65 series, the pitches were inclined to favour the batsmen, with Fred Titmus, the England off-spinner, often creating merry havoc among the South African batsmen, especially in the first two Tests. It was in this series that Trevor finally scaled the slopes of batting success to put together his only Test century, at the Wanderers, where his 112 was scored in the South African second innings of 307 for three, declared. This was after he had scored 60 in the first innings of a Test that ended in a draw.

One of the telegrams of congratulation he received after scoring his century came from Penzance Junior School, where his cricket story really began; for it was here where he discovered that there were games other than the winter code of football, his sporting teething ring. By the time he was 11, cricket had taken its rightful place at the head of his list of sporting priorities. Although diphtheria delayed by a year his first cricket season at Durban Boys' High, he soon made his way into the senior ranks and was in the school's First XI for three of the four years he attended Boys' High. He rightfully earned places in the 1948 and 1949 Natal Schools sides, attending the annual Nuffield weeks, and in the 1949 week, held in Salisbury, he won a South African Schools cap, taking three for 62 with his left-arm spin (it was only a couple of seasons after matriculating that he switched to seam bowling), while fellow Natal teammate Arthur Tayfield had a handsome haul of six for 86 in a Rhodesian innings of 230. It was during the 1949/50 season that Jim Laker, then on a coaching mission in Durban, spoke highly of the talented left-handed all-rounder who would one day, if his skilful endowment continued to blossom, play Tests for South Africa. He did more than that.

Trevor, also a prolific run-scorer at Currie Cup level, became the first South African to score 10 000 runs and take 500 wickets. In a career of 41 Tests spread over 15 seasons – two of them in England – he is also the only South African to score 2 000 runs and take 100 wickets.

While these prosaic facts illustrate the greatness of the brilliant left-hander's 18-year career, a closer examination of the statistics places him in a small group of elite world-class all-rounders, with a batting average of 40.75 and an economical bowling average of 21.65. These remarkable figures rank alongside those of Michael John Procter, who had the benefit of a career in county cricket, and the great Aubrey Faulkner (25 Tests and 1 754 runs at 40.79 and 82 wickets at 26.58), whose mantle he rightfully assumed. Trevor would be the last person to proclaim his greatness; like Jackie McGlew he is far too modest for that. But there was no doubting his ability. His batting could be either free flowing or doggedly determined, depending on the circumstances. I remember a Currie Cup B Section match I umpired in the 1966/67 season, between North-Eastern Transvaal and Natal B, and how former Test bowler Goofy Lawrence (now living in Perth, Western Australia) grumbled at having to bowl to the tall left-hander.

'I can't bowl around the wicket to him, he knows where to put you. And look what happens when I go over the wicket.'

Goofy was a giant, said to be the tallest man to play for South Africa, a fraction over two metres, and when he brought the ball over high, the trajectory from his right arm made the ball bounce quite sharply. He had the respect of most batsmen, getting the ball to lift, but on this particular day at Berea Park the ball didn't get up enough. Although he did his best to swing the ball both ways, his natural delivery – the outswinger – was inswing to the left-hander, and Trevor, the batsman that day, had the measure of his man. He scored 51 before Lawrence finally removed him late in the day, caught by Natal B opener Trevor McDonald in the gully. This followed a remarkable display of seam bowling earlier in the day, when Trevor picked up four for 11 off 10.4 overs of tight bowling.

During this match a mix-up in names caused some hilarity in the Natal B camp, but Jim Pressdee, the North-Easterns captain, felt there wasn't much to smile about at the time. Trevor Goddard was in the slips, with Jackie Botten bowling to Trevor McDonald, while Trevor Rolfe patrolled the mid-wicket fence and I was the square-leg umpire at the time. McDonald attempted a hook, the ball skied off a top edge, the call came: 'It's all yours, Trevor!' Only *which* Trevor was a mystery, until Trevor Rolfe, realising it was him, made a mad dash to take the catch, but he started too late to take the ball and it moved away from him at right angles. McDonald found it amusing, Trevor looked at his feet to hide his smile and Trevor Rolfe was miffed at missing the catch. Pressdee was even less impressed by the series of incidents that led to the catch being grassed that Saturday afternoon. But McDonald didn't escape for too long, falling for nine, the same score he had made in the first innings, with 26 on the board.

If the man of the match award had existed in those days, Trevor would have collected it, as he followed his first-innings four for 11 with five for 64 in the second, as well as scoring a first-innings total of 51. Twice in one over he foot-faulted, and immediately rectified his run-up by moving his marker a fraction to his left. He was the ideal example of a bowler who knew what he was doing, ducking the ball both ways, looking for the edge and bowling with such accuracy that the batsman was never certain what line the tall left-hander was forcing them to play next. He always tested the batsmen, looking to see how they would react. Cricket is a sideways game where a bowler such as Trevor Goddard was always probing the off-stump or, in a sense, cleverly interrogating the batsman's reaction to his line, length, swing and cut. His knack for consistently placing the ball in the right area was the hallmark of his ever-dependable line of attack, and as such placed him in the company of brilliant fast-medium seamers such as Alec Bedser, Bill Johnston, Alan Davidson, Sir Richard Hadlee, Fred Trueman and Vintcent van der Bijl. Thus there is no explanation as to why Trevor Goddard has been ignored for so long as one of the great Test all-rounders. In a similar way Athol Rowan – brother of that stormy cricketing son of the veld, Eric – a class off-spinner from 1947 to 1951, has also been overlooked by most writers of the game. Yet in some respects Athol, whose slow ambling run was the result of war wounds from the desert campaigns, was one of the best South African spinners produced since the end of World War II. Of course, it will always be argued that Hugh Tayfield was better because of his consistency and his superior record in terms of wickets. Yet in 1947 Athol Rowan was considered the best spinner in England.

Trevor's big chance to play for Natal arrived in 1952/53 when players such as McGlew, Tayfield, Roy McLean, Headley Keith and John Watkins were in Australia with Jack Cheetham's side. This was after his transformation to a seamer as a result of his club captain wanting him to 'keep an end tight with the new ball'.

He had seen the 1949/50 Australians in action as an 18-year-old, and remembered the fluency of that fine left-hand opening batsman, Arthur Morris. Trevor's main interest in that game – Australians against a South African XI – was because his friend and schoolmate Arthur Tayfield was playing. But that 1952/53 season for Natal, where he scored a century and performed with moderate success as a bowler, was almost his last, as the return of the members of Cheetham's side found him battling for a place. He toyed with the idea of forgetting the provincial scene and concentrating on club games, because of what he felt was niggardly treatment and the frustration of playing a minor role in a particularly strong Natal side. He hardly batted, and bowled only a few overs. But McGlew, mindful of the feelings of the talented left-hand all-rounder, offered him the post of opening batsman for the Natal match against the New Zealanders. It was the start of a partnership that was both rewarding and profitable for the two, as their batting styles suited each other, to the extent that they regularly opened for South Africa, beginning with the 1955 tour of England.

But that first union against the New Zealanders gave no hint of what was to come as Trevor faced a bowling attack led by the lanky Tony MacGibbon, the prototype Richard Hadlee, who also relied on swing and cut to take his wickets. Dismissed for six and 29, he soon gained retribution by scoring 174 in a friendly against Western Province, opening the batting. In the return game against the Kiwis he found himself down the list, but batting five is as important as opening, and his 78 not out was the passport he needed to become McGlew's more regular partner.

A serious, dedicated sportsman who didn't smoke and rarely drank anything stronger than orange juice, Trevor set his own standards of excellence, which in turn enabled him to produce high levels of stamina and concentration.

For instance, at Headingley, Leeds in 1955, McGlew entrusted the finely tuned left-hander to shoulder the brunt of the Springbok bowling attack in the crucial England second innings of the fourth Test of that series. South Africa needed to win to level at 2–2, and a victory here would be unprecedented, as South Africa had never before won two Tests in a series in England. It was a bowling performance that is one of the finest in all Test cricket, and has become part of the game's folklore.

Younger generations, unable to savour the success of that fine 1955 South African team, have been fed so much of the glorious era of the 1960s that anything before would appear commonplace. But what happened on the fifth day of the fourth Test is as stunning a piece of cricket as there is ever likely to be in terms of South Africa–England rivalry in the summer game. At the start of the morning's play Peter Heine, already nursing a bruised ankle, found he couldn't bowl from the Kirkstall Lane end at all, because of the footmarks worn by the bowlers during the first four days of the Test. As it was, Neil Adcock was sidelined with a broken bone in his left foot, leaving McGlew with only three recognised front-line bowlers. It was a far from happy position. But McGlew's greatness as a captain, and Trevor's stamina and skill as a bowler, served South Africa admirably that day. McGlew was now faced with winning a match with only two front-line bowlers: Trevor Goddard and Hugh Tayfield. Great bowlers they were, two of the finest to represent the country. With Heine ruled out because he was unable to bowl around the wicket, Trevor was pressed into action at the Kirkstall Lane end, bowling over the wicket to avoid the foot holes. For a while Peter May, the England captain, batted with stirring aplomb, the first scoring stroke a boundary off Trevor that brought up the elegant May's 50 on a hot, sunny day. Batting with May was his Cambridge University blue teammate Doug Insole, and the two of them, after May's initial sword thrust to reach his 50, retired behind a defensive shield.

It was demanding cricket all right, as the batsmen worked away at gathering runs at a slow pace, waiting for the bowlers to tire. Only the South African bowlers weren't quitters. There was no talk of 'so and so pulled up that ladder and that's why we lost' in the dressing room, either. Most cricketers of that era would have been described as 'macho' today, but it was certainly no pose. A job had to be done, and the right, proper and professional thing to do was to roll up the sleeves and get on with it.

Trevor's line of attack that day was leg stump: persistently nagging, waging a battle of patience, and he won the first round when Insole, after adding 101 with May, was picked up by Headley Keith off a top-edge from a sweep shot that went wrong, with the left-armer's delivery turning sharply inwards. The ball popped up to Goddard's Natal teammate at forward short leg and gave the breakthrough the South Africans needed. The bowling was so tight to McGlew's defensive field placings that the Springbok attack placed an effective curb on the natural attacking instincts of such brilliant batsmen as May and Denis Compton, to whom England now looked for victory.

Over after over, with Percy Mansell used for a couple of overs here and there for the odd relief, Trevor Goddard and Hugh Tayfield bowled in tandem; a great partnership slowly whittling away at England's resistance. At lunch England were 204 for four – 277 were needed to win in four hours, and there was a growing view among some critics that McGlew had stretched his bowlers to the limit. It was Trevor who, brushing aside the concern of his anxious captain, said, 'I'm just loosening up, Skipper,' when fielding off his own bowling.

Four hours after his marathon spell started, Goddard's final figures read 62-37-69-5; it was one of the great bowling spells in all of Test cricket, with Tayfield returning five for 94 off 47.1. Where in today's five-day game would you find two such supermen? Measure, if you would, South Africa's bowling performance on the final day of the second Test against India at the Wanderers on 30 November 1992; India needed 303 off the now compulsory 90-overs-a-day ruling laid down by the ICC. Kepler Wessels had three front-line bowlers: Allan Donald, Brian McMillan and Craig Matthews; a fourth, Meyrick Pringle, was injured when batting on the first day, which meant pressing Hansie Cronjé into service.

McGlew had no such luxury and won.

Wessels had four bowlers, including the vaunted Donald and McMillan, and managed a forced draw, while the groan in the popular press at the time was, 'If only Pringle had been fit.'

Although the two Tests were played 37 years apart, it gives the lie to the theory that today's players are fitter, faster and more athletic, and therefore better than those of, say, 1955. In the 1955 Test in Leeds, Trevor scored 74 when opening the innings with his captain, adding 176 for the first wicket in a South African second-innings total of 500.

No wonder Jackie McGlew, when asked some years later whom he would always have a place for in his side, unhesitatingly nominated Trevor Goddard.

It was Trevor's ability to probe the batsman and test his response, as described earlier, that did much to help win South Africa the game by 224 runs with two hours of play remaining. There are few better seam-bowling sights than the left-armer's outswinger, and his uncanny employment of it that day unsettled several England batsmen who today are household names. And frankly, it is doubtful whether any modern players, Hadlee and Kapil Dev excepted, have the stamina to bowl so effectively and help win a Test to level a series, which South Africa eventually lost 3–2 to England.

Trevor was always the willing bowler to take over one end, whether in a Test, Castle Currie Cup match or even a club match, in a bid to win when there was a variety of partners at the other end. The problem is that the lower the scale of competition, the lower the standard of fielding. Too many teams rely on the skills of the superb all-rounder, and 'leave it to the pro' has become a common catchphrase in club circles. When Trevor was playing for Harlequins in Pretoria at the age of 36, and still a Test player, he was expected to bowl spells lasting two hours, and then open the batting.

Few will deny that it was mainly because of Trevor that Harlequins won the Sunday league in 1966/67 and the following summer. Some of the club players, who had perhaps stayed up too late the night before, spilled too many easy catches, especially when Harlequins fielded first. One Sunday they played in a match against Berea Park, and after a few simple slip catches were dropped, Trevor looked at the umpire, disgust etched on his sunburnt features, and raised his eyes to the cobalt blue sky.

'This is too much!' he complained, and rightly so. 'If I can't rely on these guys to catch the ball, I'm going to have to bowl this lot out.'

And that's what he did.

When the side trooped to the dressing room after the innings, he asked for the door to be closed and, looking round the room, shook his head. 'I've had enough of dropped catches and shoddy fielding from you guys. That's it. You can leave me out in future,' he said.

There was an embarrassed silence in the dressing room as George Hawkins and his fellow umpire looked at each other, and decided in the best interests of team harmony to beat a hasty retreat for lunch upstairs. Somehow the press did not get to hear about the ultimatum from the great left-hander. It was a difficult position, but dressing-room conversations are strictly off-limits to the fourth estate, no matter whether they are umpires or players. At least, that was the rule that applied in those days.

But Trevor's threats did have the effect of getting players down to the nets more regularly, and a self-imposed Saturday night curfew seemed to be in force for the rest of the season. This enabled Trevor to pick up enough wickets to challenge Jackie Botten, the long-serving North-Eastern Transvaal opening bowler, for the end of season award as the leading bowler. In the end they were pipped by Glen Hall, the leg-spinner, who had played in one Test against Mike Smith's 1964/65 team. Botten was a fine outswing bowler who also dipped the ball alarmingly at times, and cut it off the pitch at such pace that he was almost unplayable on a damp surface. He had, for years, been the leading bowler in Pretoria club cricket, and many believe he should have been capped far earlier than 1965, when Peter van der Merwe led the last Springbok team to England before isolation. How Botten missed the 1960 tour of England and failed to go Down Under in the side Trevor led in 1963/64 has always been a mystery of South African selection policy at a time when there was little question about his bowling ability.

Trevor was Jackie McGlew's vice-captain on the unhappy 1960 tour of England, where he bowled his usual excellent line and length and batted soundly against the counties. However, he left it until The Oval to show off the best of his batting wares with a solid 99, when he was given out to what some felt was a disputed slip catch by Colin Cowdrey off the bowling of Brian Statham.

But his baptism as a Test captain, at Brisbane's Woolloongabba, historic venue of the first tied Test several summers before, could not have come at a more trying time. He had watched, with mixed feelings, with McGlew at Lord's in 1960, the end of Geoff Griffin's career, when the bowler was repeatedly no-balled for throwing. Now came the next acid test. Ian Meckiff, the likeable, cheerful Victorian, whose action had been the subject of much debate in the series against Peter May's team of 1958/59, was included in the Australian side for the first Test.

The Springboks, or Goddard's Cinderellas as they were dubbed, were a harmonious team during the tour. They were also called a couple of less polite names during the visit, but after the fine win in Adelaide the Australian press was forced to acknowledge that they were a far stronger team than many were prepared to admit.

Both teams went into the Gabba Test with some apprehension over Meckiff's selection. However, judgement on his action was delayed until well into the second day after Australia, batting first, scored 435, with Brian Booth putting together 169. Umpire Col Egar, who was the Australian Cricket Board president in 1991/92, was in little doubt after passing the first delivery without comment.

'No b-a-l-l!' came the call from Egar at square leg. The crowd went numb, and a sick silence swept over them. Egar stood motionless. The Australian fielders, uncertain, looked at each other, unable to believe what was taking place. Meckiff walked back to his mark on that 7 December, cold sweat on his brow. It was about 2.06 pm. Meckiff again ran in off his short run-up ... the crowd hushed and again came the call 'No 'b-a-l-l!' from Egar. The spectators now reacted angrily and booed the umpire. It was ugly all right.

Australian captain Richie Benaud moved over to Meckiff as the atmosphere in the ground became super-charged and spectators boiled with rage.

'Well, Meck, I think we've got a bit of a problem. I don't quite know what we should do,' he said, as the catcalling of the umpires went on. 'Either bowl as quickly as you can, or bowl it slow and get through the over.'

Stunned and upset as he was, Meckiff chose the latter suggestion: he wanted the over finished and the gut-aching ordeal over. It was a 12-ball over (bowled to Goddard), with Meckiff called twice more by Egar before retiring to the sanctuary of the outfield, where he cut a lonely, disconsolate figure. Egar's actions spelt the end of another Test bowler's career, and the culmination of a controversy that had plagued Meckiff since the series against May's team.

There was a view among most journalists covering the tour that Meckiff was the final fall guy to wipe the slate clean of the game's chuckers. Overlooked for the tour of England in 1961 because of injury, he played 18 Tests, but only two at home, against the 1960/61 West Indians, before disappearing until his selection for the 1963 match in Brisbane. He had toured South Africa in 1957/58, where he played in four Tests, and India and Pakistan in 1959, but had escaped the umpire's axe until 7 December 1963.

Was there a conspiracy? Not according to Col Egar, who in 1992 in Perth, on the eve of South Africa's re-entry to Australian cricket after 28 years, denied there had been any intrigue.

But why had Meckiff been selected ... and then humiliated?

'Go and ask the selectors,' suggested the famous umpire, for whom Trevor Goddard had the greatest respect.

Meckiff's out-of-the-blue selection will always be a mystery.

The icy atmosphere in the Australian dressing room will be remembered for a long time by those who experienced it. Meckiff had become the vociferous crowd's hero and was chaired, shoulder high, from the ground at the end of the day's play with the spectators anxious to help the Victorian ease the hurt and ache inside. Ten years after the calling incident, Meckiff admitted his suspicion that he had been set up.

Shades of the Griffin affair at Lord's? Hardly. The Griffin incident took place at the height of the chucking row when the witch-hunt was on and the law under critical investigation; Meckiff's ordeal came when the wording of the law of what constituted a throw and what did not had been revised. In 1960 Meckiff, in consultation with a journalist, wrote a book called *Thrown Out*, and declared 'I DO NOT THROW,' taking offence at the opinion of the British press that he had transgressed the law.

Meckiff's action had been queried during the South African summer of 1957/58, when he toured with Ian Craig's Australians, but nothing was done about it. Yet the Springbok batsmen who faced the big Victorian in that series were all convinced he threw. In the light of what had happened over Griffin, and his being cleared for the tour of England in 1960, as well as with New Zealander Gary Bartlett in 1961/62, and much later Sylvester Clarke and Hartley Alleyne (mostly their quicker ball), South African umpires seem to be uncertain of what constitutes throwing. One of the problems is that umpires have to act as judge and jury and are reluctant to apply the law, especially as officials from some clubs make it known to the umpires how calling a bowler for throwing might affect the club's attitude toward the local umpires' association.

Johnny Wardle, a controversial character who had a distinguished Test career for England as a left-arm spinner, was in no doubt that Meckiff's mode of delivery transgressed the law. Wardle's invitation for the 1958/59 MCC tour of Australia was withdrawn after a wrangle with Yorkshire over a series of critical newspaper articles about the county. So he went instead as a journalist and, writing for the *Melbourne Herald*, said Meckiff was a chucker, and what had been a festering sore burst open.

Benaud, after being summoned in 1962/63 with other state captains to the home of Sir Donald Bradman, saw films of bowlers who had either suspect or illegal actions, and made a mental note not to use those bowlers again. Thus he declined to bowl Gordon Rorke in a match between New South Wales and South Australia, and was rebuked by the state selectors. Benaud then showed the steel behind his charismatic image. Dudley Seddon, the NSW selection panel convener, with typical Australian frankness, said the bowlers had been selected because they were known not to infringe the wording of the law. Bowlers were selected with a specific job in mind, and Benaud was reminded of this. It is reported that Benaud then said he would open the batting with Rorke, and how would the selectors like that?

Meckiff's agony at Brisbane could have been avoided on the evidence of the umpires' ruling in two Sheffield Shield matches the season before. He was called in Adelaide for the first time in his career – in a match from 11 to 15 January – by Martin Kierse, although the fast bowler did take eight wickets and was only called early in the South Australian first innings. The second time that season was at the Gabba, the scene of the Test nightmare the following summer. Walter Priem was the umpire who called Meckiff during the Queensland second innings, in a match played from 1 to 5 March.

For the most part, on that tour Trevor Goddard led from the front, batted well and bowled superbly when he decided to bowl himself. However, the tour will forever be remembered for the Meckiff fiasco at the Gabba and the two fine centuries from the then 19-year-old left-hander Graeme Pollock: 122 in Sydney and 175 at Adelaide Oval. Trevor's effective captaincy did much to help the team win that Test by 10 wickets to level the series, after Australia had won the second Test in Melbourne by eight wickets.

At the end of the fourth Test against England at the Wanderers in the 1964/65 series, after scoring the memorable only century of his career, Trevor announced that he would retire at the end of the series. The announcement came after a stinging blow to his pride at Newlands, where it was alleged that the strain of captaincy had shackled his performances against Mike Smith's team. The criticism was unfair, and it indicated careless thinking on the part of the selectors of the day. Trevor was a dedicated player, husband and father, and the claim at Newlands was in fact an unwarranted attack on his cricketing ability and his personality.

Trevor was later asked if he would captain the 1965 tour of England. It would have been his third visit but he declined, and there was no doubt that the Springboks would miss his skill and expertise as captain.

When he agreed to the call to arms when Bobby Simpson's Australians arrived in 1966/67, the selectors and the country felt considerable relief. Trevor played a major role in the 3–1 success that summer, and it is hard to believe that he took 26 wickets during the series, when he was 36. The old zip and variation was back; he swung and dipped the ball with sizzling venom. And the haul of six for 53 in the Australian second innings in the first Test at the Wanderers, his old stamping ground, did much to help South Africa go 1–0 up in the series. It was South Africa's first home victory over the tourists in 22 Tests after 64 years of trying!

Although Australia levelled the series 1–1 with a six-wicket win at Newlands, historically a hoodoo ground for South Africa, Trevor achieved the milestone of 100 Test wickets with the first wicket of the third Test of the series, when he had Ian Redpath caught by Eddie Barlow. It was more than a milestone; he became the first South African all-rounder thus far to achieve this feat at Test level. His greatness had always been assured, and now he was ranked above the giant of yore, Aubrey Faulkner.

There were times when, as a fielder, he would pounce unexpectedly and pocket some amazing gully and slip catches, which enabled him to pick up a remarkable 48 catches in his 41 Tests. In one provincial match in Pretoria he took an amazing series of four catches between gully and second slip, all cleanly and without fuss and bother.

His competitiveness, his ability to skilfully gather runs and his tight control of line and length in bowling, would have made him a sensational limited-overs player. He was a fine fielder as well, especially close in. One part of his game that thinking opposing bowlers discovered was that his batting knew two faces: one graceful and free flowing, the second determined and defensive when his side was in trouble. There were also times when his ability to pluck the ball out of the air in the manner of an acrobat saw him take a number of spectacular catches at any level. It was noticeable, too, to an outsider and an umpire, that while he was in Pretoria there was envy, which occasionally spilled into ugly jealousy of his all-round talent and expertise. Such is the pettiness of small minds.

So, why did Arthur Coy's selection panel decide to end his career at 38? Did they do it on their own, or were they coerced? The story that did the rounds months later was that Goddard was given the option of graceful retirement or being sacked; when he declined, Coy and Company knifed him out. There were also players who felt he was becoming a liability. Eddie Barlow, it was claimed, argued that it was time he should go, and Barlow had a lot to say. Ali Bacher, it appears, may have tried to cushion the axing, but there was no soft landing. As Vorster would in September 1968 when he guillotined the MCC tour after Basil D'Oliveira was selected, Goddard felt the cold blade of excommunication from the Test arena. It was far from the amicable 'pack up your tepee and go' scenario. Coy often acted as the executioner.

The early, wrong impression of Barry Richards and his non-selection in 1966/67 is a good enough example. Richards admitted that he was disturbed at the way Goddard's dismissal from the side was handled. His feeling on this subject displays a warm, human side to the Richards character, which is hidden from the public.

When Trevor went in at nine in the order in the second innings of the Wanderers Test, the third of the series against Bill Lawry's side, the selectors displayed their callous intentions. They were foolishly thinking of the future and the tour of England the following South African winter.

Goddard took two for 17 on the fourth afternoon: trick-spinner Johnnie Gleeson bowled for a duck, and Alan Connolly picked up by Barry Richards. The last act on a Test field by this gentleman cricketer was to skip down the pitch, arms in the air, expressing delight. There were no actions such as the high-five hand slaps in those days. Then, turning to umpire Jack Warner, he took his sweater for the last time and walked off the field and out of the Test arena he had graced for 15 years. Did he have to go that way? Not at all. Not ditched and pushed aside as if his years of loyal service meant nothing.

PETER VAN DER MERWE 8
Clinical Captaincy

By Jackie McGlew

Peter Lawrence van der Merwe still carries himself with a professorial air. There is a studied, deep-rooted sense of duty and earnestness about the man. There is also a quick and subtle sense of humour not often apparent at first, and he is also thorough and meticulous in all he undertakes. Whatever his calling might have turned out to be, he would have ensured that it was successful. His ability to apply himself is astounding.

Van der Merwe is a man of sterling character. He has principles and he sticks to them with a rare tenacity. This is not to suggest that he is stubborn or inflexible. He is by no means obstinate and perverse. A few years ago I was privileged to sit on a South African selection panel of which he was the convener. He was always open to discussion and constructive debate, in which he was quite prepared to consider another person's views without fear or favour.

This is why it could have been extremely funny – had it not been so unfortunate – that many so-called experts in the media saw fit to single out Van der Merwe personally for criticism, when the panel responsible for picking the 1992 World Cup side actually comprised six members. The press implied that Van der Merwe was dictatorial and imposed his will on the panel. Having served with him, I find this extremely difficult to believe. Six selectors picked the side for the World Cup, not one! Judging from the fierce criticism, one would suspect the panel comprised a sole selector.

But Van der Merwe is not the type of person who would gloat over his detractors when proved right. It is more likely that he felt a warm glow of satisfaction when the team performed magnificently at the World Cup. His happiness at Kepler Wessels's successful 'scorcher' Down Under would have been tempered with his usual modesty.

The viciousness of the attacks by prominent players and some members of the media have now receded into the past to gather cobwebs. The glory due to Peter van der Merwe and Kepler Wessels and his team have now been indelibly recorded. One of my reports commented on the South Africans' meteoric rise to fame in the World Cup:

> Where one is aware of Peter's approach to the game, what can be said is that he really required total dedication from a player. He could not suffer the thought of a player being half-hearted. Physical fitness, total commitment, loyalty to the team which would, of course, embrace team spirit itself, and unstinting selflessness were high on Peter's priorities for a man at the top and making his way through the ranks. He was what was known as a 'stickler'. This did not mean that he held personal grudges or that he had a closed mind. On the contrary, with his cheerful sense of goodwill and impish sense of humour, he was always prepared to discuss the merits and demerits of any one player.

Van der Merwe's sometimes stern and almost forbidding outward appearance conceals an open-minded geniality and constructive consideration just below the surface. Perhaps it is his tall, slim, dignified and sober mien that sometimes causes critics to draw the wrong conclusions.

Peter van der Merwe was delivered by his great-uncle, Dr Frank Bester, on 14 March 1937 in the maternity ward of the Paarl Clinic. The family moved around quite a lot when he was young. From approximately 1940 to 1943 he lived in Calvinia, then in Stellenbosch from 1943 to 1950. Here, when he was a scholar at the famous Paarl Gymnasium, Peter's father decided to give his prep school son a treat.

The latter-day South African captain's passion for cricket was firmly implanted when Van der Merwe senior, a bank manager, took Peter from Stellenbosch to the beautiful Newlands ground to watch his first big game at the tender age of nine. This was the beginning of a lifelong romance with the game.

Van der Merwe still has vivid memories of that exciting outing. The match was Western Province's annual derby. It was a Cape Town encounter against a powerful Transvaal team, which included household names such as Eric Rowan, Ken Viljoen, Denis Begbie, George Fullerton and other notables. This took place on 1, 2 and 3 January 1947.

He relates with nostalgic pride that he saw Syd Kiel score a fine 87 for Western Province, and also watched some local heroes such as Jack Cheetham, Georgie Georgeau, Jack Plimsoll, Martin Hanley, Ernest Witte and Clive van Ryneveld (then still a schoolboy) in action. Syd Kiel might well have become a South African opening batsman had World War II not broken out.

Another fine Western Province player who also scored 87 in that game and might well have gone on to greater heights was middle-order batsman WBH Foley. In this encounter, Western Province emerged as victors by six wickets.

Peter van der Merwe was 'hooked', and he firmly believes a father should foster with enthusiasm, but without pressure, a son's interests and hobbies. Well, he certainly has a great debt of gratitude to his father for the famous cricket figure he finally became.

It is notable that during this game the young Van der Merwe was watching two fine cricketers destined to become his managers on two overseas tours: Ken Viljoen during the Springbok tour to Australia and New Zealand in 1963/64, when Van der Merwe was vice-captain to Trevor Goddard; and Jack Plimsoll, who managed the 1965 tour to England when Van der Merwe was captain.

In this particular game Viljoen and Plimsoll both registered excellent performances. Plimsoll captured six wickets for 160 runs off 71 overs, while Viljoen, batting at number three for Transvaal, scored 36 and 53; both respectable contributions. Peter was captivated by the scenes at Newlands and the atmosphere of cricket at this impressionable age. They were to generate far-reaching attainments in later years.

On leaving Paarl Gymnasium, the young Van der Merwe went to the famous St Andrew's College in Grahamstown. Here his cricket flourished. It culminated in Peter being selected to captain the Eastern Province Nuffield Schools team in 1955. After matriculating, Peter returned to the Western Province and studied for a Bachelor of Arts degree at the University of Cape Town. However, before he arrived in the Mother City he had proved himself to be a model scholar at St Andrew's College, as well as a talented all-round sportsman. His major feat in batting for his college was 89 not out against Beaufort, a side that included Ron Delport, and his best performance with the ball was versus Kingswood College in a fine spell of left-arm spin bowling. Despite all his later achievements, these and many other special occasions are recalled even today with particular relish by Van der Merwe.

Peter van der Merwe's days at university were happy ones. He attended UCT from 1956 to 1960, captaining the varsity in his last two years. Unfortunately in his years as captain he had to forego the pleasure of playing in the intervarsity week because of work pressure. There is little doubt that if he had played, he would have captained South African Universities.

Van der Merwe freely admits that England and Middlesex off-spinner Fred Titmus, and Jimmy Gray of Hampshire, both had a profound effect on his development as a cricketer, as did Harry Birrell when he was a scholar at St Andrew's College. Jimmy Gray was the UCT coach in 1959/60, and Fred Titmus occupied the same post during the 1960/61 season. In both Van der Merwe's years as captain the university won the Cape Town league. Taking his university side to the top of the league two years in succession was no mean feat, because in those days university students were considered somewhat 'uppity'. Van der Merwe never exhibited this quality, being confident but not arrogant. However, this would not have protected him from the hostility that emanated from certain cricketing circles; there must have been quite a few clubs that would have loved to put the student side in its so-called place.

Like his contemporaries Eddie Barlow and Joe Partridge, Van der Merwe wore spectacles, which together with his genuine modesty gave him an air of dignity. The likeable six-footer was such a versatile sportsman that he was honoured with a blue in hockey, as well as in his beloved cricket. He was also something of a physical fitness fanatic. He probably felt he owed this not only to himself, but also to his teammates. There is no doubt that he has an almost military belief that a sportsman has a far better chance of success if he is fully fit and in good shape. I agree with him.

Van der Merwe played a great deal of his early cricket under the leadership of Gerald Innes. He speaks in the fondest possible terms about Innes, a man beloved by teammates and opposition alike wherever he played. He was gentle in nature, but also keenly competitive. Innes possessed an extremely keen sense of humour. His brother-in-law, Kevin Commins, related a few of Gerald's stories in a tribute after Gerald's untimely death from cancer. Two of the remarks attributed to Gerald include: 'I would have been the Bishops shot put champion if only I could have lifted the iron shot!' and 'I would easily have been the long-jump champion if I could have reached the sandpit from the take-off board.'

Innes was a scholar at Bishops in Cape Town. He would often quip that he was the only Bishops boy to score a try against his own school. This happened when a huge schoolboy forward, Victor Wilkens, playing at lock for Paul Roos, engineered an outstanding breakaway movement. Gerald, a great deal smaller, leapt onto the giant lock's back and they both went over the Bishops line for a 'joint' try. Innes could keep an audience entertained for hours with his witty ad-libbing. He was a real Danny Kaye of the cricket circuit. Peter van der Merwe must have enjoyed many cherished moments with Innes, whose gentlemanly demeanour will be remembered with deep affection.

Van der Merwe's provincial career was notable for many highlights. After representing the University of Cape Town for five seasons, he had the distinction of playing for Western Province from 1957/58 until he went to Australia for the 1963/64 season. During his time with Western Province, he played four years for Alma after UCT. On his return to Port Elizabeth, Peter played for Eastern Province from 1966/67 to 1968/69. He captained both Eastern Province and Western Province.

His first game as captain of Western Province, against Border, quickly established him as an incisive thinker, which became evident when he moved point to leg slip where a catch was taken to close the Border innings. He first played for South Africa when he was selected as Trevor Goddard's vice-captain to Australia and New Zealand. Peter mustered 75 runs for an average of 18.75 against the

Australians in his five Test matches. In the overall first-class averages he did considerably better, with a return of 448 runs and a healthy average of 34.46. The highlight of his tour was when he stole the honours on the second day of the match against New South Wales on the famous Sydney Cricket Ground.

Graeme Pollock had already captivated the crowd with a scintillating 121 on the first day. Now Van der Merwe helped the South Africans to record the highest total against New South Wales in 52 years, when he put together a soundly played 114 runs in 184 minutes. Peter's main accomplice was the ever-useful David Pithey who, in scoring 40 valuable runs, was involved with Van der Merwe in a seventh-wicket partnership of 115 runs made in only 85 minutes. This, together with good fielding off the swing bowling by the late Joe Partridge, brought about a grand victory for the Springboks one hour from time. This was a great morale booster.

Partridge was one of the finest swing bowlers ever to wear the green and gold. He should have represented the Springboks in many more Tests than he did. Partridge wrought havoc with brisk, late inswingers to the right-hander, which, of course, became extremely dangerous outswingers to the left-hander.

The Rhodesian bowled an impeccable length and line. The dramatic lateness of his inswingers was most disconcerting. If he had a green, lively pitch, Joe Partridge became an instant match winner. He exploited the new ball to its fullest. On the New Zealand leg of Goddard's tour, Peter van der Merwe had only four innings and averaged 14.50. Nevertheless, the experience he had gained in both Australia and New Zealand was to stand him in good stead for the future. Being the avid student of the game that he is, Van der Merwe made it his business to soak up knowledge like a sponge. He possessed a searching mind.

Peter van der Merwe's sense of humour always lurked beneath the surface, and he delights in describing two amusing interrelated events in Australia. Clive Halse, Springbok opening bowler, sent a wild delivery over the batsman's head, and on bouncing it squirted with great velocity past the groping gloves of wicketkeeper Waite, shooting through for four runs. Eddie Barlow's voice rang out, 'Sundries Waite!'

This became a stock joke, with people referring to Waite as 'Sundries Waite'! However, Waite had an opportunity for his own bit of merriment. When an Australian batsman smote the first ball of an Eddie Barlow delivery right over the wall of a certain area of the ground, Johnnie Waite swiftly quipped, 'Humpty over the wall Barlow.' So from then on it became 'Sundries' Waite and 'Humpty over the wall' Barlow.

This trip to Australia was the 'university' training ground for bigger things still to come. In conjunction with the MCC tour of South Africa under MJK (Mike) Smith's leadership, it taught local players a great deal. Van der Merwe learnt clever, subtle tactics from his own playing experience, as well as from his adversaries. I am sure he studied the methods of MJK Smith very closely.

Van der Merwe's tour of Australia and New Zealand might not have been earth-shattering considering his personal performance, but he did everything required of him to the best of his ability. And as always he did it without fuss or fanfare. He remained fiercely competitive at all times, and yet he placed a refreshingly high premium on friendship and the enjoyment of the game.

Another humorous incident occurred before the tour of Australia, but this time it concerned Clive Halse. The side had not yet departed, and a South African journalist was given the assignment of interviewing Clive Halse. Clive was a big man and, at times, appeared slightly overweight. Clive was living on the Natal South Coast, and the discussion apparently went something like this:

JOURNALIST: 'Clive, I believe you have been training very hard for the forthcoming tour of Australia.'
CLIVE: 'Yes, that is true.'
JOURNALIST: 'I heard, furthermore, that you run 15 miles along the beach every morning before showering and going to work.'
CLIVE: 'That sounds very good. Please keep the rumour going!'

Although Van der Merwe originally made his mark as a left-arm slow bowler, he was destined to peak as an astute captain and a dependable middle-order batsman. In addition he commanded versatility as a fielder, which permitted him to field in any position with complete confidence.

Thus, when he took over the captaincy of South Africa from Trevor Goddard for the tour of England in 1965, the team possessed a clever captain, a middle-order batsman who could defend dourly and attack aggressively when occasion demanded, and an all-round fielder of top quality. And in his earlier career, as stated, he bowled left-arm spinners capturing 82 wickets at 25.18 apiece. Peter's best bowling figure was six wickets for 40 runs versus Orange Free State in the 1960/61 season.

In the English summer of 1961, Peter toured the United Kingdom with the Fezelas. Roy McLean captained a young team, many of whom became Springboks at a later stage, such as Peter Pollock, Eddie Barlow, Denis Lindsay, Jackie Botten, Colin Bland of legendary fielding fame and Chris Burger. It was a most successful tour and the sponsor, Stanley Murphy, must have felt great pride in blooding so many of South Africa's future stars. They certainly were a good investment.

It is reputed that Peter van der Merwe received his nickname 'Murphy' on this trip. Peter will confirm that this tour was a very important part of his cricketing learning curve. The sobriquet 'Murphy' probably came about for two reasons. He was touring under his patron, Stanley Murphy, and at the time the famous (or infamous) Van der Merwe jokes were doing the rounds by the millions, and the Van der Merwe in the joke was often referred to as 'Murphy.'

Mike Smith captained the MCC side to tour South Africa in the 1964/65 season. He was invited to lead the team when 'Lord' Ted Dexter decided to stand for parliament. Mike Smith was a shrewd leader of men in a most unostentatious way. When he arrived in South Africa he had made almost 25 000 first-class runs, with 43 centuries to his name.

Apart from his cricketing prowess, Smith was a double blue (cricket and rugby) at Oxford University. When he graduated he joined Warwickshire. The touring MCC party to South Africa was pretty powerful, and the line-up was as follows: Mike Smith (Warwickshire) captain, Ken Barrington (Surrey), David Allen (Gloucestershire), Mike Brearley (Middlesex), Geoff Boycott (Yorkshire), David Brown (Warwickshire), Tom Cartwright (Warwickshire), Bob Barber (Warwickshire), Ted Dexter (Sussex), Robin Hobbs (Essex), John Murray (Middlesex), Ian Thomson (Sussex), Peter Parfitt (Middlesex), Jim Parks (Sussex), John Price (Middlesex), Fred Titmus (Middlesex), Donald Carr manager.

This list of outstanding competitive internationals gives some idea exactly what Peter van der Merwe was up against in his very first two Test matches played at home in South Africa (he participated in only the fourth and fifth Tests). Van der Merwe batted only twice. On the first occasion he was not out for five, and in the fifth Test at St George's Park he scored an excellent 66 before Barrington caught him off the bowling of Ken Palmer. Thus he ended the series with the handsome average of 71. This fine performance led to his selection as captain of South Africa. The announcement of the 15-man Springbok party to make the half-season tour of England in the summer of 1965 was made in somewhat unusual circumstances. The names came over the loudspeaker at St George's Park at about half past four on the last day of the fifth Test, when it was obvious that there would be no further play in the series. The team announced was: Peter van der Merwe (WP) captain, Eddie Barlow (EP) vice-captain, Ali Bacher (Tvl), Colin Bland (Rhodesia), Jackie Botten (NE Tvl), Harry Bromfield (WP), Norman Crookes (Natal), Richard Dumbrill (Natal), Dennis Gamsy (Natal), Denis Lindsay (NE Tvl), Mike Macaulay (Free State), Atholl McKinnon (Tvl), Tony Pithey (Rhodesia), Graeme Pollock (EP), Peter Pollock (EP).

Jack Plimsoll's appointment as manager had been announced earlier in the season. He was a popular choice and became successful, with the players holding him in great respect.

Ian Woolridge, of the *London Daily Mail*, had this to say: 'Peter van der Merwe is a capable captain, but the real driving force behind the touring team is likely to be Eddie Barlow. He is a pugnacious, attacking cricketer who hates drawn matches almost as much as he despises being beaten.' As true as those words might have been of Eddie Barlow, there can be no doubt that Peter van der Merwe stamped his own authority on the tour.

Peter's exciting success on that tour is now history. He handled his team with competence, and his complete faith in his players led to a pulsating victory in the first Test at Trent Bridge in Nottingham. The Springboks then held on to this lead to win the series 1–0. Thus the words I wrote at the end of my book *Cricket Crisis* were timely indeed:

> Finally I feel sure that Peter van der Merwe and Mr Jack Plimsoll should prove a happy alliance as captain and manager, and all South Africa hopes of course they will be successful where for so long we have failed. For the Springboks have not won a series against England since Herby Wade's touring side toured their land in 1935. Thirty years without success is a long, long time.

Another sentence in the same book was equally timely: 'As far as I am concerned, I thought that the national selectors Messrs Arthur Coy, Dennis Dyer, Alan Melville and Lindsay Tuckett had done an excellent job.'

Although the details of the 1965 England versus South Africa series have been chronicled elsewhere in this book, let me make it abundantly clear that this tour belonged to Peter van der Merwe. It is a tour he can hug to his cricket bosom with relish and ecstatic delight for the rest of his days. Oh, what joy to beat England in England in a Test series!

However, let the captain relate in his own words that glorious chapter in the annals of South African cricket. Peter van der Merwe has kindly given permission to reproduce his personal account of that memorable Test of the series at Lord's:

> When the 17th South African cricket team to go on an international tour landed at Heathrow Airport on 16 June 1965, we were met by Dick Twining, President of the MCC, and Billy Griffiths, the secretary of that body.
>
> As the latter greeted us, we said 'Happy birthday, Billy!' and gave him a tour tie as a present. This happy and auspicious beginning, we hoped, would mark the start of a 'tour with a difference'. Every cricket captain hopes that his tour will be different, that the pre-tour promises will be kept, and that his team will emerge victorious, popular and happy. Our team had three months previously lost a boring series against the formidable MCC team led by Mike Smith by 1–0, with four draws. Since then, Trevor Goddard, our captain in that series, John Waite, and Tony Pithey had retired, and in any team that would leave a big hole. Their replacements had promise and ability but obviously lacked experience.
>
> Despite these losses, and despite the further handicap of having only one man with previous experience of an England tour, he being Atholl McKinnon,

our feeling was one of tremendous optimism and anticipation. Six of us had been on the 1963/64 Australian tour, but from my viewpoint a wonderful help would be that the same six had been in the Fezelas XI on a two-month invitation tour of England in 1961. It had been sponsored by that far-sighted philanthropist, E Stanley Murphy, managed by CO Medworth, sports editor of the *Natal Mercury*, and captained by that robust Springbok, Roy McLean. Roy and Chris Burger had already played for South Africa, but of the other 12 in the team no less than seven were soon to receive their colours.

At 26 my team was the youngest South African team ever to go on tour. We had, through the Nuffield Schools tournament, the South African Universities cricket week, Currie Cup cricket, and now international cricket, played with and against each other a good deal. Team spirit was evident before we even set off.

Our manager was to be Jack Plimsoll. A penetrative medium-paced bowler under Alan Melville in 1947, he was considered such a threat that Denis Compton and Bill Edrich were detailed to hit him out of the Test eleven. But now Jack proved equal to the occasion. His relationship with the officials and the press was excellent and the fact that our tour was so happy and incident-free was very much due to him. He was an outstanding manager.

Why though the eager anticipation of the three-Test series? We wanted revenge. England had beaten New Zealand 3–0 in the first half of the season, and had performed impressively. We had lost our first match to Derbyshire. This did not bother me, as my ambition was to win the Test series. An unbeaten tour record had a low priority.

It is normally harder to win away from home, but we genuinely felt we had a great chance of avenging our 1–0 defeat. The pitches in South Africa had been so flat that four Tests had been drawn, with little hope of either side getting on top. Taking personalities into account, I concluded that the more responsive English pitches would improve our chances as compared with England's, and also the home team would be under the close scrutiny of their highly critical press.

A tremendous boost to our fortunes came a few days before the first Test was due to be played at Lord's, with the news that Ted Dexter had broken a bone in his leg and was out of the series. Boycott's rate of scoring suited us, Cowdrey we respected, Barrington we knew we'd have to prise out, but Dexter we feared. He was the one England player I'd rather not have played against, and here he was out. I regret to admit my sympathy for him was heavily tinged with delight.

Our itinerary had designated Lord's for the first Test after seven county matches had been played. None of us had played at Lord's before, not even

Atholl McKinnon, and great sportsman that he was, Atholl never mentioned the fact until all the Lord's matches had been concluded. Attitudes like his made for our unbeatable team spirit. A few years later, an England side of which nearly every member had previously played at Sydney, was unhappy at having to play a Test there without a warm-up match. I think we had a better case than they did, but we weren't interested in controversy.

The umpires for the Test were announced as Syd Buller and AOE 'Dusty' Rhodes. The procedure for the appointment of umpires for the series was that a panel was nominated and then the secretary of the MCC would inform me who had been appointed. I would then have three days in which to lodge a protest, and then the press would be informed. Interestingly, on all three occasions my letter of notification arrived after the press had the names.

But that did not matter. We were not going to complain about any umpire because we were determined not to have our energies and concentration dissipated by acrimonious matters. Umpire-baiting is a favourite sport of players: I have yet to see the players win in the long run. Before we left South Africa Eric Rowan had said to me: 'Cultivate the umpires, ask their opinions, and you'll learn a lot.' How right he was. Even when there were wrong decisions we did not worry, as we felt they were genuine errors of judgement; and they somehow helped the game along in our favour.

The combination of Buller and Rhodes could have been trying for both, as Syd had no-balled Dusty's son Harold in our Derbyshire match for throwing. This was a touchy subject in those days. We South Africans had our share of that limelight in 1960 when Buller had called Geoff Griffin. However, if they had their differences, neither Buller nor Rhodes showed it.

By the time the first Test came we had not run into form. The weather had interrupted nearly all our matches and by and large we had not settled into an efficient rhythm. The three pre-Test games at Bristol, Jesmond and Leicester proved less than helpful for most of us. Only Ali Bacher really benefited, scoring centuries in most un-testlike conditions.

The selection committee, consisting of Eddie Barlow, Graeme Pollock and myself, with Jack Plimsoll as chairman, had a difficult task with so little to go on. As Jack Botten and Harry Bromfield had at that stage shown greater steadiness than Macaulay, McKinnon and Crookes, Jack came in to partner Peter Pollock with the new ball, and Harry took over the spinner's role. This left us without much variation as the whole attack was now right-armed. Two of the three alternatives were left-armed, but our policy in this match was to try our hardest, try for victory, but at the same time take no gamble. We could only do better in the later Tests after more time for preparation. England 1–0 up would be almost impossible to beat; England 1–0 down would be at their most dangerous, England 0–0 would still be complacent. And so it proved in the end.

This is not meant to be an indictment of the leadership of Mike Smith. He was always an intelligent scheming captain, a gentleman, and a pleasure to play against, but there was a lack of urgency in English cricket. It was the professional approach to pace oneself until the final straight. We did not have the experience to pace ourselves: it had to be flat out, hoping not to be left behind initially, and hoping to get a sufficient lead before the urgency of the matter goaded the opposition into performing completely positively when, I knew, they would be at their best. History proved me correct, for only on the last day of the third Test, when England HAD to square the series, did they get stuck in, and then the rain prevented a grandstand finish.

My first game as captain of Western Province was against Border in East London, and Mike Macaulay had won the match for us with his zip and swing. In his only Test, in March 1965, he had aggravated an injury to the pad of his right heel. The pain was so intense that Mike had to change his run up to the wicket and his whole delivery, with the consequence that for a while he could no longer bring the ball back into the batsmen. After countless, fruitless lbw appeals the story from the umpires was always the same: 'Can't you get him to bring the ball in?' Would that Mike had not tried so hard on the rock-hard Bloemfontein strip and then at Port Elizabeth. But that was Mike, always giving his best.

Before you think Jackie Botten got his Test place by default, let me say that ever since I had seen him play for South African Schools in January 1956, I had admired his bowling ability. On the Fezelas tour in 1961 he had proved devastating, and his slower ball was quite lethal. Now the edge was slightly off that particular delivery, but no one could trifle with him, and in the whole series he was as consistent as his dress was impeccable.

Norman Crookes could spin his off-breaks more than Harry Bromfield, though less accurately. He had nearly bowled the South African Colts XI to victory over the MCC at Benoni in November in 1964 when my team – through illness and injury – had at times six substitutes on the field. Barry Richards and Lorrie Wilmot had chickenpox, Botten, Macaulay and Tony Tillim had muscular problems, and at times others also went off. Field placing became somewhat difficult when the MCC objected to substitute number five, Jim Pressdee, fielding at short leg. Through all this Norman bowled his 37 overs unchanged, never flagged, and oh so nearly got through.

Early in the tour Atholl McKinnon negated much of his left-arm spin by bowling from very wide of the stumps. He simply could not get closer. This meant that his arm ball either struck the pad outside the line or went down the legside. Atholl's flight was tantalising and later on he bowled with almost mechanical accuracy. He had a wonderful sense of humour and he did a great deal to ease the tensions of the tour and keep the smile on our faces.

Dennis Gamsy was the fourth player to be left out of the Test team. A more eye-catching wicketkeeper than Denis Lindsay, perhaps because of his soccer goalkeeping days, he did not have Lindsay's century-scoring potential, besides which Lindsay was now to embark on a sequence of Tests where he hardly put a foot wrong behind the stumps and in the next series against Bobby Simpson's Australians, scored three wonderful centuries and aggregated the most runs ever by a wicketkeeper in a series.

However, the team had weaknesses. There was no settled opening partnership, or number three, and no Goddard to close up an end. Our main weapons to counter these weaknesses were to be enthusiasm and unwearying determination. I tried to instil a sense of urgency in my players and told them they HAD to enjoy what they were about, for it did not fall to the lot of many players to undertake more than one tour.

My pre-match preparation was always to have a discussion with the team about our own play and that of the opposition. All the batsmen were analysed and lines of attack settled, so that on the field everyone knew the tactical plot even though he might be patrolling the distant boundary. When fielding we decided to attack the off-stump or outside, in the belief that this would be a considerable variation to the county line of attack which we found to be middle stump veering to leg.

Geoff Boycott we decided to reduce below even his accustomed rate of scoring by pitching everything well up and blocking his on-side push and his drive past point, thereby hoping to frustrate him. To Bob Barber it was either wide of the off-stump, or at leg-pin, hoping for a snick from a slash, or a gap between bat and pad. With the ominous threat of Ted Dexter gone, we were almost pleased to welcome John Edrich at three, even though his last Test innings had been 310 not out against John Reid's New Zealanders. John showed no liking for Peter Pollock's pace, and our plan was to give him nothing to hit, by aggressive field placing inhibit his strokeplay even further, and then slip in the odd bouncer.

At four was Colin Cowdrey, and I confess that right to the end of the series we had no plan against him, so complete a batsman was he. Our biggest effort was to make him wonder why we did certain things, hoping thereby to undermine his confidence, or at the very least stop him from taking command at the crease. While Colin was diffident we lived in hope.

Ken Barrington had given the Springbok bowlers, and for that matter the Australians, such uphill in their respective countries that we had no illusions about the task that lay before us. But I felt that Ken was better away from England and with his favourite shots blocked, might be helped into indiscretions, especially as he had been dropped for slow scoring against the New Zealanders.

Mike Smith was not due to get anything to aid his exceptionally strong on-side style, and Jim Parks would not get anything short: it had to be well up to tempt his handsome drive. The field placing for both was to be 6:3 and the line off-stump or outside, but the actual positioning of fielders varied completely. For instance, for Smith I was as straight as possible at mid-off; for Parks I was where extra cover usually is, with all the other offside fielders correspondingly further round.

At number eight came Fred Titmus, my old friend and mentor from my Cape Town University days. He and Jimmy Gray, of Hampshire, had each spent a season coaching the university team of which I was captain at that stage, and had materially contributed to our winning the local league in those two seasons. So my relationship with Fred was one of great respect and friendship but with an overpowering desire to 'show' him. We decided to attack his off-stump – a mistake – as later we switched to leg stump, with better results.

To round off the England batting line-up came David Brown, David Larter and Fred Rumsey. The former we knew to be an honest hard-working seam bowler, but the latter two were quite new to us. Even so, we had kept our ears open, and they were quite thoroughly discussed. In my schooldays I had learned a soul-searching lesson under my coach, Harry Birrell, that the last wicket is the most important of the lot, and ever since losing a schoolboy match, I had begrudged the last wicket pair any runs at all.

The Springbok batting line-up was headed by Eddie Barlow. From the time that he came on the Fezelas tour as a last minute replacement for David Pithey, Ed had become a household name to South African cricketers. His self-confidence coupled with no mean ability, and a desire to attack and get on top of the opposition bowlers from the first ball bowled, paved the way for the stroke-players further down the list. Eddie's bowling was later to develop, but right now he struggled to get wickets.

To go in first with him was Tiger Lance. An all-round sportsman who excelled at soccer, hockey and cricket, Tiger was a great character. His tough exterior hid a pair of shrewd eyes, and his pronouncements were made in terms destined to go down in cricket lore. Tiger was basically a front-foot player, with a straight bat and a long reach and was better at number six, but for the sake of the side he took on this job.

Denis Lindsay was to go in at three. Fearless, quick on the hook, not scared to play the lofted drive, he too was out of place, but prepared to do anything for the side.

Graeme Pollock and Colin Bland were at four and five. Upon their shoulders lay the task of ensuring a good score. I would choose Graeme for any team that I might ever lead, and Colin was not far behind in batting skill. If one adds his fielding prowess, then Colin couldn't be left out of any team either.

Ali Bacher, who later on was promoted to No. 3, was at six now. He had scored hundreds against Minor Counties (at Jesmond) and Leicestershire in difficult circumstances. He kept his head right down over the ball and was always difficult to dislodge.

I came next. My form was completely patchy, not aided by run-outs and curious ways of getting out, but I hoped that I might be able to rise to the occasion.

At eight came Richard Dumbrill. A great theorist, he believed that the ball that swung in to leg, pitched and then cut away to hit the top of the off-stump, was the only one to bowl. His failures in his attempts to bowl this ball made entertaining telling until he got rid of Colin Cowdrey that way, but that is to get ahead of my story. As a batsman Richard scored many valuable runs. Peter Pollock, then a sucker for a leg-break (but no-one told the English until too late), Jack Botten and Harry Bromfield completed the batting order. Jack had made 90 against Leicester, a score which gave us high hopes of him.

Were I then to select one team from the two sides, I would have included four of my players and seven Englishmen, so in theory we were on a hiding. Fortunately theory was a minor suit in this match.

To a newcomer the change rooms at Lord's are a little forbidding. The hard shiny benches have an air of knowing tolerance for the mental and physical anguish that was about to be experienced, and the slightly musty smell the rubber mats exuded prepared one for possible rain. My first walk through that holy of holies, the Long Room, was marred by it being completely empty. Somehow, suddenly, I was in the wrong season. Later on, going out to bat, I could only look straight ahead when confronted by the large number of members, all highly knowledgeable I presumed, who thronged the room. I must mention one other place: the player's balcony. To sit out there in full view of the whole field was another special moment.

After breakfast at the Grand Hotel in the Aldwych I usually found the weather worse than before getting up, as though the sound of bath water touched a responsive chord in the sky. And so it was this first day of the Test. By the time we reached St John's Wood things were much better, though nothing like what we South Africans would regard as a great day for cricket.

A quick warm-up, then the moment for the toss arrived: my first Test as captain of South Africa, the 100th Test to be played between England and South Africa, and it is at Lord's of all places. The small boy who had received

Walter Hammond's *Cricket my Destiny* for his 10th birthday (after his father had first read it!) now had his dreams materialise.

Mike Smith came wandering down the corridor to look for me: I was putting on my blazer, broad green and thin gold in vertical stripes, so fashionable a decade or more ago, but even now the pride of my wardrobe. Off we set down the stairs, me mindful of the story of Peter Heine tripping and falling in a heap through sheer nerves at the end of a Test.

During a visit to a home in Adelaide, South Australia, I had noticed a small sign on a wall. It read: 'Heads you win, tails you lose'. I had ever after, when I really wanted to win the toss, called 'heads', and now the adage held true. The winning or losing of the toss is but a way of getting the game started, but it is beloved of journalists as a bone to be picked at for ages, so that the controversy over the decision to bat or field can virtually obscure the course of the game itself. In one respect I was not happy to win the toss: the conditions were not ideal, and it might have been easier for my players to ease into the Test arena by fielding first. However, I had decided that even though the pitch was inclined to be lively early on, we had to bat. I conveyed my decision with a touch of my hand on my thigh, which gesture put Eddie Barlow right on edge. He was extremely keen to do well, and he now became quite introspective, not at all the irrepressible soul he normally is.

With more than usual apprehension we wished Barlow and Lance well. We just had to ensure we did not fall at the first hurdle.

Rumsey and Larter took the new ball. Very soon Fred got one to lift into Barlow's body and Eddie steered it straight to Barber at leg gully, a smartish catch, so easily taken that one could only gulp, look straight ahead and hope that it was the last excellent catch. It wasn't – there were to be four more in the innings. Lance went to a reflex-action catch by David Brown off his own bowling and then Lindsay slashed at Rumsey and saw Fred Titmus at gully dive far to his right and bring off a fabulous one-handed catch.

This brought Graeme Pollock and Colin Bland together at 75 for three. The moment was crucial: if they failed we might not get to 150. Like thoroughbreds they warmed to their task, and soon got going. An hour after lunch, at 140 three, just as they really got into gear, the rain came down. How unwelcome it was, for on resumption 20 minutes later, neither could recapture the momentum and were soon out. Bacher, Dumbrill and I came and went, and it was left to Botten and Peter Pollock to get us to 227 for eight at close. We had not won round one.

Next day the weather only allowed two and a half hours' play. A last-wicket partnership of 39 between Pollock and Harry Bromfield regained a lot of lost ground. Mike Smith persisted with pace against these two, until the pavilion critics became audible in the 'middle'. Bob Barber then took just nine balls to have Pollock stumped. Our final score of 280 was quite satisfactory, taking all into consideration.

And now it was England's turn to bat. The spirited resistance offered by our last three had put us in good heart, so the last-minute team talk had an optimistic air about it. Boycott and Barber began their innings well after tea, with everything to lose and precious little to win. On this occasion they stayed undefeated despite all Peter Pollock and Jack Botten tried. Once a ball popped from what I thought at square short leg was Boycott's forearm, but the way some of the team reacted it appeared to have come off his glove. While I got a hand to the ball I couldn't hold it. The second day closed with England at 26 without loss and we were level pegging.

Saturday July 24, 1965 dawned clear but with high-flying clouds and a fair breeze. It was Peter Pollock's birthday and I hoped this was a good omen for so much depended on him. When our team for the tour had been announced in Port Elizabeth in March he had sized up the importance of the job he had to do, and he had turned to me and said, 'Don't worry, Skip, I won't break down and I won't let you down.' It is history now how he lived up to his promise.

When we took the field we all had on our slipovers, by now normal dress for all but the bowlers who usually sported long-sleeved sweaters. The crowd simply streamed into the ground, and by 11.30 there wasn't much seating left. I have always found that to play in front of a large knowledgeable crowd inspired me, and this day was no exception. All my team also responded and were absolute tigers in the field. Little did we know when Syd Buller called 'play', what a dramatic day's play was about to begin. As an early breakthrough did not materialise, I entrusted the nursery end to Barlow, switching Botten to the pavilion end. Just as things were becoming gloomy Jack got Boycott to edge one to Barlow at first slip. He made no mistake: in fact I doubt he dropped any catches on the whole tour. Eddie on his 1965/70 form was as good a first slip as I have ever seen. The 82 for one was a good start for England with their long batting line-up.

Harry Bromfield then came on at the nursery end. He was an amazingly accurate off-spinner, not accustomed to getting much turn on his home track, Newlands. The extra turn he obtained in England encouraged him to try for even more, unfortunately at the expense of some accuracy. Be that as it may, Harry was a great trier and an outstanding gully fielder, and this day he got the next wicket. Facing him Barber became frustrated at having his best shots cut off, so he skipped down the pitch, caught the ball on the full and sent it whistling past mid-on for four. Next ball he tried the same thing but must have lifted his head slightly, for he missed, and the ball went through between bat and pad and hit the leg stump.

John Edrich came down the pavilion steps to much applause, for most of those present were aware of his last Test innings of 310 not out. As this immaculate batsman – he received an award as one of the best-dressed men that year – got to the crease, Peter Pollock was already warming up, for we had decided the moment John got to the nursery end he'd have to deal with Peter. John didn't look happy this day, and before he could get off the mark he played back to Peter and was plumb lbw. It was 88 for three. Could we get another quick wicket? We had been 75 for three.

Ken Barrington and Colin Cowdrey had other ideas. Both were in form and their 56-run stand came in an hour. Then, bowling from the pavilion end, Richard Dumbrill took his first Test wicket, the prize scalp of Colin Cowdrey, bowled for 29. It was a great ball, making haste off the pitch, and it quite surprised both Colin and the critics.

While we made Mike Smith struggle hard for runs, Barrington played with great freedom, and many fruitless chases were made to the shortish boundary in front of the tavern. As Ken sped along past 50, 60, 70, 80, he looked thoroughly relaxed and enjoying himself. We took the new ball shortly before tea, but again a breakthrough eluded us.

After tea Jackie Botten tried again from the nursery end. He over-pitched a slower ball on about middle and off, and Ken drove the ball firmly wide of mid-on. He set off for his comfortable single. I ran from mid-off to take the return, but before I could get near the stumps I sensed something was 'on', for Colin Bland had anticipated the shot. Two long arms stretched out, intercepted the ball, and then, off-balance and with only one stump to aim at, being now at what would have been point the next over, he threw the wicket down. Pandemonium! Ken on 91 looked dumbfounded at being robbed of his century, as well he might, but we had seen Colin too often to expect anything else. Higher praise than that matter-of-fact statement I cannot give.

In the same over Botten had Smith caught by Denis Lindsay, and 240 for four had become 240 for six. We were right back in there. In Jack's very next over we were certain we had Jim Parks taken by Lindsay, but 'Dusty' Rhodes didn't agree. This was a great disappointment, for with that wicket down we would have been right on top and might well have wrapped up the innings there and then and had a lead.

As it was, Parks and Titmus came on far too merrily and shortly before 6.30 they passed our score. At the close it was 287 for six, giving 261 for six wickets off 108 overs in the day. The crowd must have gone home well satisfied with the fare offered: attacking batting, tight bowling, tigerish fielding, and Bland's wonderful solo performance, of which the Sunday papers next day rightly made great play. The pendulum had swung slightly in favour of England.

On the Monday my mentor, Fred Titmus, completed his 50 but only after Colin Bland had performed the second of his now famous run-outs, the victim this time being Jim Parks. The ball was played backward of square leg and Colin had to run round Syd Buller and throw the ball at the far wicket. Again I had a perfect view, backing up at mid-off. The ball passed through between Jim's legs as he strode out for safety and smashed the stumps with Jim well out. Again the stands erupted at Colin's brilliance, and again we players got that tingle – feeling goose pimples all over. It was great to have such a man in one's team.

Normally I was meticulous about placing my fielders, and making sure that they did not wander, but to Colin I gave full licence and left him to do his own plotting. He was a great student of the game and knew just where all the opposition played their shots. These two dismissals had a profound effect upon the whole series, inhibiting the taking of short singles by England's batsmen and ensuring our financial success as an attractive team to watch. Colin's timing for maximum favourable impact was perfect. England's innings closed half an hour before lunch at 338, 58 ahead. All my bowlers had stuck to their allotted tasks, none more so than Peter Pollock, despite figures of one for 91. At the start of the tour, in order to help him realise his promise not to break down, he and I decided that irrespective of the situation in county matches he would bowl in spells of five overs, gradually lengthening to six, seven and eight so that by the time of the Tests we could do 25 or 30 overs a day without strain. Our chances would have plummeted to zero had he broken down. In the next Test his figures were to be 10 for 89, but he didn't try harder or bowl better than his one for 91 this day.

Richard Dumbrill had the best analysis – three for 31 off 24 overs, a splendid effort. Richard was in many respects a 'moon' player; whether the moon was in the right quarter or whether it was the inspiration of his first Test that elevated his game, this Lord's Test gave him his finest hour.

Our second innings was by no means a flowing affair. At no stage were we able to take the initiative. Eddie Barlow got 30 before Tiger Lance got off the mark. Then at 55 David Brown put his mark on the game by taking the wickets of Lance, Barlow and Graeme Pollock for nine runs off 10 overs: 68 for three was very unhealthy, and the scales had tilted decisively in England's favour. But we weren't so downhearted that the spirit of fun had deserted us. Eddie lay down on the couch to recover after his swashbuckling 52 and to read the afternoon papers. The fact that he had hardly a stitch on was too much for Lance and Macaulay, who promptly set fire to the newspaper. Ed's consternation was a sight to see.

A determined Lindsay and Bland plus bad light saw us climb to 120 after tea, and then the former went, caught by Parks off Larter. Our final nasty blow for the day came when Colin on 70 miscued a ball from Barber and Edrich at mid-wicket took the catch – 170 for five. When I went out to bat 20 minutes before the close the sky was overcast and I found great difficulty in judging the flight of Bob Barber's leg-spinners bowled from the nursery end. The pavilion, though darker, at least gave some benefit of perspective to the narrow sight screen in use. All I could do was stretch forward, bat handle well over the ball, and hope. At the other end Ali Bacher mainly jabbed, with the occasional pull for four, and the two of us stayed there till stumps. Up on the scoreboard below Father Time our fortunes stood at 186 for five, or 132 ahead with six hours to play. The dressing room was very quiet that evening for we all realised the odds had lengthened against us.

The sky was still overcast when Ali and I resumed next morning to the bowling of Barber and Titmus. My main aim was to stay at the crease for as long as possible. For a while all went well, but then Ali attempted to pull a ball pitched further up than he thought, and paid the penalty, bowled by Titmus for 37. He had done well in his first Test.

Fred Rumsey came on to bowl with the score at 225 for six, or 171 on. I was feeling a little better for if we could last the 90 minutes to lunch we'd be out of the woods. Fred straightaway winkled out Dumbrill and Botten off successive balls, but Peter Pollock hit his hat-trick ball for four and together we lasted half an hour. Then what possessed me to try and slash past point off Rusmey I shan't know. Fred was happy though as Ken Barrington took the shoulder-high catch at third slip. Fred's spell had yielded three for 15 off nine overs. Next over Pollock tried to steal the strike, only for Boycott to emulate Bland with a direct hit on the stumps at Bromfield's end. Our score was 239.

Ever since I had seen Ian Craig's 1957/58 Australian team annihilate the Springboks I had held the firm belief that the team that scores the most runs at six, seven and eight would prove the stronger. Craig's trump cards were Ken Mackay, Richie Benaud and Alan Davidson. Now England had a formidable trio in Smith, Parks and Titmus in those positions, and so I feared for our success.

The final target was thus 191 runs in 235 minutes. You may well imagine the tension in the dressing room and the exhortation, the encouragement and the summoning of adrenalin for the task ahead.

Another of my beliefs was that to bowl for wickets usually resulted in runs, while to bowl for maidens earned wickets. We settled for maidens in the

25 minutes before lunch, and this was where England lost a trick. They played into our hands by scoring only eight runs off the seven overs bowled. Positive play in this period would have spelled 'finis' to our hopes. At near a run-a-minute we had a chance, especially without Dexter and not an England batsman prepared to chance a single anywhere near Bland.

The caterer for Test cricketers must sometimes wonder how players grow so big, for many chaps either peck at their food or eat nothing. On this day no-one felt hungry, and our chief encouragement came from Jack Plimsoll, who had just the right word for each man.

Three and a half hours to go, perhaps 60 overs to bowl, 183 runs to get. 'Right chaps, no more than two runs an over,' I said at the door of the dressing room. Each over yielding less than that was like gaining an inch in a tug-of-war; each boundary was a horrible wrench at the rope. Botten's first over yielded 11 runs, but then Barber left, chasing a wide one.

John Edrich still had his treble Test century on his back and couldn't fathom Peter Pollock who had prepared himself to bowl non-stop to the end. To one short one John barely ducked in time, then he ducked to one not as short and received a dreadful crack on the side of the forehead. By the time I had got to him from short cover there was already a lump the size of an egg. John decided to go off and Barrington replaced him. The score mounted but we were gaining slowly, in terms of time.

Richard Dumbrill replaced Pollock at the pavilion end and soon got rid of Boycott who, attempting a hook, got a top edge and the ball dollied up on the off-side. I shouted for Richard to take the catch, on the basis that self-interest would ensure the best chance of success, and Richard proved me right: he never looked like dropping this vital catch for 70 for two. Richard kept an absolutely immaculate length and the overs ticked by. Then he produced an excellent ball which cut back and kept low, and Barrington playing back was sunk 79 for three.

Cowdrey and Smith got things moving in the last half-hour before tea, taking the score to 109 with some smart running and good placements, mainly off Eddie Barlow's bowling. The 101 runs for three wickets in 125 minutes was good cricket on our part, for the target was now 82 in 85 minutes. We were by no means out of the woods: in fact I would have been most disappointed not to have won had I been captain of the batting side.

During the tea interval I warned the chaps against relaxing after their intense efforts. I decided to bring Peter Pollock on from the pavilion end and to switch Dumbrill to the Nursery End. Ten minutes later Richard got Smith to snick one and Lindsay made no mistake. Now came the supreme moment: half an hour of Jim Parks could spell the end of our hopes. I had a very real respect for his attacking abilities, and had I written out the England batting order Jim would have featured much higher. He flashed one through the covers for four, a beauty. Then he got a low full-toss from Dumbrill which he hit so hard that amazingly it was still in the air when I caught it at ankle height at deep wide mid-off. I had actually set myself to catch it on my right, but it swerved and I eventually took it outside my left ankle. There was more relief than exultation as I found the ball stuck in my hands.

Now for Cowdrey and Titmus. Fred's aggressive 69 in the first innings was still in the mind and the target of 70 in 65 minutes still favoured England. Peter Pollock then had Cowdrey lbw, a decision which Colin accepted with very good grace as there were suspicions that he had got an edge of his bat to the ball. If he had, then that made up for the decision that went against us in the England first innings when we were convinced that Parks had snicked a ball from Botten early in his innings.

Fifty minutes to go and 56 runs to get. Here, in retrospect I did err. I was not aware John Edrich would take no further part in the game, and having listened on the radio how Bert Sutcliffe, of New Zealand, had hit 80 in double-quick time after a blow on the head from a ball from Neil Adcock, I preferred to play safe and sorry rather than sorry and 1–0 down. So I kept the game Pollock and Dumbrill going for a bit longer. Then with the light going I gave Bromfield and Graeme Pollock a go, and though Graeme had David Brown at first slip, Fred Titmus and Fred Rumsey defied us to the end, the former taking most of the strike. In the last 85 minutes England had scored only 36 runs for four wickets, thus ending 46 runs short. The pitch had lasted very well and was a worthy Test strip.

So ended the 100th Test between the two countries at the home of cricket, and my first as captain of South Africa. Later Tests would yield higher standards of play and more satisfactory results, but few would equal this one for its fluctuating fortunes and enduring tensions. Our tour had been made by Colin Bland's feats in the field and by the wholehearted efforts of my team. What more could a captain want?

Yes, this was Peter van der Merwe's crowning glory. It was one of his greatest moments in Test cricket, and a spectacular triumph for a South African captain. Van der Merwe applied the principles of analysis of his opposition with painstaking care. The conditions prevailing in each match received microscopic attention. One could be sure that South Africa would not fail for want of planning.

As Kepler Wessels and the rest of the South African team embarked for England in June 1994, we should all have remembered that 29 years before, Peter van der Merwe had led what critics have described as one of the most competitive sides to tour Britain.

It culminated in the most famous of victories at Trent Bridge, which gave South Africa a 1–0 series victory; quite a turnaround from the 1–0 defeat inflicted by Mike Smith's England team when they toured South Africa earlier that year.

Van der Merwe's side had the advantage of being made up of young players who had started their overseas tour careers on the 1961 Fezelas visit to England. Six members of that happy band of young men, moulded into a side by my old comrade-in-arms, Roy McLean, were in the 1965 side. There are those who claim that the Fezelas tour had laid the foundation for the success of the sides that did so well up to the time of isolation in 1970.

Of the many Tests South Africa have won, Trent Bridge, 5–9 August 1965 always served as a rallying call in times of distress during those 21 years of isolation. While the Pollock brothers, Peter and Graeme (known in those days as Big Dog and Pooch), did much to help Van der Merwe achieve the victory by 94 runs, the ultimate triumph would always be the pinnacle of achievement for the Springbok captain.

On that tour Peter led with quiet, dignified authority, but the lasting memories are of a team spirit that virtually welded the side together and of players out to hit the ball, with the Pollock brothers and Colin Bland three key members of the side.

The victory at Trent Bridge was set up by the younger Pollock (then a strapping 21-year-old), putting together a well-crafted 125 on a pitch described by Richie Benaud as being a 'nightmare with damp patches which the England bowlers exploited'.

In that particular game the Pollock fraternal partnership had been without parallel at Test level, until the advent of the Australian Waugh twins, Steve and Mark. While Graeme scored 184 runs, Peter's five wickets in each innings added to the discomfort of the England side. Yet England quickly grabbed the initiative through the services of that fine seamer, Tom Cartwright.

South Africa were 80 for five in overcast conditions, with young Graeme Pollock holding the innings together in masterly fashion: his innings of 125 lasted only 140 minutes, but while he was at the crease South Africa managed 160 of their eventual innings total of 269 runs. In one of the finest batting performances in Test history, Pollock minor hit 21 fours and batted for 70 minutes before lunch (arriving when the score was 42 for three), and a further 70 minutes after the break. He offered no chances with his clean, stylish batting, adding a further 91 runs as the South African score advanced by a further 109 in an onslaught that wove its own brand of batting magic.

When England batted late in the day, Pollock major (Peter) broke through rapidly with two quick wickets – Geoff Boycott and Ken Barrington – to give Van der Merwe the edge at the close of the first day.

This continued on the Friday (the second day), when Pollock major bagged five for 53 off 23.5 overs. Apart from a stout performance from Colin Cowdrey, who scored an artistic 105 out of England's reply of 240, Van der Merwe had the lead he wanted. It may have only been a lead of 29 runs, but it was an important advantage on a pitch always helpful to the bowler.

Tiger Lance and Denis Lindsay departed quickly in the second innings, but Eddie Barlow, batting with a bruised toe, and Pollock minor added 99 for the third wicket in what turned out to be a crucial partnership.

With Ali Bacher, batting at six, scoring an important 67, the Springboks eventually ended with a second-innings total of 289, which set England a victory target of 319. Not impossible, but difficult enough, especially as England's batting had a habit of failing when under pressure.

Pollock major made quick inroads into the England second innings, and the hosts were in trouble early on the fourth day when John Snow departed with the score at 10 for three. The hosts blundered when Jim Parks, because of Snow's temporary nightwatchman slot, was forced to bat at nine in the order, which was far too low for such a punishing batsman.

Peter Parfitt and Parks did their best to put England's innings back on the rails, but too many wickets had fallen and a permanent repair job was beyond even their capabilities as Peter Pollock picked off a second five-wicket haul (this one was five for 34), while his younger brother trapped the England captain, Mike Smith, lbw for 24.

It was triumph for South Africa, and near full-house crowds for the four days of what was an absorbing game.

For Van der Merwe the lasting memory of that match was watching three teammates, several hours later, doing an impromptu lap of honour in front of the cleaning staff while wearing little more than their undershorts.

But, as Peter van der Merwe will tell you, the taste of victory is always sweet, as it was at Trent Bridge that warm August evening in 1965.

While a human being cannot be expected to deal perfectly with every facet of such an intricate game, Peter certainly deserved his appointment as captain of the national side on merit. His iron will transformed him into a match winner. His strength as a captain helped his side to tackle the task at hand in a determined yet relaxed fashion. Peter was never hostile to change, and attempted outside interference and criticism did not seem to 'faze' him.

Of course, cricket followers should not forget Van der Merwe's conquering of Bobby Simpson's touring Australians in 1966/67. It was a most interesting series that is covered more fully elsewhere. However, Van der Merwe had the great satisfaction of leading South Africa to victory in the first, the third and the fifth Tests, thus clinching the rubber for the Springboks. South Africa won 3–1, with one Test drawn.

Their victories were at the Wanderers by a mammoth 233 runs, at Kingsmead by a resounding eight wickets and at St George's Park by an equally convincing seven wickets. South Africa were certainly riding the crest of the wave and were vastly superior to the Australians, who won the second Test at Newlands and drew the fourth at the Wanderers.

I ended my book *Six for Glory* with the following remarks:

> Therefore, I prefer to quote Mr Boon Wallace, the President of the South African Cricket Association, who in the end-of-the-series impressions said: 'If one looks at the bare results of the Test series, one might be left with the impression that, compared with other Australian sides that have visited South Africa since the Second World War, Simpson's team might be classed mediocre. Yet, from every aspect, this has been the best tour ever to this country and brought maximum pleasure to both players and spectators.
>
> 'There are many sound reasons for the upsurge of interest in cricket this summer. There was the peerless batting of Graeme Pollock, some outstanding bowling performances by Trevor Goddard, and Graham McKenzie, the record-breaking batting and wicketkeeping of Denis Lindsay, and the excellent teamwork and general competence of the Springboks, so ably led by Peter van der Merwe.
>
> 'I believe, however, that the success of the Test series was basically due to the fact that both teams set out to play positive and attractive cricket and at no time deviated from their declared intentions. In this respect, I would like to give Bobby Simpson and his team full marks for the example they set. The net result was five wonderful Test matches with the real victory going to the game of cricket.
>
> 'I think the type of cricket played during the Test series had tremendous spectator appeal and the approach of both teams to the Test matches might have an excellent effect throughout the cricket world. Interest and support for the game is at an incredibly high pitch in southern Africa, and we look forward to the next series with Australia, whether it be at home or in Australia.
>
> South Africa are fortunate in the depth of established cricketers and talented young players at our disposal, but it is essential that they have opportunities of further Test cricket and overseas tours. I would welcome a more frequent exchange of visits between Australia and South Africa.'

And, with special reference to the very last sentence, who would disagree with Mr Wallace? Or, put another way, how could one possibly disagree with such sentiments after such a wonderful summer of entertainment, to which the Australians made full contribution?

I shall always be grateful for having seen such an absorbing series which had as its climax ... a Six for Glory. I would like to allot the penultimate paragraph of this chapter to a person who has become a captain of commerce and industry in his own right, Nic Frangos of Datakor. Nic was himself an outstanding cricketer who successfully represented Rhodesia on several occasions. He captained the South African Schools Eleven in 1959, then went on to the University of Cape Town where he met Peter van der Merwe. He spontaneously accepted with delight an offer to submit a tribute to Peter van der Merwe. He pens it in such a way it brings tumbling back a host of cricket's traditional qualities:

'In 1960 and 1961 I had the opportunity of playing under Peter for Cape Town University and for South African universities. Peter is an extremely serious person. Inside bursting to get out are many extrovert characteristics, a sense of humour and wonderful desire to be one of the boys. The fact that these only surfaced occasionally is probably a function of his background as it is with all of us. As a captain Peter cared deeply about the welfare of his team and is without doubt the most studious of all captains that I have played under. The fact that he rose to be a Springbok captain without the talent of the Richards, Pollocks and Procters is without doubt a recognition of the dedicated, thoughtful and excellent leadership qualities that he had. I always found Peter to be scrupulously fair and caring about the welfare of his teammates. In return he earned respect from his colleagues in the old-fashioned way.'

While it has often been said that Van der Merwe was fortunate in that he captained such powerful Springbok teams, nobody can detract from his extremely broad tactical vision and his obvious ability to plan a campaign. Van der Merwe has come in for a great deal of unfair vilification both as a captain and particularly as a selector. He has endured and overcome it all with dignity and triumph. When he stepped down before the 1992/93 season it was with the knowledge that he had set a path for other selectors to follow. And as a tribute to his standing within the International Cricket Council he was given the job of match referee in the historic Zimbabwe–India Test at Harare, along with the two one-day games – the first ICC match referee on the African continent.

His career as a match referee ended after a controversial limited-overs international series in 1998/99. England and Sri Lanka were involved in a World Series game at Adelaide Oval, when tempers spilled over as Perth umpire Ross Emerson no-balled the Sir Lankan off-spinner Muttiah Muralitharan for throwing. An angry Arjuna Ranatunga threatened a walk off for Emerson's calling of the bowler. As Murali's action, it had been proved, was a congenital problem and had been cleared by the ICC, the portly Sri Lankan captain and Van der Merwe discussed the issue. Not surprisingly, under the code of conduct Ranatunga was called on a number of charges of insubordination. In Colombo the parochial media blamed everyone, and one so-called writer became so entangled in the issue that he saw Van der Merwe as a 'paid Australian puppet'. Was this really a case of Ranatunga standing up to Australian pressure in a game that actually involved England? Or, as was pointed out at the time, was the real issue the little dog (Sri Lanka) barking at the perceived old Raj bully (England/Australia)?

What beggared belief was the way Ranatunga turned up with two lawyers at the post-match disciplinary hearing. He would not get away with such flagrant violation of the code. Coming from a political background, he knows all the dirty tricks. The fine was a soft one, which did not fit the crime: about R500 with a six-match suspension. The whole episode smacked of the sort of action that violated the ethics and code of the game, as Peter knew and played it. Peter was not interested in such semantics. He had a job to do and was stabbed in the back by a system that failed to protect ICC match referees; here the Australian Cricket Board was at fault, and Peter's comments of 'there are no winners in this issue' struck a poignant, dignified note to what was a sad episode.

BASIL D'OLIVEIRA (AND FRIENDS)
Witnesses for the Prosecution

9

By *Trevor Chesterfield*

It was quite ironic. Lunch on a Friday with two former South African captains – one black, one white – chatting and smiling and sharing a quiet drink in early October 1966. It was not in some plush hotel or city restaurant. This was in the upmarket house of a doctor in Laudium, grand apartheid's designated Indian suburb on the outskirts of Pretoria. One was Basil D'Oliveira, the other Trevor Goddard. It had been 10 years since D'Oliveira had first led the alternative body representing blacks and known by the initials Sacboc (South African Cricket Board of Control) against the Kenyan Asians. The first series was in Kenya in 1956; the second was two years later in South Africa. A frustrated decade later, he had become an England all-rounder and the centre of a growing controversy.

Goddard was head of the easily recognisable South African Cricket Association (SACA) with the Springbok as its emblem. He had led South Africa to Australia in 1963/64 and had at one time been captain of a side for which D'Oliveira played, which is why he and Basil were more than nodding acquaintances; the two had been in the same privately organised International Cavaliers side of 1962/63, which toured the Greek island of Corfu, Kenya and later Rhodesia (now Zimbabwe).

Organised by the enthusiastic English freelance cricket journalist Ron Roberts, the side on this occasion was jointly led by former England batsman Willie Watson and Colin Ingleby-McKenzie, captain of Hampshire. It included players such as West Indians Wes Hall, Chester Watson and Roy Marshall, Indians Ali Baig and Chandrakant Borde, and former England Test caps Peter Loader and Roy Swetman. It was Basil's second tour and he was enjoying the challenge. The Africa leg of the 1962/63 tour had ended, and as the side headed for India, the two all-rounders left for home; they were not going to get into India with their South African passports. Basil, though, was unaware of this at the time, and had happily gone on to his wife and parents in Cape Town.

The tour took place long before the British tabloid press dubbed him 'Dolly', and he found the sides to be a happy mix of cultures and demographics. They all smiled as best they could at the severity of some of the conditions and insults the West Indian and Indian players had to endure each time they set foot in racist Rhodesia.

'Ron knew how to organise such tours,' recalled Tom Graveney 37 years later, who had gone on any number of those tours. 'He knew how to get the right player mix as well. We always had trouble in Rhodesia, though; nowhere else ...'

In the long term, teams such as those organised by Roberts helped Basil's career, as they were part of the private tour circuit that flourished from the late 1950s to the mid-1960s. It was in the early months of 1962 that Basil first met Graveney, during the visit to East Africa and Rhodesia, and through him eventually managed to join Worcestershire (instead of Gloucestershire, who also sought his services). He had really wanted to sign for Lancashire, but the red rose county did not want him.

'A mere Saturday slogger, and we can't have that sort playing for us,' remarked Cyril Washbrook, the former England opener who at the time had much say on whom Lancashire could and could not sign.

By 1964 Basil had become what he light-heartedly called a professional tourist, travelling with international teams to gain experience and become a better player. It is always a matter of debate: promise and fulfilment are uneasy companions in sport, and combining both equally is a matter of self-belief. In 1963/64, while Goddard, now South African captain, was heading for Australia, a tour organised by former England fast bowler Alf Gover saw Basil flying with the team from Nairobi to Bombay (Mumbai), where he ran into trouble at the Indian port of entry on their way to Pakistan. The side was to stay in the teeming city overnight, but because of his South African passport the immigration officials at Bombay would not allow Basil into the country. What an ironic slap in the face for the earnest all-rounder: shunned in his own country because of the colour of his skin and banned from playing at places such as Newlands, the Wanderers and Kingsmead, he was now refused entry into India. And all he wanted was a bed for the night. Officialdom found a way around the impasse. He had to sign a form declaring that he was a South African of *Indian* parentage, put up £200 and agree that he would leave for Karachi the next day.

On his return to England he applied for and received a British passport. This eased his way to selection for England. He later said that he did not think he had betrayed his family or friends in Cape Town. He, along with more than 25 million others, was still banned by the laws of the country from representing South Africa. He was an outcast in his own country. It was common sense to become a British citizen, where his cricket skills were appreciated and without having to worry about the race paranoia of the whites.

During the first of the Roberts Cavalier safaris in Rhodesia, which included Basil, there were a number of incidents that stuck in the craw of several West

Indian and Indian players; there was some payback as well. On the way to an upcountry venue, the team stopped at Gwelo for a lunch break and a drink. Graveney went ahead and ordered four gin and tonics from the barmaid in the cocktail bar of the hotel. Two others joined him, and, as they talked, the West Indian Everton Weekes, one of the world's finest batsmen, entered. The barmaid jumped in and ordered him out.

'Get out. You know where your bar is,' she snarled.

Graveney let rip with a few choice words about so-called hospitality, and explained in less than polite terms what she could do with the drinks. The four walked out in disgust as other members of the party arrived. It was the first time Basil had seen this kind of reaction; he was not used to the kinship that existed among cricketers other than those from southern Africa. Weekes felt humiliated, and along with another West Indian great, Rohan Kanhai, wanted to quit the country.

In Bulawayo the Roberts safari was down to play a local side that included several Rhodesian players; because Weekes and Kanhai were in the side and there was, as in South Africa, a local by-law that barred blacks from playing a match in a white area, the game was shifted to a lesser venue in a black area. The grass was cut and a pitch marked out. It was a touch bumpy, but it would do.

A local, dressed in khakis, swaggered over and looked at the players as they changed in a tent.

'Say, you there … Weekes, you're going to give us a first-class performance, aren't you?' the offensive white spectator barked, wagging his finger.

Weekes retorted: 'Well, as this is a second-class venue, it'll be a second-class performance.'

The first ball Weekes faced he deliberately top-edged, and walked off without seeing whether or not it had been caught. The disgruntled bellowing of the spectator could be heard around the down-at-heel ground for the rest of the Cavaliers' innings.

On that early October afternoon in 1966, however, the efforts of Weekes were either forgotten or had been tucked into a memory box to be aired later. After lunch Goddard and D'Oliveira went to nearby Atteridgeville, a rundown black suburb with its subjugated grey apartheid face, to hold a clinic for a group of young boys; the venue was an open sports field, and those in charge had no idea what was expected of them. The boys were in awe of Basil and Goddard, and as equipment was sparse and the audience was expecting the two Test players to produce a miracle, they did what they could with what was a basic coaching session.

'It's very rough and ready and there's not much we can really do,' was Goddard's comment. 'No one seems to have prepared these kids.'

Apart from being about the only time the two men ran a joint coaching session, it was also a rare excursion across the colour line for them at a tricky time in South Africa's sports history. Had not Goddard, though, once adopted a strong non-racial stance, saying that although he was South Africa's captain, the government could not expect him to agree with their racial policies?

Basil was grateful for having been given the opportunity to coach young hopefuls and did not complain, when asked, how it would have benefited him had such a system existed when he was a schoolboy. He shrugged the question aside. He would rather concentrate his energies on what he was doing now than think about the past. Apart from what he *did* do, there was little else he could have done about that part of his life; his job was to try to help improve the future and give the youngsters some hope and something to think about.

'I was never coached when I was this age. In fact, I had no coaching at all at Signal Hill,' he said. 'We'd play in the street. And …' He hesitated. 'We might even have ended up in jail if the police had caught us …'

Basil readily sketched in some essential background. Signal Hill is in Cape Town. It was mainly a Malay quarter, where the rudiments of the game were a matter of learning to bat or bowl or field in confined spaces; there was no time to bother about such niceties as field placings or the difference between playing spin and fast bowling. Hey, the game was about *fun*. It was about running in and trying to knock off the block of the batsman. Or the batsmen knocked the ball out of the street. What did the youngsters know about such things as a World War? This was their war, their battleground; sometimes they won, sometimes they lost.

As a child, it was natural for Basil to join his father's club, St Augustine's. He agreed that the hardships he and others of his community endured meant there had to be a certain fanaticism to play the game. If fanaticism created the foundations of the career of a future South African captain and England all-rounder, there was nothing wrong with the grounding. This was not a school of technique or artistic skill; Basil was denied that opportunity. It meant working so much harder, taking that extra step and going that extra yard. Walking some 16 kilometres each summer weekend to help prepare the pitch before the game was a ritual. Matting over rolled baked clay; the outfield sandy and full of weeds – none of the fancy manicured green grass carpets and turf pitches, nothing at all of coaching and how a spinner holds a ball, or how to bowl outswing, or inswing. Often the ball was so old that it did not have a seam at all, and was, most likely, a two-piece. Four-piece balls were an unheard-of luxury: it was hard enough to find pads, gloves and a box, much less worry about a four-piece ball. A ball was used until the cover came off and the twine, which held the cork in place, unravelled as well. Basil's first experience with a four-piece was around 1948/49 when playing for Western Province (Board)[1] in a Sir David Harris tournament, and although it was an English brand name, the country of manufacture was India, imported through Kenya.

It was not all about Basil D'Oliveira either. There were others, such as Amien Variawa, his deputy in the two series against the Kenyans, and who captained the 'Test' at Kingsmead when Basil was ill. He, too, had hopes and dreams. Vincent Barnes, the former Western Province coach whose best days were long gone when unity enabled him to cross freely into a society where there were no barriers, said that there were others just as good as Basil, but who were constrained by the same laws and system of subjugation. Today youngsters are largely spoilt: ask them about a Dik Abed, or an Owen Williams, a Tiefie Barnes, Solly Chotia, Baboo Ebrahim or an Eric Petersen, and vacant stares will peer at you from under New York Dodgers caps. Oh, there were others, too. A whole lot more. Nothing is now mentioned about Eddie Barlow banning the Western Province side from visiting a restaurant in the late 1970s because Omar Henry was refused entry.

Yet, despite the disadvantaged circumstances of those years – for example, that the ground on which they played was miles from a bus route – they all happily congregated to overcome their deprived circumstances. It was about fealty to the game and its laws. At times there were as many as 11, even 12 games being played at once. It is hard to imagine, but space was tight for the bottom-rung teams on the cricket scale whose players had no hope of playing for South Africa.

One day, in the 1949/50 season, Basil went to Newlands and spent his hard-earned cash to watch the great left-handed batsman Neil Harvey, a member of Lindsay Hassett's Australian side. It was one thing to watch and another to put into practice what he saw. He did not then have the skill, technique or discipline to try to copy the Harvey style on matting; compared to turf conditions it was too far removed, and also the two-piece ball swung much more.

In December 1999, the *Sunday Times*, seeking the South African player of the twentieth century, published a series of profiles on 10 players that a select panel had chosen as worthy of such an honour. It was run in conjunction with the United Cricket Board. The list included Basil, belatedly elevating him to the status of a South African great. Here he was, 32 years after John Vorster, the ruling white minority government leader, had banned him, with an invitation to be at Newlands for a party to remember. (In the end it was Graeme Pollock who walked off with the accolade.)

It is a pity that the article published by the *Sunday Times* indulged in such platitudes as Basil being 'born in the wrong era' and how today 'a modern D'Oliveira would have been spotted early' – all so conveniently glib. No doubt something positive had to be written in South Africa about Basil, especially after the attack launched by Louis Duffus and other journalists when his banning led to the cancellation of the MCC tour of South Africa in 1968/69 and eventual isolation.

Why, Basil even had to indulge in a little deception of his own, which typically brought a finger-wagging from the South African establishment when it was discovered. He was born on 4 October 1931, which meant that by the time he reached Middleton he was 28, and getting on a bit. As he later admitted, if he hoped to attract a county, or even play for England, what selector would be interested in a 35-year-old? Did it matter that he altered the year of his birth to 1934? When he was selected in 1966, it was assumed that he was 31. The amended birth date remained until 1969, when he had it corrected as a matter of conscience. It explains why the Basil D'Oliveira story needs careful examining.

There are many misconceptions about the roles played by Basil, the MCC and their selectors, and the Vorster government in the selection impasse of August 1968.

In the mid-1970s Basil was blamed by any number of protagonists for South Africa's isolation. There was an incident in a bar in far-off Israel where Basil had gone with a group of cricketers on a private tour, and an unhappy South African tourist did not enjoy the sight of the camaraderie within the group. As he was about to leave the bar the tourist said, 'I'm not sure where you lot are from but I know all about him ...' pointing at Basil. 'He stopped *us* from playing Test cricket ...' But it was the inhumane apartheid laws that were responsible. As hard as it was for many whites to accept, only by getting rid of the repressive laws and recognising equality through emancipation could a form of normality make way for South Africa's reacceptance on the sports fields and in other areas.

One of the disturbing and sad facts of modern life is how the majority of young players attending the various development and academy systems know nothing about Basil D'Oliveira. Or, for that matter, the events he unwittingly created. If ignorance is a problem, what about the lack of knowledge of the racial administrative divide that existed for more than 200 years? The non-racial South African Cricket Board of Control (Sacboc) and its replacement, the South African Cricket Board (SACB), and their opposites, the South African Cricket Association (SACA) and the South African Cricket Union (SACU), all played their respective roles in a fractured society. People also know little or nothing about the Abed brothers – Dik and Tiny – Cecil Abrahams, Ben Malamba, Rushdi Magiet or Hoosain Ayob. Certainly the seven players who led the Sacboc and SACB teams are a mystery.

There are two reasons for this. The first is that today's youngsters would much rather watch limited-overs games available on the sports channels. A match between India and the West Indies in Jamaica is an opportunity to watch other players in action, and to learn about techniques and batting and bowling skills. It is an educational way to pass the time. The second reason is that even though few youngsters read books, there is also very little available on black, coloured and Indian cricket in South Africa.

The past generation has largely left a legacy of ignorance; the game is too important to allow such an adverse trend to continue. Yet, apart from the odd profile in such small volumes as *God's Forgotten Cricketers* (1976) and *Cricket in Isolation* (1977), both edited by Professor André Odendaal, the rich and vast cricket culture that exists within the coloured, black and Indian communities has only been recorded in part. Three recent works are Omar Henry's *The Man in the Middle* (1995), *The Other Side* (1999), edited by Krish Reddy, and *More Than A Game* (2001), by Mogamad Allie. They have filled in some of the gaps, but more needs to be written. Everything else is a blank page that needs to be filled.

* * *

It was the colonial lords, arrogant and without a thought for the future, who almost 180 years before Vorster's chilling pronouncement in Bloemfontein on 17 September 1968 had set in motion events that eventually culminated in the D'Oliveira affair. By the 1820s, the Cape Colony was their playground and the rules of law their playthings, and they turned them to their benefit.

For 20 years, from the late 1930s to the 1950s, 'non-white' cricket in South Africa was seriously splintered along religious as well as colour lines, and run by various bodies representing African, Malay and coloured interests. It was AE Docrat, whose vision was perhaps broader than most, who warned against associations formed along religious or cultural (ethnic) lines. To survive and grow, the game needed a non-racial representative body, which was the charter the Sacboc board arrived at in 1961. Yet tensions still existed, even as late as the mid-1980s, and were also felt in the disadvantaged communities. Some SACB officials continually policed the cricket community for those who wanted to cross the line and join the ranks of the opposition. While youngsters went to provincial or Premier League club nets to watch and learn, those of them who were caught often received a serious physical rebuke if they transgressed more than once.

Professor André Odendaal, who headed the United Cricket Board's Transformation Monitoring Committee, has traced the origins of Sacboc and its rise in *Cricket in Isolation*. It is a masterful study of how the sport thrived, even in the most desperate conditions. As he points out, however, the birth of a non-racial Sacboc had many midwives and occasional stillborn offspring before achieving its initial goals. To an extent, the tour of South Africa in 1956 by a Kenyan Asian side did much to help the non-racial ideal. Basil D'Oliveira was given the honour of leading the side in a series of matches, which South Africa won 2–0 at home and 3–0 in Kenya. Despite the hardships and facility problems, which were considerable, it was a side that grew in strength, ability and skill. Basil felt the honour was not only his, but also belonged to those who played in the side. It was his feeling that Sacboc reached its playing pinnacle in 1958/59, but was untested.

'I know how it feels and the frustrations involved,' he said years later. 'It was a special era, as was the side which had Graeme Pollock, Barry Richards and Mike Procter. We had some very skilful players, guys who deserved to play for South Africa. It was so disappointing to see such talent untested.'

This interesting comment was made after a luncheon during which the Nissan Shield season was launched in the mid-1980s, at a time when he and Sacboc leader Hassan Howa were on less than cordial terms. It was also a time when many white South Africans started lining up to apologise to Basil for the abuse hurled at his family and the coloured community in general after the Vorster/MCC selection debacle, which led to his banning and later the cancellation of the 1968/69 tour.

The 1960s, and even the 1970s, were times when blacks grappled with the aftermath of the Rivonia Trial in which Nelson Mandela and other prominent anti-apartheid leaders were sent to jail for life. Apart from trying to find an identity in a society bedevilled by apartheid paranoia, writing anything about someone such as Hoosain Ayob or Basil or Owen Williams was regarded as dissident. Black cricket, said an Afrikaans colleague in 1970, was revolutionary, as known communists ran the sport, just as Jack Cheetham was a communist. It would have been interesting to know the views of Cheetham and Howa, and how they felt about such comparisons.

White convention dictated that black cricket stories could appear only in newspapers catering to their community; there was no space in the white-controlled press. That was the view of many sports writers of that era, and also of those who belonged to the Rand Sports Writers Club. In the 1980s, as membership and newspapers dwindled, club management discovered how 'politically correct' it was to open their doors. Before that stage, though, the *Argus Group* of newspapers had made another 'politically correct' move. In the late 1970s they started to publish black editions in the Johannesburg and Pretoria areas; their main concern was that it might help fatten their bank balance.

Imagine the thoughts of one Lenasia-based journalist, Ameen Akhalwaya, on being told that an article he had written was 'subversive'. He had been asked to write something on 'spec', as it were, for the *Rand Daily Mail* on Doolie Rubidge, a fast bowler who in 1959 was regarded as a world-class athlete by Dolly. Subversive? What a cheek. But that was the establishment for you.

Writing anything about a 'non-white' sportsman or woman and expecting it to be published was subversive. This came from the doyen of South African sports writers of that era, Louis Duffus. Internationally respected, Duffus had written on more than 100 Tests involving South African teams since the late 1920s. He knew the establishment ropes well enough, and which one to tug for the right information. In late 1968, as England's latest Ashes series against Australia was being wrapped up at The Oval and the British tabloids were still fêting Dolly for his century, Duffus was finishing his stint as the opinions writer on the series for *The Guardian*. He wrote that if 'D'Oliveira is selected for the side, South Africa are unlikely to host the MCC tour of South Africa in the summer ahead'.

Writing from The Oval, Duffus was pragmatic about the issue. It was not a question of colour, he said, but of politics. Back in South Africa, however, he was establishment driven. He also knew that what he had written was half a lie: it was *all* a matter of colour, politics and apartheid.

Of course the SACA wanted the tour to take place with or without D'Oliveira, but with the Vorster government looking for a way to win further support as right-wing attitudes hardened, there was always going to be a scapegoat. In those dark, ambivalent times Dolly had long been viewed as an unwanted guest. Inquiries on whether D'Oliveira would be welcome as a member of the team had first surfaced 18 months before, when the British minister of sport, Denis Howell, said that 'the tour will be cancelled if there are moves to ban [D'Oliveira]'. By then a British subject, it was felt – and not only in England – that D'Oliveira deserved to be accorded the courtesy of the host country, not face threats and humiliation.

As the selection row simmered that summer, Basil was approached several times and told to make himself unavailable for the tour of South Africa. One curious suggestion was to 'make yourself available to play for South Africa', which he angrily rejected. At the dinner on the eve of the Lord's Test, it was known that a top official made a similar proposal. The 'official' was former South African Cricket Association president Arthur Coy, in England to convince Basil to withdraw as a tour candidate – or so it later transpired. Coy's confidant was Duffus, who also approached the Cape Town-born all-rounder, and later wrote a story on how D'Oliveira could 'save the tour and a lot of people many anxious hours by making himself unavailable'.

On 28 August 1968, the day after England had beaten Australia at The Oval, the side to tour South Africa was selected. There was a touch of nostalgia about the meeting: it was to be the last MCC team chosen for a tour. The selectors, headed by Doug Insole, vice-captain to Peter May on the 1956/57 MCC tour of South Africa, met at Lord's. Insole and the other selectors were unaware on that August evening of the prevailing political climate in South Africa. They were not told by either George (Gubby) Allen, the MCC treasurer, or the MCC president, Arthur Gilligan, of a confidential report from Lord Cobham, a former MCC president. Lord Cobham, while on a private visit to South Africa in early 1968, was invited to a meeting by Vorster, and during their conversation the discussion revolved around the government's new sports policy, allowing for mixed teams, and the possible selection of Basil for the MCC side. At this point Vorster made it clear that any side that included the England all-rounder would be unacceptable.

Why were the selectors not made aware of such important information? Had it been in mind all along, as it was later claimed in a copy of a report, which surfaced in 1998, that the discussion concentrated on the bowling attack rather than the batting?

Tom Graveney, the team's vice-captain, was visibly upset, as was Basil when, after approval by the full MCC Committee, the names of the touring squad were released the day after the Oval victory. What a political contradiction it revealed: in Fleet Street it was greeted with indignation; in South Africa, a packed Potchefstroom City Hall cheered when it was announced that Basil had not been selected.

Basil's omission was surprising, for he had scored 158 and had taken the crucial wicket of Barry Jarman. 'Thinking about it later, none of it made sense. An all-rounder was needed, and Dolly slotted in perfectly,' Mike Procter said when asked, not too long ago, for his views on the subject. 'There should have been no discussion about it. I was too young then to realise what trouble we were in. I thought it would soon blow over. I was young and naive; how wrong we all were.'

When the squad was announced, it was noted that Tom Cartwright, a right-arm seamer, would need a fitness test to prove to the selectors that he was fit to go on the tour. What happened after that went some way towards changing history. Cartwright's shoulder injury had failed to respond to treatment, and this showed up on 14 September, some 19 days after the announcement of the MCC side, when he played in a one-day game for Warwickshire. Two days later, Dolly was invited by the MCC selectors to join the team for South Africa.

The selection committee had blundered on two counts: the first was to say that Dolly was considered only as a batsman, and the second was to say, when he was included in the party on 16 September, that it was because Cartwright's shoulder had not responded to treatment and there was the need for a swing bowler. Twenty-four hours later Vorster became the hangman wanted by the government to rid itself of the D'Oliveira problem with one decisive jerk of the rope.

As vice-chairman of the SACA, Jack Cheetham had known months before the MCC selectors met that should Dolly be selected, it would lead to immediate problems with Vorster. If it is true what a veteran National Party politician, Ben Schoeman, admitted during a private conversation years later, four top SACA officials had known of the dangers as early as mid-April 1968. A member of the cabinet, Schoeman was present on the day the decision was taken (it was, ironically, 27 August) to ban the tour should Basil be selected. Not all were in favour of such a move; had it not been for a growing right-wing revolt, there could have been several dissenters.[2] If what Schoeman said could be taken at face value – and there is no reason to suggest otherwise – the South African captain was deliberately leaked a report citing reasons for the banning, should it be necessary. Not only would Dolly's selection cut across various apartheid laws, but it would also lead to an intolerable situation because the anti-apartheid movement would capitalise on his presence. Just the sort of insurrection needed to draw attention to the humiliating apartheid laws, which worried Vorster. As there was already a serious shift in the cabinet, where Transvaal and Free State right-wing hardliners had challenged Vorster's position, he needed to show resolve to beat off the threat, especially as there was serious concern over his sports policy speech of 11 April 1967. The speech, if studied carefully, is about as nebulous as any political doublespeak you could get out of the Nats in those far-from-halcyon days. Some seized on it as an 'enlightened landmark address'; others felt Vorster was 'playing to the international grandstand'. It was a matter of reading into it whatever one wanted. It did not impress Sacboc at all: the discriminatory laws remained.

It had been hoped that Cheetham would pass on the information about Vorster's views to those he knew in the MCC. Others who were privy to the report were Wally Hammond, a Kimberley businessman and the SACA president, and Arthur Coy, convener of the SACA selection panel. From what emerged, it seems Cheetham had not passed on the information. He knew two of the selectors, Insole and May, well enough.

Cheetham may have been a smart captain, but his administrative role and skills were blurred by inconsistency on occasions. He made one admission, though, during lunch after a meeting in 1972 between Sacboc and the SACA at the hotel next to Jan Smuts International Airport. He explained his thoughts on how to tackle the problem. Communication between the black and white bodies was essential for the long-term welfare of the sport, and if the two groups were to get around the laws of the country.

'I have to agree that it is not going to be easy and it is going to take time,' he admitted. 'We need to win their trust and have admit to them that we have made a few mistakes, which I feel has not gone down too well.'

As it was, the MCC had written to the SACA in January 1968 seeking some assurance that the tour would go ahead should the Cape Town-born all-rounder be selected. While the SACA set up a confidential study committee of three, headed by Hammond, it is no surprise that there are no reports or minutes of the meetings. Was this not perhaps the SACA realising that by the start of the next season (1968/69) they could be acting as a bereaved 'parent'? It was easier to blame the government, whereas they should have told the MCC five months earlier that there would be no tour if Basil were selected. Did the SACA vacillate over the selection issue? Did they hope that the problem would resolve itself, with Dolly losing form and the MCC selectors deciding not to pick him? By all accounts, Vorster had hoped for such a solution to the problem.

Sure, the SACA expressed 'shock' and 'deep disappointment' as they flew to England and a meeting with MCC officials on 24 September. Despite it being a lost cause, the MCC Committee still debated the matter for *four* hours. A week earlier, Vorster, acting as the hangman, had told a cheering crowd in Bloemfontein during the government's Free State congress that it was, 'No longer a team of the MCC. It is a team of the anti-apartheid movement ... We are not prepared to accept a team thrust upon us ...'

There was no alternative for the MCC other than to abandon the tour and replace it with a visit to Ceylon (Sri Lanka) and Pakistan. At least Dolly would be spared the indignity of being ostracised by a racist government and the team forced to duck for cover because of the xenophobic apartheid laws.

In the aftermath, Duffus had added, in print, his voice to the battle for and against Dolly's selection. Rereading the telexed copy, it still comes across as typical establishment jingoism, as much as Dick Whitington's chapter in his book *Simpson's Safari* attempts to express similar white-oriented sentiments. Duffus presents the glib white South African viewpoint. No black South African writer was given a forum to express an opposing view. Duffus, too, was living in a comfort zone and had not experienced the hardships created by apartheid.

He did not see D'Oliveira as just another county cricketer plying his trade to make an honest living. Here was a South Africa-born coloured who was taking on the system. He was born and had lived in South Africa, so what was he trying to prove? Any number of former players and administrators of an earlier generation, and conservative in their approach, would argue how Duffus, being the doyen of South African cricket writers, could do no wrong. As a writer he sometimes had a smooth, gilt-edged touch. To impeach his image 35 years later, when he is unable to defend himself, may smack of sacrilege to some. Yet the facts present themselves.

So, let us examine a couple of facts. One, Duffus produced volume three of the *South African Cricket History*, published by the SACA, in which he fails to acknowledge any form of black cricket. When it came to the question of the selection of black players who might previously have toured South Africa, he mentions the case of Duleepsinhji: 'A much greater cricketer could have been chosen to tour this country. He was not selected and nothing was ever heard about it.'

Oh, really? At the time, two London newspapers kicked up quite a fuss at the Duleepsinhji selection snub for the 1930/31 MCC touring team led by Percy Chapman. Duleepsinhji's uncle, KS Ranjitsinhji, had voiced his opinion in the

Evening Standard. Why Duffus ignored this pertinent fact is unknown. Perhaps in September 1968 it seemed the 'politically correct' thing to do. In any case, illness forced Duleepsinhji's premature retirement from the game in late 1932; his frail health was given as one of the (bogus) reasons for his non-selection in 1930. There was also the theory held by a couple of British writers – journalist and historian Thomas Moult being one – that 'colour prejudice alone was responsible for his exclusion'.

Moult was a rare breed in those strong establishment-conscious days between the two World Wars. He tackled prickly issues few cared to acknowledge. Certainly Sir Neville Cardus, the so-called doyen of world cricket writers, rarely strayed from the norm. Only when John Arlott, the eminent British broadcaster, journalist and author, started making ripples on what was a large institutionalised old boys' pond was the morality of South African policy against mixed sports teams seriously questioned.

Duffus was not, of course, the only sports writer to follow the party line. There were those who preferred to pay court to the establishment and rebuke those who stood against it, in this case Sacboc and Dolly. How Duffus railed against the British government's decision to throw out Colin Bland, a citizen of Rhodesia, a country whose white minority government under Ian Smith had grabbed power through an illegal declaration of independence. If this was the Duffus standpoint, then he was pro-Rhodesian (white), and it stood to reason that he would see D'Oliveira as the problem, rather than South Africa's apartheid laws.

In an article that appeared in the *Argus Group* of newspapers at the time of the tour cancellation, Duffus wrote that he did not believe that the MCC had succumbed to pressure over their initial decision to leave out Dolly, or when it was decided to include him when Tom Cartwright failed a fitness test. 'I believe this body [MCC] which exists solely to further the interests of cricket made the most crippling decision in the history of the game through blatant ignorance or deliberate ignoring of South African conditions. Because of one cricketer the great players produced in this country and the game itself have both been victimised.'

What should be asked is, had Dolly not been victimised? He had had to quit South Africa and, through friends, arrange to play for the Central Lancashire League side Middleton. No mention is made of this in the *Cape Argus* story. Or that Dolly was now a British citizen. Duffus, of course, could not see into the future. If he could he would not have suggested how, in time, 'posterity will surely marvel how a player helped to go overseas by a charitable gesture of white contemporaries could be the cause of sending the cricket of his benefactors crashing into ruins'. He also referred to Dolly in another article as being 'politically motivated and an opportunist with an axe to grind'.

Dolly has never been backward in thanking those who, in 1960, had helped raise the funds to get him to Middleton. Brother-in-law Frank Brache, then a Western Province Cricket Board member, helped form a three-man fund-raising committee. He tells the story of how a local Indian sports writer, Damoo 'Benny' Bansda, first made the cricket world outside Africa aware of the Basil D'Oliveira legend. There was also help from the gentle and humorous Western Province provincial batsman Gerald Innes. One of the unsung heroes of Cheetham's side to Australia in 1952/53, Innes was one of the few whites who understood the plight of the Sacboc players. Although he felt as aggrieved as Dolly had felt distraught and disillusioned when the West Indies side that Sir Frank Worrell had organised to tour South Africa in 1959/60 was aborted after black politicians stepped in and applied pressure, it was understood that a team of black players touring South Africa would further have demeaned the dignity of the black people, as well as given credibility to the white regime's apartheid policy. It was not a sports issue; it was a political and race issue. Forget the rhetoric of the whites, who would have clamoured to watch the side.

It is interesting to note how several white sports writers at the time (Duffus and Eric Litchfield, the former *Rand Daily Mail* sports editor, among them) questioned the need for such a tour. Worrell was as much a gentleman as Innes, and gracefully (as he explained later) withdrew the side; he was not initially aware of the possible harm such a tour of South Africa would cause. Everton Weekes, Gary Sobers, Conrad Hunte and those 'old pals of mine, (Sonny) Ramadhin and (Alf) Valentine', were among the Test players contracted. Imagine, though, the interest among the whites wanting to see Weekes, Sobers and Worrell. Newlands, Kingsmead and the Wanderers may not have been available, but no matter: venues such as Curries Fountain (Durban) and Natalspruit (central Johannesburg) would have overflowed with black supporters.

Apart from Innes, who had offered coaching advice to black cricketers in the late 1950s, and Peter van der Merwe, a future South African captain, there were several other whites who turned out and defied the apartheid laws, playing in the game that would help swell the coffers for the £450 needed to send Basil to Middleton: the first step to what became a new life.

Since then he has carried fond memories of the days in February and March 1960. He talked of them briefly in 1996, during the South African A team tour of England, while chatting to an interested group at the New Road ground in Worcester. There were, he said, people of all creeds and colour who did much to help him; among them were Innes and Tom Reddick, a former Nottinghamshire coach and Lancashire League player. Always the considerate gentleman to others who were less fortunate, Reddick coached D'Oliveira for most of the month, treated him as an equal and gave him pertinent advice. Although privately Reddick had his doubts on whether Dolly would make a success of being a professional cricketer, he quite happily acknowledges that he was wrong in his initial assessment.

As the SACA hid behind their curtain of subterfuge that summer of 1968/69, and found the Australians willing to tour the country in early 1970, Cheetham and Arthur Coy went to England in September 1968, more to seek assurances that the 1970 tour of England would go ahead than to tell the MCC what they already knew. There was a certain irony as well, as Sir Alec Douglas-Home, a former British prime minister, had been led astray by Vorster's pre-tour comments and these had been passed on to the SACA. Dolly also visited the politician and was told that there was concern that the 1970 tour was in jeopardy. Duffus wrote in August 1969 how 'friends in England and leading MCC officials contacted, have assured me the 1970 tour will go ahead without a hitch'. This was after Peter Hain (later a senior cabinet minister in Tony Blair's government), a leading anti-apartheid activist and anti-tour leader, had vowed to stop the tour, and used the visit by the South African rugby team to prove that he could. To achieve this, Hain mobilised a group called Hart (Halt All Racist Tours) and was highly successful.

In the aftermath of the abandonment of the 1968 tour, the SACA suddenly recognised that there was something called black cricket and a body known as Sacboc, run by a militant sports administrator by the name of Hassan Howa. As paranoia set in, the SACA launched a trust fund of R50 000 (then about US$22 600) for black cricket, just the sort of tokenism Sacboc and Howa were not prepared to accept. Why had the SACA suddenly launched this gambit? Was it something that had come out of the meeting with the MCC at Lord's? Or was it to belatedly salvage their conscience after almost 80 years of neglect?

The white media howled their indignation – especially the Afrikaans press – at 'the ungracious snub black cricket had offered the SACA'. Howa was seen as a maverick for telling the SACA what to do with the trust fund, which was 'founded in good faith to assist the levels of black cricket', according to a letter published in an afternoon paper called *Die Vaderland* [The Fatherland]. Nothing was mentioned about this being white cricket's first genuine offer to address a problem they had shunned since the SACA was first formed in Kimberley in 1890. Somewhere someone may have smiled at the irony. The fallow fields that Sir Abe Bailey and Sir William Milton had created for black cricket to languish and wallow in while the SACA prospered were showing signs of positive growth.

Australia informed the SACA that if the South African tour of 1971/72 was to go ahead smoothly, one or more black players would have to be selected; this was later denied by the Australian Cricket Board. Yet two seasons later, at the Basin Reserve in Wellington, Australian all-rounder Doug Walters told a different story. During the first Test of the Kiwi leg of the 1973/74 twin tours, Walters said that their board had told the players in February 1971 that the South Africans hoped to include one or more black players in their team for the tour. Later these turned out to be all-rounder Dik Abed and the spinner Dolly felt was a Test natural, Owen Williams.

With two tours aborted and a third likely to go the same way, there were problems ahead for the SACA. Now internationally ostracised and under pressure, Cheetham and his board had approached the two talented Sacboc players without consulting either Sacboc or Howa. The government would have none of it, and understandably the two players were offended by the offer. They were not prepared to be window dressing. Williams said he wanted to be 'selected on merit and not as some glorified baggage master'. It required some cheek for the SACA to go this particular route, and in black cricket circles it was seen as another discourteous move by them to enhance their image.

The SACA were now running on empty, their credibility collapsing on all fronts and isolation looming. Amid all this was another touch of irony – it was the man at the centre of the original storm, Basil D'Oliveira, who tried to act as peacemaker between the two boards, who eyed each other with suspicion. In 1973, as the talks between the two bodies collapsed, the SACA clung to the faint hope that one day there might be some accommodation reached between the two. It was also a time when most white sports writers were perceived to be part of the SACA establishment, and Hassan Howa eyed them with distrust; trying to get a face-to-face interview was hard work.

When moves towards unity did come, the hawk, Hassan Howa, had given way to the dove, Rashid Varachia. The South African Cricket Union was formed, and the brief unity of 1976/77 was launched. Something, however, was missing. Although there had been events such as the forming of a 'normal' club in Pietermaritzburg, called Aurora, in 1973, and which drew members from across the demographic divide, not many others were brave enough to follow this example. Brian Bassano, in East London in 1976/77, was founder member of the short-lived Rainbow Cricket Club. It caused some Sacboc members to ask 'why?' Surely, if there was to be genuine trust and added emphasis in this quiet revolution, more clubs such as Aurora were needed to light the way. Club members were under pressure from various establishment sources; threats to family, as well as possible court action and physical damage to property, were part of the harassment routine. It did not only happen in Pietermaritzburg. Attempting to take coaching equipment into areas such as Atteridgeville and Mamelodi and running into officialdom created problems, as did trying to establish firmer links with acquaintances in Laudium. Standing up against government policy in the treacherous 1970s marked many as subversive, and survival was characterised by the use of deception.

Howa was not the only one who was far from happy about how the unity process worked. Off the field nothing had changed: the Group Areas, Job

Reservation and Separate Amenities Acts remained, the black population was still disenfranchised and the 'whites only' signs still existed to humiliate two-thirds of the country's population. How then can you play normal cricket in an abnormal society? Yet, as in the 1950s, egos often got in the way of progress. When the remnants of the old Sacboc met in Kimberly on 25 September 1977, the plan was to resuscitate the board. It then ran into a legal wrangle over the use of the name Sacboc. The objection was clear enough: Sacboc was one of three boards disbanded the previous year to form the South African Cricket Union, and the name could not be used. It needed pragmatic thinking, and by November 1977 the South African Cricket Board had been formed, with Howa and Krish Mackerdhuj the senior executives. In November 1990, Mackerdhuj spelt out his board's long-term message. It was six weeks before the Port Elizabeth meeting, which set up the mechanism to form the United Cricket Board, and he made no issue about what he believed.

'What we at SACB attempted to do was to commit our forces as a sports body, and one representing blacks, to developing a progressive sports culture,' said Mackerdhuj. 'Our aim was simple enough: transformation through our members to become involved in the politics of sport.'

Howa, SACB president between 1977 and 1984, was a high-profile administrator and apt to issue statements and comments in terse assertive language; unfortunately his robust style of delivery hid his quixotic and warm personality. Not many administrators within the SACB or SACU saw this side of him, yet South Africa was in need of such a firebrand to stir the comfortable white conscience. It came as a shock when he was unceremoniously elbowed out of a system for which he had fought so hard. It was all a matter of position, perception and duplicity by the predators among SACB officials. There were those who had long wanted to get rid of Howa but had not succeeded; the cunning fox had all too often outmanoeuvred them. His meeting with Dr Ali Bacher, the SACU's managing director, in early January 1987 gave them their opportunity. It would surprise many, after their long stand-off, how the two intractable foes somehow found common ground for discussion. It was a minor matter: a question of a R1 million sponsorship for the game at junior level.

Ever down-to-earth in his assessment, Howa later said, 'We need each other. They cannot get into international cricket without us, and we can't realistically think of going it alone without them.'

Had the first steps towards accommodating the ideas of both bodies been taken? Perhaps. Strong argument suggests that this was the case. In late 1987, it was known that Howa had been thinking along those lines, urging hardliners to rethink SACB strategy. Moderate SACB members felt that had Howa not been placed on the pyre of internal retribution and allowed to continue his talks with Dr Bacher, the course of South African cricket unity would have taken a more rational, calmer path, and been achieved three years earlier. There would have been no need for the Gatting rebel tour, and no need for talks at Sun City in October 1989, at which the National Sports Council offered the SACU international recognition and tours within the year if the Gatting venture was aborted. Hardliners within the SACU rejected the offer.

From as early as June 1986, there was uncertainty about the political direction South Africa was taking. Apartheid laws were being dismantled, and beaches in some cities were opened to all. Certainly the traumatic and dramatic political upheavals and other pressures apparent from April 1989 had seeped into the psyche of an edgy white society, while the black population waited. After more than 350 years, what did a few more months matter?

For Howa, however, the spillover of acrimony from his meeting with Dr Bacher was deadly. Not so much were the knives out, but the whole cavalry charge was lined up: lances and sabres all aimed at his back in a wild rush to crush his power base. His untimely removal weakened the influence of the Western Province Cricket Board in SACB ranks, to the extent that at times it lost direction. Political malcontents, who were later seen to be in a mad gallop to embrace the UCB system, were openly antagonistic towards Howa. One was Rushdi Magiet, who was sacked as convener of national selectors in April 2002. For one thing, Howa would have demanded a quota system and would have won the battle. Howa saw cricket as a chance to create opportunities and a better life for the less privileged and marginalised in the community – the game for all. Yet there were many who wanted to be rid of him, and his meeting with Dr Bacher was their opportunity. Many of those who were in that cavalry charge are today part of the new UCB, singing his praises whenever his name is mentioned. He died on 12 February 1992, still bothered by some aspects of unity and where it was heading.

Mackerdhuj, SACB president from 1984 until it merged with the SACU in 1991 to form the UCB, and later ambassador to Japan, could be just as forceful when need be, and expressed his views clearly enough, especially during the era of the rebel tours in the 1980s. He was also more diplomatic than Howa, and was upset about how 'some in the Kingsmead crowd insulted my players' in the late 1990s.

* * *

One area where there are more grey patches than in a storm-tossed sky on a Highveld January afternoon is the matter of how many genuine captains have led Sacboc and SACB teams. There are three views, and they are as divergent as the politics of South Africa since Jan van Riebeeck landed in Table Bay. Several former players and officials suggest that there are two official Sacboc captains, while the others received colours. The late Khaya Majola, a leading SACB all-rounder, and top SACB wicketkeeper Yassien Begg offer a different view. They say five, although they agree that Basil D'Oliveira and Amien Variawa deserve special recognition, because they led Sacboc sides against the Kenyan Asians in 1956 and 1958. The 1958 tour saw two Tests against the Kenyans and one against East Africa. Durban historian Krish Reddy offers an enigmatic smile and a shrug, and has seven names on his list.

Dolly regards his captaincy of the 1956 and 1958 Sacboc sides in five Tests against the Kenyan Asians and East Africa with pride. He does not consider the games played against Eastern Province or the Rest of Sacboc XI as anything more than 'honorary colours', although his record is impressive enough: 1 019 runs at 72.79 with three centuries and six 50s, while his 10 wickets were at a cost of 21.60.

Variawa, who led Sacboc in the drawn Test against the Kenyan Asians at Kingsmead in 1956, was a stylish opening batsman, and there are those who feel that had he been as fortunate as Dolly and also gone to England instead of getting married, he would probably have matured into a better batsman than the Cape Town all-rounder. Variawa had elegance and all the strokes, and it was a tragedy for the game when he was killed in a car accident while on his way to Potchefstroom on 31 December 1985. Older Sacboc players saw Amien as D'Oliveira's natural successor. Ameen Akhalwaya wrote a glowing tribute in the *Post* in January 1986 of how as a player Amien had learnt to bat 'in the streets of the ghettos, Vredesdorp in this case'. Hoosain Ayob tells the story of his patience and tenacity. He was stylish and could be as fluent as Dolly: while not compact, he was neat and organised.

'Yet there was no mistaking his quality,' says Hoosain. 'There was a century against a white side led by John Waite at Natalspruit, and there is no doubt that it was his batting which won us that game. I think its quality and the way he batted impressed those such as John Waite. He scored it against a near Springbok bowling attack and in difficult conditions.'[3]

Natalspruit's outfield was notoriously rough, and the pitch was matting over rolled clay. Years later Jackie Botten, the former South African fast bowler, recalled the conditions as being 'not fit for a big match', yet wondered how anyone could have batted the way Variawa did. The conditions were hard, and as a batsman that meant it was essential to apply the basics.

Variawa's one Test as Sacboc captain against the Kenyan Asians at Kingsmead was brought about because of Basil's illness, and he led the side with the same flair and candour as Basil. The Sacboc side went on to wrap up the series 2–0, and the conditions were about as good as they were going to get. The following season they were to play games against an international side led by Frank Worrell, but the black politicians pulled the plug on the tour. It was, in a sense, the reason why Dolly decided it was time to move on and get a position with a league club in England. Variawa would have followed, but sponsorships were hard to get and he was not long married. He swallowed his disappointment and life moved on.

If, as the *Sunday Times* pointed out with unctuous ease in December 1999, Basil was 'born in the wrong era', what then about Natal all-rounder Gopaul Manicum? Or, for that matter, Transvaal's Abdullatief (Tiefie) Barnes, Natal batsman Mustapha Khan and Eastern Province all-rounder Khaya Majola? Were they not born in the wrong era? Would they also have been spotted in the modern development programme, pulled through the system and been turned out as future Test or limited-overs international players with bright futures? It is as easy to make such claims and predictions as it is to suggest that Justin Ontong is the next D'Oliveira.

As Sir Conrad Hunte, the former West Indies opening batsman once suggested, 'There is one Bradman, there is one Sobers; don't saddle future generations with false examples. Rather let Barry Richards be Barry Richards, Brian Lara be Brian Lara and Sachin Tendulkar be Sachin Tendulkar. To tell a left-hander he's going to be the next Lara is telling a lie. He is as good as he is going to be.'

Gopaul Manicum, a North Natal all-rounder who was a special player, had no mirror image. An energetic sort, he bowled off-spin with loop and guile, and there was a flair about his bowling; Tiefie Barnes, like Variawa and Majola, was in a special class, a legend in Sacboc/SACB pavilions and on the playing fields. Barnes, the diminutive Transvaal all-rounder, always had a ready smile, accepted all challenges and often swallowed his disappointment. Twice in the early and mid-1970s he withdrew from matches for the South Africa Invitation XI against the Derrick Robins XI,[4] as it cut across Sacboc principles. He would not forsake the merit selection policies laid down in the Sacboc constitution – tough choices to make in an era where merit selection was the genuine passport to playing in a South African side.

In 1976 came the unity talks. Cricket was prepared to go where no other South African sport would: throw the doors open to all. Finally, the chance came to turn out for the South African XI against the International Wanderers touring side, brought to South Africa in the 1975/76 season by Richie Benaud. There was the debut at Newlands, followed by a game at the Wanderers; an injury kept Abdullatief out of the side for Kingsmead. Sure he was happy to be able to experience playing at this level of competition; he knew he was good enough, and as with all Sacboc players, given more exposure he would have achieved more. Similarly Mustapha Kahn, who in 1985/86 led the Rest of SACB against the Howa Bowl champions and the following season played for the President's XI. Another honour was selection for a Sacos XI in the Sacos Festival Games. An all-rounder who played league cricket in England, Mustapha managed a rare double in the Howa Bowl competition: he scored 2 000 runs and took 200 wickets.

Another player who in a 'normal' society would have achieved much, and possibly have played for South Africa, was Khaya Majola. Watching him in action for Eastern Province against Transvaal in Lenasia was an entertaining experience. Although past his best, here was a talented and skilful bowler, and it would have been interesting to know how many more there were like him. Or how far he and others would have gone.

In February 1989, sneaking into an Indian suburb on the outskirts of Johannesburg was an intriguing exercise. To some the ground was the Varachia Oval; to others it was Lenz Stadium. Dr Goolam Karim enjoyed his Sunday afternoons watching Howa Bowl games, and was quite happy to extend an invitation to those sincere enough to want to make the journey with him. Khaya was perhaps a little rotund, but enjoyed bowling at the opposition. On that Sunday he picked up several wickets before rain wrecked the rest of the afternoon. Two years later, there had been any number of exciting changes to the face of the game and the shape of politics. By then a more than cheerful Khaya had already moved to Johannesburg, and the vision he had hinted at in January 1989 was taking shape. Through the agreement fashioned by the unity talks of 16 December 1990 in Port Elizabeth, Khaya had joined Dr Ali Bacher to continue a development scheme to benefit all, especially the previously disadvantaged in areas under SACB control. He now had an office and staff at the SACU offices at the Wanderers Club.

Dr Karim, the articulate chairman of the Cricket Association of Transvaal (CAT), was again the host. A soft-spoken man who had studied medicine at Trinity College in Dublin, he firmly believed in the egalitarian principles Lord Harris had taken to Bombay. Khaya was equally soft-spoken, and when he talked about his work with Dr Bacher, a broad smile creased his sweat-lined face.

'We need to create trust,' Khaya said, 'to get all the black kids into this system without them feeling awkward. I didn't feel awkward when I first started, but I know there are going to be those from some areas who are going to feel shy ... The secret is to let them know that all are equal.'

Here was the burning ambition of a man who as a player knew his career was behind him; destroyed by the uncompromising apartheid laws, which had wrecked so many dreams and lives. He wanted to turn it around. The evolution process he talked about years later would come from the revolution, but it had to be harnessed correctly. No one must feel alienated by the system. It is all a matter of working together. Working for the common cause. What sort of a player was he?

'He would have gone a long way had we been given the opportunity,' Hoosain Ayob said. 'He had such a passion for the game, and his all-round skills were good enough to attract the attention of overseas people. He turned away from all that and joined Sacboc.

'I don't think people realise what black talent there was in South Africa, and how in a normal society players such as Khaya would have had an impact. We all had the dream of playing Tests for South Africa. There are many out there who will never know how good a player like Khaya was, because of the conditions we all played in. It was hard and we all felt it.'

Selected in 1974 for a Derrick Robins tour of England under the leadership of Clive Rice, Khaya made a visible impression as a bowler and lower-order batsman. He had already made a name for himself in the John Passmore Week, and his caring father and mentor, Eric Majola, felt great pride. A double (black) international in cricket and rugby, he knew that his son was a quality player. Should he not go to England and try his hand playing in one of the leagues? Follow his dream?

Khaya did not want the glamour. Sure he wanted to aim high, to go places and learn. But if others of his race could not do that, why should he turn his back on them? Life in apartheid South Africa was hard and demeaning, and the cricket facilities were just as disheartening for someone with such talent. He shrugged it off. In a career spanning 17 years, he played 85 games for Eastern Province (Sacboc and SACB teams), the most by any of their players, and his 216 wickets at 16.27 showed he was a seamer of rare talent. They were the most games played by any cricketer in the non-racial leagues.

What was the standard of these games? Well, as they were played in oppressed and disadvantaged areas, and as the majority of whites have no idea what it was like to play on matting surfaces and corrugated outfields, a visit to places such as New Brighton would make for interesting comparisons. Then again, it should also be remembered that as a schoolboy Sir Donald Bradman played on matting over concrete strips; in such cases batsmen often had the advantage. There are a few upcountry areas in New Zealand, Australia and Sri Lanka where games are still played on matting and from where Test players have emerged. It refutes the argument that such conditions marginalise players and handicap their skills.

These conditions gave Khaya the insight and belief that the development programme he had started with Dr Bacher in the early weeks of 1991 would in time produce quality as well as quantity.

While not quite in the same context as Dr Martin Luther King, Khaya Majola also had a dream, and although he lived some of that dream, he would have asked those who travelled the road with him if it had all been worthwhile. It is a pity that, because of his tragic and untimely death on 28 August 2000, he did not live to see the dream fulfilled of the UCB repealing the quota system. His transformation initiatives and development strategies in the game have gone a long way to creating a new dimension, and Mfuneko Ngam and Makhaya Ntini are the first of many who are benefiting.

As Omar Henry, the convener of the national selection panel, pointed out, there are five players of colour in the national squad for the first tournament of the 2002/03 season in Tangiers, Morocco. There are five players of colour in the South African side attending the Africa Cup, and nine in the national academy side heading for Australia. There is also the South Africa A side to be selected for a series of limited-overs games against Australia, where a possible five black players will be included in the squad. It gives the four sides a total of 24 players of colour. And the sports minister and his overweight ministry want to quibble about ditching quotas.

10

ALI BACHER
Quality Leadership

By Jackie McGlew

Aron Bacher, affectionately known to the cricket world as Ali, is South Africa's most famous 'Mr Cricket'. Others, of course, have been given this label, including the cricket patriarch Joe Pamensky. Ali Bacher would be the first to acknowledge that he learnt a great deal about the administration of the game from Joe Pamensky. Pamensky, an astute chartered accountant, has in many ways been Bacher's mentor in the execution of his duties in the administrative field. He has always been on hand to offer spontaneous guidance and advice, if so requested. His direction is always solid and unbiased.

None of these observations detracts in any way from Ali Bacher's inherent astuteness as an administrator. He has a flair all of his own in this area. It would not stretch a point to say that he ranks alongside the great administrators this game has produced in any era and anywhere in the world. Furthermore, his astronomical success has been achieved despite the most diabolical difficulties. Bacher has faced many adverse situations, and he has surmounted them.

The major reason for his success has been his deep, abiding love of cricket and everything associated with this noble game. He has piloted Transvaal and South African cricket to countless achievements both on and off the field.

Ali Bacher started school at Yeoville Primary, then went on to King Edward VII School. While at KES he was chosen to represent the South African Schools XI in 1958 and 1959. The young Bacher set his sights on becoming a medical doctor. With his now well-known, dogged determination and application to the task in hand, he qualified as a doctor with an MBChB at the University of the Witwatersrand. He completed his internship at Baragwanath and Natalspruit hospitals in 1968 and 1969.

He has tackled everything he turned his hand to with an intense dedication. Bacher is a visionary, but paradoxically he is also a hard-nosed pragmatist. He is a genuine 'doer'. So, when he took over as managing director of the Transvaal Cricket Council in 1981, Bacher turned the whole set-up into a truly professional outfit. He has the rewarding knack of surrounding himself with capable and enthusiastic people. There is no doubt that this springs from his efficiency and enormous enthusiasm. In the affairs of the Transvaal Cricket Council, Bacher was the able convener of the Transvaal selectors when the now-legendary 'mean machine' of the 1980s was spawned. This team, under the leadership of Clive Rice, fed off the other provinces like a foraging great white shark off the Great Barrier Reef. Coming up against Transvaal was a case of 'and just when you thought it was safe to go back into the water ...'

Bacher had the foresight to sign up the two great West Indians, Alvin Kallicharran and Sylvester Clarke. They both performed outstandingly. Just imagine a Transvaal line-up reading something like this: Jimmy Cook, Henry Fotheringham, Alvin Kallicharran, Graeme Pollock, Clive Rice, Kevin McKenzie, Alan Kourie, Ray Jennings, Neal Radford, Vintcent van der Bijl, Rupert Hanley.

That is enough to make any opposition gasp! Many an international team would have taken a drubbing from such a powerful combination at its peak. When Alvin Kallicharran left in 1983, Sylvester Clarke was enlisted. Clarke was an awesome sight in full flight. Kallicharran had served the province well and his West Indian flair brought excitement to all the grounds he graced. But it was Clarke, the giant West Indian paceman, who struck terror into the hearts of his opponents. In one Currie Cup season alone Sylvester captured 52 wickets. This Transvaal record was later broken by Steven Jack, who had a massive haul of 54 wickets in the 1990/91 season. Had it come one season later, this effort would have earned Jack a trip to the World Cup.

The preamble about the 'mean machine' and the two vibrant West Indians indicates just how Transvaal cricket prospered under Ali Bacher's leadership – even after his fruitful years as Transvaal's captain. Basically, cricket has been Bacher's whole life. He was convener of the national selection panel from 1982 to 1985. Again he distinguished himself in the way he discharged his duties. And Bacher now plays the leading role in the Cricket World Cup organising committee, after relinquishing the post of managing director of the United Cricket Board in 2000.

Insofar as Bacher's actual playing days are concerned, he made his first-class debut at the tender age of 17, during the 1959/60 season. This was the start of an illustrious career that lasted 15 years, from the 1959 season to his grand finale in 1973/74. When he finally retired from first-class cricket, Bacher was a household name. He had led South Africa to a resounding 4–0 victory over Bill Lawry's touring Australians in 1969/70, and was chosen to captain a powerful team to England in the (British) summer of 1970. This tour was cancelled at the eleventh hour for political reasons, which involved government intervention. Since then Bacher has worked with a diligence bordering on fanaticism to remove all racial barriers in sport, particularly his beloved cricket. And he has been successful.

Bacher has spoken out on countless occasions about human rights and equal opportunity. He has expressed his views whenever the occasion has presented itself, on TV, radio and in public appearances. He could not have known in 1970 that his last day of Test match cricket would be at St George's Park, Port Elizabeth, on 10 March. In this Test his contributions were 17 in the first innings and a fine 73 in the second innings.

South Africa were in a rampant mood, scoring 311 and 470 for eight wickets declared. Australia's modest response was 212 and 245, mainly because they could not contend with the South African pace bowlers. In the match, Mike Procter had a superb bowling analysis of nine wickets for only 103 runs. A splendid effort, as was the efforts of the rest of the pace bowlers. Between Peter Pollock, Eddie Barlow, Tiger Lance and Pat Trimborn, they picked up the remaining 11 Aussie wickets.

This concluded a whitewash in what was one of South Africa's finest cricketing hours. It was only fitting that Ali Bacher took the final catch to close the Australian innings when he pouched Connolly off the bowling of Pat Trimborn. The other three Test matches went as follows:

FIRST TEST. Newlands, Cape Town. 22, 23, 24, 26, 27 January 1970

	SOUTH AFRICA	AUSTRALIA
First innings	382	164
Second innings	232	280

South Africa won the first Test by 170 runs, which gave them a tremendous psychological advantage.

SECOND TEST. Kingsmead, Durban. 5, 6, 7, 9, 10 February 1970

	SOUTH AFRICA	AUSTRALIA
First innings	622 (for 9 wickets)	157 (2 declared)
Second innings	Did not bat	336

South Africa ran out winners by a mammoth innings and 129 runs. It was in this Test that Graeme Pollock established a South African Test record when he scored 274. Pollock's great achievement took him only 417 minutes and 401 balls as he machine-gunned the Aussie attack. The Australians just could not contain him, and his run-making fluency was like a tidal wave rolling on relentlessly.

THIRD TEST. Johannesburg. 19, 20, 21, 23, 24 February 1970

	SOUTH AFRICA	AUSTRALIA
First innings	279	202
Second innings	408	178

In winning this Test, South Africa made sure they had won the rubber. It was no doubt a proud moment for Ali Bacher. In some ways it was a sad Test, because it was Trevor Goddard's last appearance for South Africa. He was replaced by Pat

Trimborn in the fourth Test. Nevertheless, Trevor had the consolation of taking a wicket with his final delivery in a Test. This was when Connolly, who was involved in a last-ditch stand with Taber, was eventually caught by Richards off one of Goddard's left-arm deliveries. Goddard had given his country yeoman service and is still rated by many cricket followers as South Africa's number one all-rounder: a class bowler, top front-line batsman and fine fieldsman. Alas, he was not to play in the glorious fourth Test at St George's Park, Port Elizabeth, where Ali Bacher's powerful team 'took Australia to the cleaners', thus concluding with an historic whitewash. Bacher must have been as proud as a peacock.

FOURTH TEST. St George's Park, Port Elizabeth. 5, 6, 7, 9, 10 March 1970

	SOUTH AFRICA	AUSTRALIA
First innings	311	212
Second innings	470	246
	(for 8 wickets declared)	

These were the truly golden moments of Bacher's playing days. He was 28 years old at the time, and although he had had a successful career since 1960, this phenomenal, crushing defeat of Australia must have been his crowning glory. In this series he stamped himself as a great captain and, although his average was 31 with a highest score of 73, he was always 'there at the right time'. I have heard many people claim that Bacher's only qualification was his brilliant captaincy. This is patently untrue. He was well worth his place as a reliable and consistent number three or even opener. For that matter, he could bat anywhere in the order without creating embarrassment. Ali was predominantly a back-foot player who scored the bulk of his runs on the on-side. His preference for the leg-side was probably due to his closed grip, which was strangely not unlike Sir Donald Bradman's. In fact, like Sir Donald, he began scoring runs at a very tender age. In only his second season he impressed when he scored hundreds against Natal and Rhodesia, both of whom had powerful bowling attacks. This led to a string of constantly steady scores. Certainly, he had his bad patches, as all cricketers do, but he was technically a batsman of calibre and rare determination. He never threw away his wicket lightly.

It is still something of a mystery why his potential was not recognised by selecting him for Trevor Goddard's tour of Australia during the 1963/64 season. He had such promise, it is my guess he would have made a 'packet' of runs on the hard, true Australian pitches.

Bacher delights in telling the story about his being one of only two players known to have scored three ducks in one first-class game (the other being West Indian Viv Richards in 1969 when he was an 18-year-old). For Bacher it happened at Newlands. He was out for a duck in the first innings against Western Province. Over the weekend, Mackay Coghill 'opened a book' in great fun among the team that Bacher would bag a pair in the second innings.

Early in Bacher's second innings, before he had got off the mark, he chopped a ball down to slip-gully position. The ball struck Hylton Ackerman full on the toe, kicked straight up and Hylton held the catch. On appeal Bacher was given not out. He alleges that at this stage he strolled down the pitch to batting partner, Brian Bath, and claimed, 'Now they'll never get me out.' In all fairness, he had not seen exactly where the ball had bounced and that is why he stood his ground. Shortly afterwards he got a 'nick', and this time was given out. Counting his duck in the first innings, Bacher claims that he is the only man he knows to lay three eggs in one first-class game!

Bacher's first tour was to England in the northern summer of 1965. Peter van der Merwe was captain of that team, which won a three-match Test series 1–0. This splendid victory came in the second Test at Trent Bridge in Nottingham, and it was the 11th match of the trip. Much has been written over the years about Graeme Pollock's superb 125, which set South Africa on their victory course. It was an innings acclaimed by such greats as Denis Compton, Sir Donald Bradman, Sir Garfield Sobers and many others, and what a triumph for Peter van der Merwe.

In the South African second innings, Ali Bacher contributed an invaluable 67 runs before he was lbw to Larter. Bacher shared a 99-run partnership with top scorer Eddie Barlow (76), who had dropped down the order with a badly bruised toe. It was obvious that Bacher, who had been bowled by John Snow for only 12 runs in the first innings, did not allow himself to be overawed by the occasion.

Bacher was, in fact, batting at number three for South Africa, which proves the earlier statement: he was value for money wherever he batted. The claims of those who did not see him bat and glibly state that he only made it because of his captaining abilities are blown to smithereens when one takes into account that he was selected for all three Tests. Furthermore, in the third and final Test he put together 70 hard-fought runs in 166 minutes. This innings included five fours, and it brought his aggregate in the Tests to 218. It meant that he ended the three-match series third to Graeme Pollock and Colin Bland in the batting averages, with two 50s to his credit.

Ali Bacher has an independent soul that burns fiercely and with single-minded purpose. He proved this on countless occasions. Yet he is the first to admit that he had the good fortune to play in many particularly formidable South African teams. This series, in its own way, set a new era in motion: a golden era in which selfishness and 'opposition anxiety' had no part.

Later Bacher played in even better South African sides, and captained the Springboks in his final four appearances. Four years before he was chosen as captain, Bacher represented South Africa in all five Test matches against Bobby Simpson's touring Australians. Peter van der Merwe was once again his captain. Bacher probably developed a good deal of his tactical shrewdness by observing Van der Merwe, although he was recognised as a born leader from his early school years.

In those five Tests, Bacher was consistent in averaging 30.50 with a top score of 63. Yet he gave the Australian team good cause to remember him forever. The occasion was in the Transvaal match played at the Wanderers on 11, 12, 14 and 15 November 1966. In this memorable match, watched by more than 37 000 spectators, there were many magic moments, but none more so than Bacher's 235 in Transvaal's second innings. On reaching this personal milestone, Bacher set a number of records. It was the highest score against any touring team sent to this country by England, Australia or New Zealand. The only other Springbok to score a double century against an Australian touring team was Dudley Nourse, who made 231 against Victor Richardson's Australians in a Test match at the Old Wanderers. To have beaten this superstar batsman's record was a truly memorable feat.

Bacher's remarkable innings set Transvaal up to shatter a 64-year-old record. It was the first time an Australian cricket team had been beaten in South Africa. Springbok all-rounder Tiger Lance shared in a fourth-wicket stand of 273 runs with his captain. Tiger's contribution to the partnership was 100, and he was eventually bowled by Hawke for 107.

It was about 10 minutes before time on the final day that Tony Tillim bowled Hawke round his legs with a googly to inflict an historic defeat upon Australia. Left-hander Jim Hubble and Hawke had survived for an hour, and it looked as though Australia might just save the day. Earlier Australia had enjoyed the benefit of a spate of dropped catches. Somehow, Tillim produced the ball that was magic for Transvaal but the death knell for the Australians.

Those who witnessed the game claim that the young Bacher exhibited completely uninhibited strokeplay. It was an innings of instinctive footwork and perfect timing. This feat must have been one of monumental concentration and application. His innings of five hours 23 minutes contained one six and 37 fours. Simple arithmetic tells us that 154 of the mammoth 235 runs came from sweetly timed boundaries. Ali was equally formidable on plumb pitches or grassy, moving tracks. This stemmed from a steely determination. In the same game he took a phenomenal catch at silly mid-on to dismiss Bob Cowper off Atholl McKinnon's bowling. The freeze-frame picture portrays the Transvaal captain on the point of toppling over onto his back with the ball firmly clutched in his left hand, just above his shoulder. The media raved about this incredible catch. The game ended amid delirious scenes among Transvaal spectators and players. The euphoria had to be seen to be believed – it was certainly a moment to be savoured.

Back to the Test match scene. Ali Bacher had the privilege of witnessing Denis Lindsay plunder the Australian attack to the titillating tune of 606 runs in only seven innings. This enabled him to finish the series in storybook fashion with the handsome, Bradmanesque average of 86.57. Records far too numerous to mention here tumbled like skittles in a ten-pin bowling alley. Denis notched up three brilliant centuries with a top score of 182. He was like an incoming, unstoppable tide.

This was a peak period in Lindsay's career; it was a fairytale, once-in-a lifetime series for him. Not only did he sparkle with star quality while savaging the bewildered Australian bowlers, he also shone brightly and acrobatically behind the stumps. Lindsay had been an outstanding soccer goalkeeper, and this was evident in his incredible agility as a wicketkeeper.

In that first Test at the Wanderers, Lindsay equalled the world record of six wickets in an innings. It was an unusual coincidence that this record had been established on the same ground by the great Australian wicketkeeper, Wally Grout, during Ian Craig's tour of South Africa in 1957/58. Lindsay's opposite number, Brian Taber, also had a field day on this occasion when he bagged five South African wickets in the first innings and three in the second; Lindsay also claimed eight victims in the match. Incidentally, all 24 of Lindsay's sacrificial lambs were caught behind. There were no stumpings, but with a performance like that who needs stumpings?

Lindsay's century in the fourth Test was a lightning product. His pyrotechnic display generated an unforgettable century. His 100 came in only 108 minutes – reputed to be the third-fastest Test century in post-war cricket. The one bowler Denis Lindsay pillaged mercilessly was the lanky opening bowler, Dave Renneberg. Strangely enough, Renneberg appeared to stumble into a mental block when Lindsay arrived at the wicket. Dave seemed to believe that a local rule had been introduced; the rule being that he, the bowler, was not permitted to pitch the ball over the halfway mark of the strip. Another analogy would be the 'yips'. This is when a golfer freezes on his putts. Renneberg's deliveries seemed to undergo deep-freeze treatment at the sight of the boy from Benoni.

Consequently Denis Lindsay received an over-abundance of short-pitched deliveries. This was meat and drink to one of the finest hookers of anything short. Denis thrived on these delicious consignments. He would nimbly resort to his back foot and viciously despatch the ball to the boundary with a swift sabre-like cross shot, which we all commonly know as the 'hook'.

About the only time Dave Renneberg got a strong measure of revenge was at Newlands. Lindsay, in attempting a violent hook, was struck a resounding blow on his forehead. As if this was not sufficient damage, Denis had the misfortune of being caught and bowled by a sprawling, diving Dave Renneberg. After striking

Lindsay painfully on the head, the ball had rebounded down the pitch with sufficient loop and air in it for Renneberg to bring off a spectacular catch.

Records were mentioned earlier. On their own these records would form a chapter. Even the umpires set records! The likeable Hayward Kidson had the distinction of standing in all five Tests, thus becoming only the sixth South African umpire to do so in a series at home. One could go on ad infinitum about the exciting and notable deeds of this tour, which fired the imagination of the cricketing public. As it was all part of Ali Bacher's continued rise to fame and glory, it will be sufficient to table the Test results:

FIRST TEST. Wanderers, Johannesburg. 23, 24, 26, 27, 28 December 1966

	SOUTH AFRICA	AUSTRALIA
First innings	199	325
Second innings	620	261

South Africa won by 233 runs.

SECOND TEST. Newlands, Cape Town. 31 December, 2, 3, 4, 5 January 1967

	SOUTH AFRICA	AUSTRALIA
First innings	353	542
Second innings	367	180 (for 4 wickets)

South Africa lost by 6 wickets.

THIRD TEST. Kingsmead, Durban. 20, 21, 23, 24, 25 January 1967

	SOUTH AFRICA	AUSTRALIA
First innings	300	147
Second innings	185 (for 2 wickets)	334

South Africa won by 8 wickets.

FOURTH TEST. Wanderers, Johannesburg. 3, 4, 6, 7, 8 February 1967

	SOUTH AFRICA	AUSTRALIA
First innings	322 (for 9 wickets)	143
Second innings		148 (for 8 wickets)

Australia forced to follow on. Match drawn.

FIFTH TEST. St George's Park, Port Elizabeth. 24, 25, 27, 28 February and 1 March 1967

	SOUTH AFRICA	AUSTRALIA
First innings	276	173
Second innings	179 (for 3 wickets)	278

South Africa won by seven wickets.

These statistics indicate just what a triumph the tour was, particularly for captain Peter van der Merwe. They are quoted here to chart the midway course of Ali Bacher who, I am sure, would readily admit that Van der Merwe was inspirational in his leadership and also instrumental in Bacher's approach to international contests during this five-match clash. Peter van der Merwe's line-up for the final Test at Port Elizabeth reads like any captain's dream: Peter van der Merwe (captain), Trevor Goddard, Eddie Barlow, Ali Bacher, Graeme Pollock, Herbert (Tiger) Lance, Denis Lindsay, Mike Procter, Jackie du Preez, Peter Pollock, Pat Trimborn. Enough to make any skipper turn green with envy! Van der Merwe had every reason to be proud – especially as he was now a highly senior and respected skipper guiding the fortunes and future of the likes of Ali Bacher.

These figures show just what a great distance Bacher had travelled since captaining the Yeoville Primary first cricket, soccer and tennis teams. At that stage he was considered something of a schoolboy prodigy.

He was only 15 years old when he played for King Edward VII High School. In that year Bacher eclipsed a record aggregate of runs previously held by the hard-hitting Paul Winslow, when he hit 829 runs. Apparently this record has not been broken since.

He captained Transvaal schools for two consecutive years, and in the same two years he had the distinction of being selected for the South African Nuffield XI, playing against the provincial teams of Transvaal and Natal. Bacher also represented KES at rugby in the flyhalf berth. Shortly after graduating from KES, Ali made his provincial debut for Transvaal, but it was in the 1960/61 season that he really made his presence felt in provincial circles. He enjoyed a highly successful season, which was an omen of greater honours and accolades just around the corner.

Ali Bacher's mother, Rose, a refugee from the tyrannies that engulfed Lithuania in the late 1920s, cultivated a feeling for the game as she charted her son's progress up the cricket ladder of success at KES and later Transvaal and South Africa. She was a delightful woman, full of old-world grace and charm, and very proud of the achievements of her famous son.

When her son was in his early teens she bought him the famous coaching book by Sir Donald Bradman, *The Art of Cricket*, underlining phrases such as 'the ball must never be hit in the air but on the ground' in red pencil, and leaving the book on his bed to find in the morning, read the message and memorise it. This routine during the summer months of his school life became as habitual as brushing his teeth and combing his hair.

Because of her parental interest, Rose became such a keen student of the game that Ali would often, in later years, have copies made of stories he knew would interest her ever-inquiring mind. Coming from a country such as Lithuania, Rose didn't have the luxury of growing up with a cricket background and may have found the sport strange at first, but she developed a great affection for it. The scrapbooks she built up of Ali's playing and administrative career are works of art as they plot his rise from a young boy, through the ranks to Nuffield, provincial and Test cricket.

It was during Ali Bacher's great triumph, the formation of the United Cricket Board, that his mother was admitted to hospital, and sadly died before South Africa's readmittance to the International Cricket Council on 10 July 1991.

At the early age of 21, Ali Bacher was chosen to captain Transvaal, a role he fulfilled with dignity and distinction. There was no doubting his shrewdness, while his elevation to the captaincy in no way stifled his growth as a player. Perhaps one could say it was the finest possible medicine to bring out the best in the good doctor. He obviously had an excellent medical brain, but my guess is that he had an even more clinical cricket brain. Ali Bacher possessed intense determination and he made a deep study of the game. He scrutinised his opponents carefully. Cleverly and quickly he observed or unearthed weaknesses. Then he would relentlessly go to work on these flaws. He was, in sporting parlance, a natural. Bacher earned respect from the teams he led, not only for the strong resolve contained within a quiet, reserved exterior, but also for the quality and quantity of his batting. Richie Benaud once described Peter May as 'hard as nails on the field, without ever slipping from the peaks of sportsmanship'. This could well have been applied to Ali Bacher. It would not be an exaggeration to say that he has left an indelible mark as a batsman, captain and administrator of his country.

But few people are aware of Bacher's competence as a first-class wicketkeeper. My guess is that he opted out of keeping wicket because he felt he could not do justice to both 'keeping and captaincy. Yet he was most capable behind the stumps.

This was shown in a match against an International Cavaliers side, during which Bacher took five catches and made one stumping in a single innings. Of course he produced many other fine performances while wearing pads and gloves. However, he decided to 'hang up his gloves' in favour of becoming an outstandingly safe slip-catcher and, in fact, a far-above-average fielder. Abandoning the wicketkeeping slot also meant that he could concentrate on captaincy.

While captain of Transvaal, Bacher earned great respect for his obvious astuteness. However, it is said that he could be very forgetful off the field. Stories of his absent-mindedness are legion, and nobody relates them more vividly and with more fondness than Kevin McKenzie, who began his first-class career under Bacher.

He tells humorously of the occasion when Transvaal were flying from Jan Smuts Airport to some important fixture. Ali had just got married and his delightful wife, Shira, decided he should dress like a sedate, professional doctor. So the casual captain totally stunned his teammates when he pitched up in a smart new suit, matching tie, handkerchief, shoes, etc. His colleagues realised that this was the influence of his attractive new wife.

However, when Ali sat down on a bench among his Transvaal teammates and neatly adjusted his trouser legs, he was mortified to see that he had forgotten to put on his socks that morning. The players apparently ragged him for a long time after the event.

Kevin McKenzie also claims that Ali had the ability to leave the bathroom looking as though it had been struck by a monsoon. A shaving brush covered with cream would lie in one corner, the razor in another and so on. Furthermore, he had the ability to read the morning newspaper in the bath. McKenzie thinks that Ali must have read the articles from the bottom upwards because most of the newsprint was damp at the base, and as he finished each page he would just discard it on the bathroom floor!

All these eccentricities seemed to endear him to his side. They had the effect of creating additional team spirit, if indeed any were required. His colleagues found him refreshingly different.

Bacher himself relates an amusing story that concerned him and his late mother. Ali was still a schoolboy, but frequently played for the Balfour Park first team on Sundays. At this stage he was being compared to the great Sir Donald Bradman. This was probably because Ali had a closed grip, not unlike Sir Donald, and because he was a schoolboy prodigy with the tendency to consistently accumulate runs. The Australian journalist, Dick Whitington, often described Ali as another Donald Bradman.

But it seems that on this occasion such lavish comparisons were not justified. Bacher had not been making that many runs, and on this particular Sunday he had been dismissed without scoring. When he got home his mother opened the door and said something to the effect of, 'Huh, Donald Bradman, they say. Rather Donald Duck!'

This probably helped to keep the schoolboy prodigy's feet firmly on the ground. However, his single-mindedness ensured that he would make a lasting mark on, and contribute greatly to, Transvaal and South Africa as a player, captain and administrator, whose last administrative job has been as director of the 2003 World Cup Committee.

Alan Melville

Dudley Nourse

Jack Cheetham

Clive van Ryneveld

Jackie McGlew

Dudley Nourse, the team manager, with Jackie McGlew, the captain, 1960

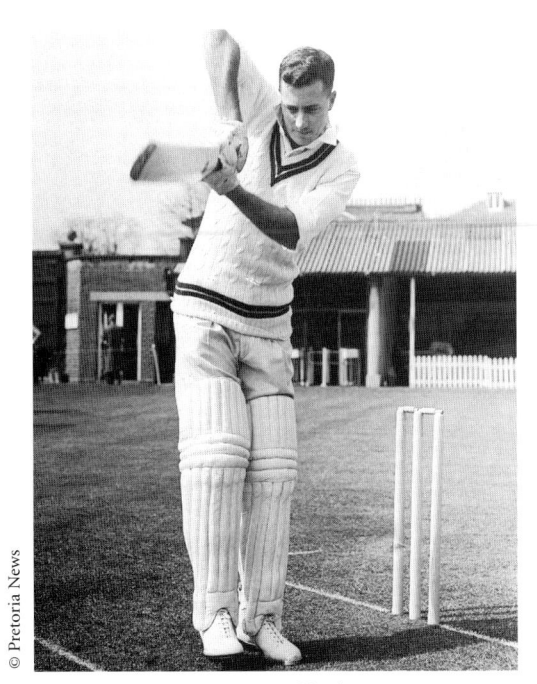

Trevor Goddard

Peter van der Merwe

Basil D'Oliveira

Ali Bacher

Barry Richards

Mike Procter

Jimmy Cook

Peter Kirsten

Clive Rice

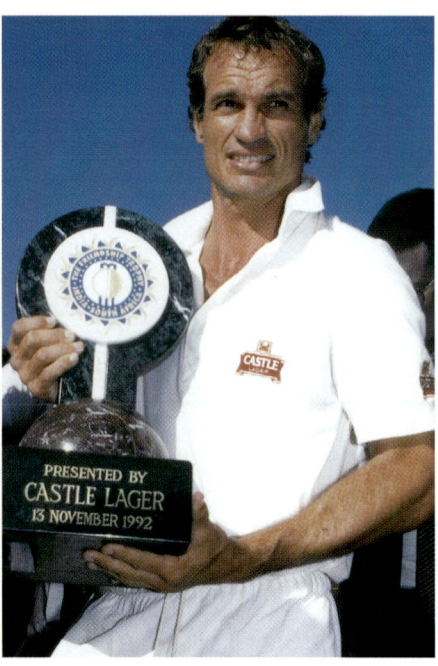

Kepler Wessels

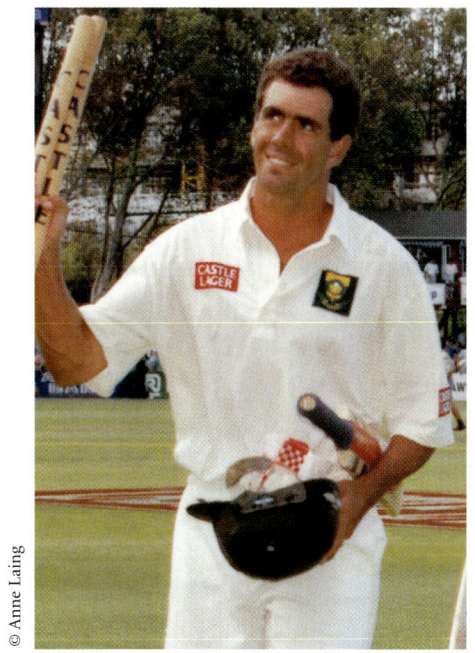

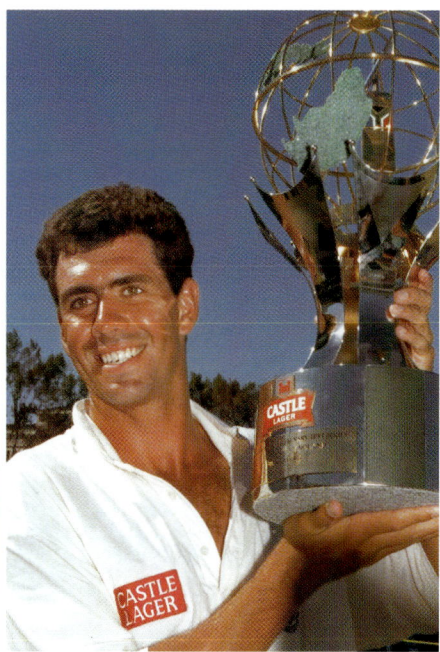

Hansie Cronjé

Gary Kirsten

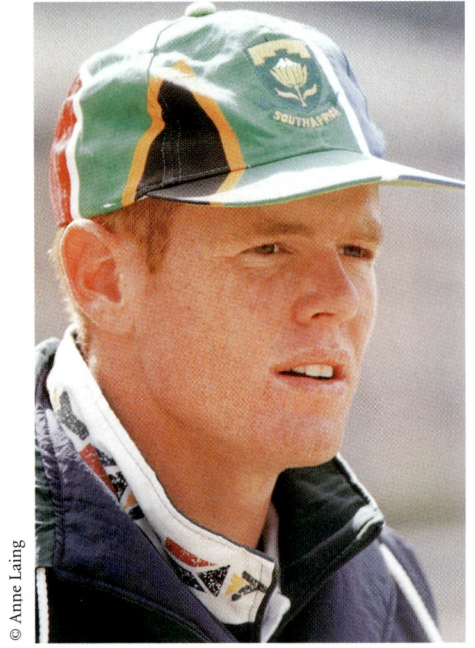

Shaun Pollock

Mark Boucher

THE REBEL ERA   11
Politics of Isolation

By Trevor Chesterfield

It could hardly be called the age of scandal, as cricket has gone through any number of them since the 1680s, when betting was first allowed on games (although the laws of cricket did not exist for a further 40 years). A match in Kent was 'bought and sold' by landed gentry in Maidstone as a way of reimbursing the innkeeper for damages caused by a brawl among the players in the bar. Indian bookmakers, too, might have learnt a few tricks more than 150 years before Cronjégate, when players were known to have 'sold' a match by bowling badly. In 1932/33 there was England's 'bodyline' tour of Australia, where leg-theory fast bowling was used as a means to curb Donald Bradman's batting genius, causing a major political rift between the two countries. In the 1990s there were ball-tampering rows involving Pakistan and England, the match-fixing scandal, and, more recently, the highly publicised contractual dispute between the international body and the players involved in the Champion's Trophy tournament in Colombo, Sri Lanka, in 2002.

To suggest that South Africa's cricket isolation began in September 1971, and that the ensuing rebel tours of the 1980s were a result of the 1948 election and the apartheid policies pursued by the Nationalist government over the next 40 years, is stretching credibility. South African sport had been isolated from inception. As Lord Milner outlined in one of his reports after the 1899–1902 war, who cared about long-term results or where the nation was heading? In 1904, short-term success was what really mattered. Long-term benefits (for the whites) would follow.

The race problems faced by the SACU after unity dissolved in late 1977 were created by the sins of the country's undemocratic past and the unhealthy legacy left by the SACA establishment.[1] As the SACU discovered, the actions of their white predecessors had laid such treacherous foundations that racial tensions would remain. This was despite concerted efforts of goodwill and racial harmony within a (cricket) society starting to examine itself more closely. Were the rebel tours of the 1980s worth it? If they were, who genuinely benefited? The tours were unofficial and gained no recognition within the ICC or from South Africa's disadvantaged communities, who were largely disenfranchised in any case.

A controversial aspect of the rebel era was that many of the games received first-class status, and the sport the sort of profile it had once enjoyed in the pre-isolation days. The first-class tag and records accorded by *Wisden* and statisticians throughout the world did not, however, sit well with certain officials in the English Test and County Cricket Board or the ICC. In 1993, an English tabloid writer, wanting to embellish a story, sought the opinion of Lieutenant-Colonel John Stephenson of the TCCB about the century scored by Graham Gooch for the rebel SAB XI against the South African XI at the Wanderers in March 1982. It became a matter of principle when, in line with policy, the TCCB refused to recognise Gooch's century. Stephenson, in true British military bluster, dismissed the innings as one of no consequence.

The matter arose when it was discovered that Gooch was on the verge of his 100th century while on a tour of South Asia. On 23 January 1993, he scored 102 before retiring hurt against an Indian under25 team in Cuttack; it took the ICC a week to confirm Stephenson's view that, in their opinion, the earlier century was not made in a first-class match. Sensibly, *Wisden* and other cricket authorities thumbed their noses at the ICC/TCCB opinion, and regarded the game as first class.

Did *Wisden*'s reaction suggest that while rebel tours were morally wrong, matches should be considered first class? Not at all. It was a matter of trying to keep an organised profile in difficult times. As the precedent had been set almost a century before, it became a matter of conscience. In the context of the game, where it was played and the strength of the opposition, it is hard to argue against the first-class status of the match played at the Wanderers in March 1982. A bigger question mark should hang over the first Test at St George's Park in March 1889, and the one at Newlands a few days later. But that is another matter: protocol of what was and what was not 'first class' did not exist in those days.

For 10 years, and leading to the events that shaped the D'Oliveira affair and eventual isolation, South Africa's global cricket relations had become increasingly tenuous. During the 1950s, as the international boundaries and expectations changed, so did the demographics in British Commonwealth politics; for one thing, cricket administrators in India, Pakistan and the West Indies were more vocal about the lack of merit-selection policies. This led to a warning in January 1958, when an Australian Cricket Board official told the SACA board members at Newlands of a proposal by the Imperial Cricket Conference[2] to upgrade the junior members – New Zealand, the West Indies, India and Pakistan – to equal status. The West Indies, a collection of former British-ruled islands in the Caribbean, and Pakistan wanted an end to all tours to and from South Africa by whites-only teams; they considered it an affront to the ICC and against the constitution. The SACA again used subterfuge to state their case: until the laws of the land were changed, they could do nothing. Whether they had thought of challenging the laws is unlikely. Writers such as Louis Duffus, Eric Litchfield and CO Medworth were cursing because the status quo had been challenged. It was a matter of 'How dare the ICC dictate to South Africa, a founder member, what they should do?'

Duffus criticised the attack on the 'imperial bastions ... because they stand for order and democracy in the region as we know it'. He forgot to mention that it was the white man's 'democracy' and the white man's 'order' being assailed by those representing the disenfranchised millions who were of colour and were part of the same organisation.

When the question of non-racial membership and merit selection arose during a meeting in early 1973 with the SA Cricket Board of Control and the SA Cricket Association, SACA member Wally Hammond, driven into a corner, commented that nowhere in the association's constitution did the word 'white' occur.

Whether Hammond's remark was designed to appease SACA members, who were under pressure at the meeting, or explain the establishment's viewpoint, is unclear. By that stage white establishment cricket was grappling with the knowledge that unless there was a concerted joint effort to stand against the government's brutal race laws, the game, internationally, was in trouble. Without genuine unity, cricket could not move forward. Tours such as those by Derrick Robins XIs were cosmetic and attracting noticeably dwindling audiences.

Freed of the manacles of the Raj, India and the British Caribbean took the hard-line approach that, until there was full emancipation, there would be no links with racist South Africa.

The formation of the SACU altered little internationally. There was sympathy and encouragement, but generally nothing had changed; the game was still essentially white run and the apartheid system was in control.

Ten years after the first rebel tour, Gooch admitted that he had no 'genuine regrets' about undertaking the venture, although there were times when some ghosts would unexpectedly pop up. Such as the smiling youngster who, in the early 1990s, asked for his autograph and said, 'My dad once called you a traitor.' During an interview at the vast Melbourne Cricket Ground on 11 March 1992, Gooch said, 'Look, what happened, happened. I took the decision and lived with it, and served out my three-year ban, which I should add was quite painful as I thought it was harsh and an over-reaction, and did so without complaint.'

What did hurt was Bob Willis's decision to go back on his offer to captain the rebel side. Given the leadership role, Gooch suddenly copped the blame for organising the tour when he had had nothing to do with it. The labels that stuck were 'Gooch's Dirty Dozen', 'Gooch's Rebel Gang' and 'Gooch's Pirate Army'. He grimaced as he walked away from the interview. He was the England captain again and had recovered his respectability, but for years the shadows of the past lurked in the corners.

At the time of unity in 1976 the country was in the throes of an identity crisis, and the white establishment had, for a change, been genuinely shaken. Soweto was under siege and in flames as brave schoolchildren took to the streets in defiance. It was a time when the country had to ask itself where it was going. It would never be the same again. The uprising and its cost in blood and lives would see to that.

As Barry Richards articulated in 1992, the rebel route was not willingly adopted by the SACU. At the time, though, they saw no alternative. The game had become so deeply embedded in the quagmire known as isolation that something radical was needed to rattle the ICC's foundations and regenerate domestic interest. It was a sport in decay, as schools began to turn away from its elitist image. This was further highlighted in 1979 in a social study for a marketing company, which discovered that in Johannesburg cricket was now a sport for the yuppies in the northern suburbs with their fancy cars and well-heeled girlfriends.

Internationally, the start of the rebel era had the opposite effect, with any number of ironic situations. South African-raised and educated Allan Lamb could play for England, but Gooch, Geoff Boycott and others were banned for three years for playing in rebel tours against South Africa. And whether or not the SACU liked it, internationally they were viewed as an organisation in a racially driven renegade state that enjoyed government privileges. The mood at SACU level was one of defiance and rebellion, and it caught on: the (white) public generally enjoyed hoisting the pirate flag, and adopted an almost gung-ho approach.

Richards did not see things the same way; nor did Mike Procter, Peter Kirsten, Clive Rice and Jimmy Cook. They were the five men who led the South African XI during the seven rebel tours spread over eight summers between 1981/82 and 1989/90. To them it was matter of uplifting the standards of the game, taking it into a new era and rescuing it from slow strangulation.

'From where we are now, a decade after it started, I don't want to downgrade the tours, but again, it didn't feel right,' said Richards on a Sunday night in Bowral, four days from South Africa's opening World Cup game against Australia. 'Sure I was very happy to be part of leading a Springbok team; but again it didn't really have the absolute seal of world cricket approval; it wasn't official, and so there was no euphoria. Deep inside we all knew it and felt it.'

The British Press – and in this case it was mainly the non-establishment tabloids, along with *The Independent* and *The Guardian* – were not overly sympathetic to the rebel tours. Yet many writers championed the right of the individual to carry on regardless. Inside South Africa, the establishment saw it differently: while justifying the tours, there were also those who wondered about the moral issue, and questioned whether they were not perhaps grappling with something akin to the curate's egg.[3]

What did keep South Africa out of the ICC at that stage was the impasse between its white and coloured members; it seemed the conscience of the white establishment had not been overly bothered by the concerns or opinions of the two Asian countries and the West Indies. The curate's egg was becoming more unpalatable. On 14 July 1961, under the ICC constitution, South Africa's delegate, granted observer status, had to withdraw from the meeting when the membership question was raised. This was because South Africa, no longer a member of the British Commonwealth, had automatically ceased to be a member of the ICC. Had South Africa remained a republic within the Commonwealth, their status would have been challenged. But long after the fateful Commonwealth prime ministers' conference in 1960, when the Canadians demanded that South Africa abandon its apartheid policies or get out, the question of South Africa's ICC status was still the subject of much behind-the-scenes discussion. In 1961 the membership issue was debated for 90 minutes without a decision; in 1962 the expected amendment to the constitution, allowing South Africa to rejoin as a full member, did not take place.

This was when Pakistan forwarded their motion, supported by the West Indies, opposing any effort to readmit South Africa, even with junior membership status, as the international body faced its first major internal battle. If the SACA were not prepared to play matches against all members on a normal, merit basis, as required by the sport's own creed and conduct, there should be no Tests, whether official or unofficial.

South African newspapers – particularly Medworth in *The Natal Mercury* in July 1962 – complained about how 'colour in politics is now barring our way to the rightful resumption of ICC membership'.

By 26 August 1968, a distinctly unpleasant odour of vocal cordite had wafted around South African and England cricket circles, as it had done for most of that year. At the time, all-rounder Mike Procter, at first unaffected by the row, was enjoying his first full season with Gloucestershire thanks to the special registration by the counties, which attracted many top Test players from South Africa, New Zealand, the West Indies, India and Pakistan. On the political front, behind-the-scenes forces had been at work since January 1968, looking at the implications and then putting on the blinkers on the possible selection of Basil D'Oliveira for the MCC tour of South Africa in 1968/69. In the end, the forces assembled in the cabinet meeting room at Pretoria's Union Buildings and in the SACA offices would not only limit the Test career of one of South Africa's finest modern all-rounders, but also allow him only one more series to display his talents.

There was a misguided view in apartheid government circles that Bill Lawry's Australians of 1969/70 would not be the last official tourists; that somehow a satisfactory arrangement would be made between the SACA and its ICC allies, the MCC, Australia and New Zealand. But the bluff and bluster of the government when tours were cancelled were shown up as a clever façade. They had made concessions for rugby in 1970, when New Zealand toured for the first time with Maoris, and the French the following year. The reason why rugby was favoured was political: the sport was the Afrikaner domain. This was forced home on a biting cold July evening in 1974 at a dinner hosted by the Department for Sport and Recreation in Pretoria for white sports administrators. Harry Stavridis, then president of the national badminton body and once a member of the banned Liberal Party, felt that he was attending a rally in Nazi Germany in the 1930s.

'I was appalled at the way he [Vorster] spoke that night,' Stavridis recalled. 'It was a reforming of the sports laager. I wondered what had happened to [Minister of Sport] Dr Piet Koornhof's vision of 15 months before, when he expressed hope for what for him was a broad dream of mixed sport.'

It had been six years since the D'Oliveira affair, and the hardening of political views gave Stavridis a ringside seat to the thinking that ruled a white minority now handcuffed to a principle based on racial superiority. Vorster admitted that rugby would always be the exception because of its strong influence in Afrikaner society.

'There is little doubt that rugby was near and dear to the government because they were brought up within its culture at their schools,' Stavridis said. 'Although he [Vorster] did concede, amid much laughter of course, that they did allow the English to play it as well.'

Vorster's message on that July evening was a reminder of the government's doctrine; or what it presumed was the overriding panacea for the country's traditional ills: 'Do not think for one moment that we will waver from our path of separate development. And do not think for one moment that we will give up our birthright in order to allow you to invite teams or sportsmen or sportswomen who are not of our thinking or our persuasion.

'This is our country. We will not change for the sake of a few overseas sports teams. We will tell you who can come and who cannot … This is our policy. It is the wish of the *volk*.'

The right-wing hardliners had won, and the sports policy of April 1967, in which the prime minister had made what appeared to be surprising concessions, had been crushed, if in fact it had ever existed.

Early on 8 September 1971, the white minority government led by Vorster and his henchmen reacted with typical arrogance to the Australian Cricket Board's decision to withdraw their invitation, banning the 1971/72 tour, and thereby effectively slamming closed South African cricket's only remaining international door. Yet what did they expect? Words such as 'indignant' and 'righteous' flooded the Afrikaans media, and Afrikaans colleagues accused English-speaking sports writers, especially foreigners, of being anti-South African. If this meant anti-government, it was a fair accusation.

While there had initially been public support for the tour, the threat of protest action could have led to serious danger and injury. Banning the tour was a decision that Sir Donald Bradman, as chairman of the Australian Cricket Board, years later admitted was the hardest he had to make. What helped convince him that the tour was wrong was when he was taken to see a rugby game between Australia and South Africa in Sydney, where the ground was ringed with police and barbed wire. South Africa's rugby tour of New Zealand in 1981 was a fair example of the costs involved in preventing anti-tour groups from protesting. Many families in the shaky isles were seriously divided into pro- and anti-tour groups, and the repercussions lasted for more than a decade. While there are many in South African rugby still snivelling over the result of the game at Eden Park in Auckland, which was flour-bombed by a light aircraft, what Bradman did was correct. To pay possibly millions of Aussie dollars to mount an effective law and order programme was not logical. Especially when it would be to protect a team from a country where the majority of people were disenfranchised and denied basic human rights.

* * *

By early September 1971, on the day the Australian tour was called off, Mike Procter faced the stark realisation that he would never again play for his country in an official Test series. To his credit, and in many ways South Africa's good fortune, he did not decide to go and settle elsewhere, as had Tony Greig and later Allan Lamb, Kepler Wessels and Robin Smith, all chasing the dream of a Test career. No one can blame this particular quartet for taking that road.

But if Procter could not play Test cricket for South Africa, he was damned if he was going elsewhere. Again, no one could blame him, or Clive Rice or Barry Richards, for joining the Packer World Series Cricket circus in 1977/78.[4] It was not just another way of earning extra money – it also gave him a chance to play against the best, and it helped him lift his game to meet the challenge. Yet to realise, as you enter the peak of your playing career, that you will never play another Test is numbing. As numb as Basil D'Oliveira felt when the West Indies tour of 1959 was aborted.

There was no one of comparable ability to Mike Procter when the politicians shut down South Africa's Test aspirations on 10 March 1970 for almost 22 years. World standards may change and star players rise and fall with each decade, but the standard set by the former Hilton College pupil and South African Schools vice-captain, and the talent he displayed as a developing teenager, was not so much precocious as self-belief in a rare talent. He was a specialist pace bowler and a class batsman who scored six successive first-class centuries in 1970/71, only 12 months after his fiery pace bowling had, with Peter Pollock, done much to rout Lawry's Australians in their 4–0 hiding.

Procter's love and enjoyment of the game stemmed from his parents. His father, Woodrow Procter, while still a schoolboy, was a member of the Eastern Province side that played Walter Hammond's MCC side in 1938/39. Mike's early skill was as a batsman, and there was an innings of 210 for the Natal under13 side against old rivals Transvaal. Any interest in bowling in his formative years only stretched so far as his wicketkeeping gloves would allow in taking the ball – until the need to boost the fast-bowling ranks at Highbury Preparatory found a willing would-be future Test bowler, eager to experiment. That was when the world first caught sight of the open-chested fast bowler who appeared to deliver the ball from the wrong foot. Those who know the game well realise that this is a technical illusion, because the open-chested arm action gives the impression that in his delivery stride he came down on the right foot (not the left as right-arm bowlers should do); what in fact happens is that the feet seem to change in mid-air, which in reality they don't. Technically it may be wrong, but no one is going to complain with 41 Test wickets in seven matches at an average of 15.37, or 1 407 first-class wickets in a career of 19 years at 19.37. At Hilton College, Procter was an above-average all-round sportsman, skilful in hockey, tennis and rugby. In many ways cricket is like a game of chess. It forces you to think ahead and plot carefully how to get rid of a batsman or score runs off a particular bowler. An all-rounder like Mike has to be especially gifted, with insight in field placings when bowling or batting, and over long periods of time, such as in five-day Tests. In this respect he came through his two Test series with a reputation that marked him for the next 12 years – from 1966 to 1978 – as one of the world's great players of his age.

Procter was well prepared for his life as a professional player by that tough cricket academy, the Coca-Cola Nuffield Week: in 1963 he was vice-captain to Barry Richards on a tour of England, and he played the same role the following year, although there was no tour. This gave him invaluable experience. His first season with Gloucestershire in 1965 partly prepared him for the demanding county circuit. The irony of the 1965 South African tour of England was that at one point, with Procter and Richards batting for Gloustershire, there were 13 South African players on the field, and the only Englishmen were the umpires. None of this was lost on the inquisitive press, especially the South African media, which took great delight in detailing the facts. This was a euphoric summer, to be repeated only twice more; the first time in 1966/67, when the 20-year-old Michael John Procter, a world star of the future, was suddenly elevated from Currie Cup level. He served an apprenticeship when he was 12th man for the first two Tests at the Wanderers and Newlands; South Africa won the first and Australia the second before changes were made after the Newlands defeat, with Atholl McKinnon (left-arm orthodox spin) and Richard Dumbrill (all-rounder) making way for Mike and Natal teammate Pat Trimborn.

On 14 January 1967, while playing Eastern Province in a Currie Cup match in Port Elizabeth, Proccie was taken aside by Jackie McGlew, his mentor and provincial captain, who quietly uttered the magic phrase: 'You're in the Springbok team, Mike.'

Five days later, on a stifling Durban afternoon at a packed Kingsmead, Procter did not have to wait too long to bag his first Test wicket – it was the Australian captain Bobby Simpson for six, with 14 on the board. Denis Lindsay took the catch – an outside edge as the ball seamed off the pitch, and the Kingsmead crowd roared their approval of their young hero. In taking the first of 15 wickets at 17.53 in the three Tests he played in that series, Procter showed himself to be a venomous bowler who knew how to tame the tourists. Their soft underbelly that summer was a disappointing middle order and lack of a balanced bowling attack.

Thwarted by politics in 1968/69, Procter was not denied in 1969/70, when the Australians surprisingly agreed to a visit after their tour of India. It was a series that started under a cloud. Many believed it would be the last time they would see an official Test series. Procter took 26 wickets at 13.57 in the series, his devastating pace always having the cutting edge over the Australians, ending in a career-best six for 73 at St George's Park, Port Elizabeth. His last wicket was John Gleeson, bowled for a duck.

As the years of isolation stretched uncertainly ahead, Procter took up a lucrative offer from Rhodesia, which may have given him financial security, but there was an ache in watching county teammates and friends regularly playing Tests for other countries. The best opposition he and others could expect were matches involving the Derrick Robins tours, as well as the International Wanderers visit in the mid-1970s. There were also the Datsun double-wicket tournaments: cosmetic affairs doomed to an early death, as were the equally futile two matches the SA Blacks played against the Datsun Shield champions, Natal and Eastern Province.

The short-lived unity of the 1976/77 season was a rare glimmer of light before the grey blanket of isolation was again lowered. No matter how much a mistrusted government tried to patch up the murky areas, it was not enough. The apartheid laws remained, enforced by vigilant police and security forces. There were several aborted efforts in the late 1970s and up to September 1980 to get sides of Test standard for a tour of between six and seven weeks with any number of top names; some of them, like Geoff Boycott, were factual, while others, like Viv Richards, Michael Holding, Andy Roberts, Ian Botham and Clive Lloyd, were highly fanciful.

Early in February 1982, Ian Todd of the *Sun* phoned his contact at the *Pretoria News*, asking bluntly, 'Is anyone in South Africa aware that some members of the England team in India have agreed to tour South Africa in March? I'm told Chris Old knows about it.' He insisted that the rumour was genuine, and that names such as Botham, Graham Gooch, Geoff Boycott, Derek Underwood, John Emburey, Keith Fletcher, Alan Knott and David Gower were on the list. It was an impressive group of players. Contact was made with Old, who was then in Pretoria where he was playing for Northern Transvaal. His enigmatic response was, 'Yes ... March may be an interesting month,' but he warned that this was 'not to be repeated to anyone'. He was not prepared to make an off-the-record statement either ... perhaps in a week or two, 'but not now'. The problem was the difficulty in distinguishing between fact and rumour; as Old said later, financially there was just too much involved.

England were then in Sri Lanka after losing a six-match Test series 1–0 to India; behind the scenes South African officials were talking to a new sponsor, keeping details close to their chest. Having resorted to chequebook tactics to lure the players, the SACU were aware of stormy days ahead when, on 27 February 1982, Gooch and six others flew from London to Jan Smuts International Airport. It came as no surprise that the England Test and County Cricket Board and the ICC were stunned and outraged by the audacity of the coup. Peter Cooke, born in Lancashire but by then living in Johannesburg, was the team's manager. Operation Chess Match had been concluded, and the rebel era was launched.

When referring to the rebel tours, it is easy to criticise what was written in cloying jingoism in magazines, newspapers and books, such as the *Cricket Annual*, in the 1980s. But comments such as 'South African cricket, as a collective unit, was treated as a leper to be avoided at all costs' were highly emotional and should have been avoided, as they ignored the fact that it was the politicians and the SACA establishment that had turned the game into a leper, and not the players. The players had already made their views known on 3 April 1971, when they said, 'We cricketers feel that the time has come for an expression of our views. We fully support the South African Cricket Association's application to include non-whites on the tour of Australia if good enough and, furthermore, subscribe to merit being the only criterion on the cricket field.' That the SACA had made the approach without Sacboc approval was overlooked by the SACA when they made the announcement.

It is interesting to note that no other South African sportsmen (Gary Player included) other than the cricket players had until then openly stated that merit was the only criterion in terms of selection. They had led the way all those years ago. In a final gamble, the SACU sanctioned the first of the rebel tours, with Mike Procter appointed the first captain for the series.

Overtures to South Africa's first pirate venture had begun more than 12 months earlier, when Cooke, travelling on a British passport, arrived in the West Indies in early February 1981, where England were playing the first Test of the series in Port-of-Spain, Trinidad. Cooke was an old friend of Boycott's, and in an ironic turn of events Boycott started his talks with the prospective rebels in Guyana at the time Robin Jackman faced deportation from the South American country for his years of playing and coaching in South Africa and Rhodesia. This was on the eve of the second Test, and Jackman, the central figure in the deportation row, had been flown in as a replacement for the injured Bob Willis. Chris Old, along with the future national coach Bob Woolmer, Les Taylor, Geoff Humpage and Arnie Sidebottom, were all in South Africa under playing or coaching contracts, and joined the rebels. The talks, held in a Georgetown hotel while the politicians argued over Jackman's fate, ended with Boycott wanting the players to sign a handwritten letter showing interest in the venture. After several previous failures, where vast sums of money were discussed but nothing materialised, the venture was dismissed as another fly-by-night scheme.

In October 1981, when Stuart Banner, representing Holiday Inn, threw a figure of £500 000 on the table, Gooch, Mike Gatting and Graham Dilley knew the offer was genuine, even if the details of whom they were to play remained sketchy. The tour plans seemed to fall apart in late January 1982 when Holiday Inn withdrew as sponsors, as it became known that Ian Botham and David Gower were not available. Yet even after new sponsors were found, contracts signed and the players had arrived in Johannesburg, details of the itinerary had not been finalised. But Joe Pamensky and Ali Bacher insisted on playing a full series of three four-day rebel 'tests' and three one-day international matches.

The side was always a quality batsman short, and the injury to John Emburey, who would have caused any number of problems for South Africa's batsmen, sidelined this quality off-spinner. Thus the tour was disappointing, as the team was rarely at its best in terms of strength. Yet it certainly caused a rumpus in world cricket circles. Two full ICC member countries, Pakistan and India, demanded some form of immediate retribution, disallowing Gooch to play, even for his county Essex, against whichever teams objected to his being in an opposing side.

At the time of the first rebel tour there were those who viewed it with scepticism because of the aggressive and defiant message it presented: credibility to a government that had barely shifted in its rigid apartheid policy. There was also the knowledge that something had to be done to keep the game in a healthy state, as the years of isolation continued to dry up the well of local talent. As the SACU saw it, the cause of the problem was reaction within the ICC to the report on South Africa and its recommendations, made during its 1979 fact-finding mission. The report had been received and noted by the members but no action was taken. With spectator numbers and interest in the tertiary and Coca-Cola Nuffield weeks showing a serious decline, it was decided that something had to be done to arrest the slide. Part of the remedy was the planned day/night series involving the five Currie Cup provinces.

As Joe Pamensky, the acting SACU president, said in April 1982, it was 'never going to be that simple'. He agreed in an interview with the *Pretoria News* that 'they were hard times, difficult times, and they [the ICC] were warned but chose to ignore that warning'.

Gooch, known for his stoicism, admitted that the first one-day rebel international at Port Elizabeth was an emotionally charged event, as South Africa took the field after Mike Procter had won the toss and opened the bowling. This was the venue where South Africa had made their official exit 12 years before. Procter, Barry Richards and Graeme Pollock were the surviving members of that side, which had beaten Australia by a record margin of 323 runs. Gooch scored a flowing 114, as a crowd of around 16 000 saw South Africa in action again. Euphoria reigned as Procter led his side to a seven-wicket victory. Pollock's undefeated innings of 57 drew as much comment from the British press covering the tour as did Vintcent van der Bijl's first wayward overs. The balding giant's career was drawing to a close, the prospect of playing in even a rebel series beyond his dreams. But here he was bowling to Gooch, who regarded him as the finest bowler of his style in the world at the time.

Procter played in only two more matches before injury ruled him out: the opening four-day rebel 'test' at the Wanderers, and the second of the three one-day rebel internationals at Kingsmead. His luck with the toss continued at the Wanderers. What did rankle is the way some newspapers referred to Jimmy Cook's innings of 114 as an 'historic century'. What was 'historic' was that it was the first century in the rebel 'tests', but nothing more. South Africa won by eight wickets while Van der Bijl, with five wickets apiece in each innings, collected 10 for 104. Gooch's 109 propped up the English rebels' reply. In fact, Gooch was the only batsman among the tourists who seemed to know how to handle local conditions.

But for rain at Newlands, the rebel 'series' may have been shared 1–1; the one-day games went 3–0 to the South Africans. Graeme Pollock, of whom much was expected, was a major disappointment in the four-day matches, with only 100 runs in five innings.

Mike Procter's career against rebel teams was almost over. He played only one more match: against Lawrence Rowe's West Indians at the Wanderers in the limited-overs series during their second tour. It was a day/night match that exploded in acrimony on the field and over money off it. Played on 7 December 1983, Procter's helmet was dislodged by a particularly nasty bouncer from Sylvester

Clarke in what was a display of ugly aggression in a bad-tempered bullring before an uncouth crowd.

Procter resumed his international links as the coach of the first South African side in world cricket after 22 years with a whistle-stop tour of India, with three games and one victory in New Delhi. It was followed by the pace-setting World Cup and then the West Indies tour, followed by the historic home series of four Tests against India, which South Africa won 1–0. Then there was the Total International Triangular series.

He hung on as coach until after England in 1994, when in the aftermath of the defeat at The Oval – where Devon Malcolm demolished South Africa's second innings with his impressive and hostile nine wickets – he lost his post to Bob Woolmer. In March 2002 he was appointed an ICC match referee. There are many who prefer to remember him for his swashbuckling batting and often terrifying bowling: his six successive first-class centuries in 1970/71 equalled the world record, when he joined Charles ('CB') Fry and Sir Donald Bradman, the only other two batsmen to perform such a feat. The achievement captured the imagination and headlines, as did the five consecutive sixes off Ashley Mallett when batting for Western Province against the Australians at Newlands in 1969/70.

* * *

Barry Richards's career is always linked with Procter's, as they shared the load of isolation for years. It is far from easy to classify something as personal as individual skills when it comes to the art of batting. Six batsmen who stand out as being on a higher level than any other are Sir Donald Bradman, Sir Leonard Hutton, Sir Frank Worrell, Sir Garfield Sobers, Sachin Tendulkar and Barry Richards. The author's memories of the Don, although fleeting, recall that merciless streak which was all too apparent in his strokeplay. His footwork was amazingly nimble, and the sight of a 41-year-old advancing down the pitch to drive was enough to make any bowler wonder if there was an easier way to spend a hot March afternoon.

Hutton's footwork, too, was something special, although his approach to run gathering was as economically calculating as you would find from someone brought up on wet pitches and in the stoical confines of a thrifty Yorkshire community. Sure there was a richness in the way he batted, but a damaged arm from World War II meant there were times when the England opener batted with the handicap of one arm being about four centimetres shorter than the other.

Sir Frank Worrell's near flawless style and elegance and great captaincy was the hallmark of all that is flamboyantly different about the game in the Caribbean. Sir Garfield Sobers, who took over the West Indies leadership from Worrell, was liquid in motion with all the artistic flair of a greatness that few have matched.

From the author's memories of that Test record innings of 365 in Kingston, Jamaica in early 1958, Sobers combined domination with impressive flair. He could be as ruthless as Bradman and as dominant as Hutton. Indian Sachin Tendulkar bears a strong resemblance to Bradman in style and strokeplay: the batting idol of millions on the vast sub-continent, there is majesty in his driving, and, like the Don, the pull shot is purposeful and controlled.

Watching Barry Richards, though, was always a special event. As a youngster he had studied the batting techniques in Bradman's classic coaching book *The Art of Cricket*, a Christmas gift from his mother, and which gave the game possibly the most perfect technician and stylist in 50 years. Here was a young man with a big reputation: little wonder, when the author saw him for the first time in the nets at the Harlequin Club in Pretoria in October 1966, memories of Bradman's footwork emerged from a distant past. Noticeable was that free-flowing driving, with all the aggressive emancipation of a batsman who had matured years ahead of his time: a classical example of textbook perfection.

The one genuine regret Barry Anderson Richards had when interviewed in 1992 was that his young son Mark has been unable to share in his career, as there is little memorabilia to show his schoolmates. Yet he is the first to admit that there are two sides to Barry Richards: the truth and the myth. He was particularly thrilled the night South Africa beat Australia at the Sydney Cricket Ground when they made their long awaited re-entry into world cricket in the World Cup on 26 February 1992. Most of the time he floated between the media centre, where the overseas press were gathered, and the officials' box.

'What a night,' was his first frank assessment. 'It has been worth waiting all these years to be here and see this victory.' He nodded with enjoyment at Peter Kirsten's drive on the up when planting Mike Whitney wide of mid-off; and a square cut the little South African maestro whipped past a deep gully brought a wry, approving grin. A firm pull from Kepler Wessels backward of square also brought a nod of appreciation. 'It's going to be a good victory. I like the way they have played: so controlled and disciplined.'

There were a lot of South Africans around that night, as well as some New Zealanders and Australians who had played against South Africa: Bert Sutcliffe and John Reid, Neil Harvey, Ray Lindwall and Doug Walters, along with Bill Lawry and Ian Chappell. There were the West Indians (Everton Weekes and Clyde Walcott popped up everywhere) and a few Englishmen, including Mike Gatting. All was forgiven and forgotten, handshakes all round and time for Barry to reflect on the irony of it all.

Many media and former players considered the paradoxical aspects of that night, including Steve Tshwete: 'All the years I spent on Robben Island I never cried, but I'm crying tonight.' It was indeed an incredible event: cricket history stretched out a welcoming hand and acknowledged the past. Barry was from the past, with a staggering talent and an appetite for runs. He had scored a century when South Africa had last played Australia officially, from 5 to 10 March 1970 at St George's Park in Port Elizabeth. The 126 was his second century of the series, and when he was caught by Ian Chappell it was with the carefree approach of a 24-year-old who had three figures next to his name on the rickety scoreboard.

Apart from the one season he played for South Australia (1970/71), when he scored a famous 356 against Western Australia in Perth (one of the few players to score 300 runs in a day's play), Barry has had an on-off relationship with Australian cricket. It was a season when his talent was given every chance to flower, and where members of the public would phone to hear if he was in the batting. He was the nearest some had seen to 'the Don' since the retirement, 21 seasons before, of the great Sir Donald Bradman. Even Ray Illingworth complained. Leading England on the tour that saw them win the Ashes Down Under for the first time since 1954/55, he often found that an innings by Richards earned bigger headlines that summer.

It was Richards's contributions, with an average of 109.86, that helped South Australia win the Sheffield Shield that season. He flew home late in March, went to Newlands for the trial to select a side to tour Australia the following season, and took part in the famous walk off. This event was the collective brainchild of five players: Barry, Procter, Peter and Graeme Pollock and Denis Lindsay. They had discussed the question of the walk off over dinner the night before the trial match between Currie Cup champions Transvaal and the Rest of South Africa. Some players wondered whether it was too late, but as Lindsay said years later, 'It probably was too late, but we had to be seen to be doing something ... no matter how futile.'

For Barry, playing for Hampshire was a means to an end, and later he welcomed the Packer era as an opportunity to spread his talents. The money was good, the cricket was good and the crowds loved it, so it did not really matter what the traditionalists thought of the advent of white balls, coloured clothing and black sightscreens. It was the all-important evolutionary phase of modernising the game.

Barry had long been disillusioned about the challenges he faced each season in the Currie Cup, and felt that the stigma attached to an average in the mid-40s was unfair. In his book, *The Barry Richards Story*, written in 1977 and published the following year, he poured out his frustrations and oft-repeated arguments. In a disarming and frank interview in 1992, he felt quite strongly that he should not have written the book.

'I had 10 years [of county cricket] and I was going nowhere. I was proving myself at the same level. At the time I knew South Africa were not going to get back in [to Test cricket], so I think in essence, the book was written as an angry young man. Out of frustration more than anything.

'I was 33 and time was running out, so I think the book must be looked on in that context. You should be smart enough to realise you should not do those sort of things. It happened, and it is a regret more than anything. A book should always be a source of pleasure: they are a source of knowledge. Looking back, this book is not a source of pleasure. I had wanted to tell the world how disappointed I was, and looking back on it, it wasn't the right thing to do.'

There is also the other side of Barry Richards, which is not seen too often. In Colombo, where he has a hand in coaching the Sri Lanka batsmen, he enjoys being able to pass on advice to a new generation. Ten years before he was wondering what lay ahead when thinking about his own career.

'In many ways I have had a deep regret about my career … I took everything so matter-of-factly that suddenly the important things in your life were just a passing phase at that time and I didn't pay any attention to it at all; absolutely none … I mean, so few knocks stand out that I have little to remind me of them: bats, or caps, wickets … even ties, or scoresheets or videos of my career …

'But really, that whole saga of the 1970s is a very sad one for me. It's a tremendous era of playing … I mean, I played some superb knocks, but I really was an immature person, and the benefits outside cricket are enormous, if you do it right. But there is so much in cricket with the history, and the heritage of the game. There are just a tremendous number of people who want to be your friends in cricket.

'And through the 70s it was so easy to pooh-pooh that … And you can see it happening again among certain players today. We all went through the angry young man stage. Yet, if you are smart enough, you can really make cricket work for you.' In Barry's view, South Africa had to take the plunge when they did and go the rebel route, despite the controversy and animosity they aroused. The dust had hardly settled after the acrimonious Packer affair, and the Test and County Cricket Board had lost a case on player restraint. This, of course, was different. Politicians from all countries, which had either full or associate membership of the ICC, were astounded at what they felt was the barefaced cheek of the first tour. Ironically, 1982 was the United Nations' official international year 'of mobilising sanctions against South Africa'.

In 1991 Geoff Dakin, first president of the United Cricket Board of South Africa, and Ali Bacher, one of the main driving forces behind unity as well as moves to get the country back into world cricket, apologised to all for the rebel era and the 'hurt and pain it caused the many people involved'.

Barry, who led South Africa in the second and third rebel tests against the SAB XI and the last one-day game, was frank and realistic about what faced South African cricket at the time.

'South Africa didn't have any option; they had to go that way to provide some sort of stimulus and impetus for the game. It is just a merry-go-round when you are playing provincial cricket all day long.

'If you take away that international incentive, it also takes away a little bit from the domestic competition ... so it was full marks to Ali [Bacher]. It was a difficult scenario, and in his heart of hearts I don't think he wanted to do it as he is a traditionalist and he knew it would tear some of traditional cricket apart. But he had to weigh that up against his knowing that it would snuff out the incentive for all the younger players, who would then turn to other sports.

'While it was a source of regret, it was also a necessity for them [the SACU]. Rebel tours filled a vacuum for the premier players; they needed it and it did give them some sort of opportunity to see where they were at ... to judge their standards.

'If I put the clock back, say, 10 years to when I was 35 or 36, I'd be a very competitive player, and have at least four or five very good years left in cricket and really have a tremendous impact on and off the field. I don't think I did. I did as a player, but I don't think I did as a leader of men.

'I have often wondered what constitutes a good captain. I suppose it is a player who can hold his place, because it is a misnomer that captains want to play just as captains ... which may have been all right in a bygone era, but with the competitive spirit around now you can't afford to carry a person that's not worth their value in the side.

'But having said that, you do need someone to have a handle on the wide spectrum of people who are going to be in the team. Not everyone is going to be playing for the same reasons, and not everyone is going to be as talented as another person; knitting that together takes a special kind of person. People tend to downgrade the art of captaincy. A good captain can't make a bad team into a good team; but he can make a good team into a very good team. Jackie [McGlew] always impressed us, but I think that was mainly because we were so young and he was a generation and a half above us; there was this mutual respect about his captaincy. I called him Mr McGlew for two seasons, and that's how it was in those days – it just wouldn't happen today.

'I think Ali was tremendous because he had what we called a "degree in people" and could read them and what their needs and wants were; he could relate to a 38-year-old who was struggling with his Test place, like Trevor Goddard was at the time, and wondering whether he was good enough, and then right down to Proccie, Lee and I who were the "babies" of the side, and in our euphoria about our first Test series were jumping out of our skins to impress everyone in sight.

'It really takes someone special to be able to blend all those people together.'

Although it was said that Barry's self-confessed immaturity cost him at least two or three Tests against Bobby Simpson's side, there is another story that surfaced in England in 1998. As a 20-year-old, Barry had stunned Simpson and his deputy, Bill Lawry, with his precocious batting talents during a supremely confident innings of 104 for a strong South African XI led by Trevor Goddard. He was earmarked as a threat should he earn a Test spot, but in an incident in East London he literally kicked away his chances. There was an invitation to a cabaret at a hotel, but on turning up late he discovered that the person who had issued the invitation had disappeared. The person had also failed to inform anyone else of the invitation, and Mike Procter, Chris Wilkins and his wife, Hylton Ackerman and Barry were unable to talk the doorman round. There were a few hard words, and Barry aimed a kick at a pot plant next to the swimming pool, sending it flying. Within seconds the bouncer hauled him into the manager's office, and a night in jail threatened until Procter contacted Deryck Dowling, a national selector, who smoothed over the ruffled feelings. The incident did not go down well with the rest of the national selectors.

The story that surfaced at Lord's during South Africa's second Test victory over England was that the selectors, such as the convener Arthur Coy, were not prepared to give Barry any sort of chance, and this was well before the East London escapade. It stemmed from a conversation Coy had had with Richards, Procter and other young SA Schools players in 1963. It was claimed that they had found a flaw in Barry's maturity and there was a belief that it would affect his batting when under pressure.

How many runs Richards would have put together at Test level will always be debatable. Former New Zealand captain John Reid has a theory that Test averages are usually relative to a particular series, because bowling strengths and pitch conditions vary from country to country; but class will always rise above standard levels. An average of, say, 40 in a season of five to eight matches (10 to 16 innings – 400 or 640 runs) is good to above average for a batsman of normal levels. For a batsman such as Barry it would be an average performance. But, as Reid had said, luck, match situations and often weather would all play a role. It would be normal for Richards to end a South African season with a 60-plus average. Yet another factor was that he played 12 months of the year, and body and mind would often go through the motions. In his Currie Cup career he played only 79 matches, yet averaged 60.40, scoring 7 551 runs with 36 centuries. South Africa's great left-hander, Graeme Pollock, scored 12 409 Currie Cup runs at 54.66 from 157 matches, with 35 centuries, or a ratio of a century every 7.45 an innings, to Barry's scoring a century every 3.88 innings.

In a first-class career spanning 18 years, from 1964 to 1982, Barry scored more runs than any other South African: 28 358 with 80 centuries, or one every 7.2 innings, which is a phenomenal record, topped by a career batting average of

54.74. It was his ability under pressure and strike rate that impressed Sir Donald Bradman, and how he wound up opening the innings for the Don's dream team.

* * *

There are those who ask, 'Is it all worth it; is cricket really more than just a game?' If they study the career of Peter Kirsten they will not only find a hero, they will discover that cricket is a whole way of life. They will also find that this gutsy, gritty and dedicated little batsman, the last playing link between the great 1969/70 side and the brave new era, has been to hell and back for his country's cricket honour, and as such played a major role in its rebirth.

While the link with the 1969/70 team, led by Ali Bacher, may seem questionable, it is a hard fact. Kirsten not only took over the captaincy of the South African team from Barry Richards and Mike Procter, he also arrived on the scene while a number of the stars of what is considered, in elite circles, a special era (from 1961/62 until 1969/70) were still able to pass on advice: Procter, Richards, Eddie Barlow, Denis Lindsay, Lee Irvine and Graeme Pollock among them. But the classy SACS sportsman was always his own man, his own batsman, setting his own standards and goals, and achieving them, often with minimal fuss and bother.

About the best example of this was Kirsten's innings in support of his captain, Kepler Wessels, on that electric and emotional night at the Sydney Cricket Ground in 1992; 49 off 90 balls with only one boundary during a partnership of 97. It helped South Africa win their great comeback match against Australia by nine wickets, as they made their official return to the international stage after 22 years; bringing cheer to an uncertain nation seeking unity and a new identity. It was one of several selfless innings the former South African and Western Province skipper made during the five-week tournament; he deserved a half-century, too, such was the skill that went into his performance. There was plenty of his grit displayed on the paddy field of Eden Park in Auckland, where he scored 90 off 129 balls, to rescue an embarrassed, embattled South Africa as the rest of the team crumbled alarmingly around him. And there was that superb, uninhibited exhibition of masterly strokeplay at Adelaide Oval when opening against India on 15 March, where an innings of 84 off only 86 balls not only won him the second man of the match award in the series, but also helped steer South Africa into the semi-finals.

If Wessels and his deputy Adrian Kuiper had not insisted, Kirsten would not have made the squad for the World Cup and later the tour of the West Indies. Who the selectors had in mind for the important role that Kirsten filled is one of the greater mysteries of team selection, as was his tragic axing all those summers ago from the captaincy of the South African team in the middle of the rebel series against Lawrence Rowe's West Indians. But he will be the first to tell you that the moment he had waited for, since playing for South African Schools against Northern Transvaal at Berea Park in 1974, had a rose-tinted glow about it. After years of waiting, he was able to strap on the pads at Eden Gardens, Calcutta, in November 1991, and walk out knowing that he was indeed representing his country at last, and it was not just another dream.

In 1982, when he retired from the county scene after five years with Derbyshire, he could have written his own epitaph: Stumped by the Politicians. In normal circumstances he would have earned 25 to 30 Test caps by then, as well as several centuries and a solid credit balance in runs around the 2 700-mark, with a handsome batting average in the 40s or better, marking him as a world-class batsman. Far better, though, to get 12 official Tests under your helmet and next to your name than end a career unhappy and frustrated. His years with Derbyshire taught him a lot, even though the club is one of the also-rans of the game. An examination of their record shows a county championship title in 1936, a NatWest trophy in 1981, the Refuge Assurance title in 1990 and nothing much else. But any county that has a racecourse as its headquarters, and where fielding in sleet in May is not uncommon, is an unlikely place to inspire anyone to make a career out of the county game. But his forced retirement had nothing to do with the conditions. There was concern over how his left knee would stand up to the rugged demands of playing seven days a week. The knee had been injured in a rugby match in 1974, and in 1982 it was felt that he had reached a crossroads in his cricket career. He was anxious to play for as long as possible, but this required a sacrifice. County cricket suffered as a result of his injury.

John Wright, a county colleague at Derby in the 1970s and 1980s, as well as a former New Zealand captain and now the successful coach of India, felt Kirsten's retirement was premature, especially as the South African had reached his batting peak in 1982 with eight centuries and was a highly respected member of the playing staff. But there were other important motivations in South Africa demanding his attention. The rebel scene had changed the face of the game. As the momentous summer of 1982/83 dawned, there was the prospect of battle.

After what was seen as the success of the Gooch rebels, Dr Bacher and the SACU went out and organised more pirate ventures. First to be raided was the island of Sri Lanka. The Arosa Sri Lankans were followed in the New Year by the West Indians. Naturally the ICC had become frustrated with such chequebook tactics, and the South African Cricket Board wondered where the game was heading. The SACU had the financial clout and expertise; the SACB had the conscience, although there was infighting in both camps.

In early October 1982, the Sri Lankan rebels under manager Tony Opatha were spirited into South Africa, with Bandula Warnapura as the captain. They later became known as 'Opatha and friends'. While their arrival made a bigger impact on the outside world than on South Africa, their ability was generally disappointing, with critics doubting their capabilities. The series flopped horrendously, and the form of Ajit de Silva was most disappointing of all. A left-arm spinner with a major reputation, De Silva arrived in South Africa as the Sri Lankans' main weapon, but the form that had earned him such a high world ranking deserted him to the extent that it consisted of either full tosses or deliveries that bounced twice.

While Kirsten's Currie Cup form was solid, with a century, several half-centuries and 500-plus runs, unfair criticism was heaped on him; it was said that the captaincy of the South African XI had placed too much pressure on his ability and robbed the side of a skilful top-order batsman. This is a bit of a joke if his Castle Currie Cup season is measured against the innings against the Arosa Sri Lankans and Rowe's West Indians in the rebel matches. A posse of press people in Johannesburg was also gunning for him; they wanted Clive Rice as captain of the rebel series against the West Indians.

Thursday, 13 January 1983 was no ordinary day: members of the press had been summoned to Jan Smuts Airport in Johannesburg to await the arrival of a West Indian rebel team, the biggest coup the South African Cricket Union had pulled off since it had been formed. While the ICC chafed angrily, Joe Pamensky uttered his famous stand on the matter of his union and the government: 'I'm not for a minute endorsing the policies of this country's ruling party. I vote against them as often as I can. My point as a former cricketer and present cricket lover is that practicalities have to be faced.'

When they emerged from the overseas arrivals lounge, the West Indians looked tired and apprehensive. Rowe and manager Armstrong were the only members of the group dressed in anything resembling suits; the rest were a very laid-back charismatic group dressed in jeans, open-necked shirts or T-shirts, sporting a variety of hairstyles from Afros to short-back-and-sides, Caribbean style. Smiling and enjoying the post-press conference chatter, Rowe made a plea for the team to be treated 'in a manner we deserve', which was a fair request, but lost on the majority of the media as there was a lot of hype about sanctions busting and misguided speculation that the side was better than the one captained by Clive Lloyd, left behind to play India.

As usual, the majority of white South Africans wanted to delude themselves. Losing to what was generally an above average West Indies B team brought them back to earth. It was a strong team in that Alvin Kallicharran was, at the time, still good enough to play in the full West Indies side; while Colin Croft (although carrying a back injury), Sylvester Clarke, Faoud Bacchus, David Murray and

Collis King had been in the West Indies touring squad the previous summer. And if the rumours were true that Desmond Haynes and Malcolm Marshall were to join the squad, it would have been a team far too strong for a South African line-up that was, in some quarters, showing its age. It was also, in some respects, lacking in experience, with the exception of Barry Richards, Clive Rice, Graeme Pollock and Kirsten, who was retained as captain for the first tour.

From the time he scored a cultured century for South African Schools against Northern Transvaal at Berea Park in 1974, the press had been on Peter Kirsten's case; and after he reeled off five in a row in 1976/77, it was either all or nothing. Kirsten was turned into a controversial character, and for some reason other than his cricketing ability. He may be a complex person and not everyone's idea of a captain, but he always did his job and took the flak when it should have been aimed elsewhere. It was not his fault that the South Africans battled to come to terms with an unaccustomed pace attack and a bowler like Sylvester Clarke, then regarded by many an English county batsman as one of the most dangerous bowlers in the game.

About the only blight on the Rowe rebels' record was their temperament, and then only when it came to money. There were chaotic scenes at the opening day/night match of the limited-overs series in the 1983/84 season at the start of the second tour. In terms of what they were wearing, the players in the Wanderers game were a motley crew. Collis King wore the official strip, but the rest batted in various shades of white. But the mostly white South African crowds loved the West Indians: they were fun and always exhibited an aggressive, often explosive, charm, which some ignorantly referred to as calypso cricket. But, as Clive Lloyd quickly pointed out, the label 'calypso cricket' is derogatory, 'a terrible misnomer, which we disown'.

South Africa lost the Wanderers day/night cash row fiasco to Rowe's rebels by two wickets on an overheated evening. The captaincy row was becoming bolder and louder, because of Kirsten's handling of the bowlers in the Rowe rebels' first innings in the first four-day game at Kingsmead, Durban. South Africa followed on and easily survived on a pitch that was fit only for a meeting of the flat earth society. Then came the second game at Newlands over the New Year. Kirsten (88) and Pollock (102) saw the South Africans through to a first-innings lead of 152, and the bowlers steered the side to a 10-wicket victory. But the bellyaching over his captaincy failed to subside. Yet Kirsten was a serious, thoughtful captain, who often made the right moves for the right reasons. His passing as leader was not mourned, but he was never given a chance, either.

While his axing resulted in Clive Rice's elevation to leadership, an unbowed Peter Kirsten ended the four-match series with a top score of 88, an average of 50.00 and the most runs in the rebel matches that season with 304. His only failure was in Port Elizabeth, where Hartley Alleyne softened up the South Africans in the second innings and Clarke reaped the benefits with a five-wicket haul.

It is still surprising how both West Indian bowlers escaped being called for throwing in South Africa. Alleyne, brought on the second tour to add muscle to the pace attack, had been no-balled in the Caribbean in a couple of Shell Shield matches as well as in the Lancashire League, and it became common knowledge that he did not play for the West Indies because of doubts about the legality of his action. When the 'Alleyne is a chucker' story broke to myopic howls, *The Citizen*, a Johannesburg tabloid, ranted hysterically that the report was based on hearsay. In fact, the Alleyne report was based on fact, with one of the umpires confirming telephonically that there were serious doubts on whether he would again be considered for Barbados. Playing for the rebels, it was suggested, was the easier option. Alleyne had played for Worcestershire and later for Kent without so much as a query, but the suspicions remained. That Clarke, like Alleyne, threw the faster ball, there is no doubt. Brian Whitfield, a former Natal opening batsman, always doubted the legality of Clarke's quicker ball.

Apart from the mental battering over the vexed captaincy issue, Kirsten also took a physical hammering from the West Indies pace attack during the second season, but withstood the onslaught far better than some teammates with bigger egos and reputations. Gritty determination was very much a Kirsten trademark, but part of the reason for Peter's doggedness may have been the intense criticism he always seemed to face. Peter's late father, Noel Kirsten, once complained that, 'if anything goes wrong, blame it on a Kirsten'. This comment, about a pitch he had prepared to instructions, held more than a grain of truth. But that fortitude not only carried Kirsten through the rebel series, but along with Rice and Cook he is the only one to have played all the rebel teams.

While Kirsten's form didn't quite produce the big bang in the first of the two series against Kim Hughes's Australian rebels, the impression he gave of being the batsman who built bridges for others to take the credit for big scores was not far from wrong. In run-scoring terms, the second Rowe rebel tour was a happier one for Kirsten, who saved his best for the New Year clash at Newlands. He scored a solid 173 to set up a South African first-innings total of 493. He played any variety of polished exhibitions against Rowe's and Hughes's teams; they were typical of a thoughtful batsman who had rediscovered a talent for delighting the purists among the limited-overs masses who flock to see the fours and sixes and wickets tumbling, and start grumbling when batsmen such as Kirsten add that extra touch of batting magic.

While all the one-day excitement against rebel teams was okay in terms of runs in the credit columns of an already illustrious career, the last of the pirate ventures, Mike Gatting's XI, showed that the game was in need of a new direction.

The political changes within South Africa had suddenly given the sport a drive and impetus that found other codes lagging far behind. International Cricket Council recognition on 10 July 1991, with backing from India and support by Australia, found South Africa suddenly taking off on an unprecedented whistle-stop tour of India, and Kirsten was part of an adventure that didn't start too well but ended with a man of the match award he'll always remember.

'Little did I think on Saturday that my next innings would be here in Calcutta,' he grinned on the day the side arrived, on 8 November 1991, in a city of teeming millions, where poverty and opulence casually rub shoulders in the dusty streets. At Eden Gardens, a fine sports venue 20 minutes' walk from the Oberoi Grand Hotel, they hung out a 'Cutta Welcomes the Return of South Africa' sign from the top tier. South Africa's return to the world cricket stage after a 22-year absence was one of the great sport stories of the decade, and occurred in a city as exotic as it was unlikely. After all, who in their right mind six months before would have considered that South African cricket, only unified on 29 June 1991, would join hands so soon with a country that had been an intractable foe for 40 years?

In Calcutta there was a fair amount of pressure on the South Africans to do well. But Kirsten's first two innings in India are not quite what he would like to remember: a seven off 29 balls in Calcutta, before being bowled by a creeper from Venkatapathy Raju; while in ancient Gwalior, about a 90-minute run from the Taj Mahal, in a match reduced to 45 overs because of fog and rain, he was shot down by an umpire who felt that after six balls and two runs it would be better for all if Kirsten sat out the rest of the match in the makeshift pavilion. It was a totally bizarre outing all round, as the ancient battlements of the local castle frowned upon the feeble efforts of the South Africans.

But a midnight flight to New Delhi, and a match at the Jawaharlal Nehru Stadium under lights 48 hours later, restored some satisfaction for the South Africans in a fairly emphatic eight-wicket victory. Kirsten won the man of the match award with another gem-like performance, with 86 off 92 balls. In truth, the match must be seen in the context of the conditions in which it was played. The venue is an athletics stadium where a third of the surface consists of an artificial running track, and no fieldsman in his right mind would dive to stop a boundary under those conditions. Kepler Wessels, who had scored a century several years before for Australia, managed a quality innings of 90 as South Africa were set to score 288 off 50 overs. These days they mostly remember the New Delhi game for the fine innings of 63 off 41 balls from Adrian Kuiper: a biff, bash and wallop affair with seven fours and a six. They forget Kirsten's class innings and bridge building that set up Kuiper's platform.

South Africa's World Cup odyssey of 1992 was tinged with nostalgia. From the opening match in Harare on 5 February 1992 during the pre-build-up stage,

Kirsten carefully established himself. On a sweltering day in Harare, South Africa found themselves 31 for two after nine overs after chicken farmer Eddo Brandes had blown away the two early wickets. South Africa was in need of Kirsten's circumspection that afternoon, and while it was not the most fluent of his innings on tour, it was a sign of things to come. Kirsten scored 64 off 123 balls: scratchy on occasions, some timing a fraction off; not up to the standard of what was later seen in Adelaide, or had been seen in Canberra a few days before, but enough to spread a little anxiety in the bowling ranks of the opposition.

In terms of the World Cup, opposing teams saw Kepler Wessels as the main danger, as not enough was known about Andrew Hudson early on in the series to assess the Natal opener. Kirsten was not so much a mystery as an enigma. It had been 10 years since he had quit the English county scene, and his only other visit Down Under was on a private expedition six years earlier, when the frustrations of isolation and political uncertainty made him think of a future elsewhere. But moving to Australia would have meant starting all over again, which is not at all easy at 30, even though Kirsten's batting talents were such that he would definitely have made an impact in Australia. It was in Adelaide that Kirsten impishly suggested he had been born 10 years too early, but it was worth waiting for what he wanted all his playing life: to be a proud South African representing a united country.

In the 1992 World Cup, Kirsten was third-highest run-scorer with 410 at 68.33, to Martin Crowe's 456 and Javed Miandad's 437, and second to Crowe in the batting averages.

After this, the West Indies tour was something of an anticlimax until the first Test and the second-innings score of 52. But Kirsten at last had that first official Test cap to his credit, and of all the South Africans who played in Bridgetown he deserved it the most.

Ending his Test career at The Oval in England in 1994 was perhaps a little unfair. South Africa wanted an opening batsman, and after his grit-laden century at Leeds in the second Test indicated he was in form, he took on the responsibility. It was a farewell he does not care to remember, but it was time to move on, and there has always been Gary to carry on the Kirsten name. Peter settled into first coaching Northern Titans, and then Western Province in the shadow of the familiar Table Mountain.

* * *

Long before the campaign of the controversial 1989/90 season started, the SACU selectors were looking for a captain who they felt had the insight and flair to lead the last of the rebel teams in that traumatic summer. As the convener, Peter van der Merwe, said at the time, the selectors examined the problem of captaincy from a broader perspective than in the past. When the planning was over, they emerged with Transvaal opening batsman Jimmy Cook as their choice, ahead of the more fancied candidates, including Clive Rice, the incumbent and the Transvaal captain.

Amid bitter acrimony, and a few days after the most controversial of all pirate tours began, Van der Merwe hinted that the selectors could, of necessity, move outside the provincial captaincy spectrum to find their man. At that time the thought, which had occurred some months before and was first expressed in the *Sunday Star* in late August 1989, was that Cook, with a successful county season behind him, might be a fair long-term bet as captain for the rebel 'series'. It was an interesting theory, based more on Rice's growing sports diversification, which had spread to deep-sea fishing and motorcar racing.

At the time, Cook was still proving his worth on the county circuit for Somerset, with a fine display of class batting, while Rice's other sporting outlets meant missing one Currie Cup game, against Eastern Province at the start of the season. However, it was this match, played at the Wanderers, which aroused the selectors' interest in Cook's captaincy capabilities, if only because of the way he turned a first-innings deficit of 70 into an impressive victory of six wickets. Hugh Page took seven for 38 in the Eastern Province second innings of 148. But Cook's handling of the bowling changes and field placings as Eastern Province crumbled was intuitive, as it had been when the Transvaal attack was under pressure in the first innings. It was just the package the selectors were looking for as they began their early season discussions on the captaincy issue in what was a watershed series.

In his first season in England in 1989, Cook proved that he was more than your average overseas bangers-and-mash batsman, the sort who is good on hard pitches and has a soft touch when the ball moves around off the seam. He was the first to score 1 000 runs, then 2 000, eventually going on to score 2 173 county championship runs at 62.08. In a remarkable match against Nottinghamshire at Trent Bridge, Cook became the first batsman since 1911 to score centuries while carrying his bat in both innings of a match – 120 not out in 186 and 131 not out in 218 – and he was on the field throughout the game. With four of his 11 centuries that season scored in succession during the hot month of July, he managed 999 first-class runs at 83.25, but this slipped to 200 runs in August – just one of the form patterns that occur in cricket.

As a tribute to Cook's dedication and fitness and playing every game in the 1989 season, he was accorded the rare honour for a South African by being selected as one of the five *Wisden* players of 1989. Cook deserved this accolade; few batsmen have dominated the way he did in what was a fairly poor summer for Somerset. The county had fallen on hard times since the sacking of Ian Botham, Viv Richards and Joel Garner: big names who didn't really win much but trouble for the lads in one of the more picturesque parts of the country. But before he rejoined them in 1990, the man Van der Merwe's panel thought was 'Mr Right' for the South African captaincy found himself in the middle of a controversy not of his making. He was entrusted with an important job, and not many people envied the role that faced him in February 1990; yet he did it with all the polite, diplomatic warmth one might expect of a former schoolteacher.

From his early years, Jimmy Cook knew that cricket was his game, although he did dabble in a winter pastime. The heavy demands of the summer sport eventually gave him little option but to concentrate more on the importance of building the batting technique that would turn him into one of the most accomplished opening batsmen in South Africa from the late 1970s. His partnerships with Henry Fotheringham for Transvaal made them a feared combination, even on the tricky Wanderers pitches before lunch on the first day of a Castle Currie Cup game. That's the way it was with the Cook and Fothers opening partnerships. One complemented the other, picking up runs against difficult bowling attacks and spotting problem areas and correcting them as they went along: an inbuilt technical school designed to spot weaknesses in bowling attacks and field placings.

Cook learnt much from his father, whose coaching and guidance helped him through the early years when attention to basics is so important. England's world famous umpire Harold (Dickie) Bird also had a hand in coaching the aspirant opening batsman in his formative years as he moved into his teens, encouraging the best of batting habits without the unnecessary frippery encouraged by the one-day game. There was a particularly fine century for Transvaal B against Northern Transvaal at Berea Park in the mid-1970s, when Cook batted with remarkable orderliness. That innings in the Jacaranda City did not go unnoticed, and he found himself back in the senior side for the rest of the Castle Currie Cup season.

The A Section was a tougher learning school, and David Dyer, an above-average captain, imbued Jimmy with added run-scoring confidence. Dyer became the victim of Transvaal selection policy in the traumatic summer of 1981/82, when Clive Rice took over the Transvaal captaincy and David was dumped. But there was neither fuss nor acrimony from Dyer, who had initially welded the mean machine together. Here was another of the game's gentlemen who went unrecognised in the Transvaal glory years of the 1980s for the work he did on the field.

On 2 February 1990, as fury over the Gatting rebel tour mounted and Krish Naidoo, of the National and Olympic Sports Congress (NSC), fought for its abandonment, FW de Klerk, the country's last white president, told the world of the sweeping changes that were planned and his desire for reconciliation. All anti-apartheid political organisations, such as the African National Congress, were to be unbanned, Nelson Mandela would be released unconditionally and all remaining apartheid laws scrapped. While the Gatting tour was still a catalyst for political demonstrations and discussion, it had also become a sideshow, as had the captaincy controversy. Only a few days before, in Kimberley, Cook had been named as the captain over Rice, who had already hinted at Centurion Park a couple of weeks before the tour started that he was no longer certain of selection, let alone of being named captain.

The Cook captaincy issue was used as part of a hysterical vendetta by some writers and so-called television personalities. They wanted the head of everyone, Van der Merwe in particular, who disagreed with their own narrow vision of how team selection policy should be handled. What was also annoying was how *The Star* became guilty of exaggerating the importance of one particular issue.

At an impromptu conference after the first pre-tour net practice at the Wanderers, rebel vice-captain John Emburey repeated his comment of the previous August that he and other members of the side were confident 'of playing for England again when our bans are lifted'. The tall Middlesex off-spinner had made the comment 48 hours after the rebel tour plans were disclosed in London six months earlier. But the news editor and the sports editor, Julian Kearns, were not too bothered about filling space by tarting up an old story. So what if the British tabloids in far-off Africa could thump the drums over the story, yet hide evidence that Emburey said nothing new? One member of the non-travelling press, Barry Glasspool, even came up with a story that Rice was available to play for the tourists because of his captaining Scotland. Although Rice's tongue-in-cheek comment created much mirth in the rebel camp, Glasspool treated it seriously. Manager–player David Graveney dismissed it as 'trashy garbage that not even the rat pack would consider newsworthy'.

Cook stayed out of the captaincy row that was deliberately stirred by the media, even though he was the central figure. It became quite ugly, and while it did not divide the team, the players assembled in an atmosphere heavy with ambivalence a few days before what was to be the only rebel 'test' of the tour. The uncertainty had nothing to do with the captaincy row. The match, played at the Wanderers, was held in a surreal atmosphere as anticipation of the tour's cancellation grew.

As it was, this particular illegitimate child had been born from an ICC meeting regarding future rebel tours. On 23 and 24 January 1989, the ICC had finally tackled the rebel tour issue in a wide-ranging seven-point resolution, designed to further isolate the SACU because of the government's apartheid policies. It laid down guideline bans, as well as stating who would be affected. The ICC passed the resolution after the West Indies' proposal was seconded by Sri Lanka.

During his visits to London on the SACU monitoring exercises, Geoff Dakin was characteristically more blunt than the diplomatic Boon Wallace and Joe Pamensky. It was no longer a question of cricket ethics, as 'the laws of our land divided us and only when they go, can we think about being a member of the ICC again', Dakin said.

When he assumed the presidency of the SACU in 1989, Dakin spelt this out again in a wide-ranging interview that earned worldwide exposure long before the Gatting tour took place. In this interview he laid down a policy guideline that partly opened the door to the South African Cricket Board of Krish Mackerdhuj to join discussions in order to 'create a single entity for the game in this country', but admitted that until 'all apartheid barriers are removed, I don't see much hope ... of such a meeting taking place'.

The Gatting tour was as traumatic as it was politically explosive. It came at a time when the country seemed to be heading towards long-anticipated violence. As a cricket tour it was totally forgettable; much of the cricket was disappointing. This could partly be attributed to the protests that followed Gatting's gang around the country. Although they wouldn't admit it at the time, this placed a psychological strain on the players in both sides.

The Wanderers match summed up the quality of that ill-fated tour. It had ended early, and was being played out against a backdrop of violence and intrigue. Gatting's side was underprepared for the game, played on a pitch that did not allow for good cricket at all; in fact, it was like watching a disappointing low-key Currie Cup match. Late on the Saturday afternoon, as about 10 000 locals cheered the winning runs, the tour was in its death throes. Dr Ali Bacher had been urged to talk to a top ANC official, who in turn urged him to meet representatives of the anti-tour body to thrash out a compromise, thus ending the civil unrest surrounding the tour. The ANC had also told the NSC to work out a 'peace formula' with the SACU; this was being done as the announcement of Nelson Mandela's release was about to be made. Cape Town was to have been the rebel tour's next venue, and it was believed that the many opponents of the tour would not allow the match to take place at any price. Gatting's rebels and the South African players were not wanted in Cape Town, and as it coincided with Mandela's release, the ANC did not want the event marred by the sort of emotional violence it would attract.

Quite frankly, common sense prevailed from the moment of President De Klerk's watershed address on 2 February 1990. There is little doubt that he had not only defused a powder keg, but also created a forum for debate. On the day Nelson Mandela was released in Cape Town, the controversial disclosure was made in Johannesburg that Kepler Wessels had walked out of the side and did not want to be considered for any further matches against the rebels. This fuelled further speculation that he had been verbally abused by some members of the side during the Wanderers game. Peter van der Merwe, acting as Kepler's spokesman, read out a statement that the Eastern Province captain had prepared, but it was deliberately construed by some to be a statement made on behalf of the selectors, as it gave them a chance to attack the panel again. The Wessels episode was overtaken by far more dramatic events. At six in the morning of 13 February 1990, there was a phone call informing the author that Krish Naidoo and the NSC had not only forced the cancellation of the Cape Town rebel 'test', but had also cut the number of limited-overs matches from six to four. Port Elizabeth and Cape Town had been excluded because of the volatile political situation.

What made up Gatting's mind to agree to captain the rebels was an issue that only emerged months after the tour was aborted. Ted Dexter, chairman of the selectors, and Mickey Stewart had wanted Gatting, not David Gower, to lead England against Australia in the 1989 series. Team manager Stewart had an uncanny eye when it came to picking the right man for the right job. Anyone who knew anything about the game in England knew that Gatt was the best Test captain. In March 1989, Gatting had been told privately that he was back in favour after being badly treated by the TCCB over the planted barmaid episode the year before during the first Test against the West Indies. Imagine his disgust; from martyr to burning mercenary as the men at Lord's stumbled around and committees pulled in different directions. Po-faced Ossie Wheatley, the former Cambridge and Glamorgan captain and chairman of the TCCB's cricket committee, had applied the veto 'for non-cricketing reasons', and kept this juicy slice of information from members of the TCCB executive. But when it came to the vote at the winter meeting of 1990, despite the private discontent, TCCB ranks closed and the decision was endorsed. 'Dishonest fumbling by the old chums society' was Martin Johnson's biting quip in the *Independent*.

The last rebel tour was born out of frustration and confrontation, and when the side arrived on a chilly Friday morning in January, Jan Smuts Airport in Johannesburg was an armed fortress, bristling with police and police dogs, acrid tear gas and antagonism. It did not stop for five weeks, which is why when it was over the SACU admitted that it had been a mistake, especially as the important township programme had come under threat.

It is no wonder that the cricket during the tour was disappointing, apart from a couple of isolated performances. Adrian Kuiper played a phenomenal innings at Springbok Park in the third one-day match, where he scored 117 off 66 balls, moving from 51 to 117 off only 17 balls (or a scoring rate of 3.88 runs a ball faced). Cook's innings of 73 off 104 balls had steered South Africa to a comfortable platform of 128 after 33 overs, and really set up the Kuiper whirlwind. That was before the floodlights failed and the England innings was reduced to a shambles.

It was only Gatting's good nature, and diplomatic noises from Graveney, that prevented a well-timed broadside at the bumbling Free State officials. They battled against Allan Donald's pace, with the batsmen looking into a gaping, murky gloom. Gatting and Graveney put it down to 'a question of experience', and left it at that.

By the time Cook's 1990 season with Somerset began, moves to bridge the gulf between the SACU and the SACB had started. There was a need to talk and understand and, above all, to unify the game so that the political aspirations of all would be answered. The SACU's credibility had been damaged, and it meant there had to be a complete breakdown before a new bridge could be built.

At the end of the Gatting tour, it is doubtful whether Cook imagined that the next time he would pull on a South African cap it would be a genuine, representative one, and in Calcutta of all places on the historic official tour of India – but that was the hectic pace unity produced. He delivered a crisp, workmanlike innings in New Delhi, but missed out on selection for the World Cup, which created further controversy. The road to rehabilitation in the eyes of the national selectors was a lot easier leading up to the tour of South Africa by the Indians. This made up for some of the disappointment as he earned two Test caps, although his first-ball duck on debut at Kingsmead off bowler Kapil Dev will be remembered better than the runs he scored in the three remaining innings. This duck, the first in Test history by an opening batsman on debut, was an ugly smudge on his record. His Test career ended in Colombo, Sri Lanka, in 1993, while a stint as coach with Hampshire ended early after a run of disappointing results. Whatever the future holds, it is going to be tied up with youth and transformation, and there is much to do to ease the path of the new generation with their ambitions.

CLIVE RICE
Captain Controversy

By Trevor Chesterfield

One thing is certain: Clive Rice has rarely, in the last 31 years, been far from controversy when matters on which he feels strongly need debating. It is one of the more intriguing facets of a tough competitor who is always prepared to argue, face a challenge or put his point across. Whatever his vocation might have turned out to be, Rice would always have been a tough customer.

In 1971 there was a furore within the governing National Party when Rice accused the politicians of wrecking the game in South Africa and the future careers of promising Test players. Twenty years later there was a serious verbal clash with the national selectors, headed by Peter van der Merwe, who felt the time had come to make changes to the side after the historic tour of India. Rice and his old Transvaal teammate, Jimmy Cook, as well as Peter Kirsten, were left out of the World Cup squad when it was announced late in December 1991.[1] In January 2002 he again took exception to national selection bungling. This episode led to the farce in Sydney where Percy Sonn, president of the United Cricket Board, had to use his executive powers in order to have Justin Ontong included in the Test side to play Australia, at the expense of Jacques Rudolph. When the side was announced in November, Rudolph had been chosen as a top-order batsman, while Ontong was seen as a lower-order batsman and spinner. When the team was selected for the Sydney Test, Rushdi Magiet's panel had not, according to Sonn, followed the 'selection policy protocols'. Rice saw it differently.

As was to be expected, South Africa's Minister of Sport, Ngconde Balfour, did not take kindly to Rice's comments. They were perceived to be racist by Balfour and the Sports Ministry, because Rice did not approve of the way the selection of the side for that particular game had been handled. Rice did not see it as a colour issue, but as one where affirmative action had overridden the needs of a side already in distress. He knew, too, that he would be criticised for his views, but he gave them anyway because he saw it as his right to freedom of expression.

While the colour and shape of political parties and government policies have changed radically between the isolationist *baasskap* thinking of 1971 and the egalitarian ideals of 2002, some of the rhetoric had not. In 1971, Vorster's government had told Rice to 'stick to playing cricket and keep your nose out of politics'.

Thirty-one years later, Balfour told him to 'keep out of politics …', and to 'pack your bags and go …'.

One of the hazards in any sport is being overlooked by selectors; as Clive Rice will tell you, that is the time to start fighting back. He has always been prepared to freely debate topics such as batting standards, bowling levels, pitch conditions, selectors, team selection, captains and his feelings on umpires and administrators – even politicians with hidden agendas.

In recent years he held the position of director of coaching for his old county, Nottinghamshire, but had his contract terminated midway through the 2002 season because of lack of results. It shows just how difficult it is to devote one's life to such a precarious job, and to a side battling for survival.

From his early years as a professional sportsman, Rice often differed from others. This is not so much because he feels that knocking traditions or traditionalists is a good idea; it is more to wake people up to the realities of a game which, in South Africa's case, had been affected by years of isolation. As it was, Clive Edward Butler Rice made a living from cricket for years, selling his superb all-rounder talents because it was the job he wanted to do. He felt frustration as friends from other countries went off to play Test series around the globe. Yet, like Mike Procter and Barry Richards, Rice gave no thought to qualifying to play for England, as had, say, Allan Lamb or the Smith brothers, Chris and Robin, and Tony Greig. South Africa was his country, and during the years of isolation it sorely needed players such as the energetic and controversial former Nottinghamshire and Transvaal all-rounder and first official South African captain in 21 years and nine months, to play a role.

'I would have felt like a bastard if I went and played for another country,' Rice stated some time ago. 'It wasn't for me. South Africa's a great place, I was born here, I live here, my wife and children … I didn't need to go and play for someone else.'

For years Rice had been labelled the aggro man of South African cricket; a tough macho type with an anti-establishment axe to grind. It was, however, just an image: one carefully designed to market the game. Away from it, yet talking about it, is the true Ricey, the man who would love to have driven Formula 1 cars, but discovered the sport of burning tyres and screaming engines late in a remarkable sporting life. But he also knew that playing a game like cricket for 12 months of the year required dedication and discipline, as well as fitness and a certain amount of showmanship.

'They can love you, or hate you, but at least you have got some reaction,' he once said of spectators and administrators in general. It was his view in the late 1970s (and still is) that as they are the entertainers, players deserve payment for the job they do. Sure, most of the administrators in South Africa were unpaid officials, but many top officials were better paid than the players. That has long

195

changed. The United Cricket Board has a contractual system for national squad players, and the provinces have a contractual system in place. This was the professional cricket circuit he had envisaged from the late 1970s, when he came back from the Kerry Packer World Series Cricket games. His argument through the 1980s was that, when it did come, what would the players earn? Each province now has its own contractual system, and some are better than others. The game has come a long way in the 25 years since the Packer revolution.

Clive Rice's career started at Berea Park, that unpretentious little ground in Pretoria, which has since fallen on even harder times. It was a sunny Friday, 14 November, at the start of the 1969/70 provincial season for Transvaal B, when this youngster charged in from what was known as the Union Buildings-end, full of cocky aggression. He had already rescued Transvaal B in his debut match against North-Eastern Transvaal. At 128 for five, the visitors were in trouble and needed an outstanding performance to build a foundation for first-innings points. It was the era before bonus points, and building a first-innings lead was always psychologically important.

Ray White, a past president of the United Cricket Board and the Transvaal Cricket Board, was captain of the Transvaal B side, and with the 20-year-old Rice lifted the score to 203. The debutant top-scored with an aggressive 81 before Transvaal B were dismissed for 278. The batting was an unexpected bonus, as he had been brought into the side as an extra support bowler because of an injury to Peter Aldworth, and he took four for 56. It was a singularly impressive debut, and team manager Johnnie Waite admitted that he had seen few better, especially as Clive had had to write a university exam on the Friday, and arrived late to see Transvaal B on a wobbly 54 for two. Stan Hankey wrapped up the match on the Monday with five wickets, when the Berea Park pitch uncharacteristically broke up after lunch on the final day. With Denis Lindsay reporting ill, the game was as good as dead for the locals.

Apart from that first season of 1969/70, Clive's career, until 1991/92, ran parallel with the years of isolation, which is no doubt partly why he turned into what his former Nottinghamshire teammate, Sir Richard Hadlee, called a 'street fighter'. That is, the sort of player who is not afraid to wage a battle in the middle when his side is in need, although Rice's very competitive nature would have made him a player of the highest quality in any sphere. It was his competitiveness that was the clue to Rice's simple cricket philosophy: always have someone to answer for the mistakes, or take the rap for a string of defeats.

Hadlee rated Rice highly among the great all-rounders of the 1970s and 1980s. Although denied the chance of playing at Test level, Rice was high on any list of outstanding all-rounders. Former Pakistan captain and fellow all-rounder Imran Khan was another who agreed with Hadlee's opinion.

'After 10 years with Nottinghamshire, it was impossible not to be impressed with his ability as a player and a captain,' the New Zealander said. The pair had spent 10 summers together and became what Hadlee called 'good buddies', because they complemented each other.

On temperament Hadlee regarded Rice as being unflappable – someone who got on with the game without any histrionics, hard but fair in his approach. He felt that Rice did not always do his talents justice on big occasions, and there was a weakness against West Indian quick bowlers on the county circuit. But Rice cannot be faulted on dedication. Because of the years of isolation there was no opportunity to play Tests, and he was always out to prove himself when up against top players. The ultimate accolade of his county career was being invited to play in the MCC bicentennial match at Lord's in 1987.

When it came to captaincy, Hadlee regarded Rice as a tough and demanding leader, tactically sound without producing too much in the way of innovation. Even Sir Gary Sobers felt the all-rounder was a percentage captain. One of the problems, however, is that he has always been judged on his captaincy – not when he led South Africa in the rebel series, but when leading Nottinghamshire or Transvaal. In the early and mid-1980s, Transvaal had a great team in terms of players and experience: Jimmy Cook, Henry Fotheringham, Graeme Pollock, Alvin Kallicharran, Kevin McKenzie, Ray Jennings and Sylvester Clarke. Leading an English county was tougher because of the disparity in the competition.

Of the four times Nottinghamshire won the county championship in the last century, Rice captained them twice: in 1981 and 1987. In South Africa he led Transvaal to five Currie Cup titles between 1982/83 and 1987/88, as well as five Nissan Shield titles between 1982/83 and 1990/91, and three domestic day/night crowns – the first two in 1981/82 and 1982/83, and the third in 1984/85.

Despite obvious shortcomings over the past 20 years, both Rice and Sir Richard Hadlee feel the county circuit, by its very nature, is far tougher than it appears to those on the outside. This has become even more so since the two-division system was introduced in 2000, as the new century finally caught up with what had for long been an archaic format. As it is, the old school-tie elitism, which had for generations pervaded and run the game in England, lost touch with the more humble cloth-cap support as early as the mid-1930s. Such divisions were highlighted in an unpublished supplementary report in the late 1950s as the reason for the decline in the number of elementary and government-funded schools where the game was played, and also for fewer spectators at county level. There were exceptions in the Midlands and the north of England. The propensity of the establishment in England to ignore those it had disaffected was similar to the white Afrikaner establishment views in the same era.

Hadlee was quite frank on several counts about his county-playing relationship with Rice. He did not ponder, for example, on the disappointment of their never meeting in a Test series. As it was never a reality, 'I didn't even think about it'. As for the county scene, Sir Richard felt it had been good for them both:

> It made me a good bowler, and I found the last three seasons hard; there's no doubt that playing six days a week is demanding; but you condition yourself and it doesn't take long to find out what you need to know to survive. You really have to look after yourself. There is no denying the lifestyle is glamorous, but very demanding, so at the end of the day you have to perform on the field. If you think it's easy, you should try it for three or four seasons.
>
> You have days, however, when you struggle and other days when you do well. But you have to work at producing consistent performances – that's what being professional is all about.
>
> In many ways Clive and I were good for each other; we had this competitive thing going as bowlers, too, which was good for us. You also have to set high standards yourself ... goals, that sort of thing. For this motivation is important. Those levels of achievement are always good.
>
> The county scene is also good because you get disciplined by the players you face. There are world-class players, Test players, your good county player and the bread-and-butter ones as well ... a variety of styles and skills, and you found that among most teams in our day. I don't think it's changed too much since then, either.

In 1999 Rice agreed with Hadlee's view. At the time he was about to assume the post of director of coaching at the county, and suggested that there is a misconception in South Africa about the county game. It partly goes back to the judgement passed on by others about Barry Richards's batting performances against what were presumed to be weak bowling attacks. It was argued in some South African provincial circles that because England have put together a number of mediocre performances since the mid-1980s, county standards are weak. What advanced the theory is that some of the players seen in South Africa, who did not make a particularly good impression, later played for England. Living in grand isolation, and boosted by the opinions of sports critics who did not want to be seen to be too harsh, a large number of South Africans had the impression that the Castle Currie Cup and subsequent SuperSport Series (first class) and limited-overs standards were better than elsewhere. Much of this attitude was buoyed by successes over the rebel sides, which apart from the West Indians were not particularly good in terms of depth or strength.

South African complacency was swiftly blown away by the brief tour of India in November 1991. It was all too obvious, even after the euphoric win in a New

Delhi athletics stadium, that South Africa had much to learn in the close combat encounters then demanded by the international limited-overs games.

After the eight-day November junket in 1991, Peter Johnson of the *Daily Mail* described the South Africans in India as 'visitors from a bygone age'; indeed, psychologically, technically and physically, the side were outplayed by the Indians. The cobwebs that festooned all phases of the game were obvious, more so in fielding than anywhere else. Jonathan Agnew of the BBC, a former England Test cap, stated that he was a 'little surprised that South Africa haven't learnt at all from three matches on this tour'.

Sitting in the massive Jawaharlal Nehru Stadium in the Indian capital, Agnew felt that technically, South African fielding was light years behind even the Indians, who were fair performers, but 'not what I'd call great shakes'. Some of the field placings puzzled him as well. In fact, the field placings were embarrassingly outdated.

'I think most of your chaps have forgotten that one-day cricket has become a lot more technical,' he said. 'It's all about economy, bowling a line and to a field. I must say I had expected a lot more. After all, you do have some players who are involved in the county game.'

Five months later, when South Africa had reached the World Cup semi-finals in Sydney on 22 March 1992, Agnew had a far more complimentary view – if only because the South Africans were prepared to learn and employ their knowledge. The build-up matches to the World Cup in Australia had taught them a lot. In New Delhi, Mike Procter admitted that South Africa had much to learn, and Rice said: 'We have been shown up ... But we must learn from this. We have to rethink our whole strategy regarding the World Cup, and we need a think tank to sort out what we need to do.'

Had South Africa not been shuttled into India, the 1992 World Cup could have turned out very differently. It might have been a disaster, and the name Jonty Rhodes and the famous run-out of Inzamam-ul-Haq in Brisbane may not have taken place. How such quirks of fate can change the mosaic of team develoment and growth and selection thinking. Peter van der Merwe and the other selectors were swift to pick up on the shortcomings so obvious in India and the comments offered by Agnew, which were passed on to Van der Merwe.

It might have been very different if Rice, selected for South Africa's tour of Australia in 1971/72 at the age of 21, had not been forced to watch it all slip away. The tour, called off by the Australian Cricket Board in September 1971, could have been the start of what promised to be a brilliant international career. Not that it bothered the *baasskap* thinking of the South African politicians. They cared nothing that they had created the platform for the protesters in England, Australia, New Zealand and other countries over the discriminatory laws, often pushed through with frightening racial vehemence. One example of how the mailed fist of South African rugby trod on the face of another nation was demonstrated in New Zealand during the 1981 tour. There are those who don their 'Springbok' rugby shirt and an eyepatch at the same time, and still grumble over the Eden Park 'flour-bomb' game, yet they should also think about how that tour created serious divisions within the population of the host nation. Ten years earlier the Australian Cricket Board had seen the danger and decided it was more prudent to abandon what would have been a costly exercise. Rugby (John Vorster once described it as 'the true Afrikaner sport') cared little what harm it did. It was typical of the thinking of white South Africa in that era.

Denied the chance to tour Australia, Rice fired off a few thoughts, born of frustration, which upset Vorster and his Minister of Sport, Frank Waring. Vorster's rebuttal of Rice's comments was far from polite.

Rice had played only two summers of provincial cricket, but had made a big enough impact to be included in the last official side selected before isolation. The team was: Ali Bacher (captain), Eddie Barlow (vice-captain), Hylton Ackerman, Dassie Biggs, Grahame Chevalier, Peter de Vaal, Lee Irvine, Denis Lindsay, Graeme Pollock, Peter Pollock, Mike Procter, Barry Richards, Clive Rice, Pat Trimborn, Vintcent van der Bijl. Barlow was later forced to withdraw and Arthur Short was included instead. His selection hardly raised an eyebrow, although it was felt that David Orchard had been unlucky. The team was now a bowler short, and the young opening batsman Short was not recognised even as a net regular. Graeme Pollock was made vice-captain. This move drew comment from Eric Litchfield and CO Medworth, two former sports editors, who felt that Graeme Pollock was not equipped to hold such a post, and that the position should have gone to the younger Barry Richards.

It is interesting that three members of the team selected for Australia did not take part in the trial at Newlands, which was part of a sports festival, although there was little to be festive about. Bacher, Barlow and Biggs were not available for the trial, being replaced by André Bruyns, Richards and Short. But the selectors, led by Arthur Coy, had made up their minds about who they felt should be in the touring party. Rice's contribution as a batsman in the Newlands game was negligible. It was his performance in the 1970/71 season, with 21 wickets at 18.33 and 202 runs at 22.44, and the way they were put together, which suggested to the selectors that here was a player of the future. Little did they realise what an impact he was to have on the development of South African cricket over the next 20 years.

The row over the proposed 1971/72 tour of Australia simmered throughout the winter, as the aftermath of the Newlands walk off on 6 April and the fierce protests during the South African rugby tour Down Under created an atmosphere inimical to a cricket tour. The government's refusal to allow the SACA to select two members of the South African Cricket Board of Control for the team was made known before the match started. It later became known that the invitations were issued directly by Jack Cheetham, the SACA president, to all-rounder Dik Abed and off-spinner Owen Williams, and not through Sacboc. Both were offended by the nature of the proposal and the political implications involved. However well intentioned, the barefaced cheek of the proposal indicated that the SACA had a hidden agenda.

The government's rejection of the SACA plan, and the inclusion of Pierre Bougarel in the French side to tour South Africa in 1972, after his initial exclusion, drew vigorous condemnation from some of the English-speaking media, but not the Afrikaans press. Papers such as the *Rand Daily Mail* and the *Natal Mercury* saw this as political double standards. Waring and the government were not interested or bothered. What mattered to the government was that they had had their rugby tour.

The door to official international cricket was finally slammed shut on 8 September in Sydney, when Sir Donald Bradman, chairman of the Australian Cricket Board, announced that 'the board [has] decided to advise the South African Cricket Association, with regret, that in the present atmosphere the invitation to tour must be withdrawn'.

Geoff Chettle, editor of the *South African Cricket Annual*, vented his annoyance with the situation in the 1971 edition:

> Where do we go from here? The answer, if we persist in closing our eyes to the obvious, is nowhere – simply because no one will have us. The Minister of Transport [Ben Schoeman] attempts to console us by saying that the prospect of isolation is not the end of the world because we, at least, will be able to see our world-class players in action. What utter rubbish! And that from a senior politician who is fully aware of phenomenal changes in our political, diplomatic and social structure, and of the necessity for adjustment to attune ourselves to the world today.

Chettle then called for a forum of sports administrators to put together plans to introduce multiracial sport.

As paranoia set in, the South African newspapers of 8 and 9 September made interesting reading. The majority of English-speaking papers said it was a triumph for the protesters. Frank Waring, under pressure, offered this po-faced comment: 'Australian cricket authorities consider it was in their interests to withdraw the invitation. That is their right. The same as it is our right in the interests of South Africa to withstand the pressures applied by the anti-apartheid movement to take over the country.'

What is surprising is how most newspapers approved of such stolid *baasskap* thinking, although the *Rand Daily Mail* offered weak disapproval by saying: 'Well ... there it is. The first big achievement of Mr Vorster's sports policy. South African cricket, at the height of its brilliance, has been destroyed.' The *Natal Mercury* and *Eastern Province Herald* posed this question: 'After all we have gone through, most South Africans will ask: is [apartheid] worth it?'

As Donald Woods, at the time editor of the *Daily Dispatch*, said in 1992, the protest was 'little more than a knee-jerking exercise'. Politically, white South Africa was already facing an identity problem, and sport was only a minor part of what was an ever-growing cataclysmic scenario. Soweto 1976 was still five years away, but in September 1971 the signs were already there. The indivisible anti-apartheid forces within were growing.

Rice, like Richards, Procter, Hylton Ackerman and Lee Irvine, pondered his career without Test cricket, and accepted that the English county scene was all that was available. For Rice, first there was league cricket in the England summer, with an occasional match for the Derrick Robins XI, before his link with Nottinghamshire opened up in 1975. His leadership qualities so impressed county officials that they appointed him captain for 1978; but his signing for Packer caused a hiccup with the establishment, and caused the county to change their mind. They sacked their man, who then took them to court. Rice won the case and was reinstated as a player, but not as captain: that took another couple of seasons. The World Series Cricket circus with Packer was, in some ways, compensation for having been done out of the 1971/72 tour, which in turn explains some of the frustration Rice no doubt felt when not included in the South African World Cup squad in December 1991.

'This is what Packer offered me, and it made up my mind that I would have given up everything in England just to play for Kerry Packer,' Rice commented when reviewing that part of his career. Did 'giv[ing] up everything in England' also include the county captaincy? 'At the time – yes.'

It was after Rice's return from WSC in the summer of 1977/78 that the next row in the chapter broke out. He was labelled a mercenary by some in the establishment, and booed at the Wanderers when he went out to bat in a provincial match, a limited-overs Nissan Shield game. While the other Packer players had provincial contracts, Clive did not. After playing as a professional for Packer (and Nottinghamshire), he was now expected to turn out as an amateur for Transvaal. As his livelihood was cricket, he did not see why he should have to sacrifice principles that would take this away from him. As it was, the Packer series took place before the rebel era and gave him a measure of his all-round capabilities. He still had fierce ambition and pride, wanting to prove to others what he could do, and might have done, given the chance.

Apart from the Packer dalliance, Rice remained true to the game in South Africa. He turned down a number of lucrative offers made by Australian state teams after the peace treaty had been signed between the Australian Cricket Board and Packer. He had patriotic priorities and pride, especially when it came to cricket and its advancement. The game needed marketing, and if this meant some controversy, well and good. But while the 1970s had been a tumultuous decade for Clive Rice, the 1980s heralded the rebel tours, and the administrators came to realise that South Africa had a core of professional players who should be paid because of the time spent away from their other jobs.

It was also fortunate for South Africa that the professional school of thinking, as it existed then, had its own ways of motivating the all-rounder with his competitive spirit. It is for this reason that he is more thought of as Clive Rice the fast bowler than Clive Rice the batsman. This was vividly brought home in early November 1979 when Northern Transvaal, newly promoted to the Currie Cup A Section, were playing Transvaal, with Rice and Rupert Hanley sharing the new ball at Berea Park. Although the players had not previously thought twice about their use of the helmet, they suddenly sprouted among the Northerns batsmen like mushrooms after spring rain. Not so much because of 'Spook' Hanley, but because 'thunderball' Rice was in the Transvaal side. There was a decidedly jittery feeling in the Northerns camp before that match – perhaps it is little wonder that they were bowled out for 79 in the first innings, with Rice taking four for six in 13 overs. That was the sort of power he held over teams making their way in the Currie Cup for the first time. His combative pace in those years made him a none-too-easy bowler to face, even at the best of times.

As a batsman he took longer to mature; his first century was scored only in 1975 when turning out for Nottinghamshire, while his first in South Africa was in the 10th season after making his debut at Berea Park. Yet anyone who scores 48 centuries in a first-class career, where opportunities in South Africa are limited and pitch conditions vary considerably, could also be a world-class batsman. The reason why Rice failed to score his first South African century until the 121 not out against Western Province at the Wanderers in the 1979/80 season, was that the pitch in the bullring had earned a notorious reputation since the late 1970s. On the first two days of a Currie Cup game the surface was, it was often claimed, more spiteful than a green mamba, which is why so few centuries were scored there. During Rice's early captaincy years in the 1980s, batting first at the Wanderers was often an insecure occupation. In the 1970s, when the pitch may have been hard, a little green and bouncy on the first day, it at least gave the batsman a chance from around lunch on day two. This is illustrated with seven A-Section centuries scored there in the three seasons between 1977/78 and 1979/80. Now compare this to the six centuries spread over six seasons between

1984/85 and 1989/90, with Rice's 73 in 1987/88 the highest score recorded during that first-class season at the Wanderers.

Kingsmead had a similar reputation in the 1970s. Englishman Geoff Cook, the Northamptonshire opener, who later opened for England after a couple of seasons as Eastern Province's captain in the early 1980s, strongly criticised South African pitches for their green-top image. Certainly Mike Gatting raised more than just an eyebrow at the lottery conditions in February 1990, when the last rebel five-day match was played at the Wanderers. It was symptomatic of the age of isolation, but preparing surfaces that are bad for batting did in a sense backfire when South Africa were welcomed back to the international fold. Those limited-overs centuries so prolific in the Nissan Shield were in mighty short supply in India, New Zealand, Australia (during the World Cup) and the West Indies. In fact, the highest score was Peter Kirsten's innings of 90 on the awful Eden Park mud patch.

Naturally pitch conditions improved, as some touring sides had equal firepower to South Africa, and it would not do to prepare a typical Currie Cup-style Wanderers pitch of, say, 1982/83, 10 years later. Yet the state of the Wanderers table at various times in its life before being relaid has always created controversy. It is acknowledged that standards may fall short on some technical fault in batting make-up, but it is significant that 87 percent of Transvaal centuries between 1984/85 and 1993/94 were scored away from the Wanderers. Of these, a high percentage were from dreary draws fashioned before dwindling crowds at Newlands and Centurion Park, where it was always the opposition and not Transvaal who were 'to blame' for the dead-end result.

It almost became a matter of pride at the Wanderers for Transvaal teams to win and visiting teams to draw. And one reason why hardly anyone went to the bullring to watch a Currie Cup game was, in all fairness, because of the lack of a fair contest. Watching visiting teams being regularly rolled for paltry totals, and the batsmen treated as whipping boys, was not appealing to the crowds.

In early January 1992, when some newspaper headlines screamed 'SACK THEM' or 'BUNGLE BOYS BLUNDER' and 'KNIVES OUT AFTER AXINGS', it was the usual outburst from a hysterical media that did not want to let go of the past and welcome in the future. Their view was: 'Let's hold on to what we have.'

Rice's views on team selection were well known. They should consist of the captain and vice-captain, and either the manager or the coach. But if they foul up, you cannot blame the tea boy, either. On Sunday, 29 December 1991, there were howls of indignation from large areas of the Transvaal, Natal and parts of the Eastern Cape. An article written by the author, predicting that shocks were looming over the selection of the South African World Cup squad, was said by critics to be ill informed. As it turned out it was largely accurate, and the information was not leaked by any of the selectors but by a United Cricket Board official on condition of anonymity. The story was about the possibility that Kepler Wessels would captain the side, and both Rice and Jimmy Cook perhaps being axed, along with Peter Kirsten. The selectors were thinking of young, fit men who could last the hectic pace demanded by the World Cup's five-week programme.

Van der Merwe and the other selectors were then put on the spot when it became known that the World Cup organisers wanted an outline of the squad by 31 December for the printing of brochures. Pressed for a pre-release because of the deadline, they knew that an announcement would create the wrong impression. Ideally, it would have suited the selectors to name the final 14 on 19 January, but with the organisers forcing their hand, they were left with no option but to name a squad from which the final side would be announced. Van der Merwe, the selection panel convener, then indicated that naming the 20 did not mean that those overlooked would not be considered, and that there was still a chance for Messrs Cook, Kirsten and Rice to be included in the final line-up. But this failed to mollify the anti-selectors brigade, who demanded that Van der Merwe and the rest of the committee resign, as the two favoured Transvaal sons found themselves no longer part of the mainstream in the game they had served with distinction. Controversial or not, the choices were allegedly in the best long-term interests of South African cricket, and should be seen in that light. Events in South Africa's first World Cup seriously embarrassed the critics.

There was little doubt that Jimmy Cook did have a future – if a limited one because of his age – as a Test opener; but Rice's sacking, which amounted to a vote of no confidence by the selectors, had been partly expected. As it was, concerns had been voiced by some English journalists in India at the historic re-entry at Eden Gardens, on whether the South African captain might not battle on some of the bigger Australian grounds. At the end of the India tour, three of the English journalists, Peter Johnson, Alan Lee and Agnew, drew up their thoughts on a South African World Cup shadow squad, and had problems finding places for Rice and Richard Snell. Even Cook was on a list of doubtfuls, along with Dave Richardson and Adrian Kuiper, who failed to impress as a bowler in India.

By 3 January 1992, a nationwide petition opposing the selection of Wessels as captain and Cook's omission was drawn up by one Michael Rappaport, who would also look at 'legal means' to achieve the aims of the petitioners. Just how serious was Rappaport's rhetoric was soon discovered when the petition died a natural death. He was hoping for two million signatures, but it was doubtful whether, before that first World Cup, two million fans even existed, and much less would line up to sign a petition. It was all bluff and bluster.

When the initial squad was announced, Van der Merwe said that the selectors had opted for a fit young side for the following reasons: the congested programme of eight games in 17 days allowed little time for the players to recover physically or mentally; conditions in Australia and New Zealand required a fit squad; large grounds, especially in Australia, called for improved fielding ability; players who carried any injuries or illness would not be considered. Within 24 hours Rice was on television, blaming a personality dispute between himself and the convener of selectors for his axing, which Van der Merwe denied, saying: 'The only time Clive Rice and I have a personality clash is when the selectors leave him out of a team.'

This followed Rice's allegations, made on TV to sports announcer Glen Hicks, that the team selected was idiotic and lacked consistency. Rice said his axing had come about because he and Van der Merwe had not seen eye to eye on the selection policy for years.

'Six weeks ago I was good enough to lead a side to India, now I can't even make the squad. That side had been selected at a moment's notice. This present selection doesn't make sense to me at all. When you look at the squad that went to India, presumably to learn, and you look at the 20 guys they've named for the World Cup, things don't add up.'

Van der Merwe's reply was that his committee had been given the job of finding a squad of the 20 best players for matches of 50 overs, and that is what 'we set out to do'. But the rumblings reverberated for weeks; even when the side was doing particularly well, the sniping continued.

This was a sad episode, and it stripped away some of the gloss on the fine career of a tough competitor who wouldn't put up with second best. No one can blame him for it, or for the elation of leading the first official South African team in 21 years and eight months. The game at Eden Gardens, Calcutta on Sunday, 10 November 1991, was traumatic as well as historic: a team of South African cricketers, after years of isolation, were getting international exposure undreamt of a week before. The team visited a slum in Calcutta, and called on the Saint of the Gutters, Nobel prize-winner Mother Theresa's famous home for orphans. Here Rice quipped, after being given her business card, 'Sorry, I don't seem to have mine with me.'

In the bus on the way back to the hotel after the final practice for Eden Gardens, Rice suggested a small 'thank you and welcome back' ceremony. Initially it was to have been a jog around the stadium and waving to the crowd, but the poignant walk on and off the next morning was more than sufficient to mark an emotional and historic moment in world cricket history.

Eden Gardens, Calcutta, 10 November 1991, was more dramatic than the hat-trick all those years ago, when Rice removed the first three batsmen in the opening over of a club match. Or the dramatic spell at St George's Park against the Australian rebels led by Kim Hughes, when the South Africans won a game they had seemingly lost. Eight wickets for 12 runs in only three overs as the

Aussies capitulated, and Rice picked up five wickets for 50, with three of them being a bonus, as the tourists went on a madcap swing and swish of the willow.

Rice's one regret in his sporting career is not to have driven in a Formula 1 event. Yet in some ways there is the feeling that he has been in the driving seat since his provincial career began all those summers ago. At the start of the 1992/93 season he joined Natal, and along with West Indian Malcolm Marshall and Graham Ford faced the sort of challenge he savours. Transvaal, with Eddie Barlow as coach, made it pretty plain that he no longer fitted in with the new scenario. It was a post Rice had coveted, but denied the opportunity it was a matter of starting again in a new province, and this time under a new captain, Jonty Rhodes.

For years Rice had been classed in the Peter Pan category of South African cricket. While his playing days ended with the 1992/93 season, and the longed-for Test cap eluded him, he eagerly took up the next challenge. When the national academy was formed, Rice was appointed its first coach. Players such as Lance Klusener were in the first intake in 1995. For Rice, however, the evolution process was more important, as he felt the system was not ready for fast-tracking players of colour. There was a brief spell as a national selector along with Wessels, but in the end he was lost to the South African scene when he joined Nottinghamshire as their director at the start of the 1999 season. Now his time is his own, and there is a chance that he may yet slip back into the South African system. Rice is one of the former players – whatever the thinking of the Sports Ministry – who have something to offer the game.

13   KEPLER WESSELS
A Burning Ambition

By Trevor Chesterfield

When they flashed that impersonal, brutally cold yellow and blue message on the large electronic scoreboard at the Sydney Cricket Ground on Sunday, 22 March 1992, it was like reading a death sentence:

> **SOUTH AFRICA
> TO WIN
> NEED 22 RUNS
> OFF 1 BALL**

For several minutes before that fateful message was flashed, a hum of confusion reverberated among the nearly 29 000 spectators, but as eyes now focused on the scoreboard there were howls of indignation. Disbelief reigned. It had been touch and go as the enticing battle waged in the middle reached the nail-biting stage: 32 runs off 18 balls was the equation (not even two runs a ball). England bowler Chris Lewis started the 43rd over of an innings reduced to 45 because of South Africa's slow bowling rate, with Brian McMillan facing. Runs had been squeezed out with frenetic urgency as England found themselves stretched, as the South Africans had been, to cut off boundaries on the jumbo-sized outfield. But a six by Jonty Rhodes had tilted the game marginally in favour of South Africa again. A place in the final loomed, and the impossible dream was about to come true.

Little wonder that Kepler Wessels and the rest of the South African team, leaning on the pavilion railing, were stunned as the improbable became the unthinkable. And it showed. While fast bowler Meyrick Pringle silently brushed away a few tears, the others were bewildered by the state of affairs. A large section of the crowd in front of the press box shouted their disgust. Styrofoam cups, beer and soft drink cans and bottles, as well as several cushions ripped in half in heated anger, spewed onto the grass in front of the Bradman Stand.

Cricket's image as a sport of fair play had slumped to its lowest ebb in Australia since the nefarious underarm bowling incident at the Melbourne Cricket Ground on 1 February 1981, when the Australian captain, Greg Chappell, instructed his younger brother Trevor to bowl that infamous grubber to New Zealander Brian McKechnie. The Kiwis had needed a six to tie the match, and the disgust expressed over that incident has haunted the former Australian captain ever since.

But on 22 March 1992, the crowd reacted in much the same way a little nine-year-old girl did all those years before. Tugging at Greg Chappell's sleeve, she howled her indignation: 'You cheated! You cheated!'

And that's what the crowd felt at the Sydney Cricket Ground: they had been swindled out of the chance of watching an exciting finish and a fair result, as the rain-affected match-playing conditions were readjusted to a new equation.

'Well done, Channel 9!' cried some. 'Good on yer, Channel 9!' yelled others. 'Great show, Benaud. You wanted a result ... hope you are happy with it!' came another aggrieved voice. And in the press box Chris Lander of London's *Daily Mirror* shook his head, muttering an anguished, 'Oh no! This is the most disgusting thing I've seen. It's totally obscene. It's not really true ... is it?'

In some circles the 1992 World Cup, run and organised by a committee comprising New Zealand and Australian officials, was also known as 'The Great Channel 9 Roadshow', and not without reason. It was claimed that Richie Benaud had worked out the playing conditions. A former Australian captain and a respected broadcaster and critic, he had been a successful Sydney journalist and author, and had designed the conditions to fit in with Channel 9 requirements. Because of the package deal between the Australian Cricket Board and the Packer crowd in the aftermath of the World Cricket Series fiasco, Channel 9 won what seemed to be lifelong rights to screen cricket in Australia. Benaud did a plausible job of telling the world why England and not South Africa were in the final, before the station switched to some low-key programme. At least the fade-out caught the South Africans starting their farewell lap to a standing ovation, some of the players still wiping away the tears.

It was the moment the lights went out on Kepler Wessels and the South African team's interest in the big event, and the moment when the glitter disappeared from the World Cup itself as the impossible dream became a stuttering nightmare.

But who had told Graham Gooch that, if he wanted England to be in the final at Melbourne, it was time to get off the field? Why, it was none other than Allan Lamb, and the source of this hot inside information is an umpire. An England player later unwittingly confirmed Lamb's role in getting England off the field. Indeed, common sense suffered one of the heaviest setbacks of its bruised career that night. Also, Channel 9's last vestige of credibility was severely compromised – not to mention the credibility of those who had drawn up the formula, which was used not only in the World Cup, but also in South Africa as part of its own day/night series. There was the decidedly ugly odour of culpability about the whole sad episode, which suggested that cricket's image of fair play had been forsaken for commercial interests. South Africa's slow over rate had of course exacerbated the problem, but this was overlooked at the time.

'Just whose version of the World Cup is this we are watching?' former England fast bowler John Snow asked in frustration, at the Gabba in Brisbane on 8 March, where South Africa were playing Pakistan. Rain and the 'best overs' ratio ruling suddenly saw Pakistan's required run rate soar from 4.84 to 8.28, and the revised target move from 212 off 50 overs to 193 off 36 overs – a loss of 14 overs, but a reduction of only 18 runs. There is some argument as to whether the International Cricket Council's approved Duckworth/Lewis system, which was used in the 1999 World Cup and will be used again for the 2003 World Cup, is much better. There is criticism of this system as well, and of how a team batting second may find itself chasing a target based on a hypothetical figure from the run rate. South Africa, for a time, used a system devised by Dick Clark and statistician Andrew Samson, known as the Clarke/Samson format. It was far more equitable than the Duckworth/Lewis sliding scale configurations code. The UCB did flirt with a system worked out by a Cape Town schoolboy, but on closer examination found it to be even more flawed than the Benaud/Channel 9 concoction.

India's captain Mohammad Azharuddin had asked the same question at the Gabba a week before, when they lost three overs to rain, but the gettable target was reduced by only one run to 236. India fell two runs short of beating Australia, who won on the rain-affected run rate. It didn't quite take the biscuit in the incredible rain-affected matches stakes, but it ran a close second to the England–Pakistan preliminary round match at Adelaide Oval. This was the outing where Pakistan were sent in on a green top, an unusual sight for Adelaide, after the pitch had been allowed to sweat for 40 hours as rain threatened to break a persistent drought. Pakistan were bowled out for only 74, and England were 24 for one after eight overs. The rain came, and the recalculation was 64 off 16 overs – or 40 off eight overs at five an over from what had been an initial 1.5 runs an over! And all this happened next to the pitch where, barely three weeks before, South Australia had amassed a remarkable second-innings score of 506 for six in their amazing Sheffield Shield match against Queensland.

For some reason, few can explain why left-hand batsmen are seen as being among the game's fancy stylists, their ability often embellished by the sort of showpiece labels that run through a glossary of explanations of run-making abilities. It is fortunate that Kepler Wessels was not of this school; but what a fighter – a mighty effective one, too. Wessels's second-innings 74 on the fourth day of the historic first Test against the West Indies at Kensington Oval, Bridgetown, Barbados, almost a month after the Sydney semi-final fiasco, needed neither elegance nor style to show that he was a quality front-line batsman. On a pitch where the bowlers had taken control and the irregular bounce required discipline and not fancy strokeplay, it needed Wessels's unruffled approach. It was also one of his finest Test innings and carried South Africa to the brink of an impossible dream. That the dream was extinguished the next day is only part of the recurring theme of the game's glorious uncertainty. Put it down to inexperience, but South African batting timidity on the last morning played into the West Indians' hands.

Sir Gary Sobers was quick to point out how the South Africans' defensive tactics suited the West Indies bowlers. He was not wrong. It needed more than technique and ambition on that last morning: it required a positive response, and South Africa's batsmen failed to read the signs.

Not that it was a new experience for Wessels. The tall, upright left-hander, a craggy fighter from the trenches of earlier West Indian combats, knew what it meant to battle it out for the honour and glory of his country. He had a granite exterior: cool, calculating, almost detached-looking; just the sort of batsman needed in a crisis, as he showed in Durban against India where he held the first innings together with a maiden century for South Africa.

Wessels had been doing it all of his international sporting life – taking the tougher, more challenging pathway offered by cricket as compared to, say, tennis, a sport in which he was once tipped to reach high levels of excellence. The money would certainly have been better, and the life generally more comfortable. South Africa needed his kind during the 2001/02 season, when Australia teasingly plucked the withered Protea petals and swamped Shaun Pollock's tourists 3–0 in Oz and 2–1 in South Africa. At the Wanderers, Wessels was disturbed by the sight of that capitulation at a sun-drenched stadium.

There are many, though, who would not agree with such a sentiment. Taking over as Eastern Province coach at the start of the World Cup summer was a careful option for a dedicated man. It has meant rebuilding a side with a strict regime and lots of discipline, which today's youngsters, brought up in a comfort zone, do not quite understand.

But Wessels has always favoured the harder option, and without the certainty of reaching those flawless levels demanded to achieve the ultimate – to play in a Test. This in itself created within the former Grey College pupil a burning ambition to scale a personal Everest. Hence the rigorous preseason training schedule in Port Elizabeth, which became his trademark when he was captain. It is his view that domestic trophies for a team such as Eastern Province (when he led the side) were more often than not won in July and August, not in February and March. This is when the fitness and discipline drilled into the players during the chilly winter days emerge as a solid recipe for success. Eastern Province's achievements in 1988/89 and in later seasons were put down to the demanding Wessels routine, where players trained during lunch breaks: a two-hour schedule in the middle of winter can do wonders when it counts most. It beats the slow progress from mid-August in which the less professional provinces seem to indulge, leaving them without any rewards at the end of the summer. And it is not merely road-running exercises either, but a sensible preseason programming of nets and fielding sessions. It was the sort of schedule Dick Motz, a fine New Zealand fast bowler of the 1960s, followed when not on tour; an insurance programme to earn wickets and fame, which enabled him to become the first Kiwi to take 100 wickets in a Test career.

Wessels was one of those youngsters brought up on the success of the South African teams of the 1960s under Trevor Goddard, Peter van der Merwe and Ali Bacher, and well schooled in basics and technique by that fine Grey College cricket master, Johan Volsteedt. Volsteedt is a man who has done much over the years to bring on any number of fine young cricketers, some of whom emerged from the Free State stable to earn South African Schools colours, as Wessels did on three occasions in the early and mid-1970s.

The left-hander could have made it four, but missed out in 1974 in Pretoria when the selectors excluded him for slow scoring, although there were, Wessels argued, mitigating circumstances, as it was not a particularly strong side in batting. It was also the week in which he first met Alan Jordaan, the South African team manager at the 1992 World Cup and to the West Indies. At the time, Jordaan was the Northern Transvaal captain. He too knew the sharp blade of the axe. Jordaan was replaced as provincial captain later in the season, but then recalled after two summers to lead his province to triumph by winning the old B-Section Castle Bowl in successive summers toward the end of the 1970s.

For Kepler, however, setbacks such as being overlooked for the Schools XI at Berea Park just made him more committed to win a place the next time round. Sure he was upset in 1974, but there was another time, another day.

In the 1992 World Cup, it was Wessels's typical resolve and strength that enabled him to overcome the day of trauma and drama at the Basin Reserve, Wellington, where South Africa's campaign slipped to its lowest rung with defeat by Sri Lanka. The islanders could not believe their luck on a cold, blustery February afternoon as they won by three wickets off the second last ball of the match. The South African captain would be the first to admit that his innings that day was not particularly endearing; like a bad day at the office, you have them, no matter how hard you try to avoid them. For that defeat there was a personal price to pay, as some South African supporters turned against the captain. After the defeat in Auckland, the one in Wellington was just too much. Matches South Africa should have won were lost, and fickle supporters behaved anything but honourably. The run-making champion of Sydney had suddenly become the batting miscreant of the Basin Reserve. Amid this tournament crisis the manager, Alan Jordaan, was sent a fax from the United Cricket Board, containing an article written by a Barry Glasspool in *The Star*, with the headline, 'What South Africa Expect from Wessels'.

'Kepler Wessels is turning South Africa's World Cup dream into a nightmare after successive defeats in New Zealand. South Africa should expect more from the captain and now demand a victory against the West Indies in Christchurch.' Jordaan showed the fax to Wessels and one of the selectors, Peter Pollock. Both men shrugged. Pollock, a former journalist turned minister, saw it as typical newspaper rhetoric. Lose a couple of games and out comes the symbolic guillotine.

Sure it was okay to criticise, if it was fair and open. Glasspool and several others wanted to make Wessels the whipping boy. Who were the hacks who churned out negative articles? How many World Cups had they played in to suggest with such arrogance that 'South Africa should expect more from their captain and now demand a victory ...'? They had all the answers from their easy chairs; perhaps they should lead the side?

As for the playing conditions during rain-affected matches at the World Cup, any amount of dissatisfaction was voiced throughout the tournament, including at the meeting of managers and captains after the media launch in Sydney on 19 February. It was always known that 'someone was going to end up on the wrong side of the conditions', and most umpires expressed private misgivings. This spilled over into querulous animosity on 22 March as even the strong red, white and blue painted army of England supporters, always in fine voice with their 'You'll Never Walk Alone', vented their feelings of disgust. For them anything was better than the eventual 'one ball and 22 runs to win' equation. Most blamed the umpires, just about everyone's favourites to cudgel into submission in such circumstances. But this time they were innocent bystanders as they were obliged to carry out the job, whether they liked it or not, of applying the playing conditions.

Rain and confusion aside, it was not a good tournament in terms of standards and skills. The bowling was generally mediocre, and even New Zealand captain Martin Crowe admitted that the calibre of the Kiwi attack was not of Test standard, 'but would suit the purposes of the limited-overs game'. This indicates that the masses, fed on a diet of one-day junk food, will accept anything, even the lower standards of limited-overs curiosity.

Because of this, it was frightening to hear an owlish SABC sports programme anchorman enthuse some weeks later about what he considered to be 'such a marvellous contest'. Perhaps Martin Locke can be forgiven, as his ideas of the demands of the three versions of the game were based on outdated ideas. Yet his lack of knowledge highlighted how easy it is for the public to be misinformed. One of the problems of the limited-overs game – and this is long before its cult image ballooned as a result of Kerry Packer's day/night circus in the late 1970s –

has been the lowering of technical skills. Some of this has been blamed on the needless increase in the number of limited-overs tournaments to satisfy the needs and greed of television.

This was highlighted in Colombo during the 2002 ICC Champions Trophy tournament, when the semi-finals and rained-off finals seemed to be incidental to the Sri Lanka Broadcasting Corporation's decision to screen as many commercials as possible. These often overran the start of an over, or a new, incoming batsman facing his first ball. Replays of a batsman's dismissal were cut to one, and on one occasion the umpire's referral to the TV umpire for a decision was not shown. The new batsman had faced two balls before the game returned to the screen.

In the 1992 World Cup, despite its popularity and attraction, most teams admitted they were in need, by the middle of the tournament, of a three- or four-day game to get their rested players into some kind of form. It was hard to motivate those sitting on the fringes for most of the games, and Tertius Bosch, the rangy Northerns fast bowler, would have struggled had he been called on to deliver a spell if Meyrick Pringle or Richard Snell had been injured or lost form. Van der Merwe, monitoring the team's fitness, agreed that South Africa had been fortunate to be relatively injury free. Bosch was given one game, and it was the wrong one as well. He bowled on the clay pudding at Eden Park in Auckland, when all the South African bowlers went through the thresher. After that he was highly useful as a net practice bowler, and almost a forgotten name on tour until the third LOI game in the West Indies.

As a captain Wessels was solid and steady, although he was criticised for being stereotyped. But so were most others, and mainly because their options were limited. New Zealander Crowe, by far the most innovative captain in the tournament, and the best batsman as well, left little doubt that to get as far as the Kiwis did was a miracle wrapped around a little Kenyan magic from Dipak Patel, opening the attack with his crafty off-spin. This seemed to sow confusion among most opponents on the slower New Zealand pitches, even to the extent of the bowler being cast into this role – and with some success – at Lancaster Park, one of the bouncier and faster surfaces played on during the tournament.

'You have to be prepared to take such risks in one-day cricket, and what works one day can work again the next, or the day after, against a different team at a different venue,' Crowe argued. 'But you can't try a similar tactic in a Test more than once.'

The Kiwi captain gave the impression that he would rather have won a Test series than a dozen LOI matches (apart from the World Cup, of course), as after a while there was a tired sameness about the LOI pattern. With refreshing frankness, Crowe outlined the day before their game how New Zealand were going to beat South Africa at Eden Park. He had the batsmen and the bowlers to do the job; it was all so simple. South Africa, the mystery team and therefore a dangerous side, were on a high after their victory over Australia, but had now moved across the Tasman Sea for the first time, and were not prepared for the Kiwi conditions or patterns of play. Eden Park was not the ideal ground on which to continue their World Cup campaign.

Although Derek Pringle, Phil DeFreitas and Ian Botham were the spearheads, England's bowling attack was eventually going to be shown up, and it was: twice by South Africa, once by New Zealand, and by Pakistan in that fateful final. They were stretched to the limit on 22 March, and going into the final four days later with the attitude that Richard Illingworth was a better batsman than Phil Tufnell, psychologically they had already lost. It was negative to rely on your No. 11, in this case a makeshift all-rounder, to win a match as important as the World Cup final, when the top order should have done it in the first place. It was as good as admitting they did not have the batting depth capable of carrying them through. Yet had the match been played on a smaller ground, Graham Gooch may have got away with that big pull off leg-spinner Mushtaq Ahmed over mid-wicket, and that would have made a big difference in the end.

But those who were at the 1992 World Cup came away with a special memory or two. One great moment was when Kepler Wessels led the side onto the field at the Sydney Cricket Ground. 'Led' is perhaps a misnomer, for as soon as the umpires appeared the 11 South Africans sprinted onto the famous lush sward. They all seemed a little too nervous, which is not always a good thing, for as with chess, cricket is a game where players need to be in control of their minds.

Then came that first explosive ball from Allan Donald, bowling from the Paddington end to Geoff Marsh. It was a flyer, which the West Australian edged, and in everyone but New Zealand umpire Bryan Aldridge's opinion it was a catch. Aldridge's stance behind the wicket gave those among us with years of umpiring knowledge the impression that he was still looking up from where Donald had landed in his follow-through to check for the foot fault, and had not picked up the wave of the bat at the ball and the edged catch.

It was an emotion-charged moment; there was total disappointment as the appeal went in favour of the batsman. The crowd, slowly building up, buzzed with excitement over the first-ball drama. Following the canny advice of Alan Jones, the former Australian rugby coach, who had talked to the side before the match, Wessels quickly pulled the team together. They swallowed their initial disappointment, put the incident behind them and settled down, calm but energetic. They still had to get used to the massive ground where fielding is not easy for newcomers, and where misjudging the pace of the outfield can be crucial in intercepting a ball in areas behind the wicket, such as fine leg and third man.

Wessels had to reset his field when Meyrick Pringle bowled, worried that his waywardness would cost too many runs. The opposition capitalised on the errant Western Province paceman's inability to move the ball later than usual. Pringle had done a pretty good job in the build-up matches; now he was under pressure, and so was his captain. Wessels was accused of being unsmiling and stony-faced when the South Africans arrived in Perth, which was not at all true. He wore a big grin at the reception during the sporadic applause that greeted the South Africans' arrival in Australia shortly after noon on 7 February 1992, some 19 days before their big appearance in Sydney. Those present felt a little emotional about the moment, too. Minutes later, sitting behind the battery of microphones, TV cameras and other equipment recording the historic event, Wessels was more serious, but to accuse him of being stony-faced was pure distortion.

But at Sydney the South Africans were on a high as Peter Kirsten, batting with sensible touches, and Wessels, leading from the front, steered the side home. It was an equally emotional moment as the raucous SCG crowd erupted to cheer the return of the new South Africans after 22 years in the wilderness. And what a walk of triumph from the field when it was over! The faces of Kirsten and Wessels were bathed in jubilant smiles to signal the side's conquest of the hosts under the harsh glare of floodlights brighter, bigger and better than anything in South Africa.

Was it beginner's luck? Not at all. Then that first fax message: 'Your victory is a victory for all of us over years of isolation and rejection – FW de Klerk (State President)'. What an ironic communiqué after the years of apartheid, which had caused the hardship and isolation in the first place.

Then the emotional Steve Tshwete of the ANC: 'Damn it, man, we mustn't let apartheid get in the way of such a great team. Those guys struck a political blow with their bats today. They showed the world what a unified South Africa can do. I'm a proud man, a mighty proud man.'

It was interesting that on the first day of the tournament the New Zealand captain, Martin Crowe, scored a technically skilful match-winning century against Australia; not your average one-day biff, bash and wallop effort either. There were a lot of fluent, silky classical off and on drives, and the Kiwi was not the sort of batsman who indulged in improvised limited-overs strokeplay unless they were necessary.

Mark Greatbatch's unceremonious slaughter of South Africa's bowling at Eden Park – 68 off only 60 balls on a smallish, awkward ground in fielding terms – was a display of explosive power hitting.

Then there was Meyrick Pringle's one-man devastation of the West Indies at Lancaster Park, Christchurch: four for 11 off eight overs, which shook the might of the Caribbean, disturbing their batting equanimity in an historic game where a lot of happy relationships were forged on and off the field. Here Donald Woods, the once banned South African journalist and intractable opponent of apartheid, smiled with urbane good humour, proud to be a South African, as his country swept aside the West Indies on a bitingly cold day.

But what about that run-out at Brisbane? The Jonty Rhodes dive for glory, which uprooted Inzamam-ul-Haq's stumps in spectacular fashion, has long been part of world cricket folklore. It explains why, in 1999 in South Asia, more than five million people canvassed in a poll regarded it as the single most remarkable fielding incident of the decade. At the time Inzamam had kept Pakistan in the race for victory, before he slipped and slid on the treacherously wet Gabba surface. Rhodes processed the moment analytically, then charged in from point to commit the most celebrated fielding moment at the Gabba since the run-out that had caused the famed tied Test at the same venue 31 years before. Another highlight was Kirsten's batting artistry at Adelaide Oval, where he effortlessly turned for a third in an innings of 84 against India, displaying a perfect batting technique in difficult conditions. Inzamam, oozing class and talent, scored the perfect match-winning innings against New Zealand in the semi-final at a packed Eden Park.

Another great memory of the 1992 World Cup was the bowling of left-arm seamer Wasim Akram at the massive Melbourne Cricket Ground – two wickets in successive balls as England's hopes were blasted away in the final. And what about Mushtaq Ahmed's leg-spin mystery? His twin entrapment of Graeme Hick, lbw with the googly, and Graham Gooch caught in the deep, did just as much as Akram to seal England's fate.

Throughout it all, Wessels drilled South Africa as he had Eastern Province in those mid-winter training programmes, and all with a purpose: to reach the semi-final and then to strive, if possible, for the final. The great imponderable is always whether South Africa would have reached the final as part of a miracle comeback story. There is no doubt that many patriotic South Africans with a limited knowledge of cricket would, at the time, have chorused 'yes'.

Caught up in the spectacular revival of South African cricket, by 22 March thousands of new cricket fans could, with accomplished delight, rattle off the names of the players: Kepler Wessels, Peter Kirsten, Allan Donald, Andrew Hudson, Jonty Rhodes, Brian McMillan, Dave Richardson, Richard Snell, Meyrick Pringle … along with other team members such as Tertius Bosch and Omar Henry, Adrian Kuiper, Hansie Cronjé, Mark Rushmere, Faiek Davids and Yasien Begg. The new apostles of the game had also acquired new knowledge: what outswing, inswing or a left-arm loop were useful for; could see the beauty in a cover drive and square cut; and knew what Rhodes ate for breakfast, lunch and dinner. They also knew that the entire team was basically non-smoking, and generally fonder of orange juice and diet drinks than the common drink, beer.

As a player, Wessels was not a machine-like robot – he just gave that impression. Sometimes he also gave the false impression that he was not thinking about the game, but about other matters. That was an illusion, as in the middle his thoughts rarely strayed from the game. He still demands the same concentration levels from his Eastern Province charges, just as you would expect of a former player who became a big name at international level when playing for Australia because of his drive for success.

Wessels was bitterly disappointed when, after two seasons, the Packer circus was shut down after an agreement with the Australian Cricket Board, and left him without a summer base in Australia. The two or three letters he wrote to former WSC confederates drew acid comment from Rod Marsh (Western Australia) and Ian Chappell (South Australia). A third letter, directed at Greg Chappell, Ian's younger brother and the captain of Queensland, elicited more understanding and sympathy. Before the 1979 English county season with Sussex was over, Kepler had signed a contract to play for Queensland. The young man from Bloemfontein had taken the first steps toward a Test career.

During Wessels's career, his first-class batting average slipped under 40 only twice – in 1976/77 when his 511 runs were scored at 35.60, and in 1979/80 with 623 at 36.64 in his first season with Queensland. He always displayed an enormous appetite for making runs and developing his talents, and, more importantly, playing to his strengths. Along with Allan Lamb and Peter Kirsten, he was the best South African batsman of his generation. Blessed with copious powers of concentration, he worked his way to the top of the Australian batting tree and was, for three seasons, one of the leading batsmen in the national averages, which earmarked him as a Test candidate when he qualified for Australian citizenship in September 1982. That step achieved, he had to surmount another before he was able to play for Australia. The prejudice of some officials in Oz meant he missed going to Pakistan because of his South African background and his ties with Packer's WSC circus.

What changed the situation was a tightly structured second innings of 103 for Queensland against England at the Gabba in the 1982/83 season. Not only did it help the state beat the tourists by 171 runs, it did much toward helping Kepler achieve his ambition of playing for Australia in his first Test. Greg Chappell, the captain for that series, did his best to support the young South African-born left-hander.

There was an initial setback to the start of the series when he was overlooked for the first Test at the Waca in Perth, which was drawn. But he was brought in for the second at Brisbane, after Greg Chappell had told him he deserved his chance. The Brisbane press backed their new hero, but the more vitriolic media from the southern states were none too happy that Graeme Wood had been replaced by 'that foreigner' Kepler. This slur showed just how divided the Australian press was at the time, with Peter McFarlane of *The Age*, Melbourne, stirring the political pot by commenting that the selection 'of a South African-born cricketer is not going to be well received by black countries'.

It was a measure of the comments passed at the time – all highly tainted, because there were those who did not want him in the team. What this showed was how, on his return to South Africa in 1986, there would always be verbal assaults. The reasons were his association with the Kim Hughes rebels, when he was seen as a 'South African', and his selection for the Wanderers pirate 'test' against Mike Gatting's tourists in February 1990, because of his Hughes tour link. Then came his selection as captain of South Africa for the 1992 World Cup, and the covert 'Australian' slur appeared.

England batted first in the second Test of the 1982/83 series against Australia and scored 219. Someone whose birthplace was Langebaanweg was their leading batsman with 72 – how Allan Lamb chuckled. Here he was playing in a Test for England in far-off Brisbane, and among the opposition was someone born in Bloemfontein who had been in the same 1973 South African Schools side in Bulawayo. What a small world! Then the Aussies lost two quick wickets before a now not-so-nervous Kepler and his usually aggressive captain, the elegant Greg Chappell, put together a tidy partnership, until Chappell ran himself out. Wickets fell all too regularly for comfort before Kepler found a partner in Bruce Yardley. At 97 he had an escape when the England wicketkeeper Bob Taylor bungled a stumping chance off Eddie Hemmings. The Test debut century arrived next ball, a short delivery and on line with the leg stump. What a juicy ball to get to reach that ton. It made him the 13th Australian to achieve the feat (and ironically the first South African-born player to do so). The ball had hardly reached the mid-wicket boundary when the Brisbane supporters were cheering their man and invading the field.

The crowd gave him two standing ovations in a matter of minutes; the first when he reached the magical 100, and the second when he walked off at the end of the second day's play.

Fred Trueman pondered publicly that 'if these are just two South Africans, I'd like to see the other nine'. South African newspapers made much of the Lamb–Wessels link with their 1973 SA Schools caps. What it gave was a false impression of South African batting standards below the top echelon. There were Jimmy Cook, Henry Fotheringham, Peter Kirsten, Graeme Pollock and Clive Rice, who in 1982 were the top five batsmen in the country. But the view that 'isolation has not blunted our effectiveness to give the world the best current cricketers they have seen' was a decidedly biased view. At the time it was an emotional issue, and had the writers looked a little deeper into that well of talent, they would have been surprised at just how empty the reservoir of potential had become, despite the start of the rebel era.

There is no doubt at all that on 10 February 1990, when he walked out of the South African rebel dressing room for the last time, Kepler considered his international career, rebel or otherwise, at an end. It came after a row with several members of the South African side over his Australian links. How ironic that 24 months and 16 days later he should walk onto the Sydney Cricket Ground to a standing ovation from a crowd hailing South Africa's return to the international stage in the 1992 World Cup against Australia.

It proves that the future is as ambiguous as a questionmark ...

Between those two emotional episodes lies one of world cricket's more remarkable accomplishments. Six days before the start of the last rebel 'test' in heavy, overcast conditions, and a sparse Thursday crowd at the Wanderers, the South African State President, FW de Klerk, had unbanned all political parties and organisations and announced that Nelson Mandela was to be released. He had also put in motion a chain reaction of reconciliation and reform as the term 'the New South Africa' gained currency. By the end of March the second Gatting tour had, because of long-term interests, been abandoned, and the South African Cricket Union, sharply divided over the tour, regained some credibility with their rivals, the South African Cricket Board. A meeting in May had Van Zyl Slabbert and Steve Tshwete, along with other non-sporting leaders, sit down in Johannesburg to discuss the future of the sport in the country. That men of such diverse political opinions, yet with the same goals, were able to put together a series of viewpoints, opened up a path of hope. Thirteen years on, as the 2003 World Cup looms, it has been forgotten how cricket was the first sport in the country to show faith in the long-term future and take the first genuine step towards unity.

Those first tangible signs of unity emerged on 8 September 1990, when the two boards met with Tshwete in the chair to discuss common interests. Agreement was reached on the need for further contact. In a carefully worded statement it was 'agreed that it is essential that one non-racial, democratic controlling body be formed'. Other points mentioned were: an agreement to maintain the sports moratorium; that a declaration of intent would be formulated, with Krish Mackerdhuj and Ronnie Pillay, of the SACB, and Ali Bacher and Alan Jordaan, of the SACU, working on the draft of what would become the founding document of the United Cricket Board. Within a month the SACB not only agreed to further meetings with the SACU, but the executive also 'agreed to forge ahead with plans to bring about one controlling body for all cricketers in the country'.

Bacher applauded the SACB action and added an equally important comment: 'The South African Cricket Union remains positive that unification of our cricket can be achieved to the benefit of all cricketers in this country, irrespective of race, colour and creed. Of great importance is the SACB's decision, in principle, to participate in the development programme by establishing a common trust, the details of which are to be worked out at a later date by both bodies, which would promote the game among us all, particularly in the underprivileged areas of South Africa.'

Of equal importance at that SACB meeting was the information that the body had cut its ties with the Pan African Congress-linked South African Council on Sport (Sacos), and had affiliated to the rival National Olympic Sports Congress, the sports wing of the African National Congress (ANC). It was the NSC, led by Krish Naidoo, whose confrontation with the SACU and the police during the Gatting tour played a major role in the last rebel visit being curtailed, and the second abandoned. The NSC affiliation did much to strengthen the ties between both cricket bodies, as well as to create a deeper mood for overall understanding at a tricky stage of the unity development process.

The big breakthrough came on 16 December 1990, in a hotel on the Port Elizabeth beachfront. At around 4.45 in the afternoon Bacher, then managing director of the SACU and later the first MD of the United Cricket Board of South Africa, emerged smiling, and sent faxes to all the major newspapers in the country with the following message: 'The most important press conference in 100 years of South African cricket will take place at the Elizabeth Sun, at 6 pm today.' It is ironic that on the day that symbolised apartheid, the Day of the Vow, accord on cricket unity was achieved after 100 years. Incredibly there were only three press representatives: the *South African Press Association's* local representative, the senior cricket writer for the *Argus Group* of newspapers, and the SABC. All other cricket writers had left for other venues, as they felt the meeting would only endorse progress before everyone agreed to meet again to discuss further problems of mutual interest.

A contact within the SA Cricket Union had already told the *Argus Group* senior writer that more than talks would take place this time. The statement of intent had been drafted and circulated and all but agreed on, and once agreement had been reached the rest would fall into place. That Sunday night the Elizabeth Room at the old Elizabeth Sun was an exciting place to be. South African cricket was about to be given a whole new identity – within eight months a united cricket body would be formed, a board put in place, a banquet held to celebrate the momentous event and a membership application sent to the International Cricket Council.

Smiling members of both boards emerged from the 16 December meeting, now more than mere nodding acquaintances. It was no longer 'them' and 'we' but 'us'. They were partners in a unifying force. Other sports were surprised at the swiftness with which unity was achieved. A nine-point statement of intent was released, and a commitment to unity with a clear timetable.

Now began the long haul to put it all together without too many teething problems. On 20 April 1991 agreement was reached on the date of the formation of the United Cricket Board of South Africa – a name suggested by the German ambassador to South Africa, who felt that as unity was the important component in the establishment of the board, the word 'united' should be the central point of the name of the new body.

Next came the tortuous step of winning approval from those countries who were full members of the ICC; to this purpose a visit to Harare was arranged by the ANC. Talks with the Indian and Pakistani high commissioners were held, as well as with top Zimbabwean sports officials. As the United Cricket Board prepared for an open pilgrimage to Lord's, long-retired legends such as Sir Garfield Sobers, Sunil Gavaskar, Richie Benaud and EW Swanton, a long venerated English cricket journalist who refused to have anything to do with South African cricket for more than 30 years, arrived to join in the celebrations, which gave a new life to the sport. Other major sports bodies in the country cast envious eyes in South African cricket's direction when, on 29 June, the unified board was established, the constitution approved and Geoff Dakin elected the first president. Krish Mackerdhuj was elected Dakin's deputy for a period of one year, with the roles reversed in 1992, after which Dakin stepped down.

On 10 July 1991, almost 900 days after they bolted the door on South African cricket 'for the last time', the International Cricket Council opened it again. This time, the nations that had voted in January 1989 to slap a blockade on international links did more than merely overturn their decision; they gave the United Cricket Board of South Africa a massive vote of confidence, with only the West Indians abstaining in both ballots. The first ballot was among full members, the second involved the full and associate members. When it came to a show of hands, Sir Colin Cowdrey could have called it a 'no contest', such was the overwhelming support for the UCB. There were 25 in favour and one abstention. Some time later, in the historic Long Room at Lord's, Sir Colin told the cricket world that South Africa was back. It was an emotional moment, and Ali Bacher showed his feelings as 'the United Cricket Board of South Africa, now representative of all the people of our country, celebrate this great day'.

The West Indians had abstained because the Caribbean countries had not discussed the question of the United Cricket Board's admission, but they were the first to congratulate South Africa. Clyde Walcott and Steve Camacho wanted it noted that they fully associated themselves with 'a fully representative South Africa now being part of the world cricket community'. That night, at an historic ICC dinner, the board president Geoff Dakin, vice-president Krish Mackerdhuj, as well as Ali Bacher and Steve Tshwete, sat down together knowing that their country now held the status of full membership. Both Bacher and Tshwete had played pivotal roles during their mission to England in May to see the high commissioners from the various islands that make up the West Indies, and to meet the West Indian team, including the former captain Clive Lloyd.

Wessels, a member of the pathfinding team that went to India in November, played a major role in the Charminar Challenge series. He shared the player of the series award with Sanjay Manjrekar, the glamorous Indian batsman who scored 105 off 82 balls in New Delhi, as well as 52 off 52 balls in the second game at Gwalior. Manjrekar displayed, in both innings, all the technical brilliance of a man who is strong all around the wicket. If the South African left-hander felt, however, that he was the backbone of the team's batting, he could also have felt with some justification that he was the left and right crutch as well. His 50 off 97 balls at Eden Gardens, 71 off 96 balls in the Gwalior match, and 90 off 105 balls at Jawaharlal Nehru Stadium, fully indicated his strength of purpose. He scored 211 runs in three innings at 70.33, and if anyone had doubted the Eastern Province captain's commitment to South Africa, they were given a double-barrel blast in India. He was firing well enough to top score in the three South African innings, and while Peter Kirsten's undefeated 86 was the performance that led his country to the singular triumph in New Delhi, Kepler could easily have repeated his century of a previous visit. But the umpire at Venkatapathy Raju's end no doubt felt some sympathy for the bowler as Kepler advanced down the pitch to hammer the 22-year-old left-arm spinner. The finger went up as soon as the ball hit the pad and Raju went up in appeal.

At that stage South Africa were 183 in the 35th over; 111 runs had been scored off only 114 balls as South Africa chased the 288 needed for victory off 50 overs at 5.76 runs an over. It was a match where the bowlers didn't stand a chance.

In Perth at the start of the 1992 World Cup tour, the South African team manager Alan Jordaan had set the tone for speech-making. A former advocate, his uncluttered thinking had always been incisive on the cricket field when he captained Northern Transvaal in the 1970s and into the 1980s. He showed the same talent in the boardroom when delivering an opinion on a tricky matter, and he made a big impression in Australia. At the official reception of the side at the Waca on 7 February, he talked about what Ali Bacher had described as South African cricket's 'greatest day'.

> But just what is our greatest day? Could it be the day on December 16, 1990 when a decision was made to unite? Or could it be that day at the Wanderers, on June 29 last year, when the United Cricket Board of South Africa was formed ... or July 10 when we were admitted as members of the ICC? Or was

the greatest day in Sharjah, when we were told we could play in the World Cup – which is why we are here now, playing Western Australia for the first time in 28 years.

It could be said that our greatest day was when we arrived in India last November and met India for the first time at Eden Gardens in Calcutta. Or is it here, tonight?

Perhaps our greatest day is still to come … at Sydney on February 26 when we beat you in that first game [of ours] in the World Cup. Or maybe our greatest day will be when we reach the World Cup final. I can't quite say what is our greatest day, but what I can tell you is that it is really great to be here in Western Australia.

Ten years on, Jordaan felt that while 'our greatest day' is still to come, to achieve unification in what was a politically tumultuous era had in its own way been a 'great day, in that while the door had been closed, the window was always ready to be opened'.

While the World Cup tournament was a general success, Wessels acknowledged that the West Indian tour was going to be just as demanding, if for different reasons, as the visit to India and the World Cup. But he was worried that a number of players were chronically short of real match practice. Tertius Bosch hadn't had a decent bowl for two months when the side arrived in Kingston, Jamaica, and Omar Henry was carrying rust as well, along with Mark Rushmere, Hansie Cronjé and new member Corrie van Zyl, the replacement for an injured Brian McMillan. Ideally a three- or four-day opening game would have ironed out some faults and cleared most of the cobwebs. But the West Indians weren't particularly interested. They'd taken a hammering in the World Cup and wanted to show the critical, knowledgeable West Indian crowds that they were a better side than their record showed. Thus South Africa copped it in Jamaica and Trinidad where the West Indians, with Brian Lara and Phil Simmons in full flow, made up for the Christchurch disaster in the World Cup.

There was much comment in Kingston about Meyrick Pringle, whose outswing in chilly and overcast Christchurch, along with much undisciplined batting, saw the West Indians abjectly surrender what chances they had. But the way the West Indians played, it is doubtful whether Pringle would have made that much of a difference in Kingston. For one thing there wasn't the wind, which had helped him at Christchurch, and the so-called psychological advantage will always be a matter of conjecture. What was sad was the way the Sabina Park crowd booed Richie Richardson. This was an indication of the parochialism so prevalent in the Caribbean, where the people take a fierce pride in their cricket, and when they say they are going to boycott a match, they do just that. The boycott of the first Test between South Africa and the West Indies in Barbados was sparked by the non-selection of Anderson Cummins.

The South African side for that historic first Test at Kensington Oval was: Andrew Hudson, Mark Rushmere, Kepler Wessels (captain), Peter Kirsten, Hansie Cronjé, Adrian Kuiper, Dave Richardson, Richard Snell, Meyrick Pringle, Allan Donald, Tertius Bosch and 12th man Jonty Rhodes. There was some criticism of Omar Henry being left out, as it was thought a spinner would be needed.

The absence of the spectators was keenly felt, but it was a marvellous Test re-entry. Hudson's century, the first by a South African on Test debut, did much to establish a first-innings lead to give the South Africans some leverage. But Donald, Snell and Pringle bowled wildly at times, giving away far too many runs – at least 40 in the second innings, when they should have turned the screws a little tighter. Bosch, however, who had kicked his heels impatiently in Australia during the World Cup, and was ignored for the first two matches in the West Indies when he should have played in at least one of them, bowled with fire and line. Not only was he the most economical bowler, but his knack of keeping a tight line just wide of the off-stump had the Caribbean batsmen battling.

Hudson apart, Wessels's batting in this Test was exemplary, and his first innings of 59 was a masterpiece in attacking batsmanship, showing off that famous square-cut of his to great advantage, while his pull was employed with equal effect. One unkind writer likened Hudson to Geoff Boycott, because of the pace of the innings, but it showed even then that the likeable Natal opener was developing into a world-class batsman. After Wessels went, Hudson could so easily have got himself out. But his concentration level was remarkable in this innings, after the restrictions of weeks of limited-overs games. Wessels tried to play down his own second innings of 74, saying it was one of the most difficult he had ever played. That may be so, but it was also one of his best, and there is little doubt that if he had not lost his wicket so early on the last day, the final result would have been rather different to the 52-run defeat.

Critics alleged that South Africa's batting on the last morning wasn't positive enough. Frankly, most of the players were short of genuine batting practice because of the overdose of limited-overs matches, and the restriction showed as some of them battled to come to terms with the conditions. Also, the first session of the fourth day was all too costly for the South Africans. While Curtly Ambrose and Courtney Walsh bowled with hostility and fire that last morning, the last two wickets, as well as Jimmy Adams's batting, pulled the West Indies back into a favourable position, scoring 100 runs on a pitch of dubious bounce. Some of the bowling by Snell and Pringle was a little too loose at times. It was a learning experience and South Africans, as usual, were expecting a little too much from their heroes. Test cricket is a far tougher exercise because of the demands made on skill, concentration and discipline. There is little doubt that a second-innings total above 200 was not going to be easy to achieve. Both of Wessels's innings in Barbados were mere appetisers, as he resumed his Test career without making a single false stroke.

Interestingly, the last Test South Africa had played overseas was at The Oval in 1965, from 26 to 31 August, when they drew with England and thus won the three-match series 1–0. Wessels became the 13th player, and the first since Gul Mohammad in 1956/57, to play Test cricket for two countries, and the first to have represented both Australia and South Africa. Others who played for South Africa and another country, in this case England, were Frank Hearne (1888/89 and 1891/92 to 1895/96) and Frank Mitchell (1898/99 and 1912).

Wessels has managed to play an important part in South African cricket, bridging the gap between his own torment of isolation in the 1970s and 1980s and the welcome back posters that greeted him in Calcutta, Perth, Sydney and, above all, the Woolloongabba, Brisbane. The young man from a far-off city called Bloemfontein had come a long way. Making the dream come true required a lot of hard work, and that, he will patiently explain, is what it's all about. He knew it wasn't going to be easy, and did not pretend that South Africa's re-entry to the Test arena was going to be a cakewalk ... but Kensington Oval, Bridgetown, Barbados, was a very important early signpost to a promising future under his tutelage.

There was the 1–0 Test success and the limited-overs series success of 5–2 over India, captained by Mohammad Azharuddin. Yet during the series against India, both in the Tests and in the day/night games, the general standard was mediocre. There were few batting highlights to remember and even fewer bowling gems – although the return of Fanie de Villiers to the South African attack was one of the great comeback stories of the season.

Twelve months before, De Villiers's provincial career had been brought to an abrupt end when a ball from the Barbadian and West Indies fast bowler, Ezra Moseley, hit him on the big toe of his left foot during a Northern Transvaal net session at Centurion Park. It was an undignified and painful exit for a man of courage and determination, who had worked at his game hard enough to become highly respected by his peers. De Villiers, who had had an unsuccessful summer with Kent in 1990, spent a season in England with a minor league club. De Villiers thrived, and on his return to South Africa quickly made his presence known. From uncertain beginnings, he fought his way back into the side he had once played for in the four limited-overs matches against Mike Gatting's rebels in February 1990.

With his accuracy, late away-swing and ability to seam the ball in to the batsmen, De Villiers was a success in the LOI arena against the Indians, and during the triangular Total International series.

Wessels once again proved that he is a superb accumulator of big scores when the pressure is on. In fact, he showed this often during the limited-overs series. He scored 342 runs at 48.86 against India, taking his run-scoring tally at this level to 920 runs in 22 internationals for South Africa at an impressive average of 46, with nine scores of 50 or more, including that top score of 90 in New Delhi.

It was not going to be as easy in the historic Total International, with Pakistan and the West Indies making their South African debuts. Defeat by Pakistan at Centurion Park led to a rare outburst, when Wessels criticised the number of run-outs for which South African batsmen were responsible during the competition.

'It has been unacceptable the way the run-outs have undermined our batting efforts,' he said, after losing the game by 22 runs had ended South Africa's quest to reach the final. His own run-out in that particular match came at a time when he was in the sort of form that wins matches. Sure, limited-overs games often lead to tight situations where run-outs, under the third umpire (television replays), are usually ruled in favour of the fielding side, instead of the batsman getting the benefit of the doubt in close situations. During the series, South Africa lost nine batsmen to run-outs against Pakistan, which did as much damage as the lethal twin bowling talents of Wasim Akram and Waqar Younis, the Pakistan captain and vice-captain in that series.

Twice South Africa were set to beat Pakistan, twice the batting was blown away by the in-swinging yorker. Throughout it all Kepler accepted the criticism with stoical calm. While the critics typecast him as the main offender when it came to slow scoring, they ignored the record of how many LOIs South Africa had won in the years when either Wessels or Peter Kirsten failed. An examination of the records points to two.

So, what were the critics griping about? Hardly, given the circumstances, negative batting performances. It is more likely that they don't quite understand that Wessels, the limited-overs batsman and captain, is far different to the Test batsman and captain; yet in terms of runs scored and results achieved, there is little difference.

This seems like a paradox, but that is what LOIs so often contrive to produce, and those who watched Wessels's debut Test century for South Africa in the Kingsmead match knew there was more to come. There was in fact only one more: at Lord's on what was a sultry – for England – summer's day in 1994. Usually the weather in the British Isles is about as po-faced as the manager/coach/selector Ray Illingworth's mood during the 1994 series against South Africa and the 1995/96 England tour of South Africa. Unfriendly, at times chilly, and far from urbane, Illingworth gave the impression that enjoyment was almost a criminal offence.

Ali Bacher once pointed out shortly before the 1990/91 season started that the most SA Schools caps produced during the summers of isolation had come from

Grey College. Only Wessels and the man who replaced him as captain went on to earn international caps. Boeta Dippenaar was a 12th man in 1995, but toured England and India as a member of the SA under19 team the same year. It was Jackie McGlew who had credited Johan Volsteedt in the mid-1980s with the upsurge in Afrikaans interest in the game, especially in the Free State, and the late Gerbrand Grobler often talked highly of the man both as a coach and mentor, not just as a teacher. Wessels has long acknowledged the role Volsteedt played in his outlook, especially as it came at a time, in the early and mid-1970s, when eager Afrikaans interest in the game was often given a disparaging backhander. This was similar to the selective views of the game's establishment in South Africa. Sure there was Free State input at old South African Cricket Association level, but until the rise of Grey College from around 1970, it was largely ineffectual. The Strydoms and the Cronjés were two traditional family links with the college.

From the end of the Wessels era at Grey College, other players began to grab attention for their skills, techniques and performances. It was an evolutionary, not a revolutionary process, and in this sense displayed how a system can grow from within. It is one that some South African politicians, who love to thump the innovatory drum and curse the 'lily-white' complexion of the teams, need to heed. Sure cricket is a game for all, but sometimes it takes time to achieve demographic growth.

Wessels agreed that Lord's 1994 was a special event. Winning that first Test at the world's cricket headquarters was as decisive as any Test victory before or since. In this case it was victory by 356 runs, based on the twin strengths of sustained top-order reliability and the mix of Allan Donald's pace and Fanie de Villiers's swing. This was the 'dirt in the pocket' Test. Mike Atherton's misdemeanour occurred on the Saturday afternoon, when the England captain was seen to take something out of his pocket and work it on the ball's surface. Atherton then took what can only be described as the fifth amendment by saying that the conversation between him and match referee Peter Burge 'was a private one'.

But the way in which the British media blew up Atherton's 'dirty pocket' story seemed to suggest an ulterior motive – to divert public attention away from the dust and cobwebs gathering in England's pavilions after the humiliating defeat inside four days.

When he played for Australia, Wessels was always the hero in South Africa. On returning home, the knives were quick to emerge for him, and after he became captain they were always sharp and pointed at his back. His single-mindedness enabled him to overcome the petty opinions of those who failed to understand the ultimate goal of every captain – victory. In his day Sir Donald Bradman was an unpopular captain, but he commanded respect among both his peers and his opponents. The same could be said for Kepler Wessels.

HANSIE CRONJÉ
Enigmatic Leadership

By Trevor Chesterfield

14

One glance at the solid, handsome stone and brick façade of Grey College in Bloemfontein explains its importance as an institution of learning and tradition. Many famous fathers and sons have passed through its portals. South African rugby jerseys that belong to past pupils dominate the walls of the Main Hall, among them that of Morné du Plessis, a former national captain. Honours boards, covered in gold leaf lettering, list famous names. There are also the caps, blazers and ties of the two successive South African cricket captains who once stood in the hall, sang school songs, said their prayers and learnt about traditions.

The current principal is Johan Volsteedt, whose father, the highly respected AK Volsteedt, held the post during part of the 1950s and 60s. Johan Volsteedt first attracted attention as a coach – a schoolmaster with a sensitive grasp of modern coaching methods. He knew how to handle the various idiosyncrasies of the players, and as Kepler Wessels once said, was not inclined to suffer fools of any description.

Volsteedt helped shape the lives of two of South Africa's top players of the post-isolation era. It was a rare, proud moment when he stood with Kepler Wessels and Hansie Cronjé at Lord's in 1994 as South Africa were about to play their first Test in England in 29 years. He had coached and taught his country's captain and vice-captain, and did so without fuss or bother, for he is a caring man.

Volsteedt once privately complained of how Cronjé's batting technique had changed since taking on the role of South Africa's captain. It was not so serious, he said, that it could not be corrected. There were times when Cronjé did, it seemed, consult his Grey College mentor. 'If you did not follow the well-structured coaching recipes, do not blame him,' the former South African captain once said of his first coach. 'You have to blame yourself.'

Wessel Johannes Cronjé made his Currie Cup debut after earning a South African Schools cap and captaining the side in 1987. The debut did not attract too much attention, beyond the comment that he had been the SA Schools captain and was the son of Ewie Cronjé, then the Free State cricket chairman and also a former provincial captain. His debut scores at the Wanderers in the match on 22 and 23 January were two and 16: he was bowled by Clive Rice in the first innings, and caught by wicketkeeper Ray Jennings off Rod Estwick in the second. A few days later he picked up a pair against Northern Transvaal on his first visit to Centurion Park, and was dropped for the Currie Cup final against Transvaal at the Wanderers from 11 to 15 February.

This proves that not in all cases are hereditary links a guarantee to automatic success as a provincial player. There are many famous Test captains whose career batting averages are embedded in the 30s instead of the 40s. Cronjé is one; he had to cast aside early, visibly narcissistic flaws about his technique to develop his skills.

By the time the unity talks kicked into gear, Cronjé had taken over as the Free State captain after Joubert Strydom answered a business call in Johannesburg. This time his batting talent, although not over-endowed with stylish technique, did rise to meet the challenge. When the squad was announced for the historic tour of India, the name Hansie Cronjé was to be found among those on a 'development trip', along with Jack Mannack and Derek Crookes. His inclusion in the World Cup squad was seen as a positive step; at that stage his rival for a top-order place was the Eastern Province opener Mark Rushmere, who was also viewed as a prospective national captain. In the 1992/93 season, when Rushmere's form did not match the Pollock selection panel's needs, Cronjé was on the rise and he was making all the right moves.

There were times in the early 1990s when Cronjé exuded a nervous energy, as if some extra adrenaline was pumping inside. Yet he had long been studying the methods of Kepler Wessels, and from hints dropped by Peter Pollock, the convener of South Africa's selection panel, in January 1993, Cronjé was earmarked as Wessels's heir. The team to tour Sri Lanka was announced at Kingsmead on 7 April 1993, after the pulsating final overs of the Natal–Transvaal domestic day/night final.

Weeks before, Cronjé had admitted that he owed much to Wessels, and that the left-hander had been a big influence in his life. So, when the South African selectors looked for a replacement for Adrian Kuiper, Wessels's deputy at the World Cup 16 months earlier, the discussions were brief. Wessels's recommendation won their vote of confidence. If there were thoughts of another vice-captain, they did not emerge.

In an interview in early 1993, when he was leading the South African under24 team against the Sri Lanka under24s at Centurion Park, Cronjé made it clear that Wessels was 'always going to be the man in charge'. He confirmed this the night he arrived back from the Australian tour in early 1994, with the comment, 'Look, I enjoyed standing in as captain, but it was tough. I felt under pressure because I lacked the experience, but the guys were really supportive.' It was a diplomatic response to the media, yet there was another side to this story. Asked how he saw the future if Wessels did not recover in time for the return Tests against Australia, Cronjé said, 'To skip or not to skip ... It will have to be discussed. There will have to be talks.' His eyes did not fix on the one asking the question, but focused elsewhere in the group. It was a trait that would surface again in later years, when facing the media after losing a Test. Whenever Cronjé did not look someone in the eye, it generally meant he was experiencing an emotional moment.

In February 1994, there were those within the UCB hierarchy who wanted Cronjé to take over the captaincy, and have Wessels play the role of senior advisor. It was felt that the Wessels knee injury problem might worsen before the tour of England, and they wanted a fit man to lead the side. It also gave rise to rumours of a power struggle between the selectors and certain members of the UCB executive.

Shortly before the start of the first four limited-overs matches of the South African leg against Australia came the next articulate Cronjé statement: 'Kepler is the right man to captain South Africa right now. He has an important role to play. Also, the time isn't right for me to take over ... not completely ... not now.' After his lack of form at the end of the 1994 tour of England, the time was not right either. Wessels told journalists gathered at Jan Smuts International Airport that he was not stepping down as captain, and would lead the side to Pakistan for a limited-overs series.

It was far from easy to take over the captaincy at Test level, even in a caretaker capacity, during a tour as demanding as one of Australia. So, when it became obvious in the first few days of 1994 that Kepler Wessels would have to return home after breaking the little finger of his left hand, it fell to Cronjé, as Wessels's deputy, to take over.

South Africa, at the time, were involved in the second Test of their first tour Down Under in 30 years, against Allan Border's baggy green-capped heroes of a convincing 4–1 victory over England in the 1993 Ashes series. With Australia having already humiliated a second-rate New Zealand side in two Tests, the view was that South Africa were on a hiding to nothing. Rain had ruined the long-awaited Test reunion at the Melbourne Cricket Ground over Christmas 1993, memories of which were quickly dimmed by the remarkable events of the second encounter at the smaller Sydney Cricket Ground. At the MCG the tall Cronjé, an upright right-hander, very correct and watchful, had managed a top score of 71, as the South Africans battled their way to 258 for three in reply to Australia's 342 for seven, declared. Both innings were little more than net practice sessions, although South Africa did manage to conquer the problems posed by spinners Shane Warne, then the new leg-spin wizard, and off-spinner Tim May.

This is not as surprising as it seems, for several months earlier in Sri Lanka the South Africans had discovered that they were capable of handling spinners, in conditions favourable to spin bowlers. While victory in Sri Lanka was achieved through the brute force of the blond left-arm blitzkrieg pace specialist Brett Schultz, the main lesson learnt from those three Tests was that the South African batsmen, still emerging from isolation, were rediscovering the art of playing spin bowling.

It was the sort of confidence and maturity noticeably lacking when they faced the tall spinner Anil Kumble during India's tour the previous summer, and left-armer Venkatapathy Raju. Kumble, who could serve up a fairly fast googly, destroyed South Africa's second innings at the Wanderers with superb tactical bowling that netted him six for 55. It was a remarkable display of controlled bowling in front of a packed bullring that hummed with expectation, punctuated with the continual exploding of fireworks. For a bowler relatively unknown before the tour, Kumble swiftly rose through the ranks, and his 18 Test wickets at 25.94 in that series was the start of a remarkable Test career.

To combat the menace of the tall, bespectacled craftsman, the South African middle order were required to adopt batting techniques absent for years, and there was a noticeable improvement in footwork, so crucial when facing spinners. Kumble may not turn the ball as much as Warne, but he needs careful watching. Graham Gooch would be quick to agree after England's best were humbled on the dusty surfaces in Calcutta, Madras only weeks after South Africa had beaten their Indian guests 1–0 in the first historic series.

Months later, in far-off Sri Lanka, there was a collective shiver among the thousands of new adherents since the World Cup, when at Tyronne Fernando Stadium, Moratuwa, Arjuna Ranatunga seemed to be on the brink of a famous victory and an early 1–0 lead in the three-match series. Muttiah Muralitharan, an off-spinner who manages prodigious turn, threatened to run through the South African second innings. At 47 for three, with Wessels back in the sweatbox of a pavilion, the fight for survival began as Daryll Cullinan and Jimmy Cook, now batting down the order, attempted to arrest the slide. First Jonty Rhodes and Pat Symcox, then Rhodes and Clive Eksteen, held the innings together against the spin trio of Piyal Wijetunge, Muralitharan and Aravinda de Silva.

Rhodes crafted an extraordinary undefeated maiden Test century and became the hero of the masses. Once before, against India at the Wanderers, he had scored a face-saving 91. Although given not out, he had in fact been run out in the first innings. Now he hung on grimly with Eksteen, and curbing his natural habit to attack, displayed calm and patience, nursing the side through to a draw.

Through it all Cronjé was learning. He studied Wessels's approach to the game, although it was very different to his own. So, when Wessels first injured his knee in Melbourne, and then broke his finger in Sydney, it suddenly fell into place for

Cronjé; it was as if he had been preparing for this moment since being made vice-captain before the tour of Sri Lanka.

The disappointments of the 1992 World Cup and the tour of the West Indies were finally put to rest when he was thrust into the series against the Indians at the Wanderers, after doing 12th man duties against Mohammad Azharuddin's tourists at Kingsmead in Durban. The Wanderers pitch on that first morning was the sort of strip that would have delighted a snake charmer – it spat and almost hissed as the South African top order was swept aside by the cunningly conceived swing and seam of Manoj Prabhakar and Kapil Dev. Little more than an hour had passed since Wessels had won the toss and decided to bat first. The South African captain looked on in horror as the first three wickets fell within the space of 54 minutes, with only 11 runs on the board. Prabhakar had taken three wickets in six balls, and the large pre-lunch first-day crowd at the Wanderers bellowed in anguish. It would have been four if the wicketkeeper Kiran More had taken a chance offered by Rhodes off the first ball he faced. When Wessels departed after a 52-minute battle for five runs, Cronjé set forth for his third Test innings. During the next 84 minutes, in which he faced 63 balls, the tall, upright batsman painstakingly put together just about the best single-figure Test innings scored at the Wanderers since it opened in 1955/56. Most will recall Rhodes's 91 and Brian McMillan's 98, but ask them to recollect Cronjé's contribution of nine, and a bemused glance is the likely response. It wasn't all defensive forward technique either – he was far too accomplished for that. Had it not been for a superb piece of fielding off his own bowling by Kapil Dev, Cronjé could have fashioned a double-figure innings of character.

By the time South Africa reached the Emerald City with its coathanger bridge for the New Year game, Sydney was ringed by bush fires. Cronjé had scored two Test centuries: in Port Elizabeth against India, and against Sri Lanka at the Sinhalese Sports Club in Colombo's colourful and colonial-styled, tree-lined Cinnamon Gardens. South Africa had not won a Test at Sydney; of the four previous victories Down Under, two had been achieved at the MCG and two at Adelaide. The first, in 1910/11, was under Percy Sherwell's captaincy. Wessels's tour came to an end when he dug his finger into the turf while attempting to take a low catch offered by Ian Healy off Fanie de Villiers's bowling. The incident came towards the end of the second day, and the compound fracture was not what the South Africans needed at the time.

At this point Cronjé stepped into the captaincy role, and found encouragement from the rest of the team, on and off the field. Amid the ruins of their first-innings score of 169, with leg-spinner Warne weaving his magic to take seven for 56, the tourists faced a torrid three days as their hosts reached 200 for five – 31 runs on and five wickets in hand. No wonder the South Africans were written off. It was baking hot, and the worst bush fires of the century were burning. The rain and disappointment of Melbourne were a distant memory as Cronjé's next joust with Warne went the way of the leg-spinner, who then chirped Cullinan after bowling him with a flipper that dropped on a good length and skidded into the stumps.

Jonty Rhodes, batting at six, held the South African middle order together as the tourists scraped together enough runs to set a target of sorts. It was amazing what Rhodes's score of 76 did for a side fighting to keep their hopes afloat. Craig McDermott worked his way through their top order, removing the fluent Gary Kirsten and Cronjé, on a pitch that was described as patchy and dusty, and fit for spin bowling and little else. Somehow Rhodes and Dave Richardson added 72 for the sixth wicket, while Donald joined Rhodes to add the all-important 36 runs for a beleaguered South Africa. 'For the tourists they were more precious than gold nuggets found in a worked-out mine,' wrote Phil Wilkins in the *Sydney Morning Herald* when he reviewed the match.

From the time Fanie de Villiers earned his first tour cap to Sri Lanka, there had been much speculation about when he would earn his first Test cap. Several critics said that the Northern Transvaal seamer would never play in a Test because his action was all wrong. The big-hearted bowler responded with a performance that embarrassed his detractors. The long-awaited cap arrived at Melbourne, where he lacked penetration on a pitch designed for batting rather than bowling. At the SCG, De Villiers put it all together in a history-making performance. If Warne could take 12 wickets for 128 runs to set up a likely Australian victory, could South Africa strike back? Cronjé, now in the caretaker role, had Pat Symcox and Gary Kirsten as spinners. Only, Wessels told him to trust the seamers, as they were the ones who would pull off the miracle.

The Wizards of Oz suddenly lost a little of their magic when De Villiers bowled Michael Slater for one with a late outswinger and only four on the board. But when Donald grassed David Boon off his own bowling, the portents for South Africa were not good. Looking for quick runs, Boon finally succumbed when he gave a catch to Kirsten at short-leg with the score on 51, and De Villiers took his third wicket when he trapped nightwatchman Tim May lbw with the second ball he faced.

Hope flickered when De Villiers bowled an off-cutter to vice-captain Mark Taylor and a gleeful Richardson snuffled the catch – four wickets and all to De Villiers. The Aussies were a stunned 63 for four at the close. It was an uneasy night for most South Africans, while the Aussies slept soundly, assured of a victory by five or four wickets: just 54 runs required and six wickets in hand.

There is a theory that the Australians do not chase targets too well. When the dramatic last morning was over, the inquest by the critics threw up remarks such as, 'Look at the series against the West Indies the season before; and the last Test against England at The Oval.' De Villiers put the theory to the test in an unbroken spell, watched by a nation resigned to the inevitable agony of defeat. But the scene changed rapidly. A remarkable delivery by the fast bowler Donald, which was replayed often enough on TV that summer, got rid of Border, and then the game was really on. Donald struck again and yorked Mark Waugh, and De Villiers bagged victim number five when he had Healy edge a drive into the stumps.

Cronjé then got into the act by running out Warne. Damien Martyn, whose six runs were all singles, gave Andrew Hudson a catch after a 35-run partnership for the ninth wicket with McDermott. It took Martyn another six years before he regained the confidence of the Australian selectors. With McDermott's departure, the faint glimmer of hope of the night before was now a flaming torch for those at home in South Africa watching the bizarre events. While the 12 000 spectators, admitted free, enjoyed the spectacle, it reached the white-knuckle fingernail-biting stage when Glenn McGrath joined McDermott, only to scoop the ball back at De Villiers on the third ball of the second over. Australia had been bowled out for 111. De Villiers was mobbed by his teammates. Pandemonium broke out, with a broadly grinning Wessels leading the rest of the side onto the field. Celebrations started for some of those back in South Africa, while the rest first heard the news at dawn, unable to believe that South Africa had squeezed out an incredible victory by five runs, the sixth closest on record.

Apart from Cronjé's uncertain form, there was the disappointment of losing the limited-overs series final 2–1, followed by the unhappy third Test at Adelaide, with its acrimony over poor umpiring decisions.

Cronjé quickly re-established his batting credentials with a century in the opening match of the limited-overs series at the Wanderers in 1994. He added to the run feast at Centurion Park 24 hours later, scored a record 251 off the Australian bowlers for Free State, and then put together a remarkable 122 in the first Test at the Wanderers, which South Africa won in style.

Before the side was named for England in April 1994, it was known that it was only a matter of time before Cronjé would take over from Wessels. Rumours had been circulating that Wessels did not want to tour England in 1994, and was persuaded only days before the tour to change his mind. This particular rumour was later yorked by Wessels, whose comment was that he 'wanted to end [his] international career with the tour of England'. It was Cronjé's lack of form during the 1994 tour that saw Wessels, with Bob Woolmer as the new coach, take the side on a fruitless limited-overs tour to Pakistan, where nothing went right. To make Cronjé captain now, it was felt, would add pressure he did not need. He was made captain for the remainder of that summer. He led South Africa to a convincing

2–1 win over New Zealand after a shock defeat in the first Test at the Wanderers because of a poor batting display. They then went to New Zealand where they beat the Kiwis in the only Test, but failed to impress in the limited-overs series.

From that point on, Cronjé's success was impressive against India, New Zealand and Sri Lanka. The 5–0 whitewash of the West Indies side, which had become a pale shadow of what it had once been, showed South Africa's all-round strength. There were Test setbacks against the Australians and Pakistan. But the 1999 World Cup elimination against Australia in the semi-final at Edgbaston in Birmingham, England was a body blow to Cronjé's ambitions of leading the hosts in the 2003 tournament.

There was certainly no mistaking his passion for the game and his love for the side he led, often with distinction; his tactical know-how improved to the extent that Steve Waugh, the Australian captain, admitted that playing against South Africa always added an extra dimension to his game. Even Test and former Test umpires admitted that there was 'always a buzz of expectancy' when walking down the steps and knowing he was about to lead the side onto the field.

In January 1999, Cronjé faced a moment of crisis. At the start of the 1998/99 season, with the West Indians on their first Test tour, the focus had been to beat the tourists, then to concentrate on building for the World Cup. This would be done through a series of limited-overs international games, first against the Caribbean visitors and then a tour of New Zealand. But there were those who were far from satisfied; instead of selection through natural progress and form, transformation was to be stepped up.

The idea for the West Indies LOIs was to reflect the World Cup squad, only the coach found himself reading a list containing 17 names. With Makhaya Ntini out of favour because of the rape case, Victor Mpitsang, hardly ready for such an important challenge, was thrust into the side in his place. Peter Pollock, convener of the selection panel, declined to explain why 17, and not 14 names were on the list. The view was that the selectors had pulled a basket of red herrings across their selections. Pollock then explained the simple truth to Woolmer – the government had intervened. The squad would be 17 – or 14 and three affirmative players; a bit harsh to classify Herschelle Gibbs and Henry Williams as affirmative action players, as they were good enough for inclusion on merit. The only one outside this circle was Mpitsang.

As a matter of policy, Pollock told Woolmer that one, or preferably two, players 'of colour' had to play in the side during the LOIs involving the West Indians. Despite a show of tactful equanimity, Pollock was disturbed by the orders on how to select the squad, as it cut across the norms of selection policy. In World Cup year it set a dangerous precedent. Cronjé was angry at a tactic he felt had been forced on the players. He was told that the World Cup squad was a different matter as long as they went along with the plans for the slogs against the Windies. While he waited for the victory ceremony to start after the 5–0 Tests series triumph, Cronjé's amicable façade slipped, to reveal a captain fuming at what he felt was a betrayal of policy. His discussions with Dr Bacher were far from cordial.

Dr Bacher met the team at their hotel the next day and outlined a broad global picture. The players argued against it; the transformation policy and accompanying hiccups could disrupt carefully designed strategies and team philosophies. Also, the public would not take kindly to defeat, with or without affirmative action players. The core of the argument, however, was how lesser players, filling the place of the proud men who had worked hard to play for their country, could weaken the side. Gibbs and Paul Adams were among the players expressing concern about the interference.

Cronjé had long supported the need for transformation, but not at Test or LOI levels. Dr Bacher left the room and the players looked at each other. The captain was not prepared to budge. What went through his mind was not fully revealed, but he thanked Woolmer and said he would not play for South Africa again. He felt compromised, and told the coach that he 'felt the way a chess player would if someone else was moving the pieces'. From his earliest days in cricket he had made it known that he was not a racist, but the selection policy was not going to build a tough-minded, winning team.

It took a minute before a startled Woolmer absorbed Cronjé's comments, and then he went to the captain's room to talk him round. Dr Bacher and the team's manager, Goolam Rajah, were alerted, and an angry Cronjé, skipping a golfing date, headed for Bloemfontein. Signs of a looming players' revolt emerged. There was a strong team support base in the side for Cronjé both as captain and player. The crisis may eventually have been resolved, but its residue did not subside. It spilled over into other areas, with Cronjé seeking a coaching job with Glamorgan and selection policy clarification with the new convener Rushdi Magiet. Pressures were always bubbling below the surface, mostly because of increasing policy changes.

Considering the chilled relations between Cronjé and Dr Bacher, the UCB's managing director's comments after the 2–0 Test series victory over India on the sub-continent are significant. Phrases such as, 'an extraordinary asset to South African cricket', and 'a role model for not only the youth of this country but for others to look up to' were on offer.

As had been the case when South Africa and England had met at Centurion Park in November 1995, the fifth Test of the Millennium Series was seriously affected by what weather forecasters called 'abnormal rains'. In January 2000, the first day's play started late because of the weather, after which rain of various strengths fell on days two and three. Although the weather had cleared by the fourth day, it was said that a drainage problem was at fault and underfoot conditions affecting bowlers' run-ups were hazardous. In a normal set of circumstances the fifth day's play would have been very dull fare: South Africa batting out their first innings and then England using the remaining overs for batting practice. To change this scenario on the last day, Cronjé needed the co-operation of the England captain Nasser Hussain to manufacture a result. It would have meant a declaration of the South African innings, and the forfeiture of England's first innings and South Africa's second innings, as allowed under Law 14.

Cronjé's initial comments, made at the post-match media conference over the declaration of innings deal at Centurion, were curious. He believed that there had been 'some whispers from the ICC' about his decision to forfeit the South African second innings. He expected 'it might raise a few eyebrows'. What he said next either was a red herring or meant that he had an idea others may have guessed that a deal had been done. Ground consultant Hilbert Smit, who oversaw the pitch and outfield preparations, was puzzled on the fourth day when he knew that play was possible, but the players were still discussing the options before lunch.

Cronjé said: 'I would be disappointed if this is the [ICC] attitude and do not want to be part of the game if this is their thinking. All I know is that when I arrived at the ground I found there were 22 players who wanted to get involved in a game and the mood was a positive one.

'I had been giving it some thought since Sunday when we would have had a sell-out crowd, and also again on Monday when we were unable to give the public anything. Both sides were in with a chance of winning with seven balls of the match remaining, and if this is what the game is about then I feel we have given the spectator something in return fore their support.

'Of course I am disappointed we lost, and our record of not losing in 14 matches has gone, but the choice was there and had to be taken,' Cronjé said, indicating that the icing on this particular cake was far from tasty.

Scoring 249 in 72 overs on what is the last day of a Test normally means that the target is a fair one; far higher scores have been achieved in limited-overs matches, where the overs faced are 50. As it is, the laws allow for such mechanisms as declaring an innings at any stage.

'I am playing in a very positive side and today was another chance to back their ability throughout to beat England,' Cronjé said.

Hussain wanted to 'test the water' first and see how the pitch behaved before making a decision on whether to fall in with Cronjé's idea. After half an hour the fun began when the England captain went off, and after a brief discussion with Cronjé accepted the decision.

'I would have been gutted had we lost,' Hussain admitted. 'I think we all would have been. We have been here for three months, and to lose the series 3–0 was not what we wanted. The 2–1 result is better than that. Hansie deserves every support for what he did. He gave us a chance, he gave his side a chance and we gave the public a great day,' he said.

Cronjé had wanted a 3–0 result. He also felt that had Paul Adams not been injured (the left-arm wrist spinner damaged a knuckle by pushing his hand under an advertising board to retrieve the ball), South Africa would have won the game. It was the one hunch he had gambled on to win the Test. Fate thumbed its nose at Cronjé's plan. Adams's departure had left him without a match winner.

* * *

Twelve weeks later, on a balmy April morning at Kingsmead, South Africa's efficient and helpful manager, Goolam Raja, asked all who had not been with the side in India to leave the dressing room. Five days earlier, on 7 April, New Delhi police had laid charges against Cronjé and three other team members, suggesting complicity in a match-fixing scam. In support of their allegations they released transcripts of a discussion taped from a mobile telephone. Cronjé had been caught in conversation with a known bookie, Sanjay Chawla, making a deal. The UCB moved swiftly to protect their man and issued a series of denials, including one from Cronjé. Two days later in Durban he received the full backing of the UCB and pleaded his innocence. Forty-eight hours after his 'I have nothing to hide' claim, Cronjé admitted to 'not having been totally honest'. In the early hours of the morning of 11 April he called the team's security officer, Rory Steyn, and handed over a written confession. Raja was summoned to Cronjé's room and Dr Bacher was contacted.

'At the start he was very calm and collected,' Steyn later told the King Commission. 'Then, when he began his story, he became agitated and broke down. He handed me a statement to read. It was in his handwriting. He said to me: "You may have guessed but I haven't been totally honest – some of what has been reported in the media is true." I recall words to the effect that lies were eating him up; that he wanted to come clean.'

The United Cricket Board moved swiftly: Cronjé was fired, his contract cancelled and he was on his way to Cape Town. The reaction was immense; expressions of dismay, shocked disbelief and near grief were recorded. Some people were physically ill during the traumatic hours that followed.

As a wider, uglier scenario emerged, the three-match challenge series with Australia, now only 30 hours away, was forgotten. Clouds of uncertainty and suspicion gathered over Kingsmead. The game had been booby-trapped from within by the hands of the fifth columnist, Cronjé, and it was about to be blown apart.

Hours later a stunned nation heard the stark truth. There were many who believed in Cronjé; he was the essence of the modern face of the spiritually cleansed young Afrikaner, reaching out to embrace the country's rainbow image. They discovered instead a cardboard cut-out. His admission had betrayed their trust, and the game, for the moment, was mentally broken on the wrack of lies, deceit and greed. Their white knight had been knocked off his charger.

They thought highly of Cronjé in South Asia as well. To thousands he was a man of integrity and honour. In Cronjé, South Africa had a sportsman who was above reproach. Five women with deep passionate feelings for the game, yet from vastly different cultural backgrounds, expressed their thoughts during the King Commission. Trishna Bose, a beguiling TV producer and freelance writer for an international company based in New Delhi, India, held a deep admiration for Cronjé. So did Colombo bank executive Sharmila Tharmaratnam and Nuwani de Silva, a Colombo PR company executive. Rukshan Cabral, an accountancy consultant for an Asian hotel group in Mumbai, and Colombo schoolteacher Irene Perera considered his upright image to be beyond question. They felt let down, as they saw in Cronjé the skills of a specialist, a committed person who was an international icon. They looked on him in awe, and ended up feeling disgust. They knew, too, that he was not the only one. For them, Cronjé was 'just not the sort of person who would do what he did'.

In South Africa, women who had started following cricket only because of Cronjé were increasingly distressed as events unfolded. Durban housewife Laura Landheer admitted to being shaken by the revelations; shop assistant Naomi Frost could not concentrate on her job for days; Nancy Parker-Adams, a pharmacist near the Durban beachfront, was equally distraught. They had grown to 'know' Cronjé during the 1999 World Cup, and came to respect his calm, reassuring outlook and general composure. He represented the face of modern South Africa.

If your national cricket captain could admit to dishonesty, who could one trust? Who indeed.

Against such a stress-laden background with its mendacious trappings, what price on a composed training session for a series against the World Cup champions? It was not going to be easy. As Pollock observed, Cronjé had, along with his leadership skills, been an integral part of the team's make-up and was not easy to replace. Donald was not around either, as he was on a sabbatical, playing for his old county Warwickshire. So, where do you go from here? Graham Ford took the side through the practice session. Whether the scandal affected his tight self-control and usually stoical approach, he did not let on.

Newspaper headlines expressed a nation's shame and a captain in disgrace. The scandal was the biggest bruising the game had suffered since the fallout over South Africa's launching of the rebel tours during the 1980s.

Snap judgements of events and their results all too often obscure the facts. In this respect it is all too easy to suggest that from the moment he was appointed captain, Cronjé was an easy target for Indian bookmakers. They were always looking for someone near the top or at the top to pass on information. Salim Malik and later Mohammed Azharuddin were bought with the lure of luxuries, and they used Malik's possible early influence to interest South Africa's captain. There is little doubt that Cronjé also liked to play the devil's advocate with himself and test his knowledge of the game. Sure he was embarrassed at having to give a nodded admission to Malik's comment that 'John' had called with an offer during the Mandela Cup final.

Cronjé was not an island; he desperately needed to talk to someone who could share his burden of guilt. When he looked around him, who was there to talk to in the South African side? Perhaps he felt too embarrassed, or too ashamed. He did not want to drag his family through a mentally and emotionally traumatic experience. There was, it seems, no player he could trust in the side, or one with the mental strength for him to unload his shameful information. The management also had its problems, and ego-clashes had got in the way of his relationship with coach Bob Woolmer. The selection committee, at times, was too introspective, and caught up in uncertainty brought about by politicians forcing the adoption of transformation policies.

In this sense, just as Cronjé had failed the system by talking to the bookmakers and by taking money, the system (the United Cricket Board) failed Cronjé, if not the team. The UCB had already failed the team on two occasions: the first occurred in November 1996, with the game they did not want to play, the benefit match for Mohinder Amarnath. The UCB had agreed to an Indian board proposal to upgrade the game to full LOI status. It was a smart bit of manipulation by the Indian board as ticket sales were low. But it suggests something even more sinister – a possible collusion between some members of the Indian board and bookmakers. The initial offer to the South African team by bookmaker Makesh Kumar Gupta, later unmasked as 'John', was US$250 000. It was rejected by the team, after which the meeting broke up. Several senior players remained, and it was suggested that if the offer was pushed up by a further US$100 000, it might be worth considering. This was rejected out of hand by those present, including Pat Symcox, Daryll Cullinan, Derek Crookes and Andrew Hudson.

Woolmer was stunned by such nefarious behaviour. Interviewed in May 2000 shortly before the launch of his book, *Woolmer on Cricket*, the former South African coach related how he had relayed the Mumbai incident to Dr Ali Bacher in the UCB offices. Rumours of attempts to make a deal had surfaced in South African newspapers several days after the game. This is where the UCB failed a second time. Had they stepped in then and issued warnings to the Indian board, there is a chance the corruption might have been halted.

So then, what about the admission by the Australian Cricket Board in December 1998 that they had, after an in-house probe three and a half years before, fined Shane Warne and Mark Waugh for taking money in Colombo during the 1994 Australian tour? Later there were the bribes offered by the unctuous Pakistan captain Salim Malik in Karachi to bowl badly. Sir Clyde Walcott, then ICC president, had been informed of this by Australian officials. Hard evidence? Was this not enough?

For years the ICC panjandrums had quibbled about needing hard evidence rather than hearsay and unsubstantiated rumour. Not only had the alarm button been punched years before, but it was ignored as officialdom preferred to sweep the debris of lies, treachery and deliberate connivance under a thick carpet, labelled 'culpability'. Those whispers were becoming too loud for comfort.

Why neither Cronjé nor Symcox reported the initial offer made by 'John' in Cape Town to the UCB is another conundrum. Symcox, having told Cronjé the approach was a bad idea and to forget it, left it at that. He may have thought – or had hoped – that Cronjé would have alerted the UCB to the dangers of being approached by people with dishonest intentions. It emerged that Cronjé had not told the UCB. The Mumbai incident in November 1996 also suggested that he had already compromised himself, and that he had had earlier dealings with either Gupta or his crooked cronies.

In July 1999, Ray White, then president of the United Cricket Board and a former Cambridge blue and Gloucestershire county player, seemed to be looking into a crystal ball. In what was his last annual UCB report, he said that among other matters of interest, the UCB were seriously concerned about reports of bribery and match fixing. It was disturbing to hear these allegations. While the ICC may launch their own investigation into worldwide bribery and match-fixing charges, South Africa would look at ways in which to monitor the situation in the country through what he called a 'prevention is better than cure' plan. White told delegates that the board would set up their own commission, whose members would investigate any charges 'of bribery and betting on games involving our own players'.

Although it was not a new phenomenon, White felt the board's concern was that the game had to retain its image of fair play and decency. While 'no South African player had yet been involved in any claims of match fixing', the idea was that the commission would act swiftly to investigate any accusations if and when they arose.

'I know that our players have a good record and have not ruined their reputations by being involved in such practices,' White had told the meeting. 'It is a matter of serious concern to all of us, and is one of the reasons why the UCB have decided to form a commission to keep an eye on matters.'

What happened to the commission? Indeed, before the government set up the King Commission, had the UCB established a formal internal body to audit players' thoughts, if any, on claims of malpractice within the sport? Four years earlier, bothered by growing rumours, the Australians had done just that during the quadrangular centenary series in New Zealand in February 1995. This is when the guilt of Mark Waugh and Shane Warne was uncovered, and their links with the infamous New Delhi fixer MK Gupta. They were fined by the ACB, yet as it later transpired the board's action was not recorded.

Had a monitoring system been in place (as suggested by White) after the 1999 World Cup, Cronjé's dishonesty may have been exposed before the New Delhi police were alerted by outside elements (most likely bookmakers) stung by heavy financial losses and using wiretaps to unmask him. Or was it only when the truth emerged and Cronjégate began to splash its ugly way into headlines that the UCB awoke to a scandal that not only rocked their foundations, but also the international profile of the game? The ICC could not say that they had *not* been warned. For 18 years or more, rumour, innuendo and accusation had filtered through the corridors; whispering in dusty, dark corners and furtive glances over shoulders were all part of the story. A tacit conspiracy of silence existed to shroud the crooked dealings.

Did Cronjé smile behind the grille of his batting helmet when he heard of White's comment: 'I know that our players have a good record and have not ruined their reputations by being involved in such [match-fixing] practices.'?

During the ICC Champions Trophy in Colombo in 2002, former Sri Lanka captain Arjuna Ranatunga blamed the boards in the various South Asian countries for soft-peddling on known match malpractices. Ranatunga, once investigated on similar corruption allegations along with Aravinda de Silva, said personal experience had taught him that players could be 'controlled by the right people'.

Surprisingly, though, he did not attack Australia over the Mark Waugh and Shane Warne episode where the Australian Cricket Board had also shown weakness. Instead of honesty, they bluff others that such integrity runs deep among their administrators. Perhaps this is because the Australians have largely had responsible and disciplined team management, which were dictated by the actions of the team's manager.

'A manager wanting to preserve his job and get on more tours, doesn't want to antagonise the players. This, you would find, leaves gaps in administration and team discipline,' Ranatunga commented. 'One team in a Sharjah tournament partied until after two with their coach and went on to lose the match by a substantial margin. That sort of manager is not much good to a side. I know I would not tolerate it.'

Ranatunga, described by Warne as the player who 'most often got up my nose', blamed the boards of India, Pakistan and Sri Lanka for his concerns about further infiltration by bookies. He blamed the boards for throwing out a proposal by the ICC anti-corruption unit (ACU) to have all players and administrators involved in gambling, or known gaming or casino establishments, barred from the game. In this case the boards, and not the players, were to blame for the lack of any effort to clean up the game. It was so bad that there were some board members who did not want to challenge the status quo, whether in their own country or of another board, in case they were found out.

As it was, the ACU had been gagged by Cronjé's lawyer, Les Sackstein, from revealing anything the disgraced captain may have said during their meetings. Does this mean there was more incriminating evidence, and that another list of names existed involving high-profile players and board members in other countries, as well as in South Africa? A request for a meeting with the ACU during the ICC Champions Trophy in Colombo was turned down. It was not that they did not want to talk, it was the legal agreement that shut them up. The impression was given – from a couple of dropped hints – that Cronjé's suggestions to the ACU to prevent a recurrence had been acted upon.

Ranatunga stated the obvious when he said it was widely known that Cronjé was not the only player involved. He became the scapegoat, apparently set up by illegal bookies in India and Pakistan when he failed to deliver. There are a number of former players and administrators in South Africa, India, Sri Lanka, Pakistan, England and the West Indies who are still walking free and grinning into the mirror each morning. Players are still involved in crooked dealings, but as Sir Clyde Walcott said, 'Where is the hard evidence?'

Other areas where there would have been an uncomfortable nibbling on the subconscious would have been Cronjé's own discipline in such matters. He was strongly motivated to become a captain admired for his record, and to this end he worked hard to have a better limited-overs record than the West Indian Clive Lloyd. His psyche was at times disturbed by events on and off the field. When he wanted help and guidance, he often had to rely on his own intuition. He could hardly be blamed by the bookies when India dropped catches, missed run-outs or misfielded. It happened in Kochi at the start of the limited-overs series in 2000, and again in Nagpur when Lance Klusener served up a spicy innings of 75 off only 58 balls as South Africa scored 320. Giving out information on which bowlers will open the attack, or who will be first, second and third changes, is a manipulation of the game and a way to influence the result. This, it appears, is the form of malpractice that the Pakistanis, the Indians under Mohammad Azharuddin and Cronjé used when making some of their deals with bookmakers. Or, information could be given on when a declaration would be made in a Test.

Their fingers badly singed by the Nagpur result, the bookmakers did not make contact with Cronjé again for a couple of games, when they moved in with a vengeance. Their concern was whether his information was reliable. There was further contact in Sharjah, when the wheel of fortune began to turn against the white knight. While he assumed he had escaped without detection from the series in India, his dealings with the bookie Marlon Aronstam, on the fourth day of the fifth Test at SuperSport Centurion,[1] had already been uncovered. Within hours of their meeting it was common knowledge that a 'deal had been made'. Several UCB members, including Dr Bacher and Richard Harrison (then president of the Northerns Cricket Union) were aware that Cronjé had met with a known bookie and that discussions had taken place. This was about half an hour after Cronjé had finished discussions with a financial advisor.

Aronstam, whom Cronjé did not know, phoned him and explained that he had a plan which would be financially beneficial to them both. Aronstam suggested that the South African captain 'make a game of it' to get a result, with a large sum of money involved. Cronjé agreed to meet the bookmaker, who worked with National Sporting Index Limited, a company that provided a range of betting services.

When the two met at a hotel lounge after Cronjé's dinner, Aronstam quickly outlined how he felt a result could be achieved through a 'manipulation of the rules'. It would mean setting England a target and getting Nasser Hussain to agree. The way Aronstam saw it, manufacturing a result depended on the two captains declaring and forfeiting an innings, 'as allowed by the rules'. Financial rewards were promised in return, including thousands of rands to a charity nominated by Cronjé. There was also the promise of a leather jacket for Cronjé's wife Bertha.

It was all slick and smooth talking. Cronjé went along with it, though, knowing what had already been discussed earlier in the day at the ground. What is surprising is why, after six years in the position of Test captain, he pretended to know nothing of the declaration law when Aronstam presented his proposal.

Was this a matter of testing his own knowledge of the game and its laws? Or was it case of who was trying to con who? Just where Aronstam came up with the bright idea of 'rule' changes is another matter. As it is, Law 14 (declarations) covers all forms of declaration and the mechanics involved for rolling of the pitch (Law 10). The ICC's Code of Conduct and standard playing conditions do not refer to any amendments to Law 14. It showed Aronstam's lack of knowledge when referring to the teams having to go to the middle to face a ball. This was removed in 1966 when the Law was amended by the copyright holders, MCC; apart from one minor word alteration to note one, the law has not changed since then. The first mention of declaration of an innings in the Laws was in 1889 (some 145 years after the first accepted code, the London Laws, of 1744 was published), when it was incorporated into Law 15. At no stage has the home authority or the tour playing conditions amended the law on declarations. It would be interesting to hear how the bookmaker came by such an assumption and explain it away, unless Cronjé misled him. Hussain would have also studied Law 14 and agreed to the forfeiture conditions, but to suggest they are new is a misrepresentation of fact.

(Note: Law 14 in the 2000 code of The Laws of Cricket now has three notes: 1 – time of declaration, 2 – forfeiture of an innings, 3 – notifications. The ICC code of conduct and playing conditions do not again refer to Law 14).[2]

If, as two creditable and confirmed witnesses state, some UCB board members knew of Cronjé's meeting with Aronstam, why was he not asked a few pertinent questions? Cronjé and Dr Bacher, however, had barely been on nodding terms since the row over transformation policy 12 months earlier.

Cronjé tried to explain his downfall to the King Commission as being the work of Satan, an easy explanation for those gullible enough to believe this line of thinking. Others saw it differently. Just how Cronjé and Cronjégate had affected people's lives has created its own polemic. Nor is it a matter of whether Herschelle Gibbs was led astray by a so-called mentor when he agreed to follow Cronjé's instructions that should count when reviewing the leniency of the UCB's disciplinary committee's sentences.

A former Cape Town journalist expressed her repugnance in her weekly column headlined, 'So much success, so little honour'. It is easy to understand the frustration and deep disappointment felt by Phylicia Oppelt at how two of her nation also became culpable. Her words of how 'Gibbs let himself, his team and his country down' carry the hurt and distress felt by others. No one can blame her for pointing out how, at 26, Gibbs had enjoyed 'so many good things'; he was also 'held up as a shining example of merit succeeding over affirmative action' and 'he had spoken of his awareness that he carried on his shoulders more than just the hopes of cricket lovers'.

Ms Oppelt looked on Gibbs as having 'personified black sporting achievement'. Which is a fair comment, as both represent the same community. 'As a nation we carry our sporting heroes in our hearts because each time they play they carry our hopes and our pride.' She said – and many viewed the issue similarly, 'We become angry and disappointed when our sportsmen and sportswomen accept glory without honour ...'

Cronjé asked Gibbs and Henry Williams to forgive him for coercing them into his schemes and promising them money. Why Cronjé wanted more money when with endorsements and sponsorships he cleared more than one million rand a year was not asked. That he tried to hand back the US$140 000, and subsequently gave it to a good cause, does not absolve him from blame. Like the gravy train enjoyed by certain South African selectors before the upheavals of April and May 2002, he did not want the good times to end. If he had, he would have reacted differently in Cape Town on 10 January 1995, and alerted the United Cricket Board to Salim Malik's dishonesty.

Cricket has been played for longer than 260 years to a set of laws; in the last 100 years many have been adjusted in order to meet the challenges of a changing game in a changing world. To suggest, as some have erroneously claimed, that apart from the front foot no-ball law, no physical changes have taken place in the laws since 1963, displays serious ignorance. The preamble to the Code of 2000 (written long before Cronjégate) draws attention to the spirit of the game. The role of the captain, defined as it was before the Code of 2000, is to see that the game is played 'within the spirit of the game as well as within the laws'.

For those brought up in the traditions of the game, its ethos rejects anyone who would cheat or bring it into disrepute. Malik, Azharuddin, Ajay Jadeja, Cronjé and others like them have deliberately abused their roles and the cardinals laws of cricket.

* * *

Minutes before first light on 1 June 2002, the Outeniqua Mountain range and its craggy outcrop were shrouded in mist. Driving winds pushed gusts of rain hard against the bleak rocky slopes, as the menacing forces of nature played their treacherous tricks around the wakening Eastern Cape town of George. Aboard a prop-driven aircraft flying into this hazardous weather mix on that Saturday morning were two experienced pilots, British-born 50-year-old Ian Noakes and 65-year-old Willie Meyer. Their passenger was Hansie Cronjé. Through a set of circumstances he had hitched a ride on their twin-engined freighter. Cronjé knew both men, having met them when they regularly flew cargo to the coastal town. He had arranged this ride to get home to his wife, Bertha. After a wildcat Highveld hailstorm the previous afternoon had led to the cancellation of commercial flights from Johannesburg, the chance of flying home in the freighter plane was the quickest option available.

Although the two pilots had flown in and out often enough, conditions in George that morning were highly dangerous for flying and landing aircraft. Two local witnesses, one a farmer, the other a doctor, knew from their own experience as pilots that the cargo plane was in trouble. For one thing, there is no radar at the airport, and pilots need to know the area well enough through instrument reading to pinpoint positions. As the cargo plane did not have the equipment to warn them of dangers such as high mountains in their line of flight, it was always going to be a serious risk landing in such unpredictable weather.

Bruce Jackson later indicated that the cargo plane was too near the mountain and too low, much lower than during normal flights. The roar of the engines as they were throttled back a second time was audible. It was as if the pilots, having seen the craggy face of the mountain, realised that they were too close, and attempted to veer off and try again. They may have been caught, perhaps, by a forceful downdraft; it is hard to imagine what hazards there were.

Dr John Zaaijman thought that the aircraft was off the central line and too close to the town for his liking. Like Jackson, Dr Zaaijman heard the roar of the engines a second time. Shortly afterwards, Cronjé and the pilots must have stared with mesmerised horror at the mountain, and death. Hours later, when the wreck was located, members of the rescue team were winched down from the helicopter to the wreck. The sight was one of numbing finality. The rescuers were unaware of who was on the cargo plane; the shock of discovering that it was Hansie Cronjé was immense. It had been so unexpected.

Within an hour of the confirmation of Cronjé's death, both BBC World News and SkyNews TV International led their mid-afternoon and late afternoon bulletins with the news. Later in the day SkyNews interviewed former England captain and all-rounder Ian Botham, who came down very hard on the dishonour Cronjé had brought upon the sport, his wife, his family and himself. It is easy to understand, in times of such distress, the family's anguish, and how they would point at those who wrote so accusingly two years before and who now sang a different song at the time of his death.

Initially the family did not want Dr Bacher, the executive director of the 2003 World Cup, or anyone connected with the UCB to attend the funeral at Grey College. In stepped his widow, Bertha, who had supported him during the traumatic months, bringing a touch of dignity and sensibility to the proceedings. She had forgiven where some had not. There were, however, others who were willing to sanctify his image. An untimely death such as Cronjé's has a habit of creating an emotional climate, especially as he was reshaping his life at the time.

There was talk and reports of plans to reinstate him. How this was going to be achieved, even after the 2003 World Cup, is a good question. The life ban had been upheld in the Pretoria High Court, and how the ICC would have handled Cronjé's re-involvement is hard to imagine, as emerged from conversations with ICC officials in Colombo in September 2002.

What has bothered one veteran writer is how those both within and outside cricket around the globe perceived the need of so many South Africans to try to balance their opinion. Perhaps in their own thoughts it was a desire for their own salvation. Little wonder that Frans, Hansie's brother, asked cynically, 'Why now?'

The Indian TV producer and freelance journalist Trishna Bose expressed her own thoughts and the thoughts of thousands of others when she wrote: 'There are sinners: most of us are. Some more, some less, but sinners all the same. He was a man I admired; he was a man I quickly learned to look at in disgust. But Hansie Cronjé did not deserve to die. At 32, he had just begun to live again.'

There are those, of course, who have in time forgiven him. Realistically, however, it is Cronjégate, the scandal, that will be remembered many years from now, and not his captaincy. It is a pity that the many who were involved and not named have escaped the publicity Cronjé had to endure. He knew what would happen if he were caught. His underhand dealings let down not only a nation but also the many thousands who, across the world, had admired him as a player and a man.

15

GARY KIRSTEN
The Banker

By Trevor Chesterfield

Something was not quite right. Two names were missing from the squad, and the question, 'why?' lay heavily in the room atop the Centenary Stand at the Wanderers on the afternoon of 1 November 1993. The room was full of media and interested parties, and Peter Pollock had just announced the side to visit India for the Hero Cup, followed by an Australian tour. He finished his explanation about the fitness concerns over Brett Schultz, and looked around the room at several raised hands. Media liaison officer Chris Day nodded in the direction of Peter Robinson of *The Star*.

'I take it in case of injury there is a list of supplementary players?' Robinson asked.

'Yes … we do have a list of players who will be considered.'

'Are you going to release those names?' Robinson asked.

'Not at this stage,' Pollock said. 'Perhaps later, if there is a need, but it is not our policy to release the names of players on the supplementary list. It's a matter of who is injured and getting the right replacement.'

'Would any of the three dropped from the team touring Sri Lanka be on that list?' This was from Pieter Oosthuizen, of the Afrikaans daily *Beeld*.

'No,' Pollock confirmed.

'Apart from Schultz, is there anyone else who is injured who was considered?' asked Ray Williams, of the *South African Press Association*.

Pollock shook his head.

There was a question from the *Pretoria News* writer about the two Kirsten brothers, and whether Gary's omission meant that the selectors were not interested in form.

Pollock smiled and again shook his head. 'Gary Kirsten's form shows just how much depth we do have at present and the selectors are well aware of the needs of the team,' he said.

Earlier that day Gary Kirsten had led Western Province to an impressive victory by seven wickets in their Castle Currie Cup match against Northern Transvaal at Centurion Park. The younger Kirsten brother had scored 192 in Province's first innings, and hours before the team was announced had also taken six wickets for

68 runs off 33 overs. It had been quite an all-round performance for someone looked upon essentially as a left-hand batsman who either opened the innings or, as he had at the Centurion venue, batted at three.

The second phase of the tough summer programme was the tour of Australia: a series of three Tests and a couple of state matches, along with the WSC triangular competition involving trans-Tasman Sea rivals New Zealand and the Aussies. The tour, including the Hero Cup event in India, was a lengthy 90 days, with the subcontinent the toughest section in respect of travel and accommodation. As Pollock pointed out, with 16 or 17 one-day internationals, three Tests and two state games, the emphasis was on players with top limited-overs skills as well as those who could be serious contenders for the Test side. It surprised a lot of people that the selectors did not feel Gary Kirsten fitted into this dual-purpose mould.

Axed from the squad that had been in Sri Lanka were Jimmy Cook, Clive Eksteen and reserve wicketkeeper Steve Palframan. Selection changes were all-rounders Dave Callaghan from Eastern Province and David Rundle from Western Province, with Errol Stewart of Natal as cover for Dave Richardson. The buzz of anticipation among the media had been overtaken by confusion. The exclusion of brothers Peter and Gary Kirsten made no sense, and meant that there was an imbalance in the batting. How could the selectors ignore the form of two such talented players? The keen disappointment could also be gauged in the Western Province dressing room. Rundle's selection was thought to be a plus; Callaghan's gutsy recovery from cancer was rewarded.

Pollock, facing a highly curious media, went to some lengths to diplomatically smooth over the rougher edges of team selection policy. Schultz, he explained, would join the touring party in Australia; this was expected at about the time of the match against Queensland, and would establish his fitness for the first Test at the MCG a week later. And there was nothing sinister to be read in the omission of Eksteen. He had not fulfilled his role in Sri Lanka, and it gave the selectors a chance to look at other options. Cook was no longer part of their plans, and Palframan …? There might be another chance for him at a later stage. This indicated that the young Border recruit did not fit in, or was thought to be unsuited to the team's strategy. There were still more than two years before the next World Cup on the subcontinent.

But the parochial Johannesburg media was grumbling. Well, hell, no Jimmy Cook! Others wondered whether Peter Kirsten had committed some sin. And no temporary replacement for Schultz? It could be argued that Allan Donald, Fanie de Villiers, Craig Matthews and Brian McMillan carried enough firepower until the Tests. Matthews had already sat out a domestic day/night match in order not to further aggravate a niggling thigh muscle injury. It also seemed as if Meyrick Pringle was no longer part of the selectors' plans. It was later learnt that Gary

Kirsten was on the supplementary list, and McMillan's injury at the Melbourne Cricket Ground gave Pollock's panel a chance to correct their earlier blunder.

One of the tragedies of sport is that there are those who love to knock down the image of the hero. One of the worst examples occurred in the late 1980s, when the British tabloid press ambushed the career of the England captain Mike Gatting by planting a barmaid in his bedroom during a Test in Nottingham. Then there is the other extreme. In early October 1994, as South Africa, with new coach Bob Woolmer, prepared for their first trip to Pakistan, the *Sun* concluded in a report that Kepler Wessels's South African side, after an investigation, was found to be the most boring sports team to visit England that year; the tabloid complained it could find nothing (salacious off-the-field gossip) to write about. It also described Gary Kirsten as one of the team's more 'boring players to watch: on and off the field'. In a way it is a backhanded compliment to the Kirsten family's pride and stoicism. It is also typical of the British tabloid industry.

Off the field, Kirsten prefers the quiet life to the bustle, and while he does not enjoy the attention of some of the more charismatic players such as Jonty Rhodes or Allan Donald, he is, like his brother Peter, decidedly upfront as a player. Any checklist of his career shows how he had been a captain of note at school – leading the 1985 SA Schools side is one example. One of his trademarks is a typical Kirsten trait: an ability to concentrate for hours. His Millennium Test innings of 275 against England at Kingsmead is the second longest in a Test. Another trademark is his habit of wearing the South African flag as a bandanna under his helmet when he bats, a similar sort of talisman as Steve Waugh's dilapidated baggy green cap.

In Durban, as the countdown to the Millennium was ticked off, few could blame former England opener, Geoff Boycott, for taking what seemed to be an apoplectic bite out of the lip of the porcelain teacup he had been holding. But there was the left-handed Kirsten, knocking off one of his near records. Kirsten became the man to occupy the crease longer than any other South African in a Test: all in a good cause, though. In time it should also be recognised as the last great Test innings of the twentieth century.

Few could have managed to successfully stage a production of such well structured, if timeless, batting; for sheer theatre, Kirsten and Mark Boucher lived up to their reputations. Their record-breaking rescue act was stylish with many gilt-edged touches, each batsman leaving their personal calling card: the stoic calm of Kirsten rubbing shoulders with the developing flair of Boucher's often intrepid strokeplay. If Kirsten's technique includes a certain stubbornness, it is because, having acknowledged that his side is in trouble, his teammates need his protection. In this case surrender is far from cheap. On a scale of one to 10, the Kingsmead innings would rank about nine, while the Old Trafford performance against England in 1998 would come in at around seven. In either case, both matches were drawn. Yet anyone scoring 275 in an innings deserves some recognition: Mr Durability or Mr Reliability were two apt sobriquets that spelt out the word 'endurance'. There is also the term 'The Banker', which again points to his reliability. Kirsten can be that sort of batsman: heroic yet focused, digging deep into energy reserves and finally emerging from the trenches sharing more than a couple of records. Mr Modesty is another nickname for a reluctant hero, always a touch shy to talk about his achievements.

Two double hundreds in a Test career falls to few: Kirsten's is only the second from South Africa (the other being Dudley Nourse, and his were 15 years apart). Granted there were fewer Tests then, and fewer tours as well; South Africa were isolated even then, only playing England, Australia and New Zealand. Now they have the happy luxury of also playing the other nine Test nations. Nourse's two double centuries were divided between Australia in 1935/36 and England in 1951. Kirsten's were 18 months apart, both against England: at Old Trafford in Manchester and at Kingsmead, Durban.

Boycott managed only one double century in his Test career, and was dropped against India at Leeds in 1967 because it was scored too slowly. Now Kirsten has the second longest innings on record of 878 minutes, and had earned the selectors' approval for the next Test, at Newlands in Cape Town. What's more, Kirsten shared the man of the match award with Andy Caddick; and this in the face of threats of being dropped. At Manchester his occupation time took up 10 hours and 50 minutes: at Kingsmead it was 14 hours and 38 minutes. It takes time and patience to build an epic innings to remember. It also explains why a lengthy innings is often called a mind game.

When it was over, an embarrassed Hansie Cronjé faced a bank of tape recorders, microphones and cameramen, and, near-blinded by TV lights, admitted how his puny innings of one off seven balls faced in six minutes was 'a touch embarrassing'. Well, he got that one right. Then he talked briefly about Kirsten's effort.

'We had about a five-minute chat before we went out to bat the second time because it was new territory for us, the follow on, and we needed to show guts and determination, and I think Gary's effort summed it up ... it was a fantastic effort by him, a truly great effort ...'

Cronjé was asked about Boucher's duty as nightwatchman. A century in Harare, now a second one in the same role – a record at Test level for the Border man.

'We take pride in having those who can bat all the way down the order and Mark enjoys the challenges of going up [the order] a little and spending time at the crease. Down at nine he does not always get that opportunity ...'

What about the follow on, Hansie? Was it a shock? It was, after all, the first one ...

'No. Not really a shock. You start preparing yourself ... At 24 for three, 57 for four and suddenly 84 for eight ... you think about batting again ...

'I thought it was a great challenge for us to come through second time around,' he admitted. 'I have inherited a team of great characters and people with determination ... You don't have to say too much to them. We knew we could bat through; it was just a case of doing it.

'Also, England having been in the field for two days obviously contributed a little [to our recovery]. They were very tired.'

Okay, Hansie, what about Gary's record bid?

'Well, when you look around the world today at the number of top opening bowlers there are and the way they [opening batsmen] have to fight against the new ball, sometimes with green surfaces up front, they deserve every run and every record they can get.

'When you consider that we had to follow on and then somebody can come up with that record ... well, it is just awesome. He had to get through three new balls; some very fine spells of bowling from Andy Caddick and not easy with Phil Tufnell bowling out of the rough.

'So I thought, overall, an unbelievable effort by Gary. Not only will it lift the team but it will give everyone a lot of confidence.'

Tough, though, about failing to set the record for the highest Test innings by a South African batsman? From the dressing room Kirsten's teammates did not get a good view of the delivery from Mark Butcher that helped him achieve a Test career best bowling figure. The England opening batsman and occasional light relief net bowler on a hot afternoon, tossed up a flighted leg-stump half volley, which the left-hander Kirsten at first tried to glide past Alec Stewart. But he lost his balance, missed, and the rest is history. What a delivery to bowl. It was supposed to give Kirsten the record.

Butcher's look of incredulity showed how bemused he was by the incident, as was Kirsten. Cullinan, who barely nine months before had broken Graeme Pollock's 29-year-old record, was probably more shocked than anyone. Disappointed, too, from Cronjé's comments on the incident.

'In one sense you are very disappointed for Gary, because he had worked so hard for it ... and deserved it. On the other hand, you feel pleased there are now two players in the side who share that record.

'I know that they are great mates ... And – yes, Daryll was disappointed for Gary that he had not broken the record.'

When Kirsten, at last, talked about that gentle Butcher delivery, there was a sheepish grin.

'If I had the chance again I'd probably play the same shot. It is nice to do well and exciting to break records. It is nice to have done that ... but so what? There is more to it than that,' was Kirsten's casual comment.

'It was nice to be involved in the recovery and hopefully the spirit can carry us through to the next game,' he said.

How different it was at the start of the second innings, when he agreed that there had been 'some pressure'. Yet he felt more relaxed when going out to bat a second time, knowing all along it was 'make or break for me' before he reached what was his 10th Test century – then a record for a South African batsman.

'I had not been getting any big runs so … yes, I had been feeling the pressure. I felt fairly comfortable and I decided to play and see what happened and then my confidence started growing … I started moving well … ducking well (from the bouncers) …'

And that was Kirsten's part of the after-match show: short on words, big on runs.

What was not revealed, though, is that at one stage Cronjé considered a declaration at tea on the last day to give the bowlers a light middle net. A message was sent out to Kirsten with the 12th man, Dale Benkenstein, giving him the option of breaking Cullinan's record, which he accepted. He batted through three century partnerships: 152 with Jacques Kallis for the crucial second wicket, which did so much to reduce the possibility of defeat by an innings; the 192 with Boucher for the record fifth wicket, equally important in that it took Cronjé's side past the psychological point of defeat; and the 101 runs with Lance Klusener for the sixth wicket.

There are other examples of Kirsten's batting expertise aiding South Africa's cause – some fancy limited-overs innings as well – but a more recent, noteworthy effort was at Newlands in the Test series against the Australians in 2001/02. It was a Test innings that gave the team some belief in themselves, and started to turn the game into the competitive arena again. While Kirsten may utter the odd curse about the Australian 'Nelson' of 87 – and which turned out to be the score he put together in the second innings at Newlands in the second Test – it meant South Africa were able raise their flag above its accustomed half-mast position of the previous four months. Winning three sessions in a row was the sort of slap-on-the-back stuff in which selectors and team management are quite happy to indulge themselves. A couple of beefy partnerships, some batting backbone, a 300-plus total on the board and a lead of 164 with six sessions remaining: why, there was even talk of a possible draw. Some went so far as to get totally misty eyed – and wonder if a victory was not possible. Hey … one step at a time guys! This is not the time to overdo it! Managing to bat through a day against Australia was the sort of trench warfare stuff of which epic tales and heroes are made, and that young men can one day relate to their grandchildren.

If New Zealand were able to declare in both innings against Australia at Perth earlier in the summer, why couldn't South Africa? The big difference was that the Kiwis were able to give the Aussies as good as they got throughout the series. The South Africans had rarely been able to achieve much more than play the Last Post.

What stabilised South Africa's second innings at Newlands against Australia in 2001/02 was the partnership of 99 between Kirsten and Graeme Smith, with Smith at last realising where his off-stump was and how to work the ball around. His feet started moving in the right direction as well, and along with this came the right handwork. It was a tough grind, and how much Smith owed Kirsten and Jacques Kallis, who partly played midwives to his half-century on his Test debut, can only be assumed. South Africa's batting also showed that the amoebic efforts in the bullring two weeks before, in the first Test of the return leg against Australia, were only the hiccups. The problem is that they had lasted for so long. Now the old fight and spirit was back.

It was suggested that only a couple of sessions were needed to turn the team around. Well, Kirsten did what he could to give the top order substance and confidence. He took on the Australians, and when Glenn McGrath was moved out of the attack at an early stage, the feeling was that there had been a small victory. After that it was a matter of rubbing shoulders with success. Kallis also won a battle or two as he followed Kirsten's 87 with an innings of 73; there was some handsome strokeplay as well. One hook sped off the bat between the two men posted backward of square and at fine leg, and Brett Lee must have wondered whether he had lost his turbo-booster. There were several other classic strokes as the mind games continued.

If McGrath lost the sub-plot battle with Kirsten, the leg-spinner Shane Warne, in his 100th Test, looked a touch hot and bothered and under pressure when he trooped off at the end of the day's play. A return of three for 100 off 42 overs for Warne represents a success story for the South African batsmen.

As a rule, national selectors have a clear idea of what they want when major policy decisions are made. While the choice of a new vice-captain is one area where the thoughts of the captain, coach and even a couple of senior players are sought before the announcement is made, there is still a need for consensus among the selectors. When Craig Matthews was injured in Kenya in late September 1996, Gary Kirsten was not everyone's ideal choice as a replacement. There were other options: Jonty Rhodes had captained South African Universities ahead of Cronjé. Nicky Boje and Derek Crookes had been South Africa Schools captains, and they were at the Kenya Centenary series. No one needed reminding of the younger Kirsten's credentials. They were good enough ... and he had taken over as Western Province's captain from Matthews when national demands meant he had little time for domestic playing chores.

For Peter Pollock it was simple enough: give the vice-captaincy to the man with experience. Of course it was not that straightforward – it rarely is when looking for the right replacement. Some had to be convinced.

When Pollock, a Test fast bowler and journalist turned pastor, took over as convener of the national selection panel after the 1992 West Indies tour, he talked about the need for what he saw as 'long-term visions and targets'. They could form committees and appoint chairmen, hold discussions and workshops to seek common denominators designed to meet the challenges of the game at international level, yet without success all the talks and ideas proved nothing. Pollock senior liked to think his ideas through and had his own vision of what was needed to develop a winning team. He had the ideal captain in Kepler Wessels as a driving force, as both he and Wessels had strong ambitions to have the best team in the world.

Kirsten was a solid performer as a batsman and a fielder; perhaps not as good as his brother Peter, whose outstanding leadership and fielding skills were ideal props for his batting talents. But Gary was as good a fielder as any in the side. At the time, October 1996, it made sense to make him vice-captain for the tour of India, which began with the Titan Cup.

Captaincy itself is far from easy. It also does not sit well with those who, although lacking in imagination, have leadership skills that are quickly forgotten. Critical analysts do this when they chew over a day's events and see no positive management points. Gary had a lot of good ideas and players to help him, yet there were times during the Test against Pakistan when he did not inspire confidence. It is also a matter of how hungry someone is to do the job. The selectors felt Gary was ideal; the critics were largely unconvinced.

With Cronjé, there was always the feeling that he knew what he wanted. His fielding abilities and tactical know-how had turned him into a motivational force, which others understood and identified as an all-important competitive edge. It gave his leadership style its charismatic image. Jackie McGlew and Jack Cheetham had set a high price on such fielding levels during the 1952/53 tour in Australia, and moulded it around a side of willing competitors, some of whom were more skilled than others. Instead of a heavy series defeat, South Africa levelled 2–2 against a team then regarded as the best in the world.

As Cronjé admitted after the Newlands Test in the Millennium series, it is not just about attitude. It is the importance placed on such skills and the support given to the bowlers; inspirational factors can switch a game's course. South Africa's bowling before lunch on the first day had disappointed, and Rhodes had dropped an easy chance offered by Atherton. A first-wicket century partnership followed. By the end of the day, tighter and hostile bowling – especially from Donald – quality catching and aggressive ground fielding had seen England lose their early initiative.

Australians Steve Waugh and Ricky Ponting are class fielding acts, and have had much to do with Australia's domination at Test and limited-overs levels. They know what is needed to keep them motivated to be the best side at both forms of the game. England's captain, Nasser Hussain, is another who sets a high standard on skills such as fielding, and has pulled off some entertaining catches.

When Kirsten had to take over from an injured Cronjé for the first Test against Pakistan in the 1997/98 series, the bizarre events around the match required a lot of diplomacy. Most of it took place behind the scenes. The game was delayed by 24 hours because of an alleged mugging involving some members of the Pakistan team. The public were more interested in what had happened at the exotic nightspots the Blue Orchid and Club 69 than in who won the toss or whether Azhar Mahmood would score a century. For days police searched for information amid the debris of what was little more than false trails.

There was a certain déjà vu about the events. Pakistan's visit to Johannesburg in 1994/95 had also been dipped in controversy. Led by the notorious Salim Malik, now banned for life, Waqar Younis, who took over the captaincy in 2001, was accused of dancing until 3 am at a nightspot in Sandton. It drew an angry denial from the manager, Intikhab Alam, a former Pakistan captain and leg-spinner, but it did not escape anyone's attention of just how badly Pakistan had played in that one-off Test. Rumours of match fixing hung heavily over the Wanderers media centre and were confirmed by Qamar Ahmed, the London-based Pakistan journalist.

Before the 1994/95 Test, Intikhab said Waqar was being sent home with a back injury and it would 'create a serious problem as it is going to disrupt the balance of our bowling attack'. The tourists on that occasion trained at Centurion Park, away from media attention, which was focused on the South Africans' practice at the Wanderers. The reason was the need to train without the distraction of TV cameras. It had nothing to do with the long suggested schism in the camp, the lack of discipline exhibited by some senior players or that a bookie had 'bought into the results'.

Kirsten later admitted that he had enjoyed captaining the side for a change, but that he had reservations. A different focus was required, and while it did not help his own game (he scored three and 20 not out) in what became a rain-affected draw, the side could have also done without the controversy in which the Test was played and 'all that extra fuss'. Kirsten gave the impression then that he would by far prefer his supporting role as one of the troops, and would quietly drop out as vice-captain when the opportunity presented itself.

SHAUN POLLOCK   16
Family Business

By Trevor Chesterfield

It was a far from comforting sight – certainly not the sort Shaun Pollock wanted to give his teammates on the balcony. He had lost the toss to Sri Lanka's Sanath Jayasuriya, and the pragmatism shown minutes earlier had slipped into a moment of grim reality and a shrug of the South African captain's broad shoulders. That blank stare of acceptance said it all: it was a steamy tropical morning in the coastal town of Galle, and the prospect of spending at least four or five sessions (or eight to 10 hours) in the field in blistering heat and humidity held no appeal at all. For one thing, the venue in Galle is closer to the equator than any other Test ground in the world, and the impenetrable granite face of the famed 450-year-old Galle Fort leaves a forbidding mental imprint. Toiling away hour after hour during the next two days in the quest for success would be hard enough – or about as effective as aiming a water pistol at a raging bush fire. It needed no added reminder of how appeals for an lbw decision or a possible catch behind would echo ineffectually off the daunting and inscrutable backdrop.

Towering and imposing ramparts, usually festooned by thousands of non-paying spectators, add splashes of colour to what is one of South Asia's great Test venue sights, and nudges Gwalior in India, with its fresco-like cliffs, and Cape Town with its Table Mountain, for majesty. The spectators are mostly full of good humour with their 'cheap seats' view of the game, as are the fascinating lace makers in their sarongs as they go about selling their wares. If the haggling is good-natured, the tourists can end up with a few quality bargains. Below, the sea from the bay, embraced by the Indian Ocean, slaps against the craggy grey rocks; at full tide, spray plumes high against the stonework, some worn smooth by centuries of sea water thrashing against the man-made fortress.

Pollock had visited Sri Lanka years before with the South African under24 side, where he was unofficial vice-captain to Dale Benkenstein. He learnt from the 1995 visit that it is far from easy to play in Sri Lanka. Heat, humidity, frustration caused by umpires' decisions, any variety of insects, and hard, rough outfields make conditions tough and demanding. On that tour, however, the South African youngsters did not play in the ancient port of Galle. Designated a United Nations living heritage site, and with links to Roman galleys and Marco Polo, the area has a rare place in history. First settled around 500 BC, Galle had for centuries been the country's gateway and had, like Sri Lanka before independence, known three masters. The Dutch, the colonisers of the Cape, rebuilt the then 100-year-old fort guarding the harbour on the rocky Pointe De Galle in 1658. This was after they had forced out the Portuguese at the end of what had been a long and bloody siege. Then came the British, who forced out the Dutch, and wherever the Raj and the sahibs went, so did cricket. Remnants of Portuguese, Dutch and British architecture and influence can still be seen within the fort and around the thriving town. The fortifications owe their striking presence to the work carried out by British engineers, who reinforced the battlements.

For Shaun, however, losing the toss to Jayasuriya on 20 July 2000 was, in a sense, a rude welcome to the real world of cricket. Just how rough it was going to be, he and the side were to discover when they looked into the mirror four nights later and two metaphorical black eyes stared back. It was not a pretty sight. It was the first Test of a three-match series, and surprisingly for Shaun his first taste of captaincy at first-class level. As it was, the side had already played a limited-overs match at Galle a couple of weeks earlier in the triangular series, before going on to lose the final to their hosts in Colombo. Only a Test, spread as it is over five days, is as demanding an exercise as any sports occupation can be; it requires a lot of mental strength, and for Shaun it was a genuine *learning* exercise.

'We all learnt a lot from this match. It certainly was an experience for us to play in such conditions,' he said when it was over. There was the impression then that 'defeat' was not a word in his vocabulary.

The portents leading to the start of the series did not sit too well in Shaun's mind. The side was missing Allan Donald, involved in a season in England, and whose absence, to an extent, had weakened the bowling attack. Whether the bowling was to a degree experimental, as national selection convener Rushdi Magiet attempted to explain at the end of the tour, is another matter. Little wonder the coach, Graham Ford, raised an eyebrow when asked to comment on Magiet's opinion as the team assembled for the indoor series in Australia. Both Ford and Pollock preferred to keep their own counsel on the tricky subject of bowling strategies for what turned out to be a 1–1 drawn Test series.

Also missing was Herschelle Gibbs, whose shock revelations before the King Commission, probing Cronjégate, forced his late withdrawal. His erstwhile captain, Hansie Cronjé, had already been fired by the United Cricket Board over match-fixing allegations. It meant finding a makeshift opener, and Neil McKenzie was tossed in at the deep end, making his Test debut in the unaccustomed role of opening batsman.

That first morning in Galle saw a display of such forceful and uninhibited strokeplay from the Sri Lanka captain, Jayasuriya, that Pollock was in need of an army of fieldsmen patrolling the boundary to halt the flood of runs. The left-hander's limited-overs style tactics flayed what was possibly the most ineffective bowling performance by a South African Test side since readmittance in April 1992. Jayasuriya did give an early chance, but was missed by a diving Jonty Rhodes when he was on 21 and the Sri Lanka total 36. After that South Africa did not sniff another chance until well after lunch, when the score was 191. Okay, so Rhodes misses the odd big catch. For Jayasuriya, however, there was far more to this frenetic display than a mere case of rapprochement for hurt pride or lamenting something that had happened almost two and a half years before.

All it needed was a dip into the pages of the last Test result between Sri Lanka and South Africa to explain the importance of wiping out memories of the Centurion Park humiliation. It was fresh enough for the Sri Lanka captain to extract some form of retribution of his own. He had the right theatre in which to do it as well, as he attempted to join an elite band of batsmen to score a Test century before lunch on the opening day of a Test. Whether he or his partner Marvan Atapattu were aware of the significance of this particular chapter in the Test records is open to speculation. Jayasuriya was stranded only four runs short of joining Australians Sir Donald Bradman, the immortal Victor Trumper and Charlie Macartney, and more recently Pakistan's Majid Khan, as one of those who have achieved such rare run-making luxury. The Matara Mauler enjoyed himself hugely at South Africa's expense. It is a pity that Atapattu hogged the strike in the last over before lunch, thus robbing the game of being above the ordinary at Test level.

For Paul Adams, Galle was a rough reintroduction to the Test arena. Along with six of the seven bowlers used in the Sri Lanka innings, there was much leather chasing over four-and-a-half sessions.

It is an exaggeration to refer to the pitch conditions at Galle as similar to those of a moonscape, yet the South African batsmen might have been excused had they donned lunar kit when facing Muttiah Muralitharan's bowling. On day four – and what became the last day – the unorthodox off-spinner wrapped up the innings with seven wickets, comfortably won the man of the match award, and had by then returned his second best Test bowling figures with seven wickets for 84 runs, and a match haul of 13 wickets. Daryll Cullinan was, in South Africa's first innings, the architect of one of the great centuries of modern times, as he did what he could to save the tourists from total humiliation. Rhodes also did his bit in the second innings, but Muralitharan's dominance at Galle continued.

It is a myth, though, that Sri Lanka and Muralitharan always dominate Tests in Galle, and that batting first is the talisman to guarantee victory. Why, barely a month before, Sri Lanka had lost to Pakistan by a massive innings and 163 runs, Abdul Razzaq dismembering the Sri Lankan first-innings lower order with a hat-trick, and Muralitharan's tactics were nullified by solid quality Pakistan batting. It produced the rare occurrence of four centuries in a Test innings as the visitors mounted a total of 600 for eight wickets, declared.

As a matter of interest, the Sri Lankan batting techniques, so often refined at home, were undone seven months later by the tricky bounce of the South African pitches and the fire and pace of bowlers such as Mfuneko Ngam, Pollock and Makhaya Ntini. Ford described his first sight of Ngam as 'about the most exciting thing I have seen in years' as he walked towards the Eastern Province nets at Port Elizabeth late one afternoon. He watched as the lanky, loping fast bowler fired off a succession of deliveries that would have had any local traffic cop writing out a succession of speeding tickets: he was regularly clocked at 150 km/h and Ford marvelled at the whipcord action and infectious smile. Here was a genuinely fast South African bowler of the future and one who, if he remained fit, would in time rival a Curtly Ambrose, Joel Garner or even Michael Holding.

Fifteen months after the Galle rout, Pollock's forlorn features were again shaped by similar cataclysmic events. This time it was at Adelaide Oval, a venue that has not been kind to South Africa since the country's return to Test combat against the Aussies in 1993/94. Pollock had again lost the toss, and two catches went down early on: Gary Kirsten in the slips and Claude Henderson in the gully. The glazed grimace peering from under the brim of his white floppy hat failed to mask the frustration of a game plan gone wrong. Just how important it is to hold on to catches emerged the next day. Australia might have been bundled out for around 300, and the pressure on the South African side, still trying to establish its identity, would have been a lot less.

Up steps Damien Martyn and his undefeated innings of 124, which did much to change the course of the series. When he had last faced the South African bowlers it was in Sydney in 1994, where he batted as if he were part of an uprooted trunk from a petrified forest, as Fanie de Villiers bowled the tourists to an incredible victory by seven runs. Sydney, the Emerald City, was ringed by devastating bush fires; Martyn scored six and did not play in another Test for seven years. On day two at Adelaide he was given a standing ovation. It was his elegance and style that anchored the Australian total to a more stable 439: South Africa's fielding lapses did not help the mood of the side, either.

At the end of the Adelaide Oval Test, which resulted in South Africa's second heaviest defeat since the end of isolation, by a margin of 246 runs, Shaun stepped up to the PA and offered a near repeat of what he had said in Galle: 'Yes ... it was an average performance and we need to improve.' For those reading his face for signs of what he was thinking, the triple role of fast bowler, captain and lower-order batsman in a series to decide who is number one, might have been too much for the young man. It is tough being a Test captain.

During a conversation with Bob Woolmer on the 1995 Sri Lanka tour, it was suggested that Shaun Pollock's pedigree would be enough to see him open the bowling for South Africa in the future. Woolmer hinted that it could happen sooner rather than later. It was in fact four months later, when England made their first tour to South Africa since the end of isolation. Woolmer's role as coach of the under24 side on the 1995 tour of the island was to monitor the progress of players such as Pollock. This was of course before the general South African media took a deeper interest in Pollock's career and suddenly knew everything there was to know. What they did not see was how his organised, professional approach to the game had battled the pressures and frustrations on the island. Poor umpiring decisions saw him reduced to a state of mind where he went through the motions: denied lbw appeals and catches behind from fairly thick nicks, and in intolerable heat and humidity, was a little too much to handle. No one minded genuine errors, but shades of incompetence, which you also find elsewhere in the world, were something else. Remaining positive is far from easy, and at times his body language was noticeably of someone fed up with life.

Yet, when the day's play was over and his composure returned, there were also touches of humour, which showed how he had managed to cast off the unrewarding day's labours. At the end of the first day of the under24 four-day international at P Saravanamuttu, the oldest Test venue in Sri Lanka, he presented a 'Polly Parrot' award to Jacques Kallis for the remark 'petrol for my radiator'. With temperatures in the mid-30s and humidity in the upper 80s, it is the sort of throwaway line that lightens the pressures of a hard session. Presenting such awards created the camaraderie that bonds a team and displays the character of the players in the squad. (Woolmer had bought the toy parrot during the side's stopover in Singapore with the idea of giving it out at the end of a day's play for what was voted the most amusing comment.)

Kallis and Shaun Pollock were two of the players who surfaced from that tour as future Test players. The others were Adam Bacher and Gerry Liebenberg, along with Lance Klusener, Nicky Boje and Roger Telemachus. What is interesting is how four members of the under19 South African team in England that same year went on to provide the senior squad with future key members: Mark Boucher, Neil McKenzie, Boeta Dippenaar and Makhaya Ntini were part of that side, with Ashwell Prince on the fringes; and Boucher did not even keep wicket but opened the batting. David Terbrugge was forced to return home early because of injury. Herschelle Gibbs, who had blown hot and cold after the 1992 West Indies trip with the South African youth side, was unable to convince the selectors of his batting talents. In 1995 Woolmer admitted that Gibbs's form was too erratic to convince the selectors he was likely to be a long-term prospect. When his inclusion did come along it was, to be honest, an affirmative action decision, and it did not make Gibbs at all happy.

Had the selection thinking on the under19 squad gone according to plan in April 1995, Messrs Jackie McGlew, Khaya Majola and Anton Ferreira would have found a place for Paul Adams; instead the schoolmasters would hear none of it. These days, of course, they sing a different tune.

Once when he talked about his playing preferences, Shaun Pollock fancied the bit about being an all-rounder: a touch of the cavalier, perhaps, but with reason. Winning a Test or a limited-overs international with a six, or taking a wicket with a spectacular yorker, has the flair people remember long after the headlines fade. Yet being in the front line of a battle as a Test bowler did have a special appeal. His father, Peter Pollock, had been a good bowler, so there was nothing wrong in treading the same worn paths at South Africa's Test grounds. With more opportunities he would hopefully get a few more wickets. Batting? Well, that too, lower in the order, perhaps, but it would be nice to get among the runs. There was the famous Pollock grin, too.

Families with sporting traditions who throw up quality and talent are far from rare. It is not all to do with genes, either. If what a noted British physician, Sir Anthony Humphrey, said early last century is true, bloodline and genes are just part of the equation – it goes beyond physical talent. It is the person within that counts; inherent ciphers such as temperament, emotional make-up and mental approach. There are many other facets, but Humphrey, in his study, drew on several case histories he had studied. One of them was the famed Grace family, with Martha Grace, the matriarch, seen as having the stronger personality.

There were three brothers who played for England, although the incorrigible and irascible Dr WG (William Gilbert) Grace has his special niche in history. His brothers were EM (Edward Mills) and GF (George Frederick); the three played in the same Test against Australia at Kennington Oval in 1880, with WG and EM opening the batting, and WG responsible for a century on his Test debut.

Shaun's father, Peter, had made his mark for South Africa in the 1960s, and later became national selection panel convener. There was Shaun's uncle, Graeme Pollock, a famed left-hand batsman of elegance and style, who was accorded the South African 'player of the century' award at a packed Newlands on the first day of the Millennium Test series against England. There have, in recent years, been several profiles of RGP (better known as Jeeps because of his initials). As Peter once commented, he was quite happy that someone in the family was given recognition.

What is interesting is how Shaun came through as a second-generation Test player. It is not always the second generation that makes the most impact, but the third, as in the case of Australia's Chappell brothers, Ian, Greg and Trevor. The

Chappells' grandfather was the likeable Victor Richardson, who captained the Australians on their all-conquering 1935/36 tour of South Africa. The three Chappell siblings are the sons of Jeanne, the only daughter of Richardson, who was Australia's 20th Test captain. There is the famed father and son duo, the batsmen Arthur and Dudley Nourse, and New Zealand has produced the Hadlee dynasty, with father Walter and sons Sir Richard and Dayle as the Test caps. India, Pakistan and England have produced any number of father and son combinations to grace their honours boards. Pakistan's Hanif Mohammad, who for more than 40 years held the world's highest first-class score of 499, and his son Shoaib Mohammad are a notable combination; as are India's Nawab of Pataudi, the younger better known as Mansur Ali Khan, who still played in Tests despite losing an eye in a car accident.

Shaun's grandfather, newspaper editor 'Mac' Pollock, had been a provincial wicketkeeper for Free State, and with his father and uncle regarded as world-class heroes in their day, the genes and the chip off the old granite block had to emerge somewhere. So, when watching Shaun as a budding under13 star at the 1986 Perm Week tournament at the vast LC de Villiers Stadium complex, there was already a hint that here was a quality player. A picture appeared in the *Pretoria News* the day after the tournament started in early December, in which Shaun and his cousin, Anthony (Graeme's son), were seen in a mock arm-wrestling battle. Already apparent were the bright eyes, infectious grin and occasional thoughtful frown. There was no mistaking his class either, although plotting his career from those early years through to Nuffield (now Coca-Cola) Week was an exercise that interested only those eager enough to see emerging talent. In 1991 the two cousins went on to play in the Nuffield Week side – as their fathers had years earlier – in a team captained by Nicky Boje.

For a time it seemed that both would play for the new South Africa. Anthony's star soon waned; whether it was from the weight of comparison, expectations or selection and coaching muddling, the schoolboy promise was left unfulfilled. Stylish and brilliant, Anthony did the best he could. Yet the callous and careless whispers of 'He's not as good as his dad,' could be heard around club and provincial pavilions. Shaun did not need to worry. He was always going to come through. Lean, lanky and aggressive, he has his father's spirit and dominance. What was also obvious from earlier days, before the 1995 Sri Lanka tour, is that he is his own person.

From the SA Schools side he was included in the Natal Colts team, which went to Centurion and Pretoria for the national Colts tournament in January 1992. There was selection, too, at the end of the 1991/92 season, when he played in the Natal B side against Castle Bowl champions Western Province B, and he took four wickets. His eventual inclusion in the Natal senior side the following summer was not without criticism. Natal coach Graham Ford, who had overseen Pollock's career and recognised his obvious talent, did his bit to ease his inclusion in the Natal senior ranks. At the time there were accusations flying around that the choice of Shaun ahead of Rowan Varner was because 'he was Peter Pollock's son'. The dropped player was the more experienced, but long-term prediction proved more accurate. He translated these into results as well. At the time, though, Shaun was either first of second change and usually batted at 11.

From 1992/93 Natal were blessed in having as their senior professional the West Indian Malcolm Marshall, one of the great bowlers of the modern era, and Ford. The pair struck up a close working relationship and a strong passion for what they wanted to achieve. Between them they turned around the careers of several highly talented young players. It was not just about Shaun Pollock. Working with Ford and alongside Marshall was what a budding Test player needed. What a combination: the coach and the senior pro; both the technique and the skills factors.

Names such as Dale Benkenstein, Derek Crookes and Shaun Pollock were all part of the new era; still to come was Lance Klusener. Benkenstein, captain of the 1992 SA Youth side to the West Indies, also captained the South African under24 side in Sri Lanka and the South African A side to the same country three years later.

Shaun knew from his father's and uncle's experiences what it took to reach the top: hours of practice and training. He is totally unlike his Uncle Graeme who, such was his command, rarely bothered about having a net unless he felt it was needed. It was not so much a matter of arrogance as a mark of the man's batting genius. Shaun's future as a South African fast bowler thrived on the hard work a bowler is expected to put into his game to get where he wants. Firstly, the Ford–Marshall set of standards encouraged him to learn the fast bowler's tricks of the trade. His father, Peter, agreed. He always saw the bowler rather than the batsman in his son. Secondly, the apprenticeship each budding Test or LOI player needs to experience is part of the character-building process. A fast bowler needs to work for his rewards – often the hard way. Losing a toenail becomes part of the summer ritual; nursing feet when they ache from a day's pounding on the hard turf is also part of the fast bowler's workload.

Later, watching the bowler cunningly undo a batsman's technique with cleverly disguised changes of pace and outswing is part of immersing the mind in the enjoyment of the battle in the middle. As Fanie de Villiers, Marshall and, in his later years, Allan Donald showed, fast bowling is not only about raw pace; the subtlety of swing contributes just as much exhilaration to the combat.

From the moment he was appointed vice-captain and then captain, Shaun began to understand that there was far more about team policy, game plans, selection philosophy and political machinations than the public would ever know or understand.

From the time Shaun had taken over leadership in Durban during those traumatic April days, through to Galle and Adelaide, South Africa's cricket image had been wrung out by the media and the malpractice revelations of the probe initiated by the King Commission into Cronjégate. There had been many disappointments, but mostly it was a list of impressive successes: a drawn series against Sri Lanka on the island, followed by victory at home against New Zealand and then Sri Lanka, and the unparalleled double triumph in the West Indies; there was also the easy conquest of Zimbabwe and India. Before this, there had been the matter of beating Australia in a home limited-overs challenge series while the first salvoes in the disturbing Cronjégate saga were fired, and drawing the return leg in a unique indoor setting in Melbourne. This was followed by winning yet another minor limited-overs event in Singapore. Heady stuff all right.

Yet there were signs that all was not well. Niggling at the subconscious was the disturbing thought, which first became visible in Sri Lanka in August 2000, that the team's success was not being well received in certain South African quarters. If this was so, what then was the problem? Were the selectors, headed by Rushdi Magiet, bothered by the so-called 'lack of demographics' of the sides they were selecting? Was this why there was ambivalence about the selectors' approach to certain deserving players? Those close to the team could see that not all the players were enjoying their cricket as much as they should. Lines of communication were clogged and there were obvious areas of concern; much of this came from mixed signals issued by the selection panel.[1] Nor was Magiet talking to the captain or the coach; he partly blamed them for blocking the advancement of players of colour.

By the time the side assembled for the Centurion Test against India on 22 November 2001, the political turmoil around the game and the selection of the squad for Australia had partly distracted the players' attention. Insiders confirmed that the team's confidence, slowly eroded by innuendo over selection policies, was low. Morale was further jolted when it became known that the Sports Ministry, acting for the government, was siding with the Indian cricket boss Jagmohan Dalmiya's demands to have match referee Mike Denness removed, and the UCB were backed into a corner. This was after the ongoing row between Dalmiya and the International Cricket Council president Malcolm Gray had upset the steaming curry pot in far-off Kolkata. The stand-off it created and the egos of the two main protagonists threatened to split the ICC – Asia against the rest. Adding further confusion 48 hours before the game were certain media organisations. There was the national broadcaster, the South African Broadcasting Corporation, who, instead of asking the opinion of Gerald de Kock, their senior sports commentator, sought the views and opinions of reporters who were not at the match in Port Elizabeth. Generally, though, the English media, headed by the Tony O'Reilly Independent Group of newspapers, were to an extent fumbling and stumbling in the dark. What was presented on some early afternoon SABC news wrap programme was unsound speculation. There was also a noticeable anti-South Asian bias that did not sit well with the Indian media covering the tour.

If the South African captain and coach were hoping that the Test would go ahead in a calm, coherent atmosphere, and that the team could focus on the five days ahead, they were soon noticing how behind-the-scenes political manoeuvring had left the players decidedly vulnerable. It was as if their own government was back-stabbing them. It will be hotly denied of course; politicians are good at that sort of thing. It is so easy to shift the blame. Rational thinking was not being applied either. It was no longer a case of allowing the players to get on with the game while the little men in grey suits, attempting to run the sport from their portentous political portals, sat at a table and thrashed out their differences. Just who was playing 'Nero' and fiddling while 'Rome' was burning has long been open to question.

More worrying, however, was how the squabble had been moved outside the sports arena. It had not been forgotten that India were the main supporters of South Africa's readmission to the ICC in 1991, and as such they were the first official tourists under the UCB banner for what was the 'Friendship Tour' of 1992/93. There was also a special relationship between the two boards. What was most important to the politicians was how India had supported the African National Congress during the years it was banned. Yet no one can blame the players for thinking that their government was now in agreement with the country that had wanted to prosecute Cronjé, Boje, Gibbs, Pieter Strydom and Henry Williams on the April 2000 bookmaking malpractice charges. While Shaun, Ford and the team manager, Goolam Raja, gave the impression that what they were dealing with was an everyday occurrence, the mood in the dressing room was, understandably, unsettled.

Shortly before going into their team meeting, the players had learnt from a report on a commercial radio station that Denness had been replaced by Denis Lindsay, and that Denness had gone off to Sun City to relax. While this was taking place, India and the ICC argued about the status of the game. There were at times certain bizarre touches, similar to those last experienced during the Gatting rebel tour: it was eerie and disconcerting.

Gerald Majola, the UCB's chief executive, was contacted, and conferred with the team's manager Goolam Raja about what had taken place. The message was plain enough: the UCB could not afford the cancellation of the Test match; a loss of income from sponsorship and TV rights had to be considered. In a media release, he chose his words well when he said, 'Although the crisis has not been of our making, we have received reports of protests at South African embassies in India. Our country has been caught up in this issue. The South African government, through Sports Minister Balfour, has instructed the UCBSA to take whatever action is necessary to ensure that the Test goes ahead.' Balfour also sent off a clumsily worded letter to the ICC regarding the status of the match.

Whether or nor he agreed with what was taking place, Majola had little option but to cooperate. An organised sports event, however, should not have to be played in such a confusing environment as the one that existed on Thursday, 22 November 2001. But with the government waving the big stick, Balfour was quite happy to beat the drum; it is what his bosses expected him to do. It was typical though – crass ministerial interference without consulting those caught in the eye of this rhetorical storm and brinkmanship tactics thousands of kilometres away in other countries.

From the time Rushdi Magiet took over from Peter Pollock as convener of the national selection panel in the latter half of 1999, uncertainty and cluttered thinking cloaked some of the selection policy. Where there had once been tight parameters and a philosophy understood by most, the psyche had changed to a less tangible focus. Cronjé had been put on probation, a decision that did not sit at all well with the players, as there was no clear reasoning behind it – unless Magiet, or the selectors, was trying to make a policy statement. Was it an oblique attempt to break the captain's power base? Or was it about Cronjé's reaction when he was told that more players of colour would be selected for the remainder of the Test series against the West Indies?

When appointed as convener after Peter Pollock's retirement, Magiet told the author that the 'standards have already been established by the previous panel and we'll follow those guidelines'. There was no hint of the plan to 'cut Cronjé down to size'. Magiet denied any such intention, stating that it had more to do with his batting form, and that lending 'such a sinister slant to the Cronjé story' was unfair criticism of the selectors.

Certainly the heated verbal entanglements that arose in Sydney over the team selection on 1 January 2002 could have been avoided had the signals been a lot clearer from the start of the season. Yet, as insecurity stalked the corridors of the team's hotel in Sydney, the fireworks about to be set off can be blamed on the indecision shown by Magiet's panel. It was a policy of procrastination and befuddled most logical processes. Instead of selecting Justin Ontong in September for the Zimbabwe tour as a way of easing him into the Test side, Magiet and the other five selectors had him in the limited-overs squad. Yet, with a group of experienced players around him, Ontong would have fitted nicely into the South African scenario of bringing on 'players of colour' at Test level. Magiet and Co. had missed a golden transformation opportunity.

At Sydney, it was three of the six selectors – Magiet, Graeme Pollock and Haroon Lorgat – who created the impasse that forced the UCB president, Percy Sonn, to intervene on a matter of principle: Ontong was in, and his roommate Jacques Rudolph was unceremoniously jerked out. When the side to tour Australia was announced at SuperSport Centurion after the disputed Test,[2] Magiet, supported by Graeme Pollock and Morris Garda, made the point that Ontong was travelling Down Under as a lower-order batsman and bowler, while Jacques Rudolph would be considered as a top-order batsman. It was an interesting twist to the story, as when the batting line-up at Centurion was announced, Rudolph was South Africa's new number three and Kallis was, in the absence of Daryll Cullinan, moved to four in the middle order. Somewhere between the first tour game in Perth and the Test at Adelaide, the policy changed. It was rumoured that Shaun Pollock felt uncomfortable with what he had seen in the nets of the 20-year-old left-hander's footwork. They would rather have the experience of Boeta Dippenaar than trust a rookie as the new No. 3.

In late 2001, Rudolph rattled off enough runs at first-class level to present a weighty case for selection to the South African squad in the Test series against India and the tour of Australia, but the selectors were only grudgingly aware of his presence. The last time any of the six selectors gave attention to his cultured talent was on a chilly, early October day in Laudium, Centurion, where Magiet watched South Africa A beat Kenya in a limited-overs game to honour the opening of a new international-class venue. In blustery conditions, the gifted 20-year-old left-hander scored another century, not so much to make a point as to nudge their taste buds for more of the same. Rudolph had just returned from Bloemfontein where he had fashioned his fourth first-class three-figure score with such dominance that it gagged those critics who claimed he was 'nothing more than a limited-overs player'. Yet it still needed the two SuperSport Series centuries that followed to convince the multitude. In seven SuperSport Series innings over five weeks he structured, along with 501 runs and an average of 83.50, a reputation of consistency and handsome strokeplay.

Privately, the former South African under19 vice-captain at the 2000 Youth World Cup in Sri Lanka is mature, quiet and seemingly undemonstrative. For those who know him well, the façade hides Rudolph's passion for the game, which is so reminiscent of Kepler Wessels. From the time he was a nine-year-old captaining a *Pretoria News* Development XI at a St Alban's College open day for under11s in 1991, Rudolph displayed a rare talent for one so young. When in the damp English summer of 2002 Rudolph broke a 51-year-old record for the most consecutive centuries scored in a Lancashire League season, the national selectors, restructured under Omar Henry, showed little genuine interest. Sure, he was included in a list of 30-plus players from which the final 2003 World Cup squad might be chosen, but questions would have been asked had he not been invited. The great West Indian batsman Everton Weekes had held the record Rudolph broke for his club Lowerhouse. In 1951 Weekes had scored three centuries in succession for Bacup.

What Sonn objected to in Sydney was the switch in the selectors' thinking, and he threw the team list back at them. (Ironically, Graeme Pollock had done the same once in the SACU-run rebel era, when he suggested that the selectors have a rethink). No one can blame Sonn's stance on the issue: Ontong had been selected to play as a lower-order batsman, and here was Rudolph being used in the same position. So, what had changed? And it was not as if it was a transformation issue; there were two non-white selectors and they did not ask the opinion of either the captain or the coach, or his assistant, Corrie van Zyl. This being the case, the level of the selection panel's ineptness had sunk lower than Boeta Dippenaar's batting average thus far in the series.

Clive Rice, a former selector and someone who is always prepared to argue fairly, face a challenge or get his point across, was among those who objected to how Magiet and his now discredited colleagues had handled the issue. Once told by the apartheid regime of John Vorster to 'pack your bags and go and live elsewhere' because of his 'racist remarks' after the cancellation of the 1971/72 South African tour of Australia, the Ontong episode found Rice again labelled as a racist. Sports Minister Ngconde Balfour, not one to enjoy criticism, and his spokesman, Graham Abrahams, also told Rice to 'pack your bags'. A change of government, a change of policy, but offer fair criticism and out comes the rhetoric. Rudolph's Test career had twice been hijacked: first by the Dalmiya/ICC stand-off during the time of the Indian Test, and then the Sydney fiasco. Having wrecked his confidence, they then sent the 20-year-old home, wondering if what he wanted to achieve was worth it. Hopefully the selection panel under Henry's guidance will be a little wiser. They have the opportunity to rebuild the side with young talent for the tour of England.

As the UCB and Sports Ministry wallahs moved into damage-control mode, mending fences and rebuilding bridges of trust, not all were satisfied. Support for Shaun and Ford streamed in as buckets of bouquets were heaped on their efforts. A concession was even made that former Test players had a role to play. Brickbats, though, were still flying.

A tour that has gone sour usually receives negative publicity, and the public at home was seriously fed up with the acrid aftermath of the Centurion Test fiasco. It seems an interesting point, but for South Africa the tour media breakdown in Australia appeared to have its roots embedded in the imbroglio that emerged from the Port Elizabeth Test and ICC match referee's Mike Denness's decision to fine six Indian players. That 12-day verbal fracas had been more about ego and posturing than the rights and wrongs of the case and how team morale had taken a knock. Now it was a new issue and one that the selectors had bungled. The public and players were tired of the wrangling. What about getting on with the game?

* * *

Debris from the fallout of the Hansie Cronjé scandal lay as thick as the piles of early autumn leaves at Kingsmead on that early April morning in 2000. Durban on a balmy day at that time of the year is in contrast to winter's fingers that are already stretching across the Highveld or sweeping in from the Atlantic in Cape Town. However, events that occurred over a matter of 12 hours were chilling enough, and had pushed the team's vice-captain, Shaun Pollock, often looked upon as one of the 'Aw gee …' guys of the South African team, to the captaincy. Sure, he had led the highly successful South Africans to the 1998 Commonwealth Games gold medal in Malaysia. But captain of South Africa against Australia? That was a far different story. Was there no one else? Well, there was a guy called Dale Benkenstein, the KwaZulu-Natal captain and leader of a highly successful South African A side to Sri Lanka in 1998. Somehow, though, Magiet and his panel did not want Benkenstein, along with other players who deserved a chance to play in the senior ranks.

Australians by nature are tough, competitive and uncompromising. One look at Steve Waugh's features explains what chunk of Sydney granite he had been hewn from to lead the World Cup champions. As Cronjé's deeds were exposed, a bruised South Africa needed a leader of character and strength to try to wipe the nightmare of their disgraced former captain from their minds. The selectors and a badly shaken United Cricket Board were sure Pollock could do the job in the Standard Bank Challenge series; it was going to be a tough call.

For those who know Shaun there was no mistaking the understated comment. His presentation can be as fine-tuned as his bowling; his tiredness, however, was evident. It was the morning after the defeat at Newlands against the Australians, in a series of three matches that was the definitive ending to the Millennium summer. Brown and yellowing leaves were scattered confetti-like across the hotel driveway as the wind reminded all that winter was closing in. For many it had been a long season: most players had been on the road since mid-August. Many had rested after the World Cup in late June; others continued, preferring the charm and bustle of Sri Lanka and writing about yet another limited-overs tournament and Test series to the quiet of easing into the new programme at home.

When asked whether the season had been too long, a thoughtful Pollock said, 'All I can say is that I have ten overs left to bowl tomorrow and it is all over. I can't wait.'

The small matter of being newly promoted to captain in the wake of the Cronjé scandal did not come into the equation: it seemed to be an accepted fact, part of the job. Bowling, though, seemed to be the extra burden. He may not have meant it that way and did not seek to justify his feelings for what was a tired body, weary legs and bruised feet, yet there was empathy for his thoughts. What he left unsaid was how South Africa needed to find new mental strength to overcome the psychological bruising of the five-wicket defeat at Newlands the night before, after the high of the emotionally draining victory at Kingsmead. To beat the World Cup champions and win the series at the Wanderers the next day required the players to once more lift themselves. It is far easier to think about it than to go out and do it.

Ken Jennings, a sports psychologist and one-time provincial opening batsman, and part of the South Africans' new management structure, had mentioned how tough the second game in a three-match series can be. You do not have to look too far for the reasons either; they are in a chapter of a book he wrote in 1993 on sports psychology, *Mind in Sport*. Chapter 2, 'The Psychology of Winning', outlines the extra pressure of expectations: public, media and self-motivation, worked into a 10-point plan for improved self-image. 'Think positive and you will always succeed. All these recipes and formulae make rational sense, yet often fall down at the time when most needed,' he wrote, expanding on the theory of what it means to be a winner and how to get to that point. Its antithesis is trying to deal with the blanket suffocation of defeat. The South African public had been given a good demonstration of this on their television screens.

Barely had they wallowed in the disappointment of the 3–2 limited-overs defeat in India, when they were confronted by another image on the eve of the Sharjah tournament. For days there were continual repeats of the Allan Donald run-out incident in the World Cup semi-final in Birmingham, which flooded TV screens. Support for South Africa, Cronjé and the team, however, remained high as the first rematch loomed. Only it was no longer 'Hansie and the Boys'. Going into the Standard Bank series, South Africa and Australia remained locked at 18 wins apiece in limited-overs internationals since the resumption of the southern hemisphere showdown during the 1992 World Cup at Sydney. The one result that rankled among South African supporters had been the tied match at Edgbaston.

As a result of that game, Malcolm Speed, the energetic and intuitive chief executive officer of the Australian Cricket Board, approached his South African counterpart, Dr Ali Bacher, about a rematch. As the two countries were not scheduled to meet until December and January 2001/02, the idea was to host a series of games in South Africa and Australia. Three games in five days is a punishing schedule at the end of an already hard season. Also, it was in the middle of other scheduled sporting events, namely Super 12 rugby and PSL soccer. Such was the demand, however, that the three South African venues were sold out hours after the booking agent opened ticket sales.

A little more than 30 hours before the start of the series, Pollock and other members of the squad were in shock as the first major sports scandal of the twenty-first century descended on the training camp at Kingsmead. The UCB had moved swiftly – Cronjé had been fired and his contract cancelled.

In a sense Gary Kirsten put it all in perspective with some technically skilled batting. Shrugging off the trauma of the previous 72 hours, he helped South Africa forget the recriminations of the scandal for one evening to concentrate their energies on beating Australia at Kingsmead. It led to a remarkable four-wicket victory against the World Cup champions; just what a packed Kingsmead, and perhaps South Africa, needed in a time of internal crisis. With a large local Asian contingent on hand, showing their loyalties by draping the South African flag over their collective shoulders, they came to cheer as their heroes took a 1–0 lead in the series. For others who saw the match, the result ranked alongside the historic World Cup victory in Sydney in 1992.

South Africa did what they had to do at Kingsmead to show the nation what character they have. To win against such high odds and predictions, producing a shoulder-to-shoulder effort, surprised most hostile critics. Kirsten dug deep in a hallmark display of grit synonymous with the Kirsten name during a well-paced innings of 97. In reality it did nothing to avenge the defeat at Leeds or the tie in Edgbaston during the World Cup in England months before; instead the side collectively focused on the game and pulled together in a display of true character. When victory came it was with 12 balls to spare. What made it possible was the way in which Kirsten and Jacques Kallis went about laying the foundations with a well-paced partnership of 129 for the third wicket. They mixed style and flair in a solid, if watchful, exhibition. The pitch was much faster than expected, and the bounce was as irregular as a trampoline's, which perhaps demanded the confident approach adopted by the Western Province duo.

Chasing a target of 241 for victory, it was Jonty Rhodes who ended the game with an audacious pull for four off a short delivery from Brett Lee. It was as entertaining, if flamboyant, as any innings Rhodes had played in recent months. But Kirsten's effort was full of purpose and merit. It was as if he wanted to win this match so much he was not prepared to sacrifice his wicket. That he missed his century was a matter of misjudgement, failing to pick a slower delivery from Brett Lee, which he edged into his stumps. Interestingly, Kallis was moved to four to stabilise the middle order. It indicated South Africa's willingness to experiment with the top five positions for the series, with Neil McKenzie, whose strokeplay showed he was on top of his game, at three. His six off McGrath was as authoritative as any of the South Africans' innings.

There was a time during the Australian innings at Kingsmead when, at 120 for seven at the start of the 27th over, Pollock might have pondered the prospect of South Africa chasing a total of around 150. Then, as can happen in a sport where technique plays such a major role, the game plan ran adrift as Australia's ability to dig deep into their batting reserves became the turning point of their efforts. A couple of quality partnerships helped put a brave smile on Steve Waugh's enigmatic features. As Damien Martyn eased his way along with an entertaining array of eloquent strokes, he realised that there was no need to shield his lesser-skilled partners.

The other two Cobbers in the middle, Damien Fleming and Brett Lee, had to dig in and provide a few runs themselves, as well as help build partnerships to prop up the innings. Not at all easy when the top and middle has surrendered some of the initiative with sloppy judgement.

Australia's coach, John Buchanan, tall and angular – and with a rug adorning his upper lip which may not have rivalled the one adorning Merv Hughes, but certainly made a statement – agreed frankly that it would be better to forget Kingsmead. Australia had bowled badly, their fielding lacked sharpness and the batting was anything but what you would expect from the World Cup champions.

In his deep Queensland drawl, Buchanan suggested that they would bounce back strongly in the last two games – levelling the series in the shadow of Table Mountain, and going on to the Wanderers confident of success. He implied that you need more than three or four days to find your legs in the limited-overs international arena, where the margin for error, as always, is narrow.

It seemed hard to improve on the valorous effort made from the trenches of Kingsmead, where South Africa bowled, batted and fielded as well as they had ever done. But that was what was required to beat the Australians at Newlands. Ford acknowledged that for him the Kingsmead victory was 'up there among the top two or three' since taking over from Bob Woolmer the previous August. South Africa had done what they had to at Kingsmead: they showed the nation what character they have to win against predictions.

Apart from growing into the role of captain, Pollock showed some adept tactical knowledge. He handled his bowling tactics well, leading from the front. The ploy of using Mornantau Hayward and Makhaya Ntini during the middle stages worked even better than he expected. If there were anything new to expect at Newlands, it would have been the employment of a sixth bowler. To be fair, in terms of experience Hayward and Ntini had between them played as many games as Brett Lee, Australia's least experienced player, with 15 matches. Yet at Kingsmead there was near unblemished commitment from both 23-year-olds from the Eastern Cape. They were not awed, and it showed: they were tough and competitive, which meant Pollock did not have to call on a sixth bowler.

If a packed Friday night crowd at Newlands had expected the senior troops to repeat the emotion-charged Kingsmead success, they should have remembered 1992. Kirsten and Rhodes, the old heads among the young who would lend experience, expertise and guidance in a crucial game at a time when these qualities were needed after the traumatic bruising of the previous six days, failed abysmally. From the high of Sydney to the low of Eden Park in Auckland during South Africa's first World Cup – the reality of defeat returned.

Australia had brought a squad of 13 for the series, and for Newlands made the remedial changes expected. The view that Brett Lee, after his disastrous night at Kingsmead, needed a break, did not fit in with the Australians' plans. Back for his second spell, he displayed why he was retained. In a hostile burst he ended with three for 32. He was one of the reasons why Australia bounced off the ropes and stubbed out South Africa's hopes of establishing a 2–0 lead.

It had been a long season and the signs of fatigue started to show in both camps. South Africa were feeling the brunt of a tougher end-of-season programme: India, then Sharjah. They knew it was going to be a lot harder to pull anything extra out of their physical and mental reserves. Perhaps the victory by six wickets, 48 hours earlier, had drained the side. For Australia, victory by five wickets at Newlands was as comprehensive as their Kingsmead defeat. Such was Steve Waugh's confidence, he allowed the others to get a 'middle net' and declined to strap on his pads as South Africa produced an embarrassing powder-puff effort. Now the need arose to reproduce the mental and physical self-possession of Kingsmead before the season was allowed to slip quietly into the autumn mist.

The Kangaroo hop, skip and jump on a breezy evening at Newlands had been unmistakable. The winning runs were on the board before their innings reached the halfway mark, with Andrew Symonds and Ian Harvey steering the visitors home. Whichever way it was viewed, it would have needed a particularly special, finely tuned bowling and fielding performance from South Africa if they had hoped to win in Cape Town, after scrambling to an ungainly 144 for eight after Steve Waugh won the toss and invited his hosts to have first use of the pitch. Batting second at Newlands is usually a problem. South Africa's bowling, however, was about as ragged as Australia's had been at Kingsmead. Martyn was in the sort of expansive batting mood that earned him the man of the match award, and the Wizards of Oz were rarely under pressure in chasing the meagre target.

Kallis did produce a couple of overs at the start of his new-ball spell with Pollock, which had the Aussies rocking at 21 for three at the end of the fourth over, but Martyn took charge and whatever game plan South Africa had was blown apart. Pollock knew he had few options open to him, and in the process utilised only four bowlers.

Whether winning the toss at the Wanderers favoured South Africa is debatable. By the middle of March there is no longer any grass growth in the Highveld region, which requires the groundsman to create a hothouse effect to induce the type of cover needed to produce quality conditions by what was now mid-April. Frenzied interest in the series had pushed the traditional winter sports of rugby and soccer to the inside pages of the Sunday newspapers. Cronjégate, though, was still splashed on pages one, two and three. Those thronging Corlett Drive on either side of the ground again underlined the demographic population spread that cricket attracts. Asian, coloured, black and white: the citizens of what Archbishop Desmond Tutu referred to as the Rainbow Nation waved South African flags, jeering good-naturedly at those few with Australian flags. A roar about 20 minutes after Pollock bowled the first ball signalled the fall of the first wicket to those outside the ground still trying to gain access.

Inside the Wanderers Stadium – also known as the bullring – the hype was 'support the "green machine".' Outside there were people selling yellow peaks, which read 'Forgive Hansie'.

Trying to concentrate on the action amid the seething emotions invoked by a packed, raucous bullring when Mark Waugh walked back to the pavilion needed calm assurance. Waugh had been dismissed by a particularly good Hayward delivery, giving Boucher his eighth catch of the series. The younger Waugh twin had not had a particularly good tour. Pollock, with the wickets of Gilchrist and Martyn, and Hayward with Waugh's, had made the most of the conditions: seam, swing and a bit of bounce. The Wanderers bullring was not Edgbaston; the pitch enabled the quicks to find the edge. The subconscious niggled again: what sort of carnage would Brett Lee and McGrath have created had Steve Waugh won the toss and sent in South Africa? It is the old story of how winning the toss can affect the result of the game. Had South Africa not gained a similar advantage over England at the start of the Test series six months earlier? Allan Donald and Pollock had reduced Nasser Hussain's tourists to four wickets for only two runs before lunch on the first day, and England went on to lose by an innings just after lunch on the fourth – tricky conditions for those batting first.

For the third limited-overs game it was an interesting ploy to open the bowling with Hayward instead of Kallis. His rocket-like pace had the top order in early trouble, bowling a line and length at the sort of pace that saw the speed gun clock 150 km/h. Very much the sort of human catapult stuff indulged in later in the day by Brett Lee. Two of the world's fastest bowlers working off a nice head of steam, glaring angrily at the batsmen who hit the ball for four, or the guy in the inner ring who misfielded. It was not done deliberately, the bowlers were assured; you know how it is though. As it is, runs were hard enough to get. Steve Waugh dropped anchor as best he could to try to hold the innings together with Michael Bevan. The man with an LOI average at the time of 57.04 and a ranking of 795 points – which was 43 less than at his peak of 838 in the Aiwa Cup at Galle in Sri Lanka nine months before – had not been blessed with runs in this series. Not in keeping with his average.

Australia were in desperate need of someone to reinvent the escape hatch. Perhaps Steve Waugh could manufacture something in keeping with his Leeds effort in the World Cup. He was tired though. Anyone who knows about his hard-nosed professionalism could tell you it may have been the same man, but it was not the same player. He was stretched, physically and mentally, and age was catching up with him.

He watched Bevan depart for 33, bowled by Klusener – a good ball, which scythed through the probing front-foot defences. It had been hard work to bat for five minutes longer than an hour knowing that you are not on top of your game.

Pollock switched the bowling. Ntini was keeping it tight, maintaining the form that had seen him come through Sharjah and the first game in Durban with the sort of rhetoric that says, 'Hey, I want to be noticed.'

The all-rounder they call Tugga finally departed for 51. His was the seventh wicket to fall, and with the score at 149 the Wizards of Oz were in danger of failing to bat through their overs. Not that it was the sort of shot Waugh would like to remember. He had stepped away, presumably to make room to cut a Hayward delivery; instead he watched transfixed as the bottom-edged shot saw the ball take out his middle and off stumps. The bullring erupted in elation.

It was left to Ian Harvey and Shane Warne in a partnership of 51 runs to keep the innings afloat; the Aussies knew that they may not have posted a competitive total, yet the argument remained: with the conditions the way they were, scoring the 206 needed was going to be a lot harder to get than the 214 South Africa had needed to win at Edgbaston. Harvey and Warne rotated the strike to get some spark back into their efforts before Pollock came back and ripped out the bottom order.

Twice during the South African reply there was tight nausea in the pit of the noisy bullring crowd's collective stomach; the nightmares of Headingley and Edgbaston loomed again. Brett Lee bowled Kirsten for one, and Hall, with some surprise, dug out the fastest recorded delivery in South Africa, a catapult of 156 km/h. Gibbs, after a flowing cover drive, fell lbw to McGrath, and it was 19 for two. Now it was the rookie and the veteran, both 24, trying to repair the early damage – Hall in only his second game, Kallis in his 95th, and both on a mission as an uneasy calm settled over the innings. Hall did not face a lot of the bowling, yet his driving on the up, while not as emancipated in style as Kallis's, was pretty enough to watch. When questioned on Hall's surprise inclusion in the squad, Magiet suggested that South Africa needed a little more batting muscle up front.

'He is someone who can take on the Aussie bowlers,' he explained.

An interesting remark, as Hall had sat out the first two games, suggesting that he was selected only because the Wanderers is his home turf. Kirsten's early dismissal did not help the selectors or lead Ford and Pollock to any conclusions, either.

When the innings moved into a comfort zone, with the batsmen rotating the strike, Warne was brought on and Kallis tucked into a couple of loose deliveries. Three fours flowed and the crowd roared for more. Kallis seemed to have found his footwork again. Like Inzamam-ul-Haq, he knows a trick or two about dodging a row of fast-moving three-wheelers when trying to negotiate a busy crossing. Having watched Kallis help himself to three fours, Hall must have thought playing Warne was going to be all too easy. If Kallis could almost walk on water against Warne, Hall thought he might be able to do the same. He perished though. Lured forward he drove at Warne, failing to check his stroke and his hands moving through all too quickly, for Andrew Symonds to take the catch. It really was a soft dismissal.

The choker image resurfaced as the side slipped from 91 for two to 91 for five, and then 122 for six; Hall's departure was followed by Kallis's and Nicky Boje's, setting a bleak picture. The biggest crowd in the Wanderers' history fell silent. Then there was a queasy murmur at the return of Brett Lee, and he rewarded his captain by ripping the middle apart at the seams. The bowler known as the Woollongong Whizz, bowled the second fastest delivery in the history of the game at 156 km/h – it was just a couple of kilometres slower than Shoaib Akhtar's fastest ball. Australia might win it yet.

It needed the mentally tough Boucher, who worked his way through the difficult patch with Rhodes, to do a little repair work, as South Africa had lost three wickets during a spell of 70 balls while scoring only 20 runs. And there was little surprise when Rhodes departed. Warne took his second wicket after the leg-spinner went for 20 in two overs, after which he bowled two consecutive maidens.

Klusener arrived and expectations bubbled again. The Natal all-rounder took his time, looked around, and took guard. Knowing that Pollock was the only remaining recognised batsman left, Klusener decided it was crunch time. Warne had bowled out his overs, and Steve Waugh was left with an assortment with which to juggle. He had McGrath and Brett Lee, but the support was lacking once Warne went. In desperation he called on eight bowlers during the innings. Five of them were used in trying to break the seventh-wicket partnership, but nothing went the way of the Australians. Boucher and Klusener grew in confidence, picking off boundaries, taking singles and twos and keeping an eye on the run rate.

While the Kirsten–Kallis partnership at Kingsmead had been the best batting produced by anyone during the LOIs in South Africa in what had been an extended season, the Boucher–Klusener effort was now marginally superior. Along with the triangular series involving England and Zimbabwe earlier in the season, which was marred by poor pitches and low scores leading to tight finishes, the batting skills were generally messy and flawed. If Klusener and Boucher are from different schools of technique, the results are similar, which makes them a dangerous duo: a left- and right-hand combination, which upsets bowling rhythm and disturbs careful fielding strategies. Klusener was very much in the Trent Bridge mood of the 1999 World Cup, where he made a mess of Shoaib's bowling figures when the Rawalpindi Express was recalled to deal with his batting tactics.

Lee, who had gone for 11 runs in his second spell of three overs and collected two wickets, could not believe the audacity of either Boucher or Klusener. It was a stick-up job without masks, barefaced bravado, as Lee went for 11 in his last two overs. Klusener then dished up something special for his old adversary McGrath: two boundaries off the ninth over – an off-drive of classical perfection, followed by a flowing cover drive. The big left-hander smashed the tight grip the big Australian opening bowler had held since the opening overs. Klusener's innings thrilled the partisan crowd, his 52 off 50 balls punctuated with nine fours. It was a Boucher flourish that finished it off – a flashing cover drive off Harvey sealing a four-wicket victory, which may not quite have buried the ghost of Edgbaston, but reviving an innings almost from the dead was a good enough salvage expedition.

Shaun Pollock, playing his 100th limited-overs international, felt the 'stubborn character of Klusener and Boucher' did much to ensure victory, forgetting to mention his own efforts as a bowler with his four for 37. Which supports Pollock's initial theory that 'a great all-round team effort' was the main reason for South Africa winning the series 2–1, setting up the August showdown in Melbourne's new massive Colonial indoor arena. After the comprehensive defeat, Steve Waugh agreed that South Africa had been the 'better side'.

Victory in a limited-overs series against Australia in Pollock's first attempt as captain was remarkable enough. But as he admitted on the day the side arrived in Colombo for the first post-Cronjé Test series, his 'apprenticeship' as captain was very much a trial and error experience. It was also a matter of adjustment, and as the side was in need of a new opening batsman for the three Tests and in the Singer Triangular series, which also involved Pakistan, Klusener was used a couple of times, but mainly the Kirsten–Hall combination.

If the innings defeat in the Galle Test was the low point of the tour, colourful Asgiriya, amid the mountain greenery that is Kandy, was more relaxing, although the second Test was a far more pulsating contest with several horrendous umpiring decisions that went against both sides. Gamini Silva, umpiring his first Test, botched two decisions in Chaminda Vaas's opening over to Kirsten. The first ball appeal was turned down when Kirsten should have been out, and he was given out to the next appeal when he was not. Daryl Harper got a few wrong as well.

There was also a repeat of the Wanderers Stadium partnership between Klusener and Boucher on day one. Klusener showed that he did not believe in superstitions such as the nervous nineties. He clambered aboard his own form of transport and hurtled his way to his third Test century, providing South Africa with an invaluable restructuring job in the process. There was also some discussion on whether he had scored 118 or 117, as TV and the media scorer suggested; what he did do, however, was rescue South Africa's first innings. Put in to bat and struggling at 34 for five by the 19th over, they had much for which to blame themselves. It was not a pretty sight, quibbling about umpiring decisions or cowboy-style shots, such as an out-of-character effort by Rhodes. It was suggested that with the scoreboard misspelling so many of the names, it was not the South Africans playing at all but an incognito version of the top order, and their demise could be explained away simply by suggesting that they were cardboard cut-outs.

When Boucher joined Klusener, the sorry tale of the scoreboard indicated that the cardboard cut-outs had been unable to negotiate the first tricky hour or so on a cranky pitch. Once Klusener and Boucher had sorted out the pace of the Asgiriya pitch, the eccentricity of the bounce and their focus, the innings proceeded. The Klusener–Boucher partnership prospered and profited with the sort of positive strokeplay and footwork needed to rescue South Africa. They added a record 124 for the sixth wicket, which eclipsed by two runs the previous best against Sri Lanka, held by Daryll Cullinan and Dave Richardson in 1993.

Yet for excitement and close finishes this Test was better than most, and the tightest finish South Africa had managed since Sydney over New Year 1994. In Sydney it was by five runs, at Asgiriya it was seven runs. And in a match that had almost been twice lost. Yet Arjuna Ranatunga would be highly miffed at being called the 'Fat Lady', for the rotund former Sri Lanka captain was not around when South Africa pulled off an amazing victory on an afternoon of frenetic activity. South Africa displayed character, fight and a touch of dig-deep quality to level the series 1–1, nine days after the awful drubbing in Galle.

For a while it was Ranatunga who, in his penultimate Test, almost did sing, for Sri Lanka. He carried his side to within sight of a 2–0 lead and series triumph when he was the third of Nicky Boje's victims. For Shaun Pollock's side it was the sort of comeback you dream about, Fat Lady or no Fat Lady. Boje's batting on the fourth morning, and later his left-arm spin, played an important dual role for South Africa. Ranatunga's innings of 88, however, almost freewheeled his side to victory. It was the sort of distinctive innings that ranks alongside some of the modern great efforts that failed to reach three figures.

When Sri Lanka went in pursuit of the 177 needed for victory, the drama swiftly unfolded as openers Marvan Atapattu and Jayasuriya were out to first-ball lbw decisions. They were fair enough too, each umpire in agreement as Pollock, with the first ball of the innings, dismissed Atapattu lbw, and Hayward, wrenching a decision from Silva, sent Jayasuriya back to stunned silence. When Mahela Jayawardena and Kumar Sangakkara departed in swift succession, it was Ranatunga the bold who joined Russel Arnold with the score limping along at 21 for four. Ranatunga exploded in the first hour after lunch. A half-century off only 34 balls, and with South Africa giving away 77 in the first hour, it needed some desperate measures to get back into the game.

Pollock switched the bowling and rotated the field placings, and at 113 for four he decided to give Boje's left-arm orthodox a chance. It worked like a charm. At 130 for five, and with Ranatunga still displaying a rare vintage in strokeplay, Sri Lanka were in with a chance. But at 161 Jonty Rhodes picked up the catch that counted at forward-short leg. The game South Africa seemed to have lost was being won. Boje suggested that the crucial moment was the run-out of Chaminda Vaas, with Kallis whipping in a return to Klusener. This may have been the case, yet there is a sneaking feeling that when Ranatunga departed the Fat Lady had indeed sung, and this time it was for South Africa.

Yet the victory was also a tribute to the captain and coach for the way they displayed the character needed to achieve an important victory and establish positive thought expectations at home. But it was spoilt by an anonymous e-mail from South Africa, suggesting that the umpires had 'been well paid for their efforts to engineer a result favouring the white cricket team'. Replying to the e-mail in an effort to discover the source resulted in 'administrative e-mail delivery error'. The sender obviously knew what he or she was doing. It was the first of several broad innuendoes that the win had not been well received in some circles at home. Whether the players later learnt of the anomalous reaction is uncertain – if they did, the diplomatic Pollock and the manager kept their own counsel.

At Asgiriya, Pollock smiled ruefully and agreed that while Galle had been a 'hard introduction as Test captain', it had also been something he had had to accept. Losing so badly did not go down well. It hurt; it really hurt the team's pride. In Kandy he helped them overcome their hurt pride by displaying a passion for the game that shows the deep commitment you would expect, and it rubbed off on the others. Pollock's leadership style is relaxed and about 'team building', as opposed to the frequent tense mood swings experienced under predecessor Cronjé. This should shut up the critics, many of whom have inferior if blunt axes to grind – and it shows. Some, it seems, are soured when their flawed opinions leave them open to critical analysis.

Shaun, however, also brings with him not so much the trappings of the family name, as some try to imply, as an expansive vision of his own image, and the ever-important first century of the third millennium during the third Test in the Sri Lanka series at Centurion. It is here where the family, his mentor Marshall and his own character looked set to shape and establish the team's identity. His innings at SuperSport Park was a virtuoso performance, delivered with robust style. There were touches of magic and majesty about that particular afternoon carve-up before a full house. Nor was he afraid to admit that, 'Yes, it did get a bit emotional out there' when the three figures were registered against his name on the giant electronic scoreboard. But that is the man he is – a street fighter with a sentimental streak.

There are times when, quite understandably, he wants to protect his players from an inquisitive media; he has every right to. There are too many who feel that the PR exercise is all part of the job, turning up at a media conference in the middle of a big innings and spilling his thoughts to a sceptical bunch who have spent most of the day in an air-conditioned media centre, while the batsman has sweated it out in the middle trying to place his side in a winning position. These are times when a batsman, 'grilled' about his thoughts as he worked his way towards three figures, becomes a party piece conversation for some of the scribes. Writers 30 years ago penned their own imaginative thoughts and then, only at the end of the game, might a player be asked to express an opinion on his innings and how it affected the game, or himself.

Sure, the media, or the fourth estate, pretend to represent the public and not themselves; they also have a right to tell the public the views of those attending the briefings after a day's play. The public and the youngsters in particular want to read what their heroes had to say. To suggest that Jacques Kallis was 'a spoilsport' for not turning up in Bloemfontein in mid-November 2000 after batting for all but two minutes of the first day against New Zealand, was not really clever. Pollock explained the reason for Kallis's absence, and carried on with the briefing, much as he did five months earlier at the Colombo Oberoi when, days after the King Commission had heard some of Cronjé's revelations about Asian bookies, the image of the sport had a careworn, frayed and bruised look, and was in need of calm assurances. Here was the right voice and authority to display a cool, calm front, which had solid depth rather than a false façade.

Ford, an early confidant of Shaun's, once expressed his admiration at how the lanky all-rounder slipped into the captaincy role at the most difficult stage of the post-isolation era, the fifth to assume the post since South Africa's international return in November 1991. He had also learnt much from the late Malcolm Marshall, the mentor all too many are inclined to forget. Genes are one thing, but mentoring is the sort of hands-on skill that is part of the finishing school that has much to do with the modern game. Look closely enough and you will see it too. Some of this emerged in April 2000 when, whatever his private thoughts and feelings were, Shaun had to shed the mantle of being one of the boys within hours in order to step into the captain's position and accept new responsibilities. 'Give it a couple more years, perhaps,' he had said once, when asked the inevitable. 'Not now.'

So there he was, thrust into something he had thought he might get one day in the future, and, as Ford explains, Pollock's passion for the game, along with Marshall's early guidance in the 1990s, did much to help in his preparation for the role. It was not easy, and nothing would happen overnight. What has been revealing is how Pollock has helped ease new players into the side and made them feel that they are part of the establishment.

All of which proves that he is not one to shirk his responsibilities. Okay, so he may gently rib a tired journalist, who seemed to have dozed off, with a blithe comment: 'Hey, I didn't know I was that boring!' but it is part of the Pollock charisma and charm.

There were also exigencies that presented themselves during the West Indies tour, where he led South Africa to a double triumph. Yet again there was sniping behind the team's back, and from the same sources that criticised the success in Sri Lanka. Some of this came from the dagga-smoking episode, which laid the team open to comments that they were ill disciplined. Again the Pollock diplomacy smoothed the rough areas and brought out the best in the players.

Being captain of a team has its moments, and no doubt before he quits the position there are going to be days when he wishes someone else would run the shop. After all, had it gone according to plan, he would have had a further three years in the role of vice-captain to learn what captaincy is all about. So far he has done a pretty good job of it and grown into the position, and there is more to come. The Australian nightmare will fade, and the side will get stronger both mentally and physically. Sit back and enjoy the ride; it is going to be worth it, as the game in South Africa moves into a new, exciting era.

MARK BOUCHER 17
Sense and Sensibility

By Trevor Chesterfield

It can hardly be called a tradition, yet South Africa's list of captains who have also been wicketkeepers is one of the sport's quaint conundrums. It may not be by design, or even by chance, yet the register of names of wicketkeepers leading teams home or abroad is matched only by Pakistan. South Africa is inclined to do things a little differently. From Fatty Castens in 1894 and Ernie Halliwell, the third captain who led the side in 1895/96, up to 2001/02, when Boucher took over from an injured Shaun Pollock, wicketkeeper–captains have added to a certain traditional code within the game, although it has been 70 years since the last wicketkeeper led South Africa in a series.

He was the much lamented and respected Horace Brackenbridge (Jock) Cameron, who was only 30 when he died from enteric fever, contracted as the 1935 side returned from England. It is thought that he had caught the infection in either Cairo or the Suez Canal.

Cameron's wicketkeeping skills and leadership qualities were noticed from his first Test series against England when only 21. He was barely 25 when he became a surprise choice to lead the side in the last two Tests of the 1930/31 series against England, and then captained South Africa in Australia in 1931/32. When asked who they thought should lead the last two Tests of the 1930/31 series against Percy Chapman's side, as well as the team to Australia, former South African Test captains and teammates Nummy Deane and Buster Nupen argued for Cameron. The double burden became too much in Australia, however, and he was quite happy to hand over to Herby Wade for the 1935 England visit, although he agreed to act as vice-captain.

Cameron, educated at Hilton College outside Pietermaritzburg and later at Jeppe High School, was barely 10 when he took an interest in wicketkeeping. Boucher came to the position in his later years at Selborne College in East London, where he was encouraged by Richard Pybus, his school coach, and Stephen Jones, the Border coach. Both Cameron and Boucher have earned a batting reputation, although Cameron failed to reach the levels of Boucher, who to date has scored three Test centuries.

With the great Don Bradman in the opposition for the only time in South

Africa's Tests against Australia, making a plan to take his wicket was a simple matter. Dropping catches did not help the South Africans' cause either. In the first Test, played at the Gabba, the Don was dropped at 11 and 15. Ouch! Little wonder he went on to score 229.

There is an anecdote about Cameron that, in the game against Yorkshire towards the end of the 1935 tour, he hit 30 runs off one over delivered by the great England left-arm spinner, Hedley Verity. After the second six had followed three fours, Yorkshire's wicketkeeper and noted wit, Arthur Wood, shook his head and said, 'Eh … Jock. Thar's got 'im reet in two minds, now. 'E dunno wither you wanna 'it 'im for six or four.'

'And here I thought I was hoping to improve my batting average,' was Cameron's response.

The other version is that when Verity had retrieved the ball at the end of the over, Wood said consolingly, 'Never mind, Hedley, you've got him in two minds: he doesn't know whether to hit you for a four or a six.'

Cameron found his batting form deserting him in Australia in 1931/32, and the weight of captaincy a little too heavy at times. It was a hefty problem for Cameron that Bradman was often dropped in the slips early on in his innings, and then went on to rattle off big centuries. Not that it affected his wicketkeeping standards. Highly efficient and instinctive behind the stumps, he was neither flamboyant nor noisy. His appeals were quiet and his stumpings were made with almost nonchalant ease. Certainly in 1932, former Australian captains Herbie Collins, Jack Ryder and Bill Woodfull, along with Sir Pelham Warner, a former England skipper, regarded Cameron as equal to the great Australian wicketkeeper Bert Oldfield. Considering the lofty regard there was for Oldfield, this tribute to Cameron's ability was impressive.

At least Cameron, when he first led South Africa at the Wanderers on Friday, 13 February 1931, was not confronted by the bizarre circumstances Ernie Halliwell had to handle in early January 1896. Lord Hawke's team had arrived in Cape Town in early December 1895, about the time of the Jameson Raid, which led to confusion over tour arrangements, as inland the country was plunged into chaos. All this happened while the first game was being played at Newlands. Financier Abe Bailey, one of the Randlords and tour backers, advised M'Lud and his troupe to remain in Cape Town, which they did for a further 10 days. Lord Hawke then decided to move to Johannesburg to play the scheduled game against a Transvaal XV, which received much publicity and was used to distract the locals from the growing political fracas. Among the prickly political issues of the day was the aftermath of the infamous and, for Cecil John Rhodes, disastrous raid. If this was a little like holding chariot races and gladiator battles at the Coliseum to distract the Romans, those responsible for the added publicity about the game knew a fancy Machiavellian trick or two. Terms such as 'enlightened imperialism', 'honest colonialism' and 'protection of the mineworkers' were used freely in some of the London newspapers to describe the unrest on the Reef. What was conveniently overlooked is how the dealings of Lord Milner and Rhodes were rarely progressive or frank unless it suited their political aims.

Another wicketkeeper who had to step in to fill the captaincy gap was Vivian (Boet) Neser. One of a number of South African Rhodes Scholars who earned an Oxford blue, Neser had served in the Royal Field Artillery in World War I before going up to Oxford; from 1919 to 1921 he played for Brasenose College. It is the long-forgotten unofficial series between a side selected from among the SACA provinces and one raised from England by financier SB Joel for which Neser is known as a player. He went on to become a Transvaal judge.

Neser was a member of the 1921 Oxford side, which included Douglas Jardine, captain of the England side on the infamous 1932/33 bodyline tour of Australia, and the journalist and author, RC Robertson-Glasgow. He was ideally suited for the role of captain, and was asked to take over much in the same way Cameron took over from Deane. In Neser's case it was the illustrious Herbie Taylor who had stepped down after the unsuccessful 1924 tour of England. History records the tour as a tragic disaster – the series was lost 3–0 in a wet summer.

By the end of that tour it appears as though the South African team had reached a crossroads, and the SACA were uncertain which road to take. Neser was asked to take over to give the team direction. For business reasons he had turned down a place in the 1924 side. As with many other top sportsmen in those years, he had other priorities; his professional career put a meal on the table while it cost time and money to play sport. In 1927 he retired to concentrate on his law practice.

* * *

When South Africa were invited to rejoin the international sports arena in 1991, Dave Richardson was made wicketkeeper. It meant that such worthies as Ray Jennings, whose cause the Johannesburg print media continued to trumpet, was left out. Rumour was that Jennings's omission was due to a verbal assault made on Kepler Wessels during the one-off rebel 'test' at the Wanderers, which the soon-to-be captain had overheard.

Such fanciful stories are usually devoid of truth. What South Africa's selectors wanted in November 1991 was a long-term solution to the role of wicketkeeper, rather than short-term answers. More accurately, though, Jennings's form was waning, while Richardson's was waxing along quite comfortably. Later the selectors, under Peter Pollock, added Steve Palframan (Sri Lanka 1993) and Errol

Stewart (Australia 1993/94) to beef up the batting at limited-overs level; it was to lighten the load on Richardson should the need arise. Both performed adequately.

In 1995, Palframan was the second in command as national wicketkeeper. A late replacement for the 1996 World Cup squad after Richardson was injured, he no doubt felt he had it made. But his inexperience was cruelly exposed in the quarter-final against the West Indies, a game South Africa lost. In the rush to find a scapegoat, the selectors' error in leaving out Allan Donald and Fanie de Villiers was forgotten.

Palframan, along with Nic Pothas, was part of the South African A squad that toured England in July and August 1996, with Duncan Fletcher as the coach. Palframan did not live up to his promise of 1993, and his batting fell off during the 1996 tour. That is probably why the national selectors started to take Pothas more seriously as a Test and LOI candidate, as he could bat in the top order and keep the scoreboard moving.

Strange how history plays its little tricks when least expected. Mark Boucher had already been on two under19 South African tours and had turned out at under13 and under15 levels. If he is highly regarded for his all-round abilities as a sportsman, there is another side to him that emerges on occasion – more regularly now than when he was a schoolboy. It is something to do with his self-belief and inner strength. The schoolboy innocence that peeps through and the accompanying cheeky smile hide a competitive, tough personality. And there is nothing wrong with that, either. This side of the Boucher character emerged during his last year at school, when he broke his arm a couple of months before the Schools national squash tournament. For most youngsters it would have been easier to take a break, or to use the free time studying for the all-important final year exams. Forget competing for a squash title. That would require peak levels of fitness and practising with a damaged arm. But Boucher decided on a fitness regime and mental strength to see what he could achieve. He went on to reach the final, but as with all good stories, it did not have that happy, burnished ending. Life's not always that simple.

Dave Nosworthy, now the Northern Titans coach, was Mark Boucher's first provincial captain; playing for Border B against Natal B in a UCB Bowl match in Durban. Sure he looked a class act, but as with the under19 and under15 South African tours, he did not keep wicket at that level. There was no thought of moving into Steve Palframan's position. He was just a Second XI provincial player making his young way in the world, owing his team spot to the Border selectors' philosophy that it was time to give some of the young talent a chance.

It is the old story of having to start somewhere so, in 1995/96, the first steps were taken – and not even as a wicketkeeper. The start to Boucher's provincial career was low key. He was a youngster no one really knew.

He was eased into the side with those first couple of B team matches, and he even managed to bowl. He almost took a wicket as well; but his first-class bowling statistics have not changed since that first game: three overs and 20 runs. His one possible wicket was a dropped top-edge offered by Errol Stewart, who at that stage had 200-plus. But that's the quirkiness of sport; only the net bowlers who get a rare opportunity in a match remember their first wicket in detail.

What did turn Boucher's career around was the Border selectors' decision to opt for him ahead of Palframan for the remaining four games in the domestic day/night series in 1995/96. It was not a flamboyant start to a provincial wicket-keeping career – no highlights to note. There were four catches in four matches, but his handiwork behind the stumps was remembered as being efficient and steady – and he generally did what is expected of a wicketkeeper. As his reputation grew, Border's selectors looked upon him as their next wicketkeeper. This had once seemed unlikely, as both Palframan and Carl Spillhaus were in the queue, and Ian Mitchell was also coming through the ranks. But by December 1995 Boucher had displaced Spillhaus as the B team wicketkeeper, and from what the selectors observed, a decision was made to give him a run in the senior provincial ranks.

It was not a selection that went down too well, either. One of the selectors was met by a couple of irate spectators at Palframan's club, Bohemians, and was told how the selectors had ruined a potential Test career. Strong language and accusations flowed that afternoon in the upmarket suburb of Beacon Bay where the club is situated. The point was made: who was Boucher? When in need, as a result of the Richardson injury, to whom did the national selectors turn instead of Nic Pothas for the 1996 World Cup side? There was also the 1996 South Africa A team tour of England. So, how could Boucher be considered the better gloveman?

At the time the A team for England was announced, Peter Pollock said that it had been chosen with a view to long-term options. He repeated this comment at the start of the 1996/97 season. South Africa were faced with a heavy schedule: a visit to Kenya would be followed by a tour of India, then a reciprocal visit by the Indians, and in the New Year the Australians would arrive. It meant nine Tests and 24 LOI games. The A team were to play India in a limited-overs game in Pietermaritzburg on 30 January, and Pollock would not be drawn on the names in the side.

'We have selected what we feel is the best-balanced side for this match,' was his guarded comment. 'There are a few players we want to have a look at under international conditions and this gives us the ideal opportunity. If it had been a first-class match we may have approached it differently.'

The media queries were more about the younger players who had been over-looked. They were HD Ackerman and the Northerns fast bowlers Rudi Bryson,

Steve Elworthy and Greg Smith, as well as Roger Telemachus. The selection of Boucher ahead of Pothas and Palframan was not part of the discussion. Not at that stage of the season. For a change the winter was quiet, with no A team tours. Yet had the selectors not already made up their minds? While no one looked at Boucher as the new reserve wicketkeeper, he had done enough during the previous season and during the winter programme to satisfy the selectors. He was thrown in at the deep end when the call came from Pakistan for a replacement for the injured Richardson.

At first the selection was downplayed. It was automatically assumed that Pothas would travel to Pakistan. Or Palframan ... No? So who is going? Boucher, from Border ... C'mon, be sensible. Palframan's the Border wicketkeeper ... There must be a mistake – you've got the name wrong: it has to be Pothas.

Most of the South African media were caught flat-footed and Peter Pollock, a former journalist, had to smile at his 'gentle beamer'. It showed the close attention some had paid to the previous season's averages and performances, and the fact that Palframan was looking to shift provinces.

So there he was, Mark Boucher, with nine first-class games behind his name: his CV read 36 catches, three stumpings and five half-centuries, one of which had reminded Peter Kirsten (as he recalled a couple of seasons later) of a younger, vintage Allan Lamb in the way he blasted the ball around Centurion Park. The selectors were taking a risk, and Ray Jennings was quoted on how they had got it wrong. After all, Boucher was just a kid. His record proved it. How could the selectors consider someone who, two years before, did not even keep wicket on an under19 tour of England?

Telford Vice, then with the East London *Daily Despatch*, recalled how interviewing the 20-year-old reminded him of a young man about to set off on the most important trip of his young life – yet this part of it had not quite settled in his mind. Cricket gear and piles of clothes were all over the room, and posters of pop artists adorned the walls. Here was the future wicketkeeper of the country, furiously packing before heading for Pakistan.

'It probably dawned on him when he arrived in Pakistan what he was there to do,' Vice recalled. 'Life had become a whirl, but the way he handled it all showed that he was the sort of person who really knew exactly what was happening, although it didn't quite show. Not then. Quite remarkable.'

To be transported from the gentle buzz of East London, where rush hour consists of half a dozen cars waiting at a downtown traffic light at 8.30 am, to the teeming Punjab where Shiekupura is situated, can be quite a culture shock, for those unaccustomed to South Asian conditions. The team was transported daily, the journey taking about an hour from Lahore. Considering the chaotic state of the municipal venue and the lack of protection against the rain, is it any wonder that the weather-affected Test from 17 to 21 October 1997 was the last to be played there? Sri Lankan umpire KT Francis considered the venue the most inadequate he had ever experienced during his career as a Test umpire.

Apart from Richardson ending a sequence of 38 Test appearances because of a hamstring strain, Adam Bacher scored his highest Test score of 96, and Boucher's contribution was six in 12 minutes out of a total of 402. He remained for the Golden Jubilee quadrangular series and gained further experience, as Richardson's career began to wind down on tour in Australia.

Criticism about the lack of players of colour was also emerging, as politicians voiced concern about the team's demographics. When the team list was handed out in the UCB's old boardroom, a swift glance showed that Boucher had been included in the 15. There was now no room for doubt on who was to replace Richardson when he retired. What did surprise, though, was that Telemachus was included as the extra member, or the player of colour. Would it not have been better to take Makhaya Ntini? As it turned out, Telemachus failed a fitness test and Ntini joined the touring party.

Boucher's first at-home Test was against Pakistan at the Wanderers in mid-February 1998. While rain clouds hovered, the media build-up might have had a disturbing influence on a more impressionable youngster. The Johannesburg press had long tried to make out a case for a player who was thought to be more deserving than any out-of-town incumbent or hopeful. In November 1992, there was a concerted bid to have Richard Snell from Transvaal included ahead of the other swing bowler Fanie de Villiers of Northern Transvaal in the squad for the limited-overs series against India.

While it has long been claimed that the pen is mightier than the sword, there were those who hoped that Boucher would fall on the blade. That at least was the feeling among some scribes in Johannesburg and the Cape. No doubt the young man had wise counsel and kept his peace. Whether advice came from his captain, Hansie Cronjé, the coach Bob Woolmer or older teammates who had also been put through the media mangle, is uncertain. He did a good job of smiling through it all and looked them in the eye at a press conference in Port Elizabeth. The theorists claimed that he was clumsy, and too young and inexperienced. None of the detractors wanted to suggest that perhaps it might be because he came from the wrong province.

It was Rod Marsh, the great Australian wicketkeeper of the 1970s and 1980s, who once remarked that 'keeping wicket is for the adventurous, those who bore easily and on reflection for those with just a touch of stupidity'.

Marsh pointed out how, next to the captain, the wicketkeeper is normally the most important player on the field; like the captain, he also needs to know how to judge any number of things, from the bounce and pace of the pitch to the various styles of bowling and batting. Keeping his hands safe from injury is equally important – it meant the difference between a long or short career. Selection of good equipment is very important: from the late 1860s until the late 1940s gloves had developed very little, despite changes to the law in 1863 when overarm bowling was legalised and fast bowling took on a new, dynamic dimension. Any number of English county wicketkeepers from the mid-1860s until the 1920s would end the day washing their blood-soaked inners.

The Wanderers Test involving Pakistan began in such bizarre circumstances, delayed for 24 hours, that it did not really settle into a normal game. That might explain why it had such a low public profile. Also, the bad light and rain that hung around the latter part of the game added its own gloomy scowl. Pakistan's form leading up to the Test had been erratic. Adding to the general confusion was the unresolved matter of the bogus mugging episode, initially claimed to have taken place close to their fancy Sandton hotel.

Haroon Rashid, the Pakistan coach and former Kerry Packer rebel, admitted privately in Port Elizabeth that it had been the most disorganised troupe he had had the misfortune to handle, and matters were not helped by the return of the charismatic Wasim Akram by the time the third Test was played at St George's Park.

Against this unnatural backdrop, Aamir Sohail won the toss and did the obvious by asking South Africa to bat first under clear skies. If there was a chance to win the opening match of the series, this was it. The pitch had bounce and good carry and the South Africans were led by Gary Kirsten, with Cronjé using the break to have knee surgery. Supporting Sohail's decision to send South Africa in was the strength of the Pakistan attack. It was as potent as any: pace from Waqar Younis and Shoaib Akhtar, with some lively swing and seam from the all-rounder Azhar Mahmood, and leg-spin by Mushtaq Ahmed for support. Not surprising that there were early inroads, and when South Africa were listing badly at 166 for eight, the possibility of Pakistan batting that first afternoon loomed; that was when Pat Symcox joined Boucher.

Amid the pre-match confusion it had almost been forgotten that Boucher's first Test had been against Pakistan five months before. Since then there had been the tour of Australia and Richardson's retirement; not too many remember seeing him as wicketkeeper or a batsman. Boucher's partnership with Symcox enabled the tall off-spinner to achieve a lifelong ambition of scoring a Test century, and helped to subdue the thoughts of some print media members who wanted to ambush Boucher's career.

It took time for the partnership with Symmo to gather momentum, although, as he had often proved at club level, the tall off-spinner was no slouch as a batsman. There was a need, however, to resurrect the innings and the pair went about structuring the sort of rearguard the side needed and the nation wanted.

When they started the second day, Boucher had his first Test half-century and Symcox was on 77, with the partnership worth 130 runs. It was a long way from turning in a competitive first-innings total, but the intention was there. Symcox had shown solid form in Australia and had a Test half-century on his season's CV, so what was wrong with another? The pair had shown some spirited batting; Symcox enjoyed driving in front of the wicket, and while Boucher's strokeplay was as handsome as his features, the veteran Symcox nudged the scoring rate along. His batting was at times reminiscent of his grizzled, weather-beaten features; some strokes were hewn from the Symmo brand of batting technique, others came from the more classical MCC 'Master Class' style. It is hard to beat such exuberance, care and attention to detail.

While the age gap between the two was 16 years, they displayed a maturity and understanding in running between wickets. Sohail was changing the field, switching the bowlers and generally becoming more frustrated as the growing crowd became absorbed in the battle. The records started to tumble: the best for the ninth wicket since the country's return to the Test fold; the highest at the Wanderers for the same wicket; and the 63-year-old partnership of 137 scored by Eric Dalton and Chud Langton against England at The Oval was also broken. From the start Boucher showed he was neither awed by South Africa's plight or in awe of the Pakistan bowlers. There was one handsome pull off a Waqar bouncer, which left the bowler standing mid-pitch, hands on hips, looking quizzically at the batsman and the boundary.

When he reached the upper 80s, Symmo started to bat with more prudence and manoeuvred his way towards the cherished coveted three-figure innings. Having got this far he was not about to blow it on a few extravagant shots; and as it was his big moment as a Test batsman, why not enjoy it? Records were dug up to show that only two no. 10 batsmen had previously scored Test centuries – England's Billy Read and the burly Australian Reggie Duff.[1] The push off Azhar brought up the three figures off 151 balls, and what crowd there was before lunch on that Saturday erupted in generous recognition as Symmo charged down the pitch, waving his bat and helmet in celebration with Boucher. No one can blame him for his exuberance: the century had been well fashioned under pressurised conditions, and as such was a remarkable effort, earning him a deserved place among the records. When the game was finally consigned to the pages of Test history as a rained-off draw, Symmo's moment of glory, captured as it was on television, created a refreshing glow and was seen by thousands.

Boucher's role in that significant world record ninth-wicket partnership of 190 was underplayed. His time as a Test batsman was, however, coming. When it did, it ended what had been a barren period in run-making productivity in the series against the West Indies. He arrived in Centurion on 13 January 1999 for pre-fifth Test nets and training sessions, and worked quietly on his batting. Two days later he looked up and saluted the dressing room after posting his first three-figure Test score on the big electronic board. That South Africa were reduced to 123 for six when he had joined Kallis did not bother the 22-year-old wicketkeeper.

The pair had batted with sense and sensibility, and although there are those who are troubled by Kallis's apparent laid-back approach, they do not know about the 110 percent effort he gives to his game plan. Kallis is always aware of his immense skills: standing up when driving off the front foot straight, or into the covers, or cutting with that precision admired by so many. There are times when Boucher's batting philosophy is similar to his close friend Kallis's; but, as he showed that day in Centurion, he is also his own man. In the back of his mind was how 10 weeks before he had scored a highly entertaining maiden 100 off only 102 balls in the SuperSport Series match against Northern Titans.

On the first day of that Test, he showed a dash of adventure mixed with talent, spiced with the sort of temperament that suggested he was far better than his critics were prepared to admit. It also said much for his future. Nor was he shy to admit during an interview that he owed his maiden Test century to his teammates. It went down pretty well with the crowd, while TV commentators indulged in jingoism – suddenly Boucher adds value to the Test side because he is a dab hand as a batsman.

Statistics such as becoming the sixth South African batsman to score a century at eight in the order did not mean that much. Something to ponder was the importance of the century against the background in which it was made. Scoring a century in a match where the side is 4–0 ahead in a series was perhaps much easier than had the sides been drawn 2–2: the pressure would have been far greater.

Instead of talking tactics and strategy with Kallis during their partnership, the pair had talked 'a lot of junk', which had made Boucher more relaxed. It may surprise many that Kallis talks at all when he is out in the middle, but he is the top South African batsman, and he was then only 23. It had been the second time in the series that they had batted together, and they had developed a good understanding. Perhaps being roommates also helped.

Boucher's innings was a matter of applying simple logic. He had found from his experience when playing for Border against the West Indies earlier in the tour and in the previous four Tests that they are positive and always inclined to back themselves.

'It is something you learn when playing them; size up the challenge on offer and do your best to beat it down. The West Indies are a competitive lot and that is why they can be so dangerous. I enjoy playing against them, as their style is so different. I learnt that from players like Vasbert Drakes.'

Comforting thoughts from the young man whose next two centuries were scored when he went in as a nightwatchman: the second was the more important of the two – 108 against England in the follow-on innings at Kingsmead. While Gary Kirsten played an epic innings to equal Daryll Cullinan's record individual score of 275, the partnership of 192 with Boucher for the fifth wicket was under immense pressure as the pair battled to save the Test and retain South Africa's 1–0 lead going to Cape Town. The 125 in Harare against Zimbabwe became the highest by a nightwatchman in a Test; not that it meant all that much to the wicketkeeper. As he later admitted, it all added up to his tactical thinking and playing philosophy and led to becoming vice-captain.

Events over which he had no control threw him in at the deep end a second time in his Test career, only this time most of the action was off the field and took place before the King Commission of Inquiry in Cape Town. It was Boucher who persuaded Herschelle Gibbs to tell the commission about the approach made by the captain in Kanpur. It was Boucher whose frankness before the commission showed the young man in a different light. As he saw it, he was just doing his duty. Anyone who closely followed the commission and the daily reports – and most cricket scribes did – could not help but wonder how a player such as Gibbs was sucked into the whirlpool of events. It emerged that it was Boucher's logic that won over Gibbs and had him tell his story, thereby turning the commission into a valuable inquiry and not a waste of time and money. There was one newspaper report in far-off Colombo in which the agency report quoted an SC, Jeremy Gauntlett, telling Boucher that 'The United Cricket Board will always be grateful to their vice-captain for his moral leadership in this inquiry.'

Boucher had performed as well as he might, for his conscience told him that what Cronjé had attempted to do during a conversation one night was morally wrong. He told roommate Kallis and, at another stage, the manager, Goolam Raja, of a pasta meal in Bangalore during the fateful tour when the captain had seemingly gone on a recruiting drive to see who was available to get involved in his schemes, and who was not. Yet it was hard to turn his back on a captain who, to an extent, had stood by him when some members of the media hounded the young wicketkeeper after several off-day performances.

'We cannot expect to always do the spectacular,' Cronjé had said at the Wanderers after the first Test in the West Indies series. 'We all miss catches and when the pitch is up and down, as it can be sometimes, or the bowler is wayward, stopping byes are not too easy either.'

One of the few appointments the Magiet selection panel did get right was to make Boucher vice-captain. They had been made aware that, despite his youth, Boucher commanded respect among his South African teammates and management, and read the game with calm insight. As the incident with the broken arm had shown years before, there was an inner courage and mental strength. As Shaun Pollock had discovered, it is one thing being vice-captain – it is a whole lot tougher being in charge.

* * *

There was a touch of déjà vu about Boucher leading South Africa at the Wanderers on Friday, 22 February 2001. It was the venue where he had made his home Test debut against Pakistan. Pollock had suffered a side strain. While the weather remained sunny and warm, and the argument for starting the game on the Friday instead of the Thursday was supposed to mean better crowds, too many fans had seen South Africa decimated in glorious colour on their TV screens throughout the height of summer. Spectators could no longer stomach further humiliation. Some preferred to watch the agony in the comfort of their home. The Wanderers is not a spectator-friendly venue, and officious Johannesburg Traffic Department officials are inclined to add to its tawdry reputation.

There was also a sense of inevitability about the first Test, as there had been about the third Test in Sydney seven weeks before. While smoke from the bush fires hung with ominous gloom over the Emerald City, few could blame Boucher for South Africa's continued lurch from one disaster to another. The Wanderers was not a place for stoic patriots after the 3–0 defeat in Australia.

Not since Cameron's 1931/32 side – 70 summers before – had there been such humiliation in Australia. Most remembered how well South Africa had performed under Pollock's leadership, especially in the West Indies; surely it was going to be a matter of turning up in Australia and showing them how to win? Had Australia not lost 2–1 to India in a series played on the sub-continent? Forget that Australia had just whipped England in England during the Ashes Tests. Who were England anyway?

Those telltale signs of media arrogance had emerged in early November, when South Africa had easily beaten India in the first Test in Bloemfontein. The attitude then was, 'Bring on the wimps of Oz.' It was an attitude that did not sit well with former captain Kepler Wessels, who shook his head at such naivety. It was worrying, as it was sending the wrong message to the public.

'You can see they haven't been to Australia,' he smiled grimly. 'We could be in for a surprise or two.'

For the Wanderers, André Nel was added to the attack in place of the injured Pollock, but was totally ineffectual when faced with batting that was far better than any he had bowled to before. There was also a general uneasiness about his action, and whether it met the requirement of note three (fair delivery – the arm) of Law 24. So far it has, but that attempted bouncer looks awry with question marks. If there are still problems with Shoaib Akhtar and Brett Lee, then Nel is not far behind. That he was out of his depth was obvious, and Mike Procter, then a national selector, admitted that there was concern about South Africa's bowling and its lack of penetration.

There was another side to this story, which emerged a couple of days before the first Test in Adelaide. For Wessels and the less glamorous batting Brit with Grit, Geoff Boycott, it was nothing new, and they can quite cheerfully quote chapter and verse of the mind games played by the Australian media. It is the old story of how they enjoy poking into the underbelly of the touring sides in order to sniff what coals of controversy they can rake over to disturb the opposition's psyche. If they can find what is assumed to be a flaw in the batting, bowling or fielding areas, expose it. Forget the last result; it is all about mind games.

For the game in Adelaide, much of the pre-Test hype was about Allan Donald's fitness and whether he would be fit to play, rather than about Australia's own shortcomings, as exposed by the Kiwis in Perth. The Australian media, and the Aussies at large, saw it as the centre of a psychological warfare. Hit the 'Safs' where it hurts most: keep needling them with doubts about Donald's fitness. One biting suggestion was: 'Without Donald, South Africa have only half an attack.'

It was not a matter of just how true this was, but also that without a fit Donald, and Pollock as captain, South Africa had lost their competitive edge. This also emerged at the Wanderers: Boucher looked on in dismay as Donald did what he could to throw sandbags in the way to halt the flow of runs. What he and his teammates were seeing, though, was the last of Donald bowling in a Test. Donald went down after delivering the second ball of the 16th over, and the sight of him being helped off, crippled by a hamstring injury, cast even deeper gloom. Amid all this was the matter of the street fighter in Matthew Hayden's approach, which anchored the Australian first innings. He was aggressive and stylish, if at times bullish, in his strokeplay; yet he was conservative in his approach, which left a decided and impressive reminder of his qualities. Donald's departure left a bowling attack, already limping along on a crutch and with one foot in a plaster cast, seriously depleted. Makhaya Ntini did what he could to keep the flag flying above half-mast for most of the day; he was as impressive as he has ever been at this level, and the searching experience in Oz had made him a better bowler. Hayden, though, was in no mood to be Mr Nice Guy. No doubt he remembered those early days in a tumultuous series played against the backdrop of a South Africa weeks away from the country's first democratic election, when the powder-blue sky was smudged with smoke from the burning pyres of revolution and destruction. Hayden failed to make even a dent in the memory of those who watched that Test.

South Africa's performance against Australia in the bullring was as pathetic as the paying public's, who instead of accepting defeat gracefully, booed the tourists.

They love handing it out, but cannot take a hiding. They failed to enjoy the marvellous Adam Gilchrist batting exhibition. There was a lesson in the savage manhandling of the bowling attack by Australia's wicketkeeper and man of the match; Gilchrist had scored the fastest double-century in terms of balls faced, and the South Africans buckled at the knees: a dung beetle being squashed by a Kangaroo paw. It was the sort of nightmare the South African selectors did not care to watch. Defeat by an innings and 360 runs, the heaviest in the country's history, and the second heaviest in 125 years of Tests matches.

The success in the limited-overs series Down Under merely covered the cracks in a problem that had been looming for months. Any side that loses 16 wickets in a day's play for 181 runs in a matter of 54.3 overs, knows they have been handed a hiding. Apart from it being the fourth successive Test defeat South Africa had received from the world champions, the wreckage of the lower order by Glen McGrath, with the 23rd five-wicket haul of his career, shocked the 18 000 spectators. If the South African bowling had been on crutches when Steve Waugh declared on the Saturday, the batting was cut off at the knees with a technique and style as frayed around the edges as a pair of baggy old shorts. For those who believe in superstition, the fact that South Africa started the third day on 111 for five might have wondered whether the side was standing at the precipice. They fell into it head first.

Before the Newlands Test there was a major row, which saw Daryll Cullinan quitting the side within 24 hours of being selected. At that stage, it seemed as if his Test career might be over. The rhetoric over the Cullinan episode spilled over into the Test, as some suggested that he should take over as captain; but other people inside the camp suggested that Cullinan, as good as he is as a batsman, would have been a disaster as captain.

There were times at the Wanderers when Boucher would no doubt have liked to check on the chapter in Mike Brearley's book on the art of the 'dos and don'ts' of captaincy and on how to run a bowling operation; the bowlers, however, did not help their fledging skipper. One unhappy memory amid all the Gilchrist sixes was when he was put down on 35 by Jacques Kallis. Gilchrist had added 10 runs to his overnight total, with Australia 346 for five. A wicket then would have given the South Africans some form of respite, but the slips were too far back and the ball was falling away. Kallis normally gobbles such catches, and it seemed as if the ghost of Adelaide Oval was dancing merrily amid the tombstones of yet another South African bowling graveyard.

There was, at about the time of the Newlands Test, an advert doing the rounds on the local cinema circuit, which had Herschelle Gibbs strolling out of the batwing doors of a saloon in western-style garb, his upper lip and jaw covered in a sprinkling of what resembles a two-week growth. He is aiming to draw quicker than Brett Lee can deliver a bouncer. However, the result is markedly different to what is suggested: instead of the guns popping into his hands as one would expect, he fumbles the job as easily as he fumbled the infamous Steve Waugh catch at Leeds in the Super Six stage of the 1999 World Cup. Only 16 minutes into the Newlands Test, it was a matter of watching Gibbs do what he did best that summer: gift his wicket to an Australian bowler. What followed was a fumbling effort all the way through the first 35 overs, when at 92 for six, and with Ashwell Prince heading for the pavilion, a first-innings total of 239 looked remote.

Unlike the Wanderers Test, Newlands was not entirely all gloom. Yet, ask any South African to name the two spinners, or slow bowlers for that matter, to have taken 100 Test wickets in a career for his country and there would be a scratching of the head. Until 9 March 2002, the only South African spinner/slow roller to take 100 wickets or more was Hugh Tayfield. Which is why, when Paul Adams reached the mark in his 35th Test, it was quite a scary statistic. Apart from becoming the seventh South African to take 100 or more Test wickets, the 25-year-old helped undo some of the Australian batting equilibrium of the 2001/02 season. Not that his four wickets for 102 runs were remarkable figures. Selection panel convener Rushdi Magiet admitted that they had taken a risk in recalling the left-arm wrist spinner. And at one stage, with the Australian first innings tottering and Steve Waugh one of his initial victims, the Adams factor became an important one. He had two wickets for seven runs until Gilchrist piled in and helped himself to anything remotely short or wayward. It happens, of course. Following Adams's career is a little like playing a game of snakes and ladders. Up one match and down in the muckheap the next, and not knowing if his brand of wrist spin is really effective.

Gilchrist's second three-figure score of the series was lavish in strokeplay. Reaching a Test century off 91 balls is remarkable enough; it was also a matter of common sense, with straight drives and occasional pulls. Gilchrist did his rescue act bit with help from Shane Warne.

Reasons why South Africa had failed so badly against Australia all point to the disparity between the first-class systems in the two countries. In South Africa the 11 provinces had possibly three players who might attract the attention of the national selectors. But as Magiet and Co. had their permanent favourites who earned Test or LOI caps in South Africa, it was harder to be selected than in, say, Australia, where the talent pool is bigger and the selection policy better.

Asked for his thoughts on the Test series in South Africa, former Australian captain Allan Border explained how quality and class play their parts. While form and averages are transitory, class has a permanency that keeps those players on the fringes knocking hard on the door. Is it class and then form that the Australian selectors look for when they put a side or squad together? Or is it a matter of who fits in where if the form is right? Magiet and his panel were reluctant to admit that they did not want to be seen falling over themselves handing out Test or LOI caps to worthy causes or form players. It was as if Mark Boucher knew that he was doing a holding job. For Kingsmead, the South African selectors had predictably decided that: (a) No, they did not want Steve Elworthy, with a proven record of 42 provincial wickets at 16.69 in the season as the replacement for Dewald Pretorius; (b) It was now time to recall another, almost forgotten reject in David Terbrugge, who was last sighted playing for South Africa in August 2000 in Melbourne at the Colonial Stadium. By this time Magiet's panel had, it seemed, decided that the easiest way out of their predicament was to paste a list of candidates on the dartboard, close their eyes and aim in the hope of hitting the right name.

Interestingly, it was Adam Gilchrist who decided that the only way to meet the Paul Adams threat was to take on the wrist spinner. This came after Steve Waugh had surprisingly again failed to read Adams, and was bowled. Having faced all types of bowlers on pitches that resembled the moonwalk on Mars – from Mohali, to Perth, to Lord's and any other number of Test venues around the globe – Waugh's deadpan features betrayed nothing as he walked away, displaying the grit of the man. The baggy green cap he wears may make Allan Border grimace, but it is his and the team's talisman, and will find a place in the team's hall of special souvenirs.

At a muggy Kingsmead it was Boucher who, upon leaving the dressing room, offered the comment, 'Don't worry, Pop, I'll get them for you,' as he determinedly looked at the balding, grey-haired manager Goolam Raja. Minutes later he hoisted Mark Waugh for a six, and ended the one-horse race the Test series against Australia had become. A victory by five wickets was not as tight as some had predicted. All that was wanted were 71 runs, and a whole day in which to get them with six wickets in hand; it suggested that there was no real pressure. How forgetful people can be. Pressure? Ask Kallis and Prince about pressure.

On 6 January 1994 Fanie de Villiers and Allan Donald had bowled South Africa to an improbable victory on a dusty Sydney Cricket Ground pitch; De Villiers bowled throughout the final morning when all Australia needed was fifty-four with six wickets in hand. Pressure? Those who believe there was no pressure should think again. Glenn McGrath and Brett Lee could have whipped out a couple of quick wickets. Oh, no, there was no pressure at all. People forget because a player such as Kallis makes it look so easy. Relaxed, calm and assured, he eased South Africa through the first few overs.

In what was a typically mystifying selection policy, Prince had been rejected for the limited-overs series, along with Adams and Terbrugge. The selectors brought back their favourite failure, Boeta Dippenaar, and surprisingly recalled Roger Telemachus, whose form had not been great. In the Test, Prince batted sensibly, taking his lead from Kallis. The pair negotiated their crucial partnership of 99, as South Africa's eventual total of 340 for five became the eighth highest score needed to win a Test.

When it was over there were a few words of thanks from the stand-in skipper, Mark Boucher.

'We have had some hard times and tough games and made a few friends but ... yes – it's nice to win for a change.'

Little did Boucher expect, though, to continue his captaincy reign into the World Cup season. As part of a general United Cricket Board shake-up during the off season, Omar Henry, who was in his last couple of summers as a player when Pollock made his first appearance, was given the job of selection panel convener in order to give South Africa a fresh face and find a winning formula. Henry had long been on the fringes of the national set-up through his coaching of Stellenbosch University and Boland. South Africa needed a new direction, and Henry would help drive it as part of the recuperation process. Squads were selected and a team sent to Tangiers in Morocco and Sri Lanka for limited-overs tournaments. Reaching the semi-finals of the International Champions Trophy against India in Colombo was a plus. It was, however, just the start of what has been a long season. By the time Bangladesh arrived in early October, the reconstruction process was being carefully monitored. The nightmare of the previous summer was slowly disappearing. A Pollock knee injury in the LOIs against Bangladesh meant Boucher could fill in as captain again. With a reshaped side for the inaugural Test against Bangladesh in East London it was so much simpler, with an easy victory to keep Boucher smiling.

NOTES

CHAPTER 1
1. An urchin from the streets of London's East End, his real name was Barnett Isaacs, but he changed it to Barney Barnato. He presented a trophy around which South African non-white cricket was formed in the early years of the twentieth century.
2. In a private publication, *Thoughts of Early Transvaal Administrators* (c. 1915), and edited by someone known only as CHI, the section on cricket contained several page-long biographies, two of which were of the financier and Randlord Sir Abe Bailey and former SACA secretary WM Luckin. Although some of the comments were generally of a non-flattering nature, it was pointed out how they had also advanced the cause of cricket during the first years of the twentieth century.
3. Wicketkeeper captains Jock Cameron and Boet Neser are to be found in the chapter on Mark Boucher.

CHAPTER 9
1. All Sacboc provincial bodies were referred to as boards, as opposed to unions (the SACA equivalent).
2. A document in Schoeman's possession and seen by the author in 1977 indicates that Wally Hammond and Cheetham had been made aware of the cabinet decision on 15 September, the day after Cartwright had failed a fitness test in a limited-overs match.
3. Organised by an affluent black sports administrator, SA Haque, the game was played on 1 and 2 April 1961.
4. The Derrick Robins XI was a team organised by a wealthy English industrialist, who ran sides in the UK and sent teams on tours of New Zealand, the West Indies and, in the 1970s, South Africa. The teams that came to South Africa under his sponsorship brand were designed to fill the vacuum created by international isolation; they were sides of near Test standard and matches were accorded first-class status. As these were private teams, they were invited by a provincial body such as Transvaal.

CHAPTER 11
1. True unity lasted less than a year, as there were those within the old Sacboc who did not agree with the principles that established the South African Cricket Union or the union's constitution. By August 1977 Hassan Howa had inspired a legal manoeuvre, which led to the eventual formation of the South African Cricket Board. As in 1976/77 during their first season, the SACU administration and their members were faced with the country's race laws, highlighted by the Separate Amenities Act and other Acts that segregated the races. Howa had already written that there could be no normal sport in an abnormal society.
2. Since its inception in 1909 the ICC has had three name changes, but until 1997 remained a largely ineffectual organisation; first it was the Imperial Cricket Conference; in 1965 it became the International Cricket Conference; and in 1989 the International Cricket Council. In the mid-1970s the former Pakistan captain, the Oxford-educated Abdul Hafez Khadar, threatened to 'hijack' the system and have it moved to southern Asia if only to shake up the 'Old Boys' image. In recent years, the ICC's

corporate profile has brought the sport into line with what an international body should be.
3 In 1895 the satirical British magazine *Punch* published a cartoon in which a curate was dining with a bishop and was served a bad egg. Asked how was his egg, the curate tactfully replied that it was good in parts and bad in others.
4 In the summer of 1976/77, Australian media entrepreneur Kerry Packer, owner of the television station Channel 9, set in motion a scheme to sign up some of the world's top players, including a number of South Africans. The idea was to launch a series of what were known as super Tests and limited-overs games, and screen them on Channel 9 in the 1977/78 season to rival the official Test series, which that summer involved India. It saw the use of coloured clothing, white balls and black sightscreens: the 'Packer Circus' was born.

CHAPTER 12

1 Kirsten was selected for the 1992 World Cup when Kepler Wessels (the captain) argued for his inclusion on the grounds that his added experience would give the side depth in the top order.

CHAPTER 14

1 Since it was built in 1986, the Centurion Test venue has had three names: Centurion Park, SuperSport Centurion and SuperSport Park Centurion. Many foreign and local statisticians, as well as media, confused by the proximity of Centurion and Pretoria, erroneously link the venue and the area with the former apartheid capital. The ground was erected within the municipal boundaries of Verwoerdburg (formerly Lyttelton) and therefore has had no direct link with Pretoria (as assumed in some local and international publications). The name Centurion replaced Verwoerdburg four days before the start of the first Test of the 1995/96 series against England. The change of municipal status came when the greater metropolitan area of Tshwane was created in 2001, and incorporated Centurion, Pretoria and Akasia.

2 There is much ignorance among the public and, surprisingly, the general media, TV and radio commentators, who refer to 'rules' and not laws; cricket has been governed by a set of laws since before the 1720s, when the first codes were drawn up, based on previous sets of local and colloquial conditions pre-dating 1680.

CHAPTER 16

1 Magiet expressed concern in an interview with the author in Colombo on 10 August 2000 that 'there are so few quality black players available to us [the selectors] at present'. As there was the need to select five for the 2003 World Cup when it is played in South Africa, it was important to 'increase the numbers'. He did not necessarily agree with merit selection if there was a need to look for a fifth black player who might not qualify, but felt it would not come to that. When his comments appeared on TheWicket.com, he said his views had been misinterpreted.

2 In April 2002, in what was a stinging rebuke by the ICC on what amounted to interference by the South African government through their Sports Ministry, the disputed South Africa/India match at SuperSport Centurion had its Test status withdrawn; records have, however, been recognised as those of a first-class nature.

CHAPTER 17

1 Read's century was scored in a match at Kennington (The) Oval, London in 1884, where WG Grace kept wicket while the wicketkeeper, the Honourable Alfred Lyttelton, became the 10th bowler Lord Harris tried in the mammoth Australian innings, and who took four wickets. Duff, a recognised top-order batsman, was held back in the second innings by his captain Joe Darling because of wet pitch conditions in the 1902 New Year Melbourne Test. Duff was making his Test debut.

BIBLIOGRAPHY

Adams, Ken. 'Tiefie Barnes', from *God's Forgotten Cricketers*, edited by André Odendaal (South African Cricketer, 1976).
Allie, Mogamad. *More than a Game* (Western Province Cricket Association, 2001).
Arlott, John. *Vintage Summer, 1947* (Eyre & Spottiswoode, 1967).
———. *John Arlott's Book of Cricketers* (Hamish Hamilton, 1980).
Barker, Ralph. *Ten Great Innings* (Chatto & Windus, 1967).
Bassano, Brian. *MCC in South Africa, 1938–39* (JW McKenzie, 1997).
——— (with Rick Smith). *A Springbok Down Under, South Africa on Tour 1931–32* (Apple Books, 1991).
———. *Vic's Boys – Australia in South Africa 1935–36* (Apple Books, 1993).
Benaud, Richie. *The New Champions* (Hodder & Stoughton, 1965).
Blofeld, Henry. *The Packer Affair* (Collins, 1978).
Botham, Ian. *Botham's Century* (Collins Willow, 2001).
Bradman, Sir Donald. *Farewell to Cricket* (Hodder & Stoughton, 1950).
Brittenden, Dick. *Silver Fern on the Veld* (AH & AW Reed, 1954).
———. *New Zealand Cricketers* (AH & AW Reed, 1961).
Cheetham, Jack. *Caught by the Springboks* (Howard Timmins, 1953).
Chesterfield, Trevor. *Fanie de Villiers: Beyond All Boundaries* (Penguin-India, 2002).
———. *Run Out at Edgbaston, Diaries of the 1999 World Cup* (unpublished).
Cutler, Norman. *Behind the South African Tests* (Putnam, 1955).
Davenport, TRH. *South Africa: A Modern History* (Macmillan, 1978).
D'Oliveira, Basil. *D'Oliveira, An Autobiography* (Collins, 1968).
———. *Time to Declare* (WH Allen, 1980).
Duffus, Louis. 'Trevor Goddard', from *The Great All-Rounders*, edited by John Arlott (Pelham Books, 1969).
———. *Cricketers of the Veld* (Sampson Low, 1952).
Fortune, Charles. *Cricket Overthrown* (Howard Timmins, 1961).
Frindall, Bill. *The Wisden Book of Test Cricket, Vol I 1877–1970* (Headline, 1999).
———. *The Wisden Book of Test Cricket, Vol II 1970–1996* (Headline, 1999).

Gooch, Graham. *Out of the Wilderness* (Collins, 1985).
Hadlee, Sir Richard. *Rhythm and Swing* (Moa, 1989).
Hart, Chris. *Two Tours and Pollock* (Sports Marketing, 1987).
Henry, Omar (with Keith Graham). *The Man in the Middle* (Bok Books International, 1995).
Lewis, Tony. *Cricket in Many Lands* (Hodder & Stoughton, 1991).
May, Peter. *A Game Enjoyed* (Stanley Paul, 1989).
McGlew, Jackie. *Cricket for South Africa* (Howard Timmins, 1961).
———. *Six for Glory* (Howard Timmins, 1967).
McLean, Roy. *Sackcloth without Ashes* (Howard Timmins, 1959).
Morehouse, Geoffrey. *Lord's* (Hodder & Stoughton, 1982).
Moyes, AG. *South Africans in Australia 1952–53* (Angus & Robertson, 1953).
Nobel, MA (Monty). *The Game's the Thing* (Cassel, 1926).
Odendaal, André. *Cricket in Isolation: The Politics of Race and Cricket in South Africa* (André Odendaal, 1977).
Peebles, Ian. *Straight from the Shoulder* (Hutchinson, 1967).
Perry, Rowland. *Bradman's Best* (Corgi, 2001).
Pollock, Peter. *The Thirty Tests* (Don Nelson, 1978).
Procter, Mike. *Cricket Buccaneer* (Don Nelson, 1974).
——— (with Patrick Murphy). *South Africa – the years of isolation and the return* (Bok Books International, 1994).
Ranjitsinhji, Prince KS. *The Jubilee Book of Cricket* (Blackwood, 1897).
Robinson, Ray. *Green Sprigs* (Collins, 1954).
———. *On Top Down Under* (Andre Deutsch, 1996).
Ross, Alan. *Cape Summer* (Hamish Hamilton, 1957).
———. *Ranji: Prince of Cricketers* (Collins, 1983).
Sayen, Henry (as told to Gerald Brodribb). *A Yankee Looks at Cricket* (Putnam, 1956).
Schulze, Heinrich. *South Africa's Cricketing Lawyers* (Interdoc Consultants, 1998).
Short, Graham. *The Trevor Goddard Story* (Purfleet, 1967).
Swanton, EW. *A Sort of Cricket Person* (Collins, 1973).
———. *Gubby Allen, Man of Cricket* (Hutchinson, 1985).
Waite, Johnnie, and Dick Whitington. *Perchance to Bowl* (Nicholas Kaye, 1963).
Warner, Pelham. *Long Innings* (Harrap, 1951).
Whitington, Dick. *Simpson's Safari* (Howard Timmins, 1967).
———. *John Reid's Kiwis* (Whitcombe and Tombs, 1962).
———. *Bradman, Benaud and Goddard's Cinderellas* (Howard Timmins, 1964).
Wessels, Kepler. *Cricket Madness* (Aandblom Publishers, 1987).

INDEX OF NAMES

Aamir Sohail 292
Abed, Dik 133, 134, 144, 201
Abed, Tiny 134
Abrahams, Cecil 134
Abrahams, Graham 271
Ackerman, HD 289
Ackerman, Hylton 156, 180, 200, 202
Adams, Jimmy 225
Adams, Paul 88, 237, 239, 261, 264, 299, 300
Adcock, Neil 45, 47, 52, 53, 60, 62, 63, 64, 65, 74, 75, 77, 82, 84, 86, 87, 95, 123
Agnew, Jonathan 199, 205
Akhalwaya, Ameen 136, 147
Akhtar, Shoaib 279, 280, 292, 297
Aldridge, Bryan 215
Aldworth, Peter 196
Allen, David 109
Allen, George (Gubby) 84, 137
Alleyne, Hartley 100, 185
Allie, Mogamad 135
Amarnath, Mohinder 241
Ambrose, Curtly 225, 262
Anderson, James (Biddy) 7
Anguish, Charles 2
Appleyard, Bob 47
Arlott, John 141
Armstrong, Gregory 183
Arnold, Russel 282
Aronstam, Marlon 245–6
Ashman, RGA 30
Atapattu, Marvan 261, 282
Atherton, Mike 228, 257
Ayob, Hussain 134, 136, 147, 149
Azhar Mahmood 258, 292, 293

Azharuddin, Mohammad 50, 210, 226, 233, 241, 244, 247

Bacchus, Faoud 183
Bacher, Adam 263, 291
Bacher, Ali 102, 109, 112, 116, 117, 121, 125, 145, 146, 149, 150, 152–62, 173, 178, 179, 181, 182, 191, 200, 212, 220, 221, 222, 223, 227, 237, 239, 241, 245, 246, 248, 273
Bacher, Rose 160–61
Bacher, Shira 162
Baig, Ali 129
Bailey, Abe 9–10, 11, 143, 286
Bailey, Trevor 47, 59, 60–61, 65, 77
Balaskas, Xenophon 18, 19
Baldwin, Harry 83
Balfour, Ngconde 194, 195, 269, 271
Banner, Stuart 173
Bansda, Damoo (Benny) 142
Barber, Bob 109, 114, 117, 118, 121, 122
Barlow, Eddie 85, 90, 101, 102, 106, 107, 108, 109–10, 112, 115, 117, 118, 120–21, 125, 133, 154, 156, 160, 181, 200, 207
Barnato, Barney 10
Barnes, Abdullatief (Tiefie) 133, 148
Barnes, Sid 11–12, 42
Barnes, Vincent 133
Barrington, Ken 47, 109, 111, 114–15, 119, 121, 122, 125
Bartlett, Gary 86, 100

Bassano, Brian 144
Bath, Brian 156
Beck, John 74
Bedser, Alec 20, 21, 26, 29, 55, 94
Begbie, Denis 19, 22, 23, 104
Begg, Yasien 147, 217
Benaud, Richie 42, 53, 62, 62, 65, 79, 99, 100, 121, 124, 148, 161, 209, 210, 222
Benkenstein, Dale 255, 259, 266, 272
Bester, Frank 104
Bevan, Michael 278
Biggs, Dassie 200
Bird, Harold (Dicky) 189
Birrell, Harry 105, 115
Bisset, Murray 6, 7
Blair, Bob 45, 46, 69, 70, 71, 74
Blair, Tony 143
Bland, Colin 4, 85, 90, 108, 109, 116, 117, 119, 120, 121, 122, 123, 124, 141, 156
Boje, Nicky 256, 263, 265, 268, 279, 282
Boon, David 234
Booth, Brian 98
Borde, Chandrakant 129
Border, Allan 92, 231, 235, 299, 300
Bosanquet, BJT 7–8
Bosch, Tertius 88, 214, 217, 224, 225
Bose, Trishna 240, 248
Botham, Ian 171, 172, 173, 189, 215, 248
Botten, Jackie 81, 93, 98, 108, 109, 112, 113, 116, 117, 118, 119, 121, 122, 123, 147

307

Boucher, Mark 252, 253, 255, 263, 277, 279–80, 281, 285, 288–301
Bougarel, Pierre 201
Boycott, Geoff 54, 109, 111, 114, 118, 121, 122, 125, 166, 171, 172, 173, 225, 252, 253, 297
Brache, Frank 142
Bradman, Donald 14, 20, 29–30, 31, 44, 69, 70, 100, 148, 150, 155, 156, 160, 162, 163, 169, 175, 176, 177, 181, 201, 228, 261, 285–6
Brandes, Eddo 187
Brearley, Mike 18, 109, 298
Bromfeld, Harry 85, 109, 112, 113, 116, 117, 118, 123
Brown, David 109, 115, 117, 120, 123
Brown, Freddie 28, 29, 55, 77
Bruyns, André 200
Bryson, Rudi 289
Buchanan, John 275
Buller, Syd 83, 84, 85, 112, 118
Burge, Peter 228
Burger, Chris 108, 111
Burke, Jimmy 42, 52, 62, 63, 65
Burtt, Tom 69
Butcher, Mark 254

Cabral, Rukshan 240
Caddick, Andy 253, 254
Cairns, Chris 32
Cairns, Lance 32
Callaghan, Dave 251
Camacho, Steve 222
Cameron, HB (Jock) 9, 13, 14, 285–6, 287, 296
Cardus, Neville 141
Carr, Donald 40, 54, 109
Cartwright, Tom 109, 124, 138, 141
Castens, HH (Fatty) 5, 285
Catterall, Bob 55
Chapman, Percy 140, 285
Chappell, Greg 208–9, 218, 219, 264–5
Chappell, Ian 176, 177, 218, 264–5

Chappell, Jeanne 265
Chappell, Trevor 209, 264–5
Chapple, Murray 45
Chawla, Sanjay 239
Cheetham, Jack 14, 36, 37–50, 67, 69, 71, 72, 73, 74, 75, 76, 78, 81, 90, 91, 94, 104, 136, 138, 139, 142, 143, 144, 201, 257
Cheetham, John 40
Cheetham, Norma 40
Cheetham, Peter 40
Cheetham, Robert 40
Chettle, Geoff 201
Chevalier, Grahame 200
Chotia, Solly 133
Chubb, Geoff 22, 23
Clark, Dick 210
Clarke, Sylvester 100, 153, 174–5, 183, 184, 185, 197
Close, Brian 40
Cobham, Lord 137
Collings, JC 30
Collins, Herbie 286
Commins, Kevin 106
Compton, Denis 21–2, 26, 35, 47, 48, 59, 88, 96, 111, 156
Connolly, Alan 102, 154, 155
Cook, Geoff 204
Cook, Jimmy 153, 166, 174, 185, 188–93, 194, 197, 205, 219, 232, 251
Cooke, Peter 172, 173
Cowdrey, Colin 47, 59, 60, 76, 98, 111, 114, 116, 119, 122, 123, 125, 222
Cowper, Bob 157
Coy, Arthur 49, 92, 102, 110, 137, 139, 143, 180, 200
Craig, Ian 42, 53, 55, 58, 61, 63, 64, 65, 79, 99, 121, 158
Craven, Danie 75
Crisp, Bob 32
Croft, Colin 183
Cronjé, Bertha 245, 247, 248
Cronjé, Ewie 229
Cronjé, Frans 248
Cronjé, Hansie 14, 71, 87, 96, 217, 224, 225, 228, 229–49, 253–4, 255, 256,

257, 258, 260, 268, 269, 272, 273, 274, 277, 283, 291, 292, 295
Crookes, Derek 230, 241, 256, 266
Crookes, Norman 109, 112, 113
Crowe, Martin 187, 213, 214, 216
Cullinan, Daryll 11, 71, 232, 234, 241, 254, 255, 261, 270, 281, 295, 298
Cummins, Anderson 225

Dakin, Geoff 178, 191, 222
Dalmiya, Jagmohan 267, 271
Dalton, Eric 17, 293
Darling, Joe 7
Davids, Faiek 217
Davidson, Alan 65, 94, 121
Davies, Emrys 83
Dawson, Ossie 19, 23, 24
Day, Chris 250
Deane, Hubert (Nummy) 9, 12–13, 285, 287
De Courcy, Jimmy 42
DeFreitas, Phil 215
De Klerk, FW 189, 191, 216, 220
De Kock, Gerald 267
Delport, Ron 105
Denness, Mike 267, 268, 272
De Silva, Ajith 183
De Silva, Aravinda 232, 243
De Silva, Nuwani 240
De Vaal, Peter 200
Devereaux, Louis 40
De Villiers, Fanie 88, 226, 228, 233, 234–5, 251, 262, 266, 288, 291, 300
Dexter, Ted 109, 111, 114, 122, 192
Dilley, Graham 173
Dippenaar, Boeta 228, 263, 270, 271, 300
Docrat, AE 135
D'Oliveira, Basil 11, 13, 49, 102, 129–51, 164, 167, 168, 169
Dollery, Ken 41

INDEX OF NAMES

Donald, Allan 96, 193, 215, 217, 225, 228, 234, 235, 240, 251, 252, 257, 260, 266, 273, 277, 288, 297, 300
Douglas-Home, Alec 143
Dowling, Deryck 23, 180
Drakes, Vasbert 294
Dravid, Rahul 21
Duckworth, Chris 47
Duff, Reggie 293
Duffus, Louis 11, 37, 133, 136–7, 140–41, 142, 164–5
Duleepsinhji, Kumar Shri 12–13, 140–41
Dumbrill, Richard 109, 116, 117, 119, 120, 121, 122, 123, 171
Dunell, Owen 3, 5
Du Plessis, Morné 129
Du Preez, Jackie 160
Dwyer, 'Chappie' 42
Dyer, David 23, 189
Dyer, Dennis 19, 23, 110

Ebrahim, Baboo 133
Edrich, Bill 18, 21–2, 72, 111
Edrich, John 114, 119, 121, 122, 123
Egar, Col 98, 99
Eksteen, Clive 232, 251
Elgie, Kim 85
Elworthy, Steve 290, 300
Emburey, John 172, 173, 190
Emerson, Ross 127–8
Endean, Russell 11, 19, 38, 43–4, 45, 47, 51, 59, 61, 62, 63, 78, 79, 81
Estwick, Rod 230
Evans, Godfrey 26, 29, 47, 48

Farnes, Ken 17–18
Faulkner, Aubrey 9, 11, 12, 13, 93, 101
Fell, Des 33, 81, 82
Fender, Gerald 68
Ferreira, Anton 88, 264
Fingleton, Jack 20
Fisher, Eric 69, 71, 89
Fitzpatrick, George 77
Fleming, Damien 275

Fletcher, Duncan 288
Fletcher, Keith 172
Foley, WBH 104
Ford, Graham 207, 240, 260, 262, 266, 268, 271, 275, 279, 283, 284
Fotheringham, Henry 153, 189, 197, 219
Frames, Algie 12, 80
Francis, KT 291
Frangos, Nic 127
Frielinghaus, LO 12
Frost, Naomi 240
Fry, CB 7, 51, 175
Fuller, Eddie 38, 44, 47, 63
Fullerton, George 18, 19, 40, 56, 104
Funston, Ken 38, 42, 44, 51, 52, 59, 65, 69, 78, 81

Gamsy, Dennis 109, 114
Garda, Morris 270
Garner, Joel 189, 262
Gatting, Mike 146, 173, 176, 185, 190, 191, 192, 193, 204, 219, 220, 221, 226, 252, 268
Gaunt, Ron 78
Gauntlett, Jeremy 295
Gavaskar, Sunil 222
Geary, George 55
Geddie, Doug 33
Georgeau, Georgie 104
Gibbs, Herschelle 6, 236, 237, 246, 260, 263, 264, 268, 278, 295, 298
Gilchrist, Adam 277, 298, 299, 300
Gilligan, Arthur 137
Gladwin, Cliff 26
Glasspool, Barry 190, 213
Gleeson, John 102, 171
Goddard, Trevor 33, 47, 48, 52, 59, 61, 68, 78, 79, 86, 90–102, 105, 106, 107, 108, 110, 114, 126, 129, 130, 131–2, 154–5, 160, 179, 180, 212
Gooch, Graham 164, 165, 166, 172, 173, 174, 182, 209, 215, 217, 232

Gordon, 'Mobil' 17
Gordon, Norman 17, 19
Gover, Alf 83, 130
Gower, David 172, 173, 192
Grace, Arthur 77
Grace, EM 264
Grace, GF 264
Grace, Martha 264
Grace, WG 264
Graveney, David 190, 193
Graveney, Tom 28, 47, 130, 131, 138
Gray, Jimmy 105, 115
Gray, Malcolm 267
Greatbatch, Mark 216
Greig, Tony 169, 195
Grieves, Ken 41
Grieveson, Ronnie 17
Griffin, Geoff 80, 81, 82–4, 85, 86, 98, 100, 112
Griffiths, Billy 110
Grimmett, Clarrie 14, 30
Grinaker, Ola 19
Grobler, Gerbrand 228
Grout, Wally 52, 53, 63–4, 158
Grove, Charlie 41
Gupta, MK 241, 243

Hadlee, Dayle 265
Hadlee, Richard 71, 94, 95, 97, 196–8, 265
Hadlee, Walter 54, 265
Hain, Peter 143
Hall, Andrew 278–9, 280
Hall, Glen 98
Hall, Wes 129
Halliwell, Bisset 4
Halliwell, Ernie 4–5, 7, 285, 286
Halse, Clive 107, 108
Hammond, Wally 8, 17, 18, 117, 139, 165, 170
Hankey, Stan 196
Hanley, Martin 36, 104
Hanley, Rupert 153, 203
Harper, Daryl 281
Harris, Lord 2, 149
Harris, Tony 18, 19, 22
Harrison, Richard 245
Harvey, Ian 276, 278, 280

309

Harvey, Neil 51, 52, 53, 55, 63, 133, 176
Hassett, Lindsay 35, 44, 45, 133
Hawke, Lord 4, 6, 286
Hawke, N 157
Hawkins, George 77, 97
Hayden, Matthew 297
Haynes, Desmond 184
Hayward, Mornantau 275, 277, 282
Hayward, Thomas 7
Healy, Ian 233, 235
Heaney, Tim 22
Hearne, Frank 226
Hector, Rupert 91
Heine, Peter 47, 52, 53, 62, 64, 65, 77, 81, 83, 86, 87, 95, 117
Hemmings, Eddie 219
Henderson, Claude 262
Hendricks, Krom 5
Henry, Omar 133, 135, 151, 217, 224, 225, 271, 301
Hick, Graeme 13, 217
Hicks, Glen 206
Hill, Clem 9
Hilton, Malcolm 41, 55
Hirst, George 7
Hitchcock, Ray 41
Hobbs, Robin 109
Hofmeyr, Murray 54
Holding, Michael 171, 262
Hollies, Eric 20
Howa, Hassan 136, 143, 144, 145, 146
Howell, Denis 137
Hubble, Jim 157
Hudson, Andrew 187, 217, 225, 235, 241
Hughes, Kim 185, 206, 219
Hughes, Merv 275
Humpage, Geoff 173
Humphrey, Anthony 264
Hunte, Conrad 79, 142, 148
Hussain, Nasser 13, 238, 245–6, 258, 277
Hutton, Leonard 14, 21, 25, 28, 47, 55, 56, 68, 175, 176

Ikin, Jack 28, 41
Illingworth, Ray 177, 227

Illingworth, Richard 215
Imran Khan 196
Ingleby-McKenzie, Colin 129
Innes, Gerald 38, 106, 142
Insole, Doug 59, 76, 77, 95, 137, 139
Intikhab Alam 258
Inzamam-ul-Haq 199, 217, 279
Ironside, Dave 4, 46
Irvine, Lee 181, 200, 202
Isaacs, Wilfred 40

Jack, Steven 153
Jackman, Robin 173
Jackson, Bruce 248
Jackson, Stanley 7
Jadeja, Ajay 247
Jameson, Leander 6
Jardine, Douglas 287
Jarman, Barry 138
Javed Miandad 187
Jayasuriya, Sanath 259, 260, 261, 282
Jayawardena, Mahela 282
Jenkins, Roley 26
Jennings, Ken 273
Jennings, Ray 153, 197, 230, 287, 290
Joel, SB 287
Johnson, Martin 192
Johnson, Peter 199, 205
Johnston, Bill 35, 94
Jones, Alan 215
Jones, Charlie 19
Jones, Stephen 285
Jordaan, Alan 212–13, 220, 223–4

Kallicharran, Alvin 153, 183, 197
Kallis, Jacques 255, 256, 263, 270, 274, 276, 278–9, 280, 282, 283, 294, 295, 298, 300, 301
Kanhai, Rohan 131
Kapil Dev 97, 193, 233
Kaplan, 'Kappie' 34
Kardar, Abdul Hafeez 54
Karim, Goolam 149
Kearns, Julian 190

Keith, Headley 36, 38, 44, 47, 94, 96
Kerr, Jack 45
Khan, Majid 261
Khan, Mansur Ali 265
Khan, Mustapha 148–9
Kidson, Arthur 81
Kidson, Hayward 18, 23, 82, 159
Kiel, Syd 1–4
Kierse, Martin 100
King, Collis 184
King, Derek 34
King, Martin Luther 150
Kippax, Alan 26
Kirsten, Gary 71, 187, 234, 250–58, 262, 274, 276, 278, 279, 280, 281, 292, 295
Kirsten, Noel 185
Kirsten, Peter 11, 40, 166, 176, 181–7, 194, 204, 205, 216, 217, 218, 219, 223, 225, 227, 250–51, 252, 257, 290
Kline, Lindsay 62, 63, 78, 86
Klusener, Lance 207, 244, 255, 263, 266, 278, 279–80, 281, 282
Knott, Alan 172
Koornhof, Piet 168
Kotze, JJ (Kodgee) 4
Kourie, Alan 153
Kuiper, Adrian 6, 181, 186, 192, 205, 217, 225, 230
Kumble, Anil 232

Laker, Jim 58, 92
Lamb, Allan 166, 169, 195, 209, 218, 219, 290
Lance, Herbert (Tiger) 86, 115, 117, 120, 121, 125, 154, 157, 160
Lander, Chris 209
Landheer, Laura 240
Lang, Mervyn 23, 34
Langley, Gil 42
Langridge, John 82, 83
Langton, Chud 17, 293
Lara, Brian 148, 224
Larter, David 115, 117, 121, 156

INDEX OF NAMES

Lawrence, Charles 7
Lawrence, Goofy 85, 93
Lawry, Bill 69, 92, 102, 153, 167, 170, 176, 180
Leadbeater, B 56
Lee, Alan 205
Lee, Brett 256, 274, 275, 276, 277, 278, 279, 297, 299, 300
Lee, Frank 82, 83, 84, 85
Leveson Gower, Henry 9, 12, 13
Lewis, Chris 208
Liddle, Jimmy 36
Liebenberg, Gerry 263
Lindsay, Denis 108, 109, 114, 115, 117, 119, 121, 122, 125, 126, 158–9, 160, 171, 177, 181, 196, 200, 268
Lindsay, Johnnie 19, 81
Lindwall, Ray 35, 44, 69, 176
Litchfield, Eric 142, 164, 200
Lloyd, Clive 171, 183, 184, 223, 244
Llyewellyn, Buck (Charlie) 7
Loader, Peter 59, 61, 129
Lock, Tony 77
Locke, Martin 213
Loeser, Paul 22
Lorgat, Haroon 270
Lowson, Frank 56
Luckin, MW 2–3, 4, 10

Macartney, Charlie 261
Macaulay, Mike 109, 112, 113, 121
MacGibbon, Tony 71, 94
MacKay, Ken (Slasher) 51–2, 64–5, 121
Mackay-Coghill, Don 156
Mackerdhuj, Krish 145, 146, 191, 220, 222
MacLaren, Archie 7, 13
Magiet, Rushdi 134, 146, 194, 237, 260, 267, 269–70, 271, 272, 279, 295, 299–300
Majola, Eric 150
Majola, Gerald 268–9
Majola, Khaya 88, 147, 148, 149, 150, 264
Malamba, Ben 134
Malcolm, Devon 175

Mallett, Ashley 175
Mandela, Nelson 136, 190, 191, 220
Manicum, Gopaul 148
Manjrekar, Sanjay 223
Mann, George 25, 35
Mann, Tufty 19, 28
Mannack, Jack 230
Mansell, Percy 38, 47, 96
Marais, Bill 52, 53
Marsh, Geoff 215
Marsh, Rod 218, 291
Marshall, Malcolm 184, 207, 266, 283, 284
Marshall, Roy 129
Martin, Syd 32
Martyn, Damien 235, 262, 275, 276, 277
Matthews, Craig 96, 251, 256
May, Peter 47, 48, 55–6, 57, 58, 59, 61, 76, 77, 95, 96, 98, 99, 137, 139, 161
May, Tim 231, 234
Mayne, Jimmy 5
McCabe, Stan 30
McCarthy, Cuan 28, 29, 69
McCool, Colin 35
McDermott, Craig 234, 235
McDonald, Colin 52, 62
McDonald, Trevor 93
McFarlane, Peter 219
McGlew, Jackie 11, 14, 23, 37, 47, 49, 57, 67–89, 90, 91, 93, 94, 95, 96, 98, 171, 179, 228, 257, 264
McGlew, Jacqualine 89
McGlew, Patricia 88
McGlew, Robin 68
McGrath, Glenn 235, 256, 275, 277, 278, 279, 280, 298, 300
McKechnie, Brian 209
McKenzie, Graham 126
McKenzie, Kevin 153, 161, 162, 197
McKenzie, Neil 260, 263, 275
McKinnon, Atholl 109, 110, 112, 113–14, 157, 171
McLean, Roy 27, 29, 33, 36, 38, 41, 44, 47, 56, 59, 62, 63,

65, 68, 69, 75, 76, 94, 108, 111, 124
McMillan, Brian 96, 208, 217, 224, 233, 251–2
Meckiff, Ian 62, 98–100
Medworth, CO 111, 165, 167, 200
Melle, Michael 33, 38, 67, 68
Melville, Alan 14, 15–26, 28, 35, 53, 71, 72, 80, 81, 82, 110, 111
Meyer, Willie 247–8
Miller, Keith 35, 42, 43, 44, 69
Miller, Lawrie 45
Milner, Lord 163, 287
Milton, William 3–4, 5, 6, 10, 11, 143
Mitchell, Bruce 17, 19, 21, 22, 23, 24, 28, 76
Mitchell, Frank 226
Mitchell, Ian
Mohammad, Gul 226
Mohammad, Hanif 265
Mohammad, Shoaib 265
Moir, Alex 69
Mooney, Frank 46
More, Kiran 233
Morris, Arthur 42, 94
Mortimer, John 73
Moseley, Ezra 226
Moss, Alan 40
Motz, Dick 212
Moult, Thomas 141
Moyes, AG (Johnnie) 37, 38, 43
Mpitsang, Victor 236
Muralitharan, Muttiah 127–8, 232, 261–2
Murphy, Stanley 108, 111
Murray, Anton 38, 47, 67, 70, 71
Murray, David 183
Murray, John 109
Mushtaq Ahmed 215, 217, 292

Naidoo, Krish 189, 192, 221
Nandy, Ashish 1
Nazar, Mudassar 63
Nel, André 296–7
Neser, Vivian (Boet) 287
Ngam, Mfuneko 151, 262

311

Noakes, Ian 247–8
Norton, Eric 38
Nosworthy, Dave 288, 289, 290
Nourse, AW (Dave) 7, 8, 9, 11, 30–33, 265
Nourse, Dudley 7, 11, 17, 19, 20, 23, 24, 27–36, 40, 55, 71, 72, 73, 74, 80, 82, 85, 157, 253, 265
Ntini, Makhaya 88, 151, 236, 262, 263, 275, 278, 291, 297
Nupen, Buster 13, 285

Odendaal, André 135
Old, Chris 172, 173
Oldfield, Bert 286
Ontong, Justin 148, 194, 269–70, 271
Oosthuizen, Pieter 250
Opatha, Tony 183
Oppelt, Phylicia 246
Orchard, David 200
Orchard, Ken 23
O'Reilly, Bill (Tiger) 14, 30
Owen-Smith, Tuppy 53

Packer, Kerry 196, 202–3, 213, 218, 292
Page, Hugh 188
Palframan, Steve 251, 287–8, 289, 290
Palmer, Ken 109
Pamensky, Joe 152, 173, 174, 183, 191
Parfitt, Peter 109, 125
Parker-Adams, Nancy 240
Parks, Jim 40, 109, 115, 119, 120, 121, 122–3, 125
Partridge, Joe 81, 106, 107
Patel, Dipak 214
Payne, Les 19, 23
Pearson, DB 82
Perera, Irene 240
Petersen, Eric 133
Pfaff, Brian 33, 68
Phillips, 'Ricey' 19
Phillipson, Eddie 83
Pillay, Ronnie 220
Pithey, David 107, 115
Pithey, Tony 109, 110

Pitts, Steve 18
Player, Gary 172
Plimsoll, Jack 23, 24, 104, 105, 109, 110, 111, 112, 122
Pollock, Anthony 265
Pollock, Graeme 11, 30, 32, 54, 71, 90, 100, 107, 109, 112, 116, 117, 120, 123, 124, 125, 126, 127, 133, 136, 153, 154, 156, 160, 174, 177, 180, 181, 184, 197, 200, 219, 254, 264, 266, 270, 271
Pollock, 'Mac' 265
Pollock, Peter 85, 86, 87, 90, 108, 109, 112, 114, 116, 117, 118, 119, 120, 121, 122, 123, 124, 125, 127, 154, 160, 170, 177, 200, 213, 230, 236, 240, 250–52, 257, 264, 266, 269, 287, 289, 290
Pollock, Shaun 211, 259–84, 285, 296, 297, 301
Ponting, Ricky 258
Poore, Matt 45, 71
Porter, Nyree Dawn 74
Pothas, Nic 288
Pothecary, Jim 81, 85
Prabhakar, Manoj 233
Pressdee, Jim 93, 113
Pretorius, Dewald 300
Price, John 109
Priem, Walter 100
Prince, Ashwell 263, 299
Pringle, Derek 215
Pringle, Meyrick 96, 208, 214, 216, 217, 224, 225, 251
Pritchard, Tom 41
Procter, Mike 27, 93, 127, 136, 138, 154, 160, 166, 167, 169–75, 177, 180, 181, 195, 199, 200, 202, 297
Procter, Woodrow 170
Pybus, Richard 285

Qamar, Ahmed 258

Rabone, Geoff 45, 46, 55, 57, 74, 75
Radford, Neal 153

Raja, Goolam 237, 239, 268, 295, 300
Raju, Venkatapathy 186, 223, 232
Ralph, Andrew 'Nobbie' 19
Ramadhin, Sonny 142
Ramprakash, Mark 13
Ranatunga, Arjuna 128, 232, 243–4, 281–2
Ranjitsinhji, Kumar Shri 6–7, 12, 13, 26, 140
Rappaport, Michael 205
Rashid, Haroon 292
Razzaq, Abdul 261
Read, Billy 293
Read, Walter 3, 4, 5
Reddick, Tom 9, 12, 142
Reddy, Krish 135, 147
Redpath, Ian 101
Reid, John 45, 74, 75, 85, 91, 114, 176, 180
Renneberg, Dave 158–9
Rhodes, AE (Dusty) 112, 119
Rhodes, Cecil John 5, 6, 10, 286–7
Rhodes, Harold 112
Rhodes, Jonty 4, 87, 199, 207, 208, 217, 225, 232, 233, 234, 252, 256, 257, 261, 274, 276, 279, 281, 282
Rhodes, Wilfred 7
Rice, Clive 150, 153, 166, 169, 183, 184, 185, 188, 189, 190, 194–207, 219, 229, 271
Richards, Alfred 4
Richards, Barry 11, 27, 32, 54, 85, 89, 102, 113, 127, 136, 148, 155, 166, 169, 170, 174, 175–81, 184, 195, 198, 200, 202
Richards, Mark 176
Richards, Viv 155, 171, 189
Richardson, Dave 205, 217, 225, 234, 251, 281, 287–8, 289, 290, 291, 292
Richardson, Peter 59
Richardson, Richie 224
Richardson, Victor 30, 157, 265
Roberts, Andy 171
Roberts, Ron 129, 130, 131
Robertson-Glasgow, RC 287

INDEX OF NAMES

Robins, Derrick 50, 148, 150, 165, 171, 202
Robinson, Peter 250
Rolfe, Trevor 93
Rorke, Gordon 100
Roro, Frank 10
Rowan, Athol 19, 28, 29, 36, 41, 55, 94
Rowan, Eric 17, 19, 22, 23, 24, 25–6, 28, 29, 40, 55, 72, 74, 76, 94, 104, 112
Rowe, Lawrence 174, 182, 183, 184, 185
Rubidge, Doolie 136
Rudolph, Jacques 194, 270–71
Rumsey, Fred 115, 117, 121, 123
Rundle, David 251
Rushmere, Mark 217, 224, 225, 230
Ryder, Jack 286

Sackstein, Les 244
Salim Malik 241, 242, 247, 258
Samson, Andrew 210
Sangakkara, Kumar 282
Schoeman, Ben 138–9, 201
Schultz, Brett 232, 250, 251
Seddon, Dudley 100
Sherwell, Percy 8, 9, 233
Short, Arthur 200
Sidebottom, Arnie 173
Siedle, Jack 32
Silva, Gamini 281, 282
Simmons, Phil 224
Simpson, Bobby 19, 62, 69, 79, 92, 101, 114, 125, 126, 157, 171, 180
Simpson, Reg 28
Slabbert, F van Zyl 220
Slater, Michael 234
Smit, Hilbert 238
Smith, Aubrey 4
Smith, Chris 195
Smith, CS 41
Smith, Graeme 256
Smith, Greg 290
Smith, Ian 19, 47, 141
Smith, Mike 84, 92, 98, 101, 107–8, 109, 110, 113,
115, 117, 119, 121, 122, 124, 125
Smith, Robin 169, 195
Snell, Richard 205, 214, 217, 225, 291
Snooke, Sibley 9
Snow, John 125, 156, 210
Sobers, Garfield 79, 142, 148, 156, 175–6, 197, 211, 222
Sonn, Percy 194, 270, 271
Speed, Malcolm 273
Spillhaus, Carl 289
Statham, Brian 40, 47, 48, 61, 76, 84, 98
Stavridis, Harry 168
Stephenson, John 164
Stewart, Alec 254
Stewart, Don 22
Stewart, Errol 251, 287–8, 289
Stewart, Mickey 192
Steyn, Rory 239
Strydom, Joubert 230
Strydom, Pieter 268
Sutcliffe, Bert 45, 46, 68, 73, 74, 75, 123, 176
Swanton, EW 66, 222
Swetman, Roy 129
Symcox, Pat 232, 234, 241, 242, 292–3
Symonds, Andrew 276, 279

Taber, Brian 155, 158
Taberer, Henry (Tabs) 7
Tallon, Don 42
Tancred, Bernard 86
Tancred, Louis 11
Tattersall, Roy 29, 40–41
Tayfield, Arthur 23, 59, 92, 94, 299
Tayfield, Hugh 36, 38, 43, 46, 47, 48, 51, 52, 53, 58, 59, 61, 62, 63, 64, 74, 76, 77, 79, 94, 95, 96
Taylor, Don 41
Taylor, Herbie 9, 11–12, 32, 54, 55, 57, 287
Taylor, Les 173
Taylor, Mark 234
Telemachus, Roger 263, 290, 291, 300
Tendulkar, Sachin 148, 175, 176
Terbrugge, David 263, 300
Tharmaratnam, Sharmila 240
Thomson, Ian 109
Tillim, Tony 113, 157
Titmus, Fred 40, 92, 105, 109, 115, 117, 119, 120, 121, 123
Todd, Ian 172
Townsend, Alan 41
Trimborn, Pat 154–5, 160, 171, 200
Trueman, Fred 24, 47, 48, 84, 90, 94, 219
Trumper, Victor 26, 261
Tshwete, Steve 176, 216, 220, 223
Tuckett, Lindsay 19, 33, 34, 35, 81, 110
Tufnell, Phil 215, 254
Tutu, Desmond 277
Twining, Dick 110
Tyson, Frank 47, 76

Underwood, Arthur 40
Underwood, Derek 172

Vaas, Chaminda 281
Valentine, Alf 142
Van der Bijl, Pieter 17–18
Van der Bijl, Vintcent 18, 153, 174, 200
Van der Merwe, Peter 90, 91, 98, 103–28, 142, 156, 157, 160, 187–8, 189, 190, 192, 194, 199, 205–6, 212, 214
Van Ryneveld, Clive 6, 29, 51–66, 78, 79, 104
Van Zyl, Corrie 224, 271
Varachia, Rashid 144
Variawa, Amien 11, 133, 147, 148
Varner, Rowan 266
Verity, Hedley 17, 286
Versfeld, Berry 87
Verwoerd, Hendrik 80
Vice, Telford 290
Viljoen, Ken 17, 19, 22, 23, 38, 47, 69, 74, 75, 79, 90, 104, 105
Vogler, Ernie 8

Volsteedt, AK 229
Volsteedt, Johan 212, 228, 229
Vorster, BJ 102, 133, 134, 135, 136, 137–8, 139, 140, 143, 168, 194, 200, 202, 271

Wade, Billy 23
Wade, Herby 9, 13–14, 30, 32, 110, 285
Waite, Johnny 4, 29, 32, 38, 43, 46, 47, 51, 59, 62, 63, 64, 68, 69, 72, 75, 76, 79, 82, 84, 107, 110, 147, 196
Walcott, Clyde 176, 222, 242, 244
Walker, Peter 84
Wallace, Boon 126, 191
Wallace, Merv 68
Walsh, Courtney 225
Walter, Ken 85
Walters, Doug 143, 176
Walton, Bert 41
Waqar Younis 227, 258, 292, 293
Ward, Jackie 22
Wardle, Johnny 29, 47, 58, 59, 100
Waring, Frank 200, 201
Warnapura, Bandula 183
Warne, Shane 231, 232, 233–4, 235, 242, 243, 244, 256, 278, 279
Warner, Jack 102

Warner, Pelham 6, 7, 8, 286
Warton, Robert 4
Washbrook, Cyril 21, 130
Wasim Akram 217, 227, 292
Watkins, John 36, 38, 73, 94
Watson, Chester 129
Watson, Willie 129
Waugh, Mark 124, 235, 242, 243, 277, 300
Waugh, Steve 124, 236, 252, 258, 272, 275, 276, 277, 278, 279, 280, 298, 299, 300
Weekes, Everton 20, 131, 142, 176, 271
Weeks, Ray 41
Wessels, Kepler 14, 96, 103, 123, 169, 176, 181, 186, 187, 191–2, 205, 207, 208–28, 229, 230–31, 233, 234, 235, 252, 257, 270, 287, 296, 297
Westcott, Dick 63, 64, 78
Wharton, Alan 41
Wheatley, Ossie 192
Whitcombe, Peter 40
White, Gordon 9
White, Ray 196, 242, 243
Whitehead, JP 56
Whitfield, Brian 185
Whitington, Dick 140, 162
Whitney, Mike 176
Wijetunge, Piyal 232

Wilkens, Victor 106
Wilkins, Chris 180
Wilkins, Phil 234
Williams, Bob 19
Williams, Henry 236, 246, 268
Williams, Owen 133, 136, 144, 201
Williams, Ray 250
Willis, Bob 165, 173
Wilmot, Lorrie 113
Wilson, RG 40
Winslow, Paul 47, 160
Witte, Ernest 104
Wood, Arthur 286
Wood, Graeme 218
Woodfull, Bill 286
Woods, Donald 202, 217
Woolley, Frank 26
Woolmer, Bob 173, 175, 235, 236, 237, 241, 252, 263, 275, 291
Woolridge, Ian 109
Worrell, Frank 87, 142, 147, 175
Wright, John 182
Wyatt, Bob 14
Wynne, Owen 18, 19, 25, 26

Yardley, Bruce 219
Yardley, Norman 56

Zaaijman, John 248
Zulch, Billy 86